BREAKING THROUGH

BREAKING THROUGH

The Birth of China's Opening-Up Policy

LI LANQING

Former Vice Premier of China

Translated by
Ling Yuan and Zhang Siying

OXFORD
UNIVERSITY PRESS

OXFORD

UNIVERSITY PRESS

Oxford University Press is a department of the University of Oxford.
It furthers the University's objective of excellence in research, scholarship,
and education by publishing worldwide in

Oxford New York

Auckland Cape Town Dar es Salaam Hong Kong Karachi
Kuala Lumpur Madrid Melbourne Mexico City Nairobi
New Delhi Shanghai Taipei Toronto

With offices in

Argentina Austria Brazil Chile Czech Republic France Greece
Guatemala Hungary Italy Japan South Korea Poland Portugal
Singapore Switzerland Thailand Turkey Ukraine Vietnam

Oxford is a registered trade mark of Oxford University Press

© Oxford University Press and Foreign Language Teaching and Research Press 2009

First published 2009

This impression (lowest digit)
1 3 5 7 9 10 8 6 4 2

British Library Cataloguing in Publication Data
available

Library of Congress Cataloging in Publication Data
available

Breaking Through: The Birth of China's Opening-Up Policy /author, Li Lanqing;
translators, Ling Yuan and Zhang Siying – 1 st ed.
p. cm.
Includes index.

ISBN 978-0-19-801692-2

1. China—History—1976–. 2. China—Economic history—20th century.
3. China—Economic policy—1976–. 4. China—Politics and government.
5. Political leadership—China. 6. China—Reform and Opening Policy.

Printed in Hong Kong
Published by Oxford University Press and Foreigh Language Teaching and Research Press
18th Floor, Warwick House East, Taikoo Place, 979 King's Road, Quarry Bay
Hong Kong

LI LANQING
Former Vice Premier of China

Contents

Preface to the English Edition

Foreign friends often ask me about China. This gives me the impression that the world has never been so keen on my country as it is today. It is therefore my great pleasure to tell people what I know about my motherland. I hope that my book about the early years of the opening-up policy will be of some help to those who want to know what has happened in China over the last three decades.

To know China, one must first know its changes. About a century ago, the Chinese abolished autocratic monarchy, cut off their pigtails and unbound their feet, while opening their doors to modern civilization and beginning to incorporate Western democracy and science. Born of a semi-feudal, semi-colonial society 60 years ago, New China adopted the socialist system, gradually put together an industrial and economic setup, and laid the groundwork for development in the contemporary world. Thirty years ago, the Chinese embarked on the road of reform and opening and began learning to build a market economy, run joint ventures with foreign partners, and boost international trade, and to play its role in international commerce, thereby vastly accelerating its process of industrialization and modernization.

Today, the 1.3 billion Chinese relish their first taste of affluence, nine-year compulsory education is the norm for school-age children, some 300 million are learning English, nearly 100 million are producing for the world market, and more than one million are studying in foreign countries. The Chinese market, consuming US$1 trillion worth of foreign commodities annually, has so far attracted a total of US$1 trillion of foreign direct investment. With its rate of contribution to the world economic growth exceeding ten percent, China today is in an age of all-round openness to the world.

What has made these colossal changes possible? As I see it, the answer boils down to the opening-up policy. A look at Chinese and foreign history reveals the inexorable law that a nation thrives whenever it embraces the world, and declines whenever it shuts itself behind closed doors. China's opening-up process over the last three decades is a good case in point. The road of reform and opening designed by Deng Xiaoping, the chief architect of the opening-up policy, has turned out to be a thoroughfare to national rejuvenation.

Throwing their doors wide open to the world community, the Chinese have thrown over old dogmas and closed-mindedness to learn and assimilate the advanced accomplishments of world civilization, executed the opening-up policy to stimulate reform, development and institutional innovation, and put a premium on mutual benefit and win-win results, while enhancing economic collaboration and trade with other nations, thereby pumping new vitality into both Chinese and world economies.

The opening-up policy, however, has been no cakewalk. Such a dramatic transition entails a long-term process of exploring, learning and maturing. To understand the recent 30-year Chinese history under this policy, we have to remember the four milestone years: 1978, the year the nation adopted the opening-up policy and began groping its way into the outside world and running special economic zones through trial and error; 1984, when Deng Xiaoping, convinced that special economic zones really worked in this country, opened up 14 more coastal cities to foreign investment, a move that put an initially introverted China on the world map; 1992, the year the opening-up endeavor gained all-around momentum after Deng, in remarks made during a south China itinerary, set the goal for the nation to establish a socialist market economy; and 2001, in which accession to WTO along with a maturing world-oriented home economy ushered China into a new stage of opening up to the outside world.

In short, by exploring the mutually beneficial relationship between opening up and self-reliance throughout the last 30 years, my country has been better able to push domestic economic growth through expanding global economic ties. Jiang Zemin and those of us who later entered the top-echelon of national leadership had the good fortune to work at the forefront of the opening-up policy in its early years, an experience that battle-tested our mettle and wisdom. Opening up has been a great education for every man and woman involved in it.

I became an executive of the opening-up policy right after it was adopted in 1978. In looking back at what I had gone through, I initially felt that all the historical events I had experienced or witnessed were worth writing down. However, as the Chinese saying goes, "The first step is the hardest." I decided to focus my narrative, therefore, on that episode of Chinese history that began in 1978 and ended in 1984, the year the opening-up policy took root after standing the severe test of the previous years.

I believe that no discussion of that piece of history can be complete without noting the decision-making process of the national leaders and the efforts of those who fought to carry out these decisions alongside the broad masses of people. And I chose to relive history in a storytelling fashion. Sticking to the Chinese historian's tradition of telling nothing but truth, I asked myself to write only what I knew or did, and use only those materials whose truthfulness had been double-checked and validated.

Writing this book put me in mind of the entire process in which Deng led the Chinese people to dismantle ultra-leftist taboos and dogma, central planning and, ultimately, "closed-doorism." It was a process in which the nation effected a monumental switch from seclusion or self-seclusion to a progressively thorough openness to the outside world. It was a "breakthrough" in ideological and institutional terms. That is why the title of the book is "Breaking Through," a term that reflects the harsh reality of the early years of the opening-up policy, symbolizes the daring spirit of the pioneers, and justifies the decisively trailblazing significance of the opening-up policy to the future of China.

When you have broken through an encirclement, the way out is directly ahead of you. Each minor progress in the opening-up endeavor triggered a giant stride forward in national development and brought the country much closer to the outside world. Today, the concept of openness to and respect for new approaches has been deeply engrained in our hearts. It has also become the hallmark of present-day China, and part of the Chinese spirit.

The policy of opening up to the outside world will remain a basic state policy for a long time to come. The younger generation, growing up in an open China, will have an even more open mindset as they work hand in hand with their peers in the rest of the world to begin a new page of history in which civilizations respect one another in harmony and seek common progress while preserving their differences.

As the Chinese proverb goes, "Understanding is the harbinger of love." You are bound to be touched by China if you keep observing with an open eye.

A Dialog With the Author

Publisher: We understand that you have engraved hundreds of seals since you began learning seal-cutting at age 71, including two seals carved in honor of Deng Xiaoping. What was it that you carved on them and why?

Li: After I retired in the spring of 2003, I had time to catch up on art and culture and to pick up the hobbies I had loved since childhood. After learning the skill, I felt inspired to carve some seals for Deng. One of the two pieces I did for him was the "Seal of Deng Xiaoping, Chief Architect of Reform and Opening," and the other was the "Seal of Deng Xiaoping, Quartermaster for Science and Education." Deng had held quite a few important Party and government leadership positions with official stamps from central authorities. Only these two important "posts," "Chief Architect" and "Quartermaster," were non-official. The first one was an honorable title bestowed on him by the entire Party membership and the Chinese people in recognition of his monumental contributions to Chinese history, and particularly to the great cause of reform and opening up to the outside world. He chose the second title for himself for his post-Cultural Revolution mission to end disorder and to set things right, restore the Chinese tradition of respecting teachers and valuing education, and address people's worries and problems in developing science and education. He set a splendid example for us by approaching these missions with grace and style. I believe these two non-official titles were as important as his official ones. It was with a mixture of admiration and nostalgia that I carved these two seals in memory of his historic and worthy contributions.

Seal of Deng Xiaoping, Chief Architect of Reform and Opening

Seal of Deng Xiaoping, Quartermaster for Science and Education

Publisher: *It can take a few centuries, at least, to accomplish the cause of reform and opening, whereas Deng's leadership over this cause lasted less than two decades. In what ways should we see him as the chief architect of the reform and opening policy?*

Li: It's true that reform and opening, the inevitable choice to guarantee success in developing socialism the Chinese way, is a long historical process. However, as the old Chinese saying goes, "The first step is the hardest." To that I would like to add: "It's even harder to begin a great cause." The reason Deng will go down in history with the honorable title "Chief Architect of Reform and Opening" is because the road that he charted to national rejuvenation holds great promise for the Chinese people.

Publisher: *What prompted you to write this book?*

Li: The other day, when you asked me for an interview on Deng and the 30th anniversary of the adoption of the reform and opening policy, I was absorbed in cultural interests. That is why I was slow in answering you. It was due to your repeated urging that I gradually pulled my mind back to old familiar scenes, including my involvement in the nation's foreign economic relations and trade. My treasured memories of Deng and my admiration for him also prompted me to write down the historical facts, however sporadic in my memory, about the great cause of opening up to the outside world that was initiated by the second-generation central leadership led by Deng, however patchy they were in my experience. As I began to write, memories kept flooding back, and I did not stop until I had written down everything I remembered.

Publisher: *We know you became a member of the central policy making echelon in the 1990s. Why didn't you write about the main events of your career, instead of things that happened a lot earlier, back to the days when the reform and opening policy was still in its infancy?*

Li: If you look at the history of China and foreign countries, it is clear that a nation thrives when it is open to the world and goes downhill when it cannot resist the temptation to turn inward. To mark the 30th anniversary of the reform and opening policy, we have got to write about that trailblazing episode of Chinese history as thoroughly as we can. No book of this kind would be complete without mentioning the top leaders' decisions and actions, and the process by which government functionaries at all levels carried out the decisions. A book like this should also tell stories about our pioneers who toiled right at the forefront, and in particular, about the masses of people who dared to venture into the unknown. Everyone involved in this effort should be acknowledged, regardless of their field of work; every historical fact concerning these people is valuable. These considerations moved me to write down what I knew or personally experienced in the early days of the reform and opening efforts. On the other hand, history can be put into proper perspective only when it is observed at a distance. That is why I must leave to other writers the story of the contributions of the third-generation central leadership led by Jiang Zemin.

Publisher: It is 30 years since the beginning of the reform and opening. As someone who was a long-time leader in helping the country to advance this policy, what is your take on this mighty historical process?

Li: That is a rather big question. The National Party Congresses held since the Third Plenary Session of the 11th Party Central Committee have made important summaries of the historical process and national experience in that context. My own personal sense is that the 30-year opening-up effort has been a process of ceaseless exploration, study and development, but some of the years, in particular, were pivotal to this process. These included 1978, the year the country began exploring ways to open up and went on to run special economic zones on a trial basis; 1984, the year Deng affirmed the practice of the special economic zones and decided to open 14 seaboard cities to foreign investors, bringing about an initial pattern for the opening-up policy; 1992, when the top leadership made the decision to build a socialist market economy following the remarks Deng had made during a previous south China tour – a decision that called for speeding up the opening of the Pudong District in Shanghai, adopting a strategy to open the nation's coastal regions to foreign investment, and pursuing the opening-up policy in an all-round way; and 2001, which witnessed our nation's accession to the World Trade Organization (WTO), constant progress in a highly world-oriented economic system, and the beginning of a new stage in the opening-up effort. Thanks to three decades of exploration through trial and error, we have – while upholding socialism and properly balancing the needs for opening up and for national independence and self-reliance – become more keenly aware of the need to develop home and foreign markets and resources, and we are more capable of advancing home development through stronger global economic ties. My book, however, is focused on what happened in the few years before 1984, although for the sake of clarity or thoroughness I extend my narrations on some events to circumstances before or after that period. During those years, despite all the hardships, the opening-up effort got underway, and some of the experiments scored initial success. Many of us working at the forefront at the time would later enter the ranks of central leadership; we could not have gradually deepened our understanding of reform and opening without those years of valuable practice. The opening-up years have been a period of real learning and growth, both for the nation and for those closely involved in it.

Publisher: Many books have been written about the reform and opening. What new things does your book bring to the table?

Li: I joined the opening-up effort right after it began in 1978, so this book is mainly about what I experienced and knew as a participant at the time. To make it more readable, I have written it in a storytelling fashion. The stories are meant to reconstruct that episode of history in which Deng led us to brave all obstacles and put China on the world stage. Because I was just one participant and executive, I was well familiar with some of the central authorities' decision-making processes, but ignorant of many others. Because I could only write about what I knew, my accounts cannot reflect the whole picture. Furthermore, the reform and opening form an integral whole in Deng's strategy, whereas my book is mainly about the opening-up process alone. I do mention some of the reforms, but they are all associated with the opening-up efforts touched upon in the book. The reforms, on the whole, covered a much wider spectrum of efforts. I was not in a position to write about these because my knowledge of some of them, such as rural reform, came only from reading documents and newspapers. Given the limits of my knowledge and

改革開放是我國發展史上的
重大轉折我們要沿著鄧小平同志
為中華民族開創的这条道路堅持
不懈地奮勇前進

江澤民
二〇〇八年八月一日

The adoption of the policy of reform and opening up to the outside world was a major turning point in Chinese history of development. We should forge ahead valiantly and without letup along the road Comrade Deng Xiaoping charted for the Chinese nation.

Jiang Zemin
August 1, 2008

experience, my book cannot give a complete account of the multi-faceted opening-up effort, which involves economic, political and cultural dimensions, among many others.

Publisher: The title of your book, "Breaking Through," is easy to remember. It will strike a strong chord with readers. How did you come up with it?

Li: I was using a different title in the beginning. In the course of my remembrance and writing, one fact kept coming back to me. In its early days, the reform and opening effort came up against ossified ways of thinking, established institutions, and the nation's rather flimsy economic base. People were thwarted by one obstacle after another to whatever they wanted to accomplish. The going was really tough, the risks were huge and everyone was under enormous pressure. It was under Deng's leadership that we were able to break through ideological stereotypes and central planning, to end our nation's self-imposed isolation and blaze a trail to a new age of international openness. Every small step we made in this effort meant a quantum leap forward for national economic development. I finally settled on this book title because I wanted to reflect all the trials and tribulations we had gone through, and to do justice to the boldness of the pioneers.

Publisher: I understand that you devoted a lot of time and energy to researching and collating facts and figures for your book. And you also went to see quite a few places. Could you tell us something about the process of writing the book?

Li: Well, to begin with, I wrote a hundred thousand or so words at a stretch. Then I spent some time digging into archives for new clues, and on this basis, I revised and added to the manuscript to come up with a second draft. After the editorial work began, I sorted out photos I had collected and talked to people to verify certain facts and figures. This refreshed my memory and enabled me to add a lot of newly discovered valuable documents and historical data to my book. Li Gu (93-147) of the Eastern Han Dynasty once said, "Of the multitude of things, nothing is more important than this single action*, for the nation's destiny hinges upon it." In my opinion, opening up is one such "single action" because it is pivotal to our effort to make our nation strong and prosperous. Therefore, I wrote my book in all seriousness, in which my writing ability was secondary. The authenticity of historical facts was foremost on my mind because I did not want to say anything that might mislead our readers.

Publisher: You have said that you wrote this book mainly for the younger generation. What do you want to say to those people who grew up in the years of reform and opening?

Li: China's opening-up policy is a fundamental, long-term state policy that still has a long way to go. While some problems remained unsolved as of today, new ones will inevitably crop up. Coming to grips with all these problems calls for the unremitting

---

* "This single action" refers to Li Gu's abortive cause of choosing a wise and upright prince to succeed the throne after the child emperor Liu Zuan (138-146) of the Eastern Han Dynasty (25-220) was poisoned to death by his all-powerful uncle and regent, Liang Ji (?-159). Instead, Liu Zhi (132-167), who was to marry Liang's sister, was enthroned. As a result, Li was dismissed as defender-in-chief, the de facto prime minister, and beheaded at the age of 54.

efforts of one generation after another. Our young people today were born after the 1960s. They were too young to experience those years mentioned in my book. I wanted to tell them some of the things that people of my generation have gone through and help them understand the historical background and process of Deng's opening-up strategy, as well as the relevant problems and solutions, so they will cherish the hard-won accomplishments of the reform and opening policy and carry forward Deng's great cause.

Introduction

In 1958, the First Auto Works produced China's first domestic car – a Dongfeng model. Director Rao Bin and I had the good fortune to accompany it to Beijing's Zhongnanhai, the seat of the central government, for the nation's top leaders to take a look at it. The Second Plenary Session of the Eighth Party Central Committee was in session at Huairen Hall, and our car was on display on the lawn behind it. While Director Rao attended the session as a delegate, I, together with some colleagues, including the chief car designer, Shi Ruji, waited on the lawn in case any central leaders or delegates came to see the car. That task kept us there for the duration of the session, and gave us the chance to see almost all the national leaders. Ye Zilong, director of the Confidential Division of the General Office of the Party Central Committee, went out of his way to arrange for us to attend the session as guest observers the day Chairman Mao made his keynote speech.

On one of those afternoons, two leaders came by, and we immediately knew who they were. The tall man was Peng Zhen, vice chairman of the Standing Committee of the National People's Congress and Mayor of Beijing, and the short one was Deng Xiaoping, General Secretary of the Party Central Committee. Both took a close

As the author (*first row, second from left*) looked on, Deng (*first row, right*), Peng Zhen (*center*) and other top leaders marveled at the First Auto Works' Dongfeng brand car on display at Zhongnanhai, Beijing, 1958.

1

look at the car, said something of encouragement to us, and asked us a few questions. Deng's questions sounded particularly professional. While we answered his questions one by one, we were deeply impressed by his professional knowledge. We came to know later that when Deng was studying in France decades ago, he had worked for a time at the Renault auto works. He was not just a proletarian revolutionary and military strategist – he was also something of a forefather of the Chinese auto industry! Such was my first impression of Deng.

He won me over once again with his comeback to central leadership in 1973, when the nation was caught in the throes of the ten-year chaos of the Cultural Revolution (1966-1976). At the time I was one of the builders of the Second Auto Works in Hubei Province. I could feel his tremendous impact in turning the tide by undoing all the things that had gone wrong. As a result, our factory was able to make up for the time lost in the turmoil and start production in 1975. Later, Deng came under fire for a second time for his actions against the Gang of Four, but it did nothing to tarnish my impression of him as a great man.

In 1978, the First Ministry of Machine-Building Industry appointed me to head a working panel to survey the nation's auto industry and to draft a plan on restoring it to order. During the months thereafter I left my footprints across the country, and I was shocked by the benighted condition of the industry. To change the situation, the government decided to import complete sets of advanced technology and equipment for the construction of a large heavy-duty auto plant. The ministry put me and two colleagues in charge of the preparatory work. I began my mission by negotiating with some of the world's top auto manufacturers. Toward the end of 1978, with Deng's approval, we shifted the topic of the negotiations from technology transfers to establishing a joint venture with Chinese and foreign investment. It was those negotiations that ushered me into the nation's opening-up endeavor.

After I became a member of central leadership in 1992, I met Deng in person on many occasions. During one particularly unforgettable encounter, he told me, "We have got to reform and open up; otherwise we are doomed." He had made that remark on many previous occasions, but when he said it directly to me, I regarded

The author posing for a photo with Deng Xiaoping.

it as his political admonition for members of my generation. It has since become my maxim.

Thus I traveled down the road Deng charted for reform and opening until my retirement.

Decades passed quickly by without my realizing. I look back with pride on our nation's achievements – achievements that the world was watching with great interest – over the 30 years of reform and opening. As I begin to recall those exciting early days in which Deng led the entire Party membership and the people to surmount obstacles and to open the nation up to the world, a wealth of emotions and thoughts flood my mind. Past events keep returning, clearly and vividly to my memory.

1

Opening Up Becomes a Key State Policy

T he 20th century was full of trials and tribulations for China. It was an age in which the nation fought to overcome internal turmoil and foreign invaders, and eventually embarked on a road to national rejuvenation.

The Third Plenary Session of the 11th Party Central Committee in 1979 marked a point of departure in Chinese history and ushered the nation into a new era of reform and opening and the Four Modernizations. By accurately reading the pulse of the times and seizing the opportunities open to him, Deng raised a series of important ideas and made the crucial policy decision to establish the reforms along with an open policy. Of all his logical theses, the following two had perhaps the most sobering effect on us in those days: "The world today is an open world," and "The development of China cannot do without the world." Proceeding from the Chinese reality, and drawing on international experience, he decided to open the coastal regions to foreign investors as the first step in a strategy that envisioned a China with a multi-dimensional and wide-ranging openness to the world. He then established the opening-up effort as a fundamental, long-term state policy. This laid the ideological and theoretical groundwork for opening the nation up to the outer world in an all-round way, for speeding up the modernization drive and leapfrogging the nation onto the road of strong and sustainable national development and enrichment for its people.

Chinese and foreign history has long borne out the objective law: A nation thrives whenever it swings its doors open to the world, and goes downhill whenever it dwells behind closed doors. People may ask: Then how do you explain the seclusion of China in the first 20 years of the People's Republic?

Embargo and Isolation in the Early Years of New China

Deng gave a compelling answer to the question of China's isolation:

> When Comrade Mao Zedong was still around, we had also thought of expanding international exchanges in economy and technology, including fostering economic ties and promoting trade with some capitalist countries. We had even thought of adopting foreign investment and running joint ventures with foreign partners. But circumstances did not allow us to do these things, because some countries were imposing sanctions on us. Later, the Gang of Four labeled those who wanted to open up as "worshippers of foreign things and bootlickers for foreigners," and even accused them of committing treason. By doing so they virtually excluded us from the world. It was Comrade Mao Zedong's strategic thought on the division of three worlds* that eventually charted a new road for us.

New China abrogated all the prerogatives – such as customs control, troop garrisoning and inland navigation rights – that the imperial powers had extorted from rulers of old China. That action, coupled with the advent of the Cold War in the wake of World War II, prompted the Western powers, headed by the United States, to adopt a policy of hostility and containment against New China. They refused to grant diplomatic recognition to China, and imposed upon it isolation, military encirclement and economic embargo. Thus the road to learning and opening up to the West was totally blocked for China.

To shatter the embargo and win international help for its rehabilitation and construction efforts, New China listed "inside and outside exchanges" as a major part of its basic principle for economic

---

* Mao's theory that the world is divided in political and economic terms into three worlds, that is the "first world" of superpowers (the Soviet Union and the United States), the "second world" of developed nations (including European countries and Japan) and the "third world" of developing countries.

development. Mao himself clearly recognized the necessity of this two-pronged approach. In an address to the Party's Seventh National Congress held in 1945, he said:

> We need huge amounts of capital to fuel industrial development. Where will it come from? It will come from none other than two sources, that is, we must rely mainly on the Chinese people to accumulate funds on their own, and at the same time, we must avail ourselves of foreign aid. Foreign investors are welcome, so long as they observe Chinese law and order and act in favor of the Chinese economy.

The Chairman repeated this principle of openness to foreign trade and investment four years later in his report to the Second Plenary Session of the Seventh Party Central Committee (on March 5, 1949), where leaders deliberated the fundamental policies for the soon-to-be established People's Republic:

> As for doing business with foreigners, there is no question: wherever there is business to do, we shall do it and we have already started it; the businessmen of several capitalist countries are competing for such business. As far as possible, we must first of all trade with the socialist and people's democratic countries; at the same time we will also trade with capitalist countries.

At the Preparatory Meeting for the New Political Consultative Conference held on June 15 of the same year, he declared, "The Chinese people wish to maintain friendly cooperation with the people of all countries and to resume and extend international trade in order to develop production and to promote economic prosperity." On October 1, 1949, the day the People's Republic was founded, he proclaimed:

> This government is the sole legal government representing the people of the People's Republic of China. This government shall establish diplomatic relations with any foreign government willing to observe the principles of equality, mutual benefit and mutual respect for each other's territorial integrity and state sovereignty.

Mao proclaiming the birth of New China at Tiananmen Rostrum, Beijing, October 1, 1949.

In his celebrated essay *On the Ten Relationships* published in 1956, Mao advocated learning from foreign countries, as he wrote in the chapter "The Relationship Between China and Foreign Countries":

> Our policy is to learn from the strong points of all nations and all countries, learn all that is genuinely good in the political, economic, scientific and technological fields and in literature and art. ... We must firmly reject and criticize all the decadent bourgeois systems, ideologies and ways of life of foreign countries. But this should in no way prevent us from learning the advanced science and technologies of capitalist countries and whatever is scientific in the management of their enterprises. In the industrially developed countries they run their enterprises with fewer people and greater efficiency and they know how to do business. All this should be learned well in accordance with our own principles in order to improve our work.

No one, perhaps, more keenly felt the importance of linking domestic development to the world economy than our long-time beloved Chinese Premier Zhou Enlai. As he pointed out:

Deng (*center*) visiting the Poland Economic Exhibition in Beijing, September 26, 1953.

In the presence of Mao (*second row, third from right*), Liu Shaoqi (*second row, first from right*), Zhu De (*second row, second from right*) and Nikita Khrushchev (*second row, fourth from right*), Zhou Enlai(*seated, right*) and A. I. Mikoyan (*seated, left*), Vice Chairman of the USSR Council of Ministers, signing on behalf of their respective governments the Sino-Soviet Agreement on Cooperation in Science and Technology along with a loan agreement and a protocol on Soviet aid to new industrial projects in China, October 12, 1954.

No country in the process of development, nor any country in this world for that matter, can become completely self-sufficient behind closed doors. Nations inevitably need one another, first of all, in trade and technological cooperation.

What the premier meant was that autarky and xenophobia were nonstarters in the new age. These ideas about the need to engage and do business with the outside world became the cornerstone of the foreign economic policy of post-Liberation China. This pragmatic, open attitude, however, was both principled and flexible. Zhou essentially said: We shall develop equal and mutually beneficial trade relations with other countries, provided they recognize the new Chinese government.

Under the circumstances of the time, however, when the Western countries, headed by the United States, were bent on politically isolating China, it was impossible for us to open up to every country in the world. We had no alternative but to open the door to the socialist countries led by the Soviet Union. This policy of partial extroversion was reinforced both by the outbreak of the Korean War and the subsequent blockade imposed on us by the West. Under this policy, the economic and trade relations between China and the Soviet Union and Eastern European countries made big headway. This policy was by no means one of complete self-seclusion, but it indeed held back China's effort to open up to the Western world.

In December 1949, Mao paid a two-month visit to the Soviet Union, where he spoke with Stalin about a Sino-Soviet treaty of friendship and alliance. Subsequent negotiations between Premier Zhou and Vice Premier Li Fuchun and their Soviet counterparts culminated in an agreement whereby China was to receive 156 major industrial projects from the Soviet Union and some complete installations from other Eastern European countries. Most of these projects were at an advanced world level for their time. Incomplete statistics show that from 1949 to 1960, China, in order to master the technologies involved in these imports, invited more than 20,000 experts from these countries and sent about 10,000 students and trainees abroad to those countries. These students and trainees – plus the scholars and experts who had returned from Europe and North America upon finishing their studies there – formed a staunch

Mao on an inspection tour of First Auto Works, one of the 156 Soviet-aided construction projects around the First Five-Year Plan period (1953-1957), February 13, 1958.

Liao Chengzhi (*right*) and Takasaki Tatsunosuke (*left*), shaking hands after signing the Liao-Takasaki Memorandum on Sino-Japanese nongovernmental trade relations. Premier Zhou Enlai was present at the signing ceremony, November 9, 1962.

contingent of elite scientists and technicians for New China. The central government called on government functionaries at all levels, as well as factory workers, to find ways to study culture, science and technology and management. As a result, learning new things became the call of the day across the land.

The nation embarked in earnest on the First Five-Year Plan (1953-1957), with efforts focused on the 156 Soviet-aided projects. Here are a few facts and statistics from this period:

- China fulfilled a total investment of 55 billion yuan in capital construction, outstripping the original target by 15.35 percent, and acquired 46 billion yuan worth of fixed assets, or 1.9 times the nation's total primary value of fixed assets by the end of 1952.
- Of the aforementioned 156 projects, 135 came under construction, and 68 were entirely or partially completed and started production.
- In 1957, the nation's total industrial and agricultural output value amounted to 124.1 billion yuan, 67.8 percent more than in 1952;
- The total industrial output value exceeded the original target by 21 percent and the 1952 figure by 128.5 percent;
- The steel output totaled 5.35 million tons, or nearly quadrupling what it was in 1952;
- The national income over this period went up by 53 percent;
- Workers' wages averaged 637 yuan, up by 42.8 percent, while farmers' income rose by close to 30 percent.

The First Five-Year Plan met all of its goals and laid down the initial groundwork for the industrialization of China.

During the years of the First Five-Year Plan, active efforts were made to promote economic relations and trade with neighboring countries as well as countries that had achieved national independence. In 1952, with friendly nongovernmental figures serving as matchmakers, China concluded its first nongovernmental trade agreement with Japan even though Sino-Japanese diplomatic relations were yet to be normalized. In 1962, Liao Chengzhi and Takasaki Tatsunosuke signed a comprehensive Sino-Japanese memorandum on long-term trade relations. This significantly boosted the relationship between the two countries and opened a window for bilateral contacts and exchange on a semi-governmental, semi-nongovernmental basis.

As early as the 1950s and 1960s, Hong Kong, an international harbor and trade and financial center, became a major channel for China's economic relations and trade with the outside world. The country managed to procure some badly needed materials from Western countries via Hong Kong. To reciprocate, a freshwater supply project was constructed on the East River of Guangdong Province to meet Hong Kong residents' daily needs and to help the city maintain political stability.

In the early 1960s, the Sino-Soviet relationship went sour. The Soviet side unilaterally scrapped the contracts signed between the two governments and pulled its experts out of China. Mao, Zhou and some other top leaders made the timely decision to shift the main thrust of foreign trade and the importation of technology and equipment to friendly Western countries and regions. Negotiations with these countries and regions during the 1962-1966 period resulted in the importation of more than 20 complete sets of precision machinery and equipment for the metallurgical, petrochemical, electronics and other industries, topping US$300 million in total contractual volume of investment.

These facts show that in the 17 years prior to the Cultural Revolution, it was not that we were unwilling to open our gates to the outside world, but that circumstances did not allow us to carry out an all-dimensional open policy. Even under the blockade imposed by the West, we never stopped experimenting with our opening-up effort.

Self-Imposed Seclusion Under Ultra-Leftist Ideology

The Cultural Revolution, however, plunged China into an age of self-imposed seclusion. The Gang of Four, headed by Jiang Qing, whipped up a frenzy of ultra-leftist posturing, using "anti-imperialism" and "anti-revisionism" as excuses for severing the country's connection with most countries. In 1967, in blatant violation of international norms, they instigated a riot in which the office of the British *Chargé d'Affaires* in Beijing was set on fire. At the time, people with overseas relatives or those who had studied abroad were likely to be dubbed "espionage suspects," and even those who had merely socialized with foreigners came under political scrutiny. Jiang Qing and company particularly targeted foreign economic relations and trade. They pitted self-reliance against exchanges and cooperation with foreign countries, and – resorting to sheer fabrication or exaggeration – labeled imports of foreign technology or products as acts of treason or examples of a "slavish comprador philosophy." As a result, China's foreign economic relations and trade suffered serious interference and sabotage. Zhou Enlai and other revolutionaries of the older generation waged a struggle against the Gang.

The instability at home aside, the deteriorating Sino-Soviet relationship escalated from political confrontation to armed conflicts on the borders between the two nations. This landed China in a position where it could not afford hostility from both the socialist camp and the West.

It was at this juncture that history offered China an opportunity to bail itself out of the dilemma. A shrewd and farsighted Mao seized the opportunity to mend fences with the West. Through painstaking efforts, China had its legitimate position in the United Nations restored in 1971. The signing of the Shanghai Communiqué (more informally referred to as the "Shanghai Accord") in February 1972 marked the normalization of diplomatic relations between China and the United States. Some Western European countries followed suit by gradually easing up on their embargoes and expressed a desire to develop trade with China. Following the changing world circumstances, Mao came up with his famous "Three Worlds" theory to point the way for handling Chinese diplomacy and international economic relations and trade, which set the stage for the opening-up policy.

In 1975, Zhou Enlai fell seriously ill. Deng who, with Mao's backing, had returned to power in 1973, took over the leadership of the Party Central Committee and the State Council. His broad rectification of the chaos of the Cultural Revolution, to the great gratification of the Chinese people, was crowned with success. Those of us working at the forefront felt that Deng was the man capable of stemming the tide and setting China in a new direction. Acting on Deng's instruction, the State Council, from mid-June through mid-August in 1975, held a brainstorming meeting on national planning to hammer out the principles, policies and steps for the realization of the Four Modernizations. Proposals to import new technology and equipment and increase imports and exports were raised. In his speech to the meeting, Deng became the first man in New China's economic history to elevate the introduction of sophisticated technology from foreign countries to the strategic height of "key state policy."

The Gang of Four, however, continued their efforts to sabotage. By the fourth quarter of 1975, the political situation on the home front had taken a drastic turn for the worse. The Gang went on a frenzy to "criticize Deng and counterattack the rightist trend of overturning verdicts" in an attempt to ditch the political principles and the accomplishments of Deng's leadership. Under the Gang's slogans – "Better to keep the weed of socialism than accept the sprouts of capitalism" and "Oppose revisionism and prepare against it" – China turned inward once again. Under the impact of ultra-leftist ideology, self-reliance and "pioneering spirit" were extolled to the skies. People were asked to stop learning and using advanced foreign science and technology, and the nation turned down all foreign countries' offers of economic aids and loans. As a result, the nation was robbed of a golden opportunity to develop its economy.

That episode of history illustrates that in the first few decades, despite the central leadership's good intentions, New China found it hard to open itself to the outside world. The impediments came mainly from without, but sabotage from within by the Gang of Four was definitely another important factor.

"Closed-Doorism" Sets the Economy at an Impasse

The Chinese economy was in shambles and people were hard up as a result of the decade-long calamity of the Cultural Revolution. According to *China Statistical Yearbook* statistics, China accounted for 4.7 percent of the world gross domestic product (GDP) in 1955, thanks to post-Liberation rehabilitation efforts, but the figure plummeted to 1 percent in 1978. In 1976, the Chinese consumed a per capita average of 190.5 kilograms of grain, compared with 197.5 kilograms in 1952, and workers of state-owned or collective firms earned an average of 575 yuan, compared with 583 yuan in 1966. The statistics indicate that for an entire decade workers barely had a single pay raise and their living standards were declining as a result, while the 250 million rural people, for their part, were having trouble making ends meet. The 470.4 billion yuan of GDP the Chinese people created from 365 days of work in 1976 was equivalent to what they would later achieve in a single week in 2007, the year the GDP reached 24.7 trillion yuan. In 1976, one third of the industrial enterprises across the country were losing money, and the nation's industrial profit rate was only half what it had been in 1965. Meanwhile, the nation's imports and exports totaled a meager US$13.4 billion and its foreign exchange reserve amounted only to US$580 million.

These statistics shed some light on the difficulties that China faced in macroeconomic terms, but they could hardly fully reflect the hard lot of the people during those years. The experience of economic hardship and isolation during those years may mean little to the younger generation today, but it is etched deeply in the memories of those of us who lived through it. Those were days in which almost everything was in short supply. Capital goods were allotted according to state quotas. Cooking fuel, rice, cooking oil, table salt and other daily necessities could be bought only with ration coupons that fell into 60 to 70 categories.

Grain Ration Coupons

The term "grain coupon" may sound strange to young people today, but for my generation it was for decades a harsh and inescapable reality.

The story of grain coupons dates back to my school years in Shanghai. The nation had just been liberated in 1949. The Kuomintang had just fled the mainland to Taiwan, but their dream of a comeback never died. Alternating military and economic means, working overtly or secretly, they wasted no opportunity to sabotage. "The Communists may have conquered Shanghai, but they cannot govern it. They will beat a retreat when things get really nasty," they bragged. As one of these subverting activities, underground Kuomintang agents worked hand in glove with unscrupulous merchants to disrupt the grain supply. Because grain was in short supply in those early days, the merchants hoarded the stocks to send grain prices skyrocketing, thus residents could not afford them. The municipal government countered by flooding the local market with grain shipped from other parts of the country. The resulting ample grain supply on the market quickly proved to be the undoing of the merchants. They hurried to offload their stocks, but it was too late. The people thus stood the test, and the government gained precious time for making long-term plans.

The First Five-Year Plan beginning in 1953 marked the start of the socialist industrialization of China. The large-scale industrial construction that ensued drastically boosted the cities' and industries' demand for grain. To tackle the grain shortage and to ensure people's livelihood, the Administrative Council of the Central Government issued the *Instructions on Planned Grain Purchase and Supply*, stipulating that city dwellers working in government departments, institutions, schools and enterprises should obtain their grain supply from the workplace, and the other city residents should buy their share of grain with a grain purchasing certificate or, in the absence of such a certificate, their residence registration documents. In 1955, the *Provisional Procedures for the Supply of Rationed Grain for Urban Residents* was adopted, and grain ration coupons were issued in November of that year to go with these procedures. The grain

Some grain coupons issued in different localities.

coupons came in two kinds, one for local use and the other for nation-wide circulation.

The grain coupons played a major role in guaranteeing provisions for residents in the early days when grain was in short supply. By the time of the Cultural Revolution, however, people were being asked to "voluntarily" trim their already tight rations. Grain rationing became an exercise in minute categorization, with differing values accorded to people at various job levels and ranking, and differences between women and men in each category. This made life even harsher. At the time, my monthly grain ration was 14 kilograms. Grain coupons for local use were issued in grain stores to bearers of residence registration certificates. People making business trips to other parts of the country had to convert their local grain coupons into the kind for nationwide circulation with an employer's introduction letter. Local grain coupons were good for a fixed term, so people had to use them up before they expired. As there was no deadline for the nationwide coupons, people would make every effort to convert local coupons into nationwide ones, thus turning grain coupons into "negotiable securities." As I remember it, a nationwide coupon for 0.5 kilogram of grain was worth one egg. If you had enough coupons, that entitled you to a few kilograms of grain, or if you chose to trade in the coupons, a much-coveted plastic basin.

A foreign friend working as a senior executive with a big foreign company once told me about his experience back in the 1980s when he was a Chinese major at the Beijing Language Institute. Having a penchant for Chinese culture, he was learning Chinese calligraphy from a tutor during his spare time. One day he was pedaling his bicycle home from his lesson. Dusk was gathering and, realizing he was hungry, he stopped at a restaurant in east Beijing. When he fished out money from his pocket and asked for a few stuffed buns, the waitress asked him for a grain coupon. "I am a foreigner and I don't have grain coupons," he said. The waitress insisted, saying that she could not sell food to anyone without a grain coupon. Foreigners were no exception, she told him. My friend replied in Chinese, "They sold me food without asking for a coupon the other day, when I ate in another restaurant." The waitress would not budge an inch; to use a catch phrase from today, she was insisting on "national treatment."

My friend's embarrassment was ended when a gentleman generously offered him a few coupons that were enough for a few *liang** of grain. That was my friend's first encounter with grain coupons. He was so curious about them that he kept one of them and still has it today. He was grateful to his "savior," but all my friend could remember by the time I knew him was that the gentleman was middle-aged and slim. He regretted not asking his name, so that he might have looked him up to thank him decades later. My friend's experience – nothing unusual for my fellow countrymen in those days – for him was remarkable enough to become an oft-told anecdote for years into the future.

Grain coupons did not disappear from everyday life until after the adoption of the reform and opening policy. Remarkable increases in grain output, coupled with a transformed grain sales and purchases system, eventually rendered the rationing system obsolete.

Ration Coupons for Other Food Items

Grain was not the only food item supplied by rationing. Cooking oil, meat, eggs, coal and other items were all rationed and could be bought only with coupons or certificates. Fresh fish was a rarity in Beijing's grocery stores. Once in a while, if you were lucky enough, you might come across some ribbon fish. When winter was around the corner, it was the task of neighborhood committees to urge residents to store an allotted amount of cabbage for the duration of the winter. Many articles of daily use, such as soap, were also sold only to bearers of ration coupons or certificates.

Cloth Ration Coupons

Cloth coupons were a big concern whenever people wanted to buy cloth more than three decades ago. The supply of cloth was rationed and the amount allotted to each person was meager. The cloth ration for an adult in Beijing, where winter is cold, was 5.76 meters, enough for a full-length suit, while in the south, where winter is mild, it was 2.47 meters, enough for a short suit. An additional length of cloth was granted in a lump sum to

---

*   Traditional Chinese unit of weight: one *liang* equals 50 grams.

those having a wedding or funeral. One of the ways to manage with the scarcity of cloth was to sew together empty flour bags or plastic bags for chemical fertilizers to make makeshift quilt linings. The cloth available on the market came in monochrome colors: army green, blue, gray and black. The smart look for men in the spring or autumn was a Mao uniform of light grey. Shortly after the Cultural Revolution, a blouse of flowery design came into vogue among ladies – by "flowery," I mean a kind of cloth printed with tiny red, yellow, blue and brown dots on it.

At the time, officials and intellectuals seldom visited foreign countries. Those who did go abroad on business tours had to borrow the appropriate clothing. Government institutions with foreign relations stored such clothes like stage props, so that they could loan them out to whomever was planning to go abroad or to meet foreigners in China. Due to the limited range of sizes, a good fit was hard to come by. For this reason, some people chose to have clothes made for themselves by tailors. If you think it was no big deal to have your clothes made in a tailor's shop, my personal experience might prove you wrong.

Encounters With a "Third-Class Garment-Making Department"

In early spring of 1978, I was in need of a short-sleeved shirt for summer. I combed through seven stores in one stretch, but could not find a suitable one. My wife told me not to worry. "Let's buy some material and find a tailor to get your shirt made," she said. So we bought a piece of plain-weave silk fabric, and started searching the streets, from Xidan Shopping Street to the Ganjiakou neighborhood, for a suitable tailor's shop. But none of the shops I visited wanted the job, for the single reason that they could only make clothes for people with standard dimensions – a category to which I did not belong. I was puzzled, not knowing which part of my body had gone wrong. Yes, I was slightly overweight, but that was all right for someone in his early forties. I felt helpless: I had looked high and low in vain to buy a shirt that fit me; now I could not even find a tailor to fit me! I had no choice but to continue with my hunt for a store that could do it for me.

To my great relief, I found one in the Sidaokou neighborhood in west Beijing. After the tailor took my measurements, wrote them down on a slip of paper and tucked it into my silk fabric, I asked when I could come back to fetch my shirt. "November," he said. That really left me speechless, as I wondered why it would take more than six months to get a shirt made. "Look," I said with a note of urgency in my voice, "I am supposed to wear the shirt this summer, and you're telling me now I can't get it until November. That will be wintertime. Could you be so kind as to speed it up a bit?" The man was uncompromising. "Don't you see we just have a few people on hand, but the orders are stacked almost to the ceiling," he said. "How can we get around to your order so soon?" I looked around and found out that he was telling the truth. "Why don't you hire more hands now that you have so much work to do?" I ventured. "Hire more people? You make it sound like a piece of cake. Who do you think you are, the boss of the labor bureau?" That retort brought me back to reality. In those days no firm could recruit workers without authorization.

Disappointed, I left the man and went on to try my luck elsewhere. After looking almost everywhere, I found myself standing in front of the Dong'an Emporium at Wangfujing, Beijing's busiest shopping street. At the northwestern gate of the emporium, I saw a silk store with a horizontal signboard on the wall, announcing that the shop could make clothes for clients. Delighted, I asked the shop assistant if they could make a shirt for someone of my stature. He said yes, but at the same time he pointed at the signboard, reminding me to read carefully. What I saw was the name of the store, "Third-Class Garment-Making Department." I asked what was meant by "third-class." "That's because of the poor skills of the workers," he explained, adding that his shop would not compensate if they botched someone's order in the process of tailoring. Finding the man's candor both funny and annoying, I ventured, "You are not saying you would spoil it deliberately?" "Of course not." That sounded reassuring to me, so after being told that it wouldn't take too long to get my shirt done, I had my measurements made and went through the paperwork before returning home, relieved at long last. When the date came, I returned to the shop for my shirt, but was told it was not done yet. I visited the shop a second time, and got the same answer. It was raining when I went there for a third time on the date agreed upon between us. A shop assistant took out the shirt for me to try on. I looked at it, and spotted ugly stitches aligned in irregular lines along the edges of the pocket and cuffs. When I put it on, it looked and felt as baggy as a Japanese kimono. I blurted out, "Come on guys! I can't just wear something like this! See these warped lines? I wouldn't complain if they were sewn inside the shirt, but they're all on the outside for anyone to see. It's really ugly!" To my surprise, the people in the store showed not the slightest sense of guilt. One of the shop assistants said, "We told you when you first came here that this is a 'third-class garment-making department.'" You also knew we would't compensate you for any damage, but you still insisted that we do it for you. Now you are here to accuse us when things did not go your way." When I heard that explanation, I realized that justice was not on my side. What I did not say was that I should not have come to this "third-class" tailor's shop in the first place. I had gone off on the wrong track, because I had no choice. Speechless, I took the shirt and left the shop feeling totally disappointed.

This story reminds me of a tale from *Arabian Nights*. Even I still find it unbelievable, though it happened to me 30 years ago. But it was real and not uncommon in those days.

My Share of "Shrinking" Housing

The housing problem is another embarrassing topic to dwell upon when talking about my country's recent past. Back in the early post-Liberation years, just after I had graduated from college and started work in 1952 with the First Auto Works (then under construction in Changchun), the working conditions were harsh, and winter was subfreezing. Nevertheless, thanks to the Party policy of respecting knowledge and cherishing talents, we felt we were well taken care of. Everybody worked with boundless energy. Along with factory buildings, one residential building after another sprang up. The apartments were of different sizes, but all of them came complete with such amenities as hot running water and shower rooms. At first, we could not believe that these "posh" buildings were for workers. In 1956, when I turned 24 and got married, I moved into a two-room apartment in one of the buildings. At the time, Jiang Zemin was Deputy Chief of the Auto Works' dynamic mechanics division and concurrently Deputy Chief Engineer and Director of its electricity-supply plant, but he was treated as an official at the prefecture level, and lived in a spacious apartment in a building graced with curving eaves. The good housing conditions offered by the First Auto Works struck me as evidence of the superiority of socialism.

My good days, however, were short lived. From the early 1960s, when I left First Auto Works, to the early 1980s, my residential conditions steadily worsened. I was quartered successively in an adobe with rammed-earth walls, a rundown cottage in a village, a dormitory room without a kitchen and tap water, and my own office. Even so, my housing was not the worst in those years. Many married couples lived separately in dormitories. To them, a room even without tap water or a kitchen would still be a dream come true. Those couples with the good fortune to live together were housed in single rooms that opened off on either side of a central hallway which residents typically turned into makeshift kitchens and storerooms.

Official statistics from that period reflect the severity of the nationwide housing problem: in 1977 the per capita floorspace for urban residents averaged 3.6 square meters, compared with 4.5 square meters in 1952. The situation, however, has markedly improved over the last 30 years of reform. By the end of 2007, housing space averaged 29 square meters per urban resident.

Commuting and Traveling Woes

In those pre-reform days, when people spoke of travel – around town or beyond – the refrain of the day was not "taking" the bus or train but "jostling for space" on them. I personally had taken probably the most crowded train in the world, in which seatless passengers stood in the aisles with their backs pressed against each other, with barely a single inch of breathing space. My wife, a daily commuter, had been knocked to the ground when elbowing her way onto a bus; she even suffered a broken bone on one such occasion. Bicycling thus became a convenient mode of transportation for commuters. In wintertime, bicyclists wore gauze masks to ward off the subzero cold. Bicycling in those days was not without its safety hazards, especially when you were pedaling along a street where lamps were dim. One evening, on just such a street, I was thrown off my bicycle when I ran into a half-open manhole. Later, using a much sought-after bicycle coupon, I bought a Forever brand bicycle with a dynamo-driven lamp for 180 yuan. Before long, however, it was stolen by someone who could not resist its allure. My heart ached whenever I thought of my dear, Forever two-wheeler.

Automobiles were a rarity in those years. Most of the trucks on the streets were Dongfeng brand vehicles made by First Auto Works. The output of the newly launched Second Auto Works was negligible. Though trucks were in severe short supply, the First Auto Works did not have the means to expand production and to upgrade its products because virtually all of its annual profits had to be delivered to the state, which then used them to fund other construction projects in the country. Localities had to build their own brands of trucks patterned on the Dongfeng models; because of limited investment and outdated technological know-how, however, they were no match for First Auto Works in terms of output, quality and returns.

In 1978, on assignment for the First Ministry of Machine-Building Industry, I led a nationwide survey of the auto industry to collect data for drafting a national development plan for the industry. During the survey, I found that all provinces, autonomous regions and municipalities except Tibet were running their own auto works, with output ranging from a few dozen to a few hundred or thousand. And most of the vehicles were assembled with a mix of good and bad components purchased from all over the country. These local auto works – handicapped by small scales of production and scattered sources, chaotic management and shabby product quality – were causing a staggering waste of resources, environmental pollution and safety hazards.

Our survey was not without its laughable discoveries. One of the auto plants was producing cheaper imitations of the Liberation brand truck under a name that meant something like "Forever Forward" or "Advance Bravely." I jokingly commented, "That's an ironic name for a truck that is no good." A colleague chipped in, "True to its name, this truck has no reverse gear, so it can only drive forward ."

I was also shocked to learn that people were using tractors, not as farm machinery but as a means of highway transportation, despite their extremely low efficiency, high safety risk, serious pollution, high costs and great waste of resources.

The output of cars was even lower. While localities scrambled with one another to make trucks, few were interested in cars and other small vehicles. At the time, the Shanghai brand car and the Beijing brand jeep were the only available Chinese-made sedan vehicles. The yawning gap between Chinese and foreign auto industries notwithstanding, the chaotic competition between so many local auto works was causing a colossal drain on energy and other resources. The Chinese automobile industry of today, by contrast, has come a long way in terms of both output and quality. The energy, traffic and environmental problems caused by the industry are of a different order, for these are things that come along naturally in the course of healthy development and can be tackled through legislation and progress in science and technology.

Agony in the Barbershop

Getting a haircut is a relatively minor matter, when measured against the four basic necessities of life: food, clothing, shelter and means of travel. It loomed large as a challenge in the 1970s, however, when almost every middle-aged man had trouble getting a timely haircut. People had to queue up in barbershops and patiently await their turn. At the time I was Director of the engine factory of the Second Auto Works, which was then under construction in a remote mountain valley of Hubei Province. In those years, every factory in this country functioned like a society, taking care of the everyday needs of its workers and staff members – and no society, however small, could do without a barbershop.

In my factory, the barbershop was a cause of grievance to everyone, and I was no exception. While the waiting was time-consuming, the barbers' waste of haircutting time was exasperating. If one of the barbers, in the middle of cutting someone's hair, heard that a certain fish, meat, vegetable or anything in short supply was being sold somewhere, or simply felt he had some errand to do, he would just walk away, to the agony of those still waiting their turn, not to mention the man left behind in the chair with a half-shaved head. Finding the situation totally outrageous, I decided to hold a monthly meeting with every barber to appraise his work performance, and join a collective discussion to recommend who had done well enough to deserve a monthly bonus. The idea was to improve the barbers' service and raise their work efficiency. Contrary to my best intentions, however, every time the bonus was discussed, each barber claimed he was the best. The discussion became so heated that it was impossible to make a decision. I ended up having the bonus divided evenly among the barbers, but the problem with the haircutting room remained unsolved, and people's complaints continued.

Then I introduced a piecework wage system, whereby the barbers' wages were based on the number of haircuts performed. This method paid off quickly, and the waiting line became shorter with the steady improvement in the barbers' work efficiency. The good situation, however, did not last long. Some barbers invented what was called the "blitz-speed cutting method." The number of haircuts grew as a result, but quality plummeted drastically. When one of the "victims" came to my office to complain, I immediately knew what he wanted to say. His hair was cut in such a fashion that he appeared to be wearing a wok cover on his head. Torn between annoyance and amusement, I set a ceiling for the number of haircuts each barber could perform in a workday, with no pay for above-quota services. This decision, which was supposed to contain the "blitz-speed cutting method," did not work as I hoped. The barbers went on with it, so that they could knock off ahead of time after serving their quota of clients.

What happened in my factory's barbershop was nothing new. It was, in fact, a daily occurrence in this country for a long time, and it became worse during and after the Cultural Revolution. I remember my Sunday barbershop visits after I was transferred to Beijing shortly after the incarceration of the Gang of Four. It usually took me half a day, from queuing up to getting my hair cut, despite the fact that I managed to shorten the haircutting process itself to 30 minutes by giving up shaving and hair drying. I decided to do something about it. Though I could not give myself a complete haircut, I bought a haircutter to trim my sideburns so that I could prolong the intervals between my barbershop visits. More importantly, I could use the trimmer on my children to save them the trouble of going to the barbershop. I remember thinking wistfully in those years how nice it would be if people never needed to queue up to get a haircut.

My erstwhile haircut misgivings were a microcosm of everything that had gone wrong during the period of economic shortages with "everyone eating from the same big pot."

I'm not casting blame for this and other nagging problems on government functionaries or barbers. People may argue, "The barbers in our neighborhood were not behaving like that. Their attitude was just fine, and some of them were labor heroes." Of course, every trade or profession has its heroes, and we should learn from their exemplary acts. In the past, we often believed that everybody should and could become a labor hero because our ideological and political work was so omnipotent that the problems in our system and institution did not matter at all. Practice, however, shows that problems of a universal nature must be traced back to institutional and administrative pitfalls. Only thus can we stamp out the problems. Our haircutting woes have disappeared only because the adoption of the reform and opening policy has transformed the economic system, opened up the service industry, and abolished the lifelong tenures that were part of the egalitarian practice in which everybody ate from the same rice pot. Only with good work attitude, quality and efficiency can people be duly awarded and work to save their jobs. All this has been borne out by facts.

The Cost of Chasing Fashion

In those years daily necessities, like anything else, were in dire shortage. I felt that was particularly true of children's toys. It seemed to me that the toys selling in stores were mostly celluloid dolls, tin-plate playthings, inflated balloons, and plastic geese and ducklings. Once, I was shopping around for a desk lamp, but all I could find were three kinds: antiquated lamps with a green glass shade; lamps featuring an umbrella-shaped gauze shade; and T-shaped lamps with a fluorescent tube.

Watches were not considered luxuries at the time, but they were hard to come by – you had to obtain a wristwatch coupon before you could buy one. Back then I had been wearing an oft-repaired Shanghai brand wristwatch for 20 years. Because it had become very inaccurate and worn out, I wanted a new one, but I put it off because of all the hassle of getting a coupon for it, and the fact that the domestically made watches available in stores looked very much the same. Shortly after the country began its reform and opening, Beijing released a Double Diamond watch. It had a somewhat new design and could be purchased without a wristwatch coupon, so I bought one, even though its price tag – 130 yuan – was twice as expensive as old-fashioned watches. Before long, however, an electronic watch, on which seconds, minutes, hours and dates were indicated by digital numerals, caught my fancy. These were selling for 70 yuan apiece. I bought one without hesitation. Wishing to save money, I immediately went off to a secondhand shop to trade in my Double Diamond. When the shop assistant examined the watch and the invoice, he offered me two options: to sell it on commission for 80 yuan, or sell it to the store for 60 yuan. I was surprised by both prices. Pointing at the invoice, I hastened to say that the watch was worth 130 yuan and nearly brand new – I had used it for less than three months. The shop assistant answered, "I don't doubt you're telling the truth, but you probably don't know that the intra-trade price of the Double Diamond is only 70 yuan. Who would want to buy the same watch at double the cost?" That explanation was plain enough. I had no choice but to sell the watch at a loss. The consequence of my costly chase after wristwatch fashion, however, did not stop then and there. The electronic watch stirred a lot of envy in friends and colleagues in the beginning, but less than six months later, it began to "age" prematurely. The digital display became increasingly fuzzier, the electroplated surface began to peel, and the entire watch broke down after serving me for only eight months.

In 1983, I became Vice Mayor of Tianjin. There happened to be a large factory there, producing watches in styles that had remained unchanged for decades. My penchant for watches prompted me to do something about it. When I visited the factory, I found out that the problem was less technical than institutional. In foreign countries, wristwatch components – movements, cases, hands and dials – were made by different factories along specialized lines, and the tasks of a watch plant were limited to designing, assembling, brand promotion and sales. The watch-making factory in Tianjin, by contrast, was big and all-inclusive, and made every component on its own with the outdated technology and equipment at hand. A foreign watchmaker could come up with more than 300 watch styles a year, but it took at least three years for a Chinese manufacturer to release a single new style. This problem could easily be solved by importing foreign technology and equipment. The true snags, however, stemmed from drawbacks in management and state policy. During my visits to Tianjin Watch Factory, I discovered that watch-making was a high-profit industry: it cost an average of eight yuan to produce a watch that would then sell for several dozen yuan. But given this huge profit margin, why was the factory not keen on innovation? It turned out that any profit the factory made was handed over to the state, and thus profit had become irrelevant to the well-being of the factory and its workers. More importantly, the high profit of the watch-making industry was driving localities to launch small factories to market their own watches at prices far lower than those made in large factories in Shanghai, Beijing and Tianjin. While the small factories were selling cheap, the big factories were not allowed to bring down their state-mandated prices. The market share of small factories grew unchecked, while inventories in big factories kept stacking up. It was a typical case of unfair competition, resulting from the government's approach of keeping a tight rein on big factories and giving a free hand to small ones. It was like so many ants gnawing away at a bone, pushing mainstay factories to the brink of bankruptcy. This phenomenon, ridiculous and dismaying as it was, was a living reality. The only way out was reform. Only by decontrolling production plans and prices, running joint ventures, promoting international cooperation, introducing advanced technology, and participating in competition at home and abroad, could the watch-making industry be resurrected.

Though they may sound like dust-covered fragments of history, these things really happened in our country a mere 30 years ago. I expect that young people today would find them utterly unimaginable.

People's Choice: Deng's Comeback to Power

The downfall of the Gang of Four in 1976 spelled the collapse of the Cultural Revolution. The Chinese people, having had their fill of misery during that decade-long turmoil, saw the dawn of national rejuvenation once again.

Who would bail out China and lead it on the road to rebirth? Both the nation's veteran leaders and man on the street were thinking of the same man: Deng Xiaoping. Ye Jianying, Chen Yun, Li Xiannian and other top leaders petitioned the Party Central Committee to bring Deng back to his leadership posts as soon as possible.

Deng's comeback to power, however, was no smooth sailing. In February 1977, a few national newspapers ran an editorial entitled "Learning the Documents Well and Grasping the Key Link," which emphasized: "We should resolutely safeguard *whatever* policy decisions the late Chairman Mao had made and unswervingly follow *whatever* instructions he has delivered." The "two whatevers" line was purported to justify the mistakes Mao had committed in his later years in launching the Cultural Revolution. It was also an effort to block attempts to overturn the Gang's erroneous verdicts on Deng and on the April 5, 1976 Tiananmen Incident, in which people gathered to mourn the death of Premier Zhou and protest against the Gang.

This editorial came as a straw in the wind, signaling that something was seriously wrong in the political atmosphere. The nation's veteran leaders were the first to voice their opposition against the "two whatevers," while stepping up their effort to reinstall Deng in central leadership. Ye Jianying added the following two proposals for overcoming this setback to a forthcoming speech to be delivered by Hua Guofeng (at a Party Central Committee work conference scheduled for March 10 to 22, 1977):

> First, the "Tiananmen Incident" was a sheer frame-up and those implicated should therefore be exonerated; second, regarding our appraisal of Comrade Deng Xiaoping, we should change our tone and furnish favorable conditions for him to step up and begin work again.

In a written speech delivered on March 13 at the same conference, Chen Yun endorsed this support for Deng:

> I learned that some comrades on the Central Committee, taking the needs of the Chinese Revolution and the Communist Party of China into consideration, have suggested that Comrade Deng

Xiaoping be allowed to rejoin the Party Central Committee leadership. This suggestion is entirely correct and necessary, and I stand for it with no reservation whatsoever.

In his speech, Wang Zhen condemned those bent on blocking the exoneration of the participants of the "Tiananmen Incident" and the restoration of Deng to his leadership position. He said:

> Deng Xiaoping is strong in politics and ideology. He is also a rare talent. This was what Chairman Mao said about him and was conveyed to us by Premier Zhou. Deng's achievements were remarkable when he presided over the work of the Party Central Committee and the State Council in 1975. He was the vanguard in our fight against the Gang of Four, and that is why the Gang stopped at nothing to frame him in despicable ways. The "Tiananmen Incident" was the pride of the nation and the crystallized embodiment of the Chinese people's class consciousness and awareness of the Party line. Whoever denies the essence and popular mandate of that incident is actually glossing it over for the Gang.

Through the persistent efforts of Ye Jianying and other proletarian revolutionaries of the older generation – and in response to the urgent demand of people of all ethnic backgrounds throughout the country – the Third Plenary Session of the Tenth Party Central Committee (July 16 to 21, 1977) in Beijing unanimously endorsed the *Resolution on Restoring Comrade Deng Xiaoping to His Posts*. This act reinstalled Deng as Politburo Member and Standing Committee Member, Vice Chairman of the Party Central Committee and of the Central Military Commission, Vice Premier of the State Council, and Chief of the General Staff of the People's Liberation Army. In his speech to the session, Deng said:

> It is a personal pleasure for me, in the few years left in my lifetime, to do what a veteran Communist is supposed to do for the Party, the nation and the people. Anyone setting out to work may take one of two attitudes, to be a bureaucrat or to get something done. I say to myself, who was it that turned me into a Communist? It was none other than myself. Now that I have chosen to be a Communist, it

makes no sense for me to indulge in officialdom and selfish thinking. I have no choice but to stay humble while fulfilling my obligations as a Party member and to obey the Party's arrangements.

On the evening of July 30, 1977, Deng was seen at the presidium of an international invitational soccer game at Beijing's Workers Stadium. It was his first public appearance since he was reinstalled in his official functions just about two weeks before. The 80,000 spectators were elated at the sight of him, and the entire stadium reverberated with a prolonged thunderous applause. The news electrified its way to the world in no time. His presence in the stadium also added to the excitement of the soccer game itself, which pitted the national team against Hong Kong.

That public appearance pushed Deng onto a much broader stage, where he was to direct China's advance along the road he would chart – the Chinese road of socialism toward prosperity. If the rectification campaign of 1975 – masterminded by Deng after his previous comeback to power at Mao's behest during the Cultural Revolution – was a bold exploration of the cause of reform, then all the major events in Chinese history and the everyday life of the Chinese people during the following three decades were intimately linked with Deng's reform and opening policy. At his 80th birthday banquet, Marshal Ye Jianying said of Deng, "He is the squad leader of us old marshals." Obviously, in the eyes of the founders of New China, Deng was the irreplaceable nucleus of the nation's central leadership. To put it another way, the reform and opening would have been out of the question without Deng's third and final comeback to power. It was history and the people that had chosen him.

"Emancipating the Mind" and the "Criterion for Truth"

The demise of the Cultural Revolution gave China a new lease on life. It took no less than a Herculean effort, however, to eradicate the political and ideological aftermath of this catastrophe.

China's crisis did not end immediately with the fall of the Gang of Four. The political situation remained grim. Instead of repudiating the disastrous Cultural Revolution, the man in charge of the Party Central Committee believed that the Gang's downfall was "yet another great victory of the 'Proletarian Cultural Revolution' and that China "should carry through to the end the continued revolution under the proletarian dictatorship."

It was against this background that the editorial on the "two whatevers" was released; it came as a bucket of cold water thrown upon the Chinese people who had been reveling in the overthrow of the Gang. People began to wonder: Should criticism of Deng be allowed to go on? Should the nation stick to "taking class struggle as the key link" and carry on with "continued revolution under the proletarian dictatorship"? Should the Cultural Revolution be continued, or allowed to happen once every seven or eight years? Everyone knew, however, that if the answers to all these questions were positive, China would be doomed forever.

In his quieter days before his final comeback to power, Deng had already seen through the "two whatevers." Showing a veteran's valor, he pointed out: The "two whatevers" will get us nowhere! In an April 1977 letter to Hua Guofeng, Ye Jianying and the Party Central Committee, he urged them to "apply Mao Zedong Thought accurately and completely as the guidance for the entire membership of our Party and army and the people throughout the country." On more than one occasion, he spoke openly in opposition against the "two whatevers."

In April 1977, Hu Yaobang, who had been appointed vice president of the Party School of the Party Central Committee a month earlier, organized a conference on rectifying the Party work style to address the legacies of the Cultural Revolution. (The conference did not end until September.) Considering the chaos caused by the Cultural Revolution, Hu called on the participants to reverse all of the Gang's verdicts on ideas, theories and Party line, and to restore and carry forth the Party's fine traditions and work style that had been badly corrupted by the Gang. Marshal Ye Jianying, speaking at a ceremony for the reopening of the Party School on October 9, urged the faculty and students to study Party history carefully, particularly the history of the struggle between the two lines at the Ninth, Tenth and 11th National Party Congresses. He was actually asking people to summarize the lessons of the Cultural Revolution as a whole. Acting on the marshal's call, the Party School under Hu's leadership started studying and discussing the struggle on the Party line during the Cultural Revolution, with a focus on what criteria

The Central Party School journal *Theoretical Trends* releases the landmark article "Practice Is the Sole Criterion for Judging Truth," May 10, 1978.

should be adopted to judge the rights and wrongs of certain historical issues. In this way, he shifted the main thrust of the discussions to the criterion for judging truth. At a December 2 Party School meeting to summarize the discussions, Hu set practice as the criterion. "The history of the last decade or so should not be judged with a certain document or a certain man's remarks," he said, "rather, it should be put to the test of practice. It is practice that counts." He then set two major principles. One was to understand Mao Zedong Thought comprehensively and accurately; the other was to use practice as the criterion for judging truth. On this basis, the Party School compiled the document, *On a Number of Issues Concerning the Struggle Between the Two Lines at the Ninth, Tenth and 11th National Party Congresses*, for further study among its 800 students.

This theoretical discussion found its way into a broader arena. On May 10, 1978, the Party School journal *Theoretical Trends* published "Practice Is the Sole Criterion for Judging Truth." The next day, the national *Guangming Daily* reprinted the full text of the article, under the name "Our Special Commentator," and the Xinhua News Agency released it for national circulation. The same article was reprinted again on May 12 by the *People's Daily*, the *Liberation Army Daily* and a number of provincial-level dailies.

The article came with four subtitles: 1) "Only Social Practice Can Be the Criterion for Judging Truth"; 2) "Unity Between Theory and Practice is the Most Fundamental of All Principles of Marxism";

3) "Revolutionary Gurus Are Exemplary in Adhering to Practice as the Criterion for Judging Truth"; and 4) "All Theories Must Be Put to Repeated Tests of Practice." Among other things, the article boldly proclaimed: "Wherever there is a self-styled absolute 'forbidden zone' that transcends practice, there will be no room for science and true Marxism-Leninism and Mao Zedong Thought, but only for obscurantism, idealism and cultural autocracy."

This article raised a lot of eyebrows, and caused tremendous repercussions. Before long, detractors began rebuking it from the height of Party line and what banner it was upholding. Some accused the article of committing "mistakes concerning political orientation," arguing that it was "fallacious in theory and reactionary in ideology" and that it was a political attempt to "chop down the Party's banner." Some said it had "played a downright bad role." The others argued that the article "definitely hurts inner-Party unity by exposing in the media the conflict between top leaders of the Party Central Committee."

Deng was the first to stand up for the article at this critical moment. In a May 30 conversation with Hu Qiaomu and others, he said:

> You are deemed wrong if you've said something to differ from Chairman Mao and Chairman Hua. You are deemed wrong, too, if you've said what Chairman Mao and Chairman Hua did not say. How can you do right then? Only by parroting what Chairman Mao said or what Chairman Hua said. I mean by copying either of them verbatim. This is by no means an isolated phenomenon, but the reflection of a prevailing trend of thought. Those comrades who make these kinds of statements when they talk about Mao Zedong Thought want no part of what we are now calling for: to seek truth from facts and to proceed from reality.

Deng went on, "A new problem has arisen, which is that even the saying 'practice is the criterion for judging truth' has come into question. I can't make head or tail of it!"

On July 21, Deng summoned Zhang Pinghua, minister of the Party Central Committee's publicity department, and told him, "Let's have no more taboos and forbidden zones. Let this political situation play itself out and don't hinder it. It has just come to life and is full of promise." Deng affirmed the discussions that Hu Yaobang was presiding over on the criterion for testing truth, when he spoke with Hu on July 22. "The article 'Practice Is the Sole Criterion for Judging Truth' is Marxist," he said. "The controversy surrounding it is unavoidable, and it is a good thing. The root cause of this controversy is the "two whatevers.'"

During a meeting with Minister of Culture Huang Zhen and Vice Minister of Culture Liu Fuzhi on August 19, he said again, "The article 'Practice Is the Sole Criterion for Judging Truth' is Marxist and therefore, irrefutable."

These unequivocal remarks lent forceful support to the theme of the article during a critical moment in the controversy. They also brought into sharp relief Deng's boldness, vision and insight in seizing an historical opportunity to set things right on the political and ideological fronts and in calling on people to persevere in truth.

Chen Yun and other veteran Party leaders also backed the viewpoint put forth in the article. Whenever Chen was asked to compose an inscription for someone as a keepsake, he would write down the same line: "Worship neither higher-ups nor books; worship practice. Keep exchanging opinions and making comparisons."

Deng told Hu Yaobang on July 22, 1978, "The controversy surrounding it (the criterion for judging truth) is unavoidable, and it is a good thing. The root cause behind the controversy is the 'two whatevers'."

The article also won the allegiance of the military. Addressing the preparatory meeting for an all-army conference on political work, Luo Ruiqing, Secretary-General of the Central Military Commission, put it this way:

> [The article] "Practice Is the Sole Criterion for Judging Truth" is good in that it persists in Marxism-Leninism and Mao Zedong Thought. It raises an issue that will have a major impact on the overall situation. The purpose of the All-Army Conference on Political Work is to publicize the ideological line of seeking truth from facts, to proceed from practice in whatever we do, and to promote practice as the only criterion for testing truth. We will get nowhere without thoroughly coming to grips with this issue.

When the All-Army Conference took place on June 2, Deng delivered an important speech in which he elaborated the guiding principle for seeking truth from facts; emphasized that "seeking truth from facts is the starting point and very foundation of Mao Zedong Thought"; criticized cults of personality, dogmatism and idealism; and called on the army to "restore order, set wrongs right, smash all spiritual yokes, and free up our minds in a big way."

Deng urged army commanders to be exemplary in combining Marxism-Leninism and Mao Zedong Thought with practice. With Luo Ruiqing's backing, the Party School under Hu's leadership wrote another article entitled "A Most Fundamental Principle of Marxism" to refute detractors of the ideas expressed in the article "Practice Is the Only Criterion for Judging Truth." On Mao's 85th (posthumous) birthday, *Red Flag*, the Party mouthpiece, invited Tan Zhenlin to write an article. "I am not going to limit my article to history," Tan told the editors. "I will start from reality to write about practice as the only criterion for judging truth, to show that Mao Zedong Thought is a scientific truth that stems from practice and has stood the test of practice."

To deepen the discussions, Deng left Beijing and went on a tour to promote the spirit of seeking truth from facts. The tour brought him to Sichuan and Guangdong and ended in Jilin in September. "I am spreading the flame everywhere," he said. On September 16, when hearing a work report by governors of Jilin Province, he instructed:

How to uphold the banner of Mao Zedong Thought is a paramount issue. Many people today, inside and outside the Party, at home and abroad, are in favor of upholding the banner of Mao Zedong Thought. But what does "upholding" really mean? How should we uphold it? As you all know, there is an argument promoting the "two whatevers." It's famous, isn't it? According to that line, whatever Comrade Mao Zedong did or said is untouchable. Does this argument uphold the banner of Mao Zedong Thought? Absolutely not! If that line of thinking is allowed to run unchecked, it can only ruin Mao Zedong Thought. The foundation of Mao Zedong Thought is to seek truth from facts, that is, to integrate the universal truth of Marxism-Leninism with the concrete practice of the Chinese revolution.

During his tour, Deng also stressed:

The most pressing mission for China is to develop productivity. We have been so poor and are trailing so far behind others that, to be honest, we have let the people down. Ours is a socialist country. A fundamental manifestation of the superiority of the socialist system is that it allows society's productivity to grow at a rapid speed (which our old society was incapable of) so as to meet the people's growing demand in their material and cultural life.

To tackle that pressing mission, Deng made the suggestion that later turned out to be of pivotal strategic significance: Bring mass criticism of the excesses of the Gang of Four to an opportune end, and shift the emphasis of Party and government work to the socialist modernization drive.

When addressing a central work conference on December 13, 1978, Deng reiterated the importance of settling the ideological debate: "The discussions on the criterion for testing truth are about ideology. This is a political issue with a close bearing on the destiny of the Party and the state." His "flame-fanning" tour, indeed, won him the allegiance of local governments, for all the provinces, municipalities and autonomous regions voiced their support of the idea that practice is the sole criterion for testing truth. All the army services and military zones pledged their loyalty as well.

The large-scale discussions fully demonstrated that only practice can tell whether a theory reflects reality or truth. They also showed that the point is not so much to judge whether a theory is right or wrong, but to enable people to shake off the restraints of dogmatism and cult of personality and to shift the work of the entire Party membership and the whole country away from ossified ways of thinking and toward innovation and reform – from the state of seclusion or semi-seclusion to full openness to the outside world.

The principal contribution of these discussions was that they restored the Party line of "emancipating the mind" and "seeking truth from facts." Judging from the reform and opening process over the last three decades, every advance has been a process of "emancipating the mind." In that sense, the very destiny of the Party and the nation hinged upon the political issue of an agreed understanding of the criterion for truth.

Restoring Order and Setting Things Right

After national celebrations of the fall of the Gang of Four were over, people began to ask the serious question: Which is the road to national rejuvenation? This was the same question that occurred to Deng right after he returned to power for the third time in his political career.

From a Chinese perspective, major changes had taken place on the world scene in the 1970s and Mao's diplomatic philosophy played a large role in it. On October 25, 1971, the 26th Session of the United Nations General Assembly passed with an overwhelming majority vote the resolution to restore China to all its lawful rights in the United Nations. This was a monumental victory, the hard-won result of long-term efforts on the part of China and many other Third World and sympathetic countries.

US President Richard Nixon's historic China visit, which began on February 21, 1972, culminated in the now-famous meeting between the American President and Chairman Mao. On February 28, on the basis of repeated consultations between Premier Zhou and President Nixon on the normalization of bilateral diplomatic relations and other issues of common concern, the Joint Communiqué of the United States of America and the People's Republic of China was signed in Shanghai. The communiqué emphasized that both nations agreed to handle international relations on the basis of the

Five Principles of Peaceful Coexistence. The Chinese side reaffirmed its solemn, principled stand on the Taiwan issue, while the US side declared, "The United States acknowledges that all Chinese on either side of the Taiwan Straits maintain there is but one China and that Taiwan is a part of China. The United States Government does not challenge that position." The communiqué also stipulated that both sides would facilitate the gradual conduct of Sino-US trade, as well as contact and exchanges between the two nations in such areas as science, technology, culture, sports and the press. The Nixon visit and the conclusion of the Shanghai Communiqué (also known as the Shanghai Accord) were milestones in the annals of Sino-American relations. They marked the beginning of normalized relations between the two countries, and laid the cornerstone for further improvement and growth in Sino-US relations.

China continued its diplomatic outreach to other countries that year. Japanese Prime Minister Tanaka Kakuei arrived in Beijing on September 25, 1972, for an official visit. The earnest and candid talks between the leaders of both nations on the normalization of Sino-Japanese diplomatic relations led to the signing of a joint communiqué on September 29 that put an end to the abnormal situation between the two countries and established diplomatic relations between them. That evening, Mao received Tanaka and his entourage. The joint communiqué declared that the Government of Japan and the Government of the People's Republic of China agreed to establish relations of perpetual peace and friendship between the two countries on the basis of the Five Principles of Peaceful Coexistence, and would enter into negotiations for the conclusion of a peace and friendship treaty. The normalization of diplomatic relations opened a new chapter in the history of Sino-Japanese relations.

On September 11, 1973, at the invitation of the Chinese government, President Georges Pompidou of France became the first head of state from a major Western European country to arrive in China for a state visit. The Sino-French Joint Communiqué, signed in the wake of in-depth exchanges of opinions on major international issues and bilateral relations, ushered the two nations into a new period of cooperation.

Seizing the moment of change in international circumstances, Mao orchestrated these and other major breakthroughs in China's foreign policy. In February 1974, he introduced his celebrated "Three

Worlds" strategic concept while meeting visiting President Kenneth David Kaunda of Zambia. Deng expounded on this concept in his April 1974 address as chairman of the Chinese delegation to the Sixth Special Session of the United Nations General Assembly:

> Judging from the changes in international relations, the world today actually consists of three parts, or three worlds, that are at once interconnected and contradictory with one another. The United States and the Soviet Union belong to the First World. The developing countries in Asia, Africa, Latin America and other regions form the Third World. The developed countries between the two make up the Second World.

The "Three Worlds" concept provided strategic backing for the formation of an international united front, and created an international environment in favor of China's open policy.

Deng Xiaoping, showing great vision and foresight, and seizing the opportunity of his third return to power, set about pushing the modernization drive and the initiative to open the nation up to the world. Aware that science and technology and education held the key to modernization, he volunteered to personally attend to these fields of endeavor. He convened a national forum on scientific, technological and educational work, led the work to restore order and set things right in the field of science and education, and resolutely resumed the nation's college enrollment examinations after a decade-long suspension.

Springtime for Science and Education

At the time, something lay heavily on the hearts of intellectuals throughout China, and that was the "two appraisals" in the *Summary of the National Working Conference on Education* released in August 1971. Appraisal One: The education front during the 17 years prior to the Cultural Revolution was one in which "the proletariat was under the dictatorship of the bourgeoisie," or to put it another way, the "dictatorship of the black Party line." Appraisal Two: The world outlook of the overwhelming majority of the intellectuals was "by and large bourgeois," or in other words, they were "bourgeois intellectuals."

While speaking with Wang Zhen and Deng Liqun on May 24, 1977, Deng said:

> If we are to bring about modernization, the key lies in raising our science and technology to another level. Development of science and technology cannot happen without boosting education. Empty talk brings no modernization. We have got to have knowledge and talented people. We must foster an inner-Party environment in which knowledge and talents are held in due respect.

When someone rehashed the "two appraisals" at a science and education forum that Deng was chairing a few months later (August 4 to 8), Deng pointed out:

> How should the work of the education front during those 17 years be appraised? In my opinion, it was dominated by the red Party line. During those years, the overwhelming majority of intellectuals, whether scientists or educators, worked hard and made tremendous achievements under the guidance of Mao Zedong Thought and correct Party leadership. This was particularly the case with our educators, for their work was most arduous. Almost all the best and brightest experts in various fields were cultivated in the post-Liberation years, the first dozen or so years in particular. If we cannot make this kind of appraisal of what happened during those 17 years, we have no way of accounting for all the accomplishments we have made so far.

He stressed that most intellectuals in the country were willing to serve socialism, and that the government should go out of its way to respect and to motivate the educators. "Every one of them is a laborer whether they are researchers or teachers. All those intellectuals who have been wronged should be exonerated," he said.

On September 3, an article entitled "How the *Summary of the National Working Conference on Education* Was Produced" was issued for internal reference. In it, the writer, a *People's Daily* correspondent, concluded that the "two appraisals" analysis should be completely repudiated because it had badly hurt the feelings of the educators and was a grave impediment to education development.

41

Upon reading the article, Deng lost no time in following up by issuing a directive.

Deng continued to campaign vigorously against the "two appraisals." During a conversation on September 19 with Minister of Culture Huang Zhen and Vice Minister of Culture Liu Fuzhi, Deng said that the "two appraisals" did not correspond with reality. "How could the intellectuals in their millions, or tens of millions, be completely written off like that? Isn't it true that the talented people we have today were groomed mostly during those 17 years?" He asked. "This summary should be criticized; that's the only way we draw a clear line between right and wrong. It is true that Comrade Mao Zedong once approved the summary, but that does not mean there is no problem with it. We should understand Mao Zedong Thought accurately and as a complete system."

Calling a spade a spade, Deng discredited the "two appraisals" by affirming what had been accomplished in the field of education during the 17 pre-Cultural Revolution years and recalling the socialist nature of the services the intellectuals had carried out for the nation. Shortly afterward, *People's Daily* and *Red Flag* published the article "Major Polemic on the Educational Front – A Critique of the 'Two Appraisals' Concocted by the Gang of Four," which caused a nation-wide stir. Reading between the lines, people working in education and other fields of endeavor saw signs of hope.

In March 1978, the central authorities held the National Conference on Science and, in April, the National Working Conference on Education. In his speeches on both occasions, Deng said that "science and technology are a productive force," (on another occasion he called them *the* foremost productive force), that "intellectuals are an integral part of the working class," and that "educators in the service of the people are noble and revolutionary laborers." By lifting the sobriquet "Stinking Ninth Category"* from the intellectuals in their tens of millions and restoring them to their position of high respect,

---

* "Stinking Ninth Category" was derived from the "Nine Black Categories": renegades, spies, capitalist roaders, landlords, rich famers, anti-revolutionaries, bad elements, rightists, and [ninth] intellectuals. This term could be traced to the Yuan Dynasty, when Mongol rulers imposed ten "castes" on Han people: bureaucrats, officials, Buddhist monks, Taoist priests, physicians, workers, hunters, prostitutes, [ninth] Confucian scholars and finally beggars. (*Translator*)

Deng's remarks fundamentally corrected the longstanding prejudice against the intellectuals, enhanced their social status, and promoted science and education.

At the closing ceremony of the National Conference on Science, Guo Moruo, President of the Chinese Academy of Sciences, delivered an emotional speech under the title "The Springtime of Science": "The most splendid springtime for science in our nation's history is upon us. This is a springtime for the people! And for science! Let us open our arms and warmly embrace this springtime!" These lines spoke for all the scientists and educators in this country. Indeed, the springtime for science and education had arrived!

Having personally weathered the wintertime of education, I basked in the springtime of education. When I was one of the builders of the Second Auto Works in northwest Hubei Province in the 1970s, all the colleges and universities around the country were closed down and we suffered a serious shortage of competent managers, engineers and technicians. We did have a rich pool of well-educated senior middle school graduates, but they were deprived of college education opportunities. The few college graduates we had on hand were not quite able to be themselves under the derogative "Stinking Ninth Category" label. The progress of construction work suffered greatly. After Deng's 1973 comeback to power, we began to restore order and set the construction of the auto plant back onto a normal track, but the badly needed college graduates were still hard to come by. To solve the problem, the auto works put many of its senior middle school graduates through a workers' university it had established jointly with the Central China Polytechnic Institute (the predecessor of Huazhong University of Science and Technology) and the Hubei Institute of Economics (the predecessor of Zhongnan University of Economics and Law). Many graduates from the university went on to become senior engineers and managers and to play a crucial role in building the auto works. Some of them have become top executives. Deng's emphasis on science, technology and education has, through my work experience in the First and Second Auto Works, left an indelible impression in my mind.

Restoring College Entrance Examinations

The mere mention of the restoration of college entrance examinations a year after the end of the Cultural Revolution never fails to stir the emotions of the tens of millions who experienced it. In the aftermath of the chaotic ten-year Cultural Revolution, the nation was having trouble finding successors to its aging contingent of professionals in all fields, and the dire shortage of well-educated personnel had become a drag on efforts to meet the goals of the Four Modernizations. Public attention turned to the question of when the colleges and universities should be reopened and start enrolling students.

The annual college entrance examinations were abolished shortly after the Cultural Revolution began in 1966. College enrollment was suspended from 1966 through 1969 as a result. Large numbers of "educated youths," that is, senior middle school students who were denied schooling opportunities because of it, were sent to rural areas to be "reeducated"; college teachers were driven to May 7 Cadre Schools for physical labor. Nationwide, higher education met its total collapse.

It was not until 1970 that Peking, Tsinghua and some other universities began enrolling students from among workers, peasants and soldiers. In 1971, institutions of higher education around the country followed the "16-character principle" for people to "apply on a voluntary basis with colleagues' recommendation and local leadership's approval, and be reexamined by colleges," and began to admit applicants who had worked at least two years as workers, peasants or soldiers. Because the entrance examinations had been shelved for years, the enrollees were widely divergent in education level. According to a May 1972 survey of 11 colleges in Beijing, 20 percent of the freshmen had an education above junior middle school level, 60 percent were at the junior middle school level, and 20 percent had an elementary school education. With such educational disparity in the classroom, the teaching quality was predicable.

When Deng started overall rectification efforts in 1975, he spoke on many occasions about revamping the college enrollment system and raising the quality of teaching. He asked, "What role should our colleges play? What kind of people should they cultivate? Some universities are just at the level of a secondary technical school, but why should they pass themselves off as universities?" He also said:

> How can you scale new heights in science and technology if you do not know English at all, or if you are totally ignorant of mathematics, physics and chemistry? In that case, you won't be able to climb a peak of average height, and you will still have trouble with a low mountain. We are facing a crisis. A lag in education could drag down the entire modernization drive.

Deng suggested that a number of colleges and universities give entrance examinations to senior high school students, so that those who excelled in the exams could be enrolled for further education.

On July 29, 1977, while meeting with Fang Yi, Vice President of the Chinese Academy of Sciences, Liu Xirao, Minister of Education, and others, Deng said he would convene a special discussion on science and education. He wanted the Academy and the Ministry to choose the participants. "Don't give me administrators," he said. "Just give me people who are outspoken, who have original opinions, are gifted in natural sciences, and have no links with the Gang of Four." A "man hunt" was carried out within the Academy and some universities before a list of 33 people was drawn up. It included such well-known scholars as Wu Wenjun, Ma Dayou, Tang Aoqing, Yang Shixian, Su Buqing, and Zha Quanxing.

The meeting on science and education took place from August 4 through 8. On the opening day, the Ministry of Education had just submitted to the State Council its *Proposals on 1977 College Enrollment Work*, which still followed the 16-character enrollment principle formulated during the Cultural Revolution. Naturally, this principle became the focus of discussion for the entire meeting.

The participants became all worked up as they got long years of pent-up feelings off their chests. Some pointed out that the 16-character principle for college entrance examinations should be revised because the "colleagues' recommendation" requirement was often a mere formality and "local leadership's approval" enabled back-doorism. Some felt the examinations should be put under a watchdog system. Others suggested a new version for the 16-character principle: "Voluntary application, leadership approval, strict screening, and enrollment only for those who excel in the examinations." Everyone urged the authorities to be more determined and to give the current college enrollment system a thorough overhaul. The consensus was that college entrance examinations should be restored immediately even if it might delay enrollment for two months.

During the discussions on August 8, Deng adopted the participants' proposal to change the recommendation-based college enrollment method in the near future. "Why don't we change it right away? We have enough time left this year. Let's scrap the *Proposals* and rewrite it according to our consensus," he said, adding:

> The 16-character principle needs to be reworded. Your new version, "voluntary application, leadership approval, strict screening, and enrollment only for those who excel in the examinations" sounds better, but something is wrong in the second phrase, "leadership approval." If, for instance, someone who stands a good chance of college wants to apply but his boss does not approve of it, or if his leader is bad-tempered and does not allow him to apply, what can you do? So let me eliminate this phrase and keep the other three.

He vowed to tighten up administration over science, technology and education, drawing warm applause when he added, "I am willing to be your quartermaster."

In his speech summarizing the discussion on August 8, he announced:

> Our colleges and universities have determined to resume direct enrollment from among senior middle school graduates – free from any recommendations. As I see it, direct enrollment from senior middle schools is a good way to speed up the cultivation of talents and increase the yield from education results.

A major policy decision was thus adopted.

After the meeting, the Ministry of Education followed Deng's instruction and submitted the *Report on Postponing College and School*

Enrollment and the New School Year. Accordingly, the enrollment work of colleges and secondary technical schools was to be put off until the fourth quarter of the year, and new students were to begin school toward the end of February 1978.

On August 18, Deng sent the report to the chairman and vice chairmen of the Party Central Committee, along with his suggestion: "This decision has been made through deliberation and consultation to guarantee the quality of students to be enrolled in elite universities. I suggest that we give it our approval." All the leaders approved it the same day.

On September 19, referring to the Ministry's many rigorous stipulations concerning candidates' political qualifications for college enrollment, Deng pointed out:

> Your draft document on enrollment is too wordy and too hard to understand. I have changed the enrollment requirements a little bit. As to political screening, it should be based mainly on a student's behavior. A clean personal record, love of socialism, love of physical labor, a good sense of discipline, and determination to study for the sake of revolution – these are enough. In short, let us just consider two things when enrolling students: first, good behavior; second, to choose only the best.

In line with Deng's instructions, the document on 1977 college enrollment announced, "Enrollment work shall follow the principle of giving overall consideration to students' moral character, intelligence and physical development and the principle of enrolling those who excel." The political screening of applicants was to be "based mainly on a person's behavior." Manifestations of good behavior were, to quote Deng verbatim, "to have a clear personal record, support the Communist Party of China, love socialism and physical labor, be well-disciplined, and determined to study for the sake of revolution." These revised stipulations on political screening met with positive public responses.

In the past, political screening was focused on a candidate's family background and social relations. This deprived many promising young people of valuable schooling opportunities. The changed criteria set the stage for fair competition and enabled many talented people to go to college. More importantly, these changes quickly spread to military conscription, factory employment, and promotion in rank and position, thereby setting the tone for efforts to stop dogmatic thinking throughout the Party and society, abolish the concept of "taking class struggle as the key link," and correct ultra-leftist mistakes.

Deng delivered the Ministry of Education's amended *Report on the Proposals on 1977 College Enrollment Work* to Hua Guofeng on October 3, and a draft document for these proposals to be transmitted and released by the State Council. In his note on the documents Deng wrote:

> This is an urgent issue. After you have finished examining both documents, please have them printed and transmitted for endorsement at the Political Bureau. My suggestion is that we convene a Politburo meeting to discuss these documents along with the *Red Flag* commentator's article on education (previously transmitted to you).

Hua then had the documents printed and transmitted to other Politburo members. Two days later (October 5), the Political Bureau held the proposed discussion session, made further amendments to the *Proposals*, and passed the document in principle.

New arrivals at Peking University after national college entrance examinations were restored in 1977.

On October 7, Deng wrote another instruction on the twice-amended *Proposals*: "In my opinion, this will do. I hereby suggest that the document be examined by Chairman Hua and comrades [Ye] Jianying, [Li] Xiannian, [Wang] Dongxing and Fang Yi, and returned, along with their instructions, to the Ministry of Education for execution." Hua and the other leaders put their marks of approval on the document the same day.

Five days later (October 12), the State Council issued the *Proposals on 1977 College Enrollment Work*, with the ruling that from then on, the college enrollment system was to be transformed and standardized entrance examinations would be restored. All the applicants should have a high school education or a similar education level; they were to send in applications voluntarily and sit for standard entrance exams. Accordingly, workers, farmers, educated youths who had either settled down in villages or returned to cities, demobilized soldiers, and graduates fresh from high school could apply for college entrance exams provided they met the application conditions.

The good tidings soon spread all over the country.

Young people, many of whom had seen their schooling opportunities delayed for more than a decade, hastily dusted off their textbooks and began studying to prepare for the college entrance exams. That year, 5.7 million entered their names for the exams, and 273,000 were enrolled. Because the number of applicants far exceeded the expected figure, for a time the authorities could not procure enough paper to print the exam papers. The problem was not resolved until the central authorities made the urgent decision to ship in all the paper previously allocated for the printing of the fifth volume of the *Selected Works of Mao Zedong*.

Of all the events unfolding during the year the college entrance examinations were restored, one particularly worth mentioning was the expansion of college enrollment at the Central Conservatory of Music.

On December 9, 1977, Li Chunguang, Yang Jun and four other teachers wrote to Deng that the high academic level and large number of talents among that year's 17,000-plus applicants were something that the conservatory had never experienced since the founding of the People's Republic. Some 400 applicants had passed the preliminary and reexamination rounds, the teachers reported, but a lot of those who had been eliminated were professionally better than those already studying in conservatory. The problem, the letter said, was that only 135, or a meager 0.8 percent, of all the applicants could eventually make it to the 28 faculties. This meant that many of the 400-plus finalists could not be recruited. The emergence of this vast pool of musical talents is a "windfall" for the conservatory, the teachers claimed. "They are young, have great promise in music, and should be further cultivated in good time. It will be devastating to these young talents if they are not enrolled," the letter emphasized. "If that happens, they will probably never get another opportunity to pursue music. Some of them will lose their confidence in music and turn to other careers. The cause of music will incur irreparable losses." They suggested removing the enrollment quota and taking in those who had both promise and talent and were up to the entrance standards, so that more and better artists could be groomed for the country.

Two days later, Deng issued the instruction: "I am delighted to learn what is reflected in this letter. I would like to suggest that something be done to help the conservatory. Please deliver this letter to the Ministry of Culture after Chairman Hua, [Li] Xiannian, [Ji] Dengkui and Ulanhu have read it." The conservatory finally enrolled 213 students. Thus it was with Deng's support and blessing that more aspiring musicians saw their dreams of a college education come true.

The public supported Deng's decision to restore college enrollment, for it brought hope not only for national rejuvenation, but also to numerous young people thirsty for study and knowledge. The nation's limited resources, however, were already stretched thin to take up all that had been left undone for so many years, and it was impossible to meet every young person's demand for college. During a business trip to Wenzhou, in Zhejiang Province, in the 1980s, I was spending the night on Yandang Mountain. While taking a stroll the next morning, I saw three young nuns reviewing school lessons. When I asked them what they were reading, they smiled, and showed me the books, which turned out to be third-year high school Chinese textbooks. "You are taking cultural courses in the temple?" I asked. "No. We have just graduated from high school but we failed this year's college entrance exams. We became nuns at the temple because it gives us time to review the materials and prepare for the exams next year." Upon hearing that explanation, I really felt for the girls and admired their keen desire to continue their studies. How nice it would be for our people and country, I thought, if the economy could grow to a point where higher education is available to more young people. Today, after 30 years of development, college enrollment in China has expanded vastly. According to the statistics, it grew from 273,000 in 1977 to about 5.7 million in 2007, with the enrollment rate rising from 4.8 percent to 56 percent. Today's expanded higher education has paved the way for the younger generation to pursue successful careers and continues to develop valuable human resources for the modernization drive.

Redressing Frame-Ups and Other Miscarriages of Justice

While the nation exposed and condemned the Gang of Four, the authorities faced another urgent task: to respond to the people's demand for redressing all the trumped-up charges and mishandled legal cases left over from the Cultural Revolution, and for rehabilitating the victims.

On March 14, 1977, Hu Yaobang called on Deng at his residence. The two of them exchanged opinions on what steps to take to implement the policy on Party and government functionaries and to redress miscarriages of justice. Shortly afterward, under Hu's supervision, 90 or so Party School faculty members who had been wrongly labeled "rightists" were acquitted.

Nine months later, on December 10, Hu was appointed minister of the Organization Department of the Party Central Committee. With the backing of Deng and Chen Yun, he immediately started pushing the work of redressing the past wrongs. In the years that followed, Party organizations at all levels joined efforts to rehabilitate the victims of the Cultural Revolution in the spirit of seeking truth from facts. More than 600,000 Party members participated in the effort. By the end of 1982, the nation had acquitted some 3 million wronged Party and government functionaries, restored 470,000 citizens to Party membership, and exonerated 540,000 "rightists." Large numbers of innocent people were reinstalled in leadership positions, which greatly boosted the morale of officials and intellectuals across the land.

Sounding Out the Outside World

The central authorities – while busy making studies and investigations, setting things right, redressing miscarriages of justice and readjusting the Party line – also sent top leaders on fact-finding tours of foreign countries to see how things stood out in the world and to draw on their development experience.

Gu Mu Goes on a Western European Tour

In May 1978, a Chinese delegation arrived in Western Europe for a visit. Headed by Vice Premier Gu Mu, it was the first official economic delegation headed by a state leader ever to be dispatched abroad by the People's Republic of China. Members of the delegation included leading members of the Ministry of Water Conservancy and Power Industry, the State Construction Commission and the Ministry of Agriculture and Forestry, and representatives of Beijing municipality, Guangdong and Shandong provinces. Before the delegation left Beijing, Deng met with Gu Mu and told him to establish extensive ties, look deep into certain issues, find out about the host countries' industrial modernization levels, and bring advanced economic management expertise back to China. For two months (from May 2 to July 6), the delegation toured France, the Federal Republic of Germany (West Germany), Sweden, Denmark and

Gu Mu (*first row, sixth from right*) posing for a picture with members of a Chinese delegation for a West European tour, May 1978.

Belgium, where the members came into wide contact with political, economic and other major figures. Apart from talks and exchanges, they visited factories, farms, cities, harbors, research institutes and families.

Just after the delegation members arrived in West Germany, the Chinese Embassy showed them a documentary about that country's postwar reconstruction efforts. Postwar West Germany had been in ruins. In many cities, half or two thirds of the buildings had been razed to the ground, leaving many residents homeless. With little to eat, many people drove horse-drawn carts to the countryside and scavenged to survive. Victims of famine and subfreezing weather were everywhere. In the short span of a dozen or so years, however, the country restored its economy and accomplished modernization by promoting new industries and international trade. Thirty years after World War II, the Federal Republic of Germany was already a thriving developed country, where electrification and automation were the norm. The delegation members were stunned by the yawning gap between China and the Western European countries in economic terms, and in science and technology, but the visit also boosted their confidence in the possibilities for revitalizing their own country.

During the five-nation tour, Gu Mu was deeply impressed by the strong desire of local officials and entrepreneurs to develop economic relations and trade with China. At a meeting with President Giscard d'Estaing, Claude Arnaud, the French ambassador to China, told Gu, "We've heard that your country plans to build 120 large construction projects. My country is willing to do something for you. Can you give us ten of these projects?" In West Germany, some state governors said they could provide China with loans ranging from billions or tens of billions of US dollars. Gu Mu could sense some urgency in his hosts' voices as they explored the potential for new markets in which to invest their surplus and idle capital. Later, upon finding that our country could ill afford all the 120 large projects, the authorities dealt with them on the principle of "readjustment, reform, consolidation and improvement." The situation at home and abroad, however, indicated that it was feasible to utilize foreign investment to spur domestic economic development.

After the delegation returned home, Deng met with Gu Mu to learn the details of his Western European visit. Their conversation involved the opening-up policy and the introduction of advanced foreign technology. Deng emphasized that: first, we must bring in foreign technology; second, we should determine to borrow some money from foreign countries to invigorate construction; and third, we should race against time. Another meeting was arranged afterward, at which the vice premier delivered a detailed report on his visit to Hua Guofeng, Ye Jianying, Li Xiannian, Nie Rongzhen, Ulanhu, and Wang Zhen. That meeting lasted seven and a half hours (from 3:30 p.m. to 11:00 p.m.), while Gu Mu reported on three topics. First, he stressed that Western European countries had come a long way in economic growth and especially in science and technology after World War II, and extensive use of electronic technology had enabled them to raise their levels of modernization and labor productivity in industry, agriculture, transportation and telecommunications. Second, most of the host countries were friendly toward China, and because they had surplus funds and wanted to find new markets for their technology and commodities, they were interested in developing economic relations with China. All the countries the delegation visited believed that China was a major stabilizing factor in the world, and that the world situation would be much better with a powerful China and a powerful Europe. The political stability and unity China enjoyed after the fall of the Gang of Four boosted their confidence, and the vast Chinese market held increasing appeal to them. Third, in developing international economic relations, China could adopt many established international conventions – including seller's credit, buyer's credit, compensation trade, absorption of foreign investment and cooperative production – which could alleviate foreign exchange payment difficulties and speed up national economic development. In their interpositions or independent remarks at the meeting, the six leaders spoke highly and enthusiastically about what they had heard. They asked Gu Mu to submit a summary to the State Council for further deliberation.

In early July 1978, leaders of the relevant ministries and commissions gathered at the State Council for a brainstorming meeting. Gu Mu delivered a report on his Western European tour and presented his opinions on opening up to the outside world. Emphasizing that the international situation offered opportunities for China to assimilate the scientific and technological accomplishments of the capitalist world, he said:

Comrade Deng Xiaoping initiated the major policy to step up technology imports and boost exports as early as 1975. It is high time that we carried it out in a meticulous and methodical way. We have got to free our minds and open the way in this regard. On no account should we impose seclusion on ourselves and let the opportunities slip through our fingers.

The meeting lasted for more than 20 days, at which the participants summarized the experience and lessons of New China over the past three decades and carefully studied the advanced accomplishments of foreign countries. Development, however, was the focus of discussion throughout the meeting. Every one was asking the same questions: How was it that the two defeated nations – Japan and West Germany – were able to rise to their feet so soon? How come Switzerland, which its people claim "got nothing from God but sunshine and water," could stand proudly among developed countries? Why couldn't China – not in the least inferior to Switzerland in material conditions and even better in many other respects – do the same? Many participants declared that the Chinese people should be determined and do whatever they could to catch up in economic development. In a lengthy speech at the meeting, Li Xiannian raised suggestions for restructuring the economy and adopting a policy to open the nation to the world. He pointed out that the current world situation, with European and North American countries and Japan struggling to bail out their slumping economies, was tilted in China's favor. "We should have the guts and ability to boost development by utilizing their technology, equipment, funds and management expertise. We cannot afford to lose this rare opportunity. Self-reliance does not mean shutting ourselves behind closed doors and turning a blind eye to advanced things in foreign countries."

The impact of Li's speech was so obvious that after the brainstorming meeting was over, it was adopted as one of the documents for deliberation at the forthcoming Third Plenary Session of the 11th Party Central Committee, and it played a key role in the formation of the reform and opening policy.

Japan Saves Itself With Quality Products

The rise of Japan was the talk of the international economic community in 1979. In 1945, the year Japan proclaimed unconditional surrender during World War II, General Douglas MacArthur, Commander of the Allied Forces in the Pacific Theater, told a *Chicago Tribune* reporter something to the effect that Japan had degenerated to such a fourth-rate country that it could never rise as a world power again. In 1955, China accounted for 6.5 percent of the world GDP, while the figure was a lowly 2.5 percent for Japan. By 1960, however, Japan had already overtaken China. Nevertheless, nobody was taking Japan seriously into account at the time, because the image of Japanese products as cheap and shabby goods was deeply ingrained in people's minds.

I remember buying a plastic soap box at a Japanese products expo in the Beijing Exhibition Center in the 1960s. I took a great fancy to it, but to my dismay, its inviting pinkish color soon faded to a drab gray, and the plastic clasp attached to its lid was broken. That experience confirmed my impression of Japanese goods as cheap imitations. Later, while reading an eminent Japanese politician's memoirs, I came to a passage where he recalled that during one of his visits to the United States, he wanted America to expand imports from Japan in the hope that this could help deliver postwar Japan from its economic quandary. To his surprise, his host said that the Americans had never bought directly from Japan. "We did obtain some of your products, but that was through transit trade, and we stopped doing so because of quality problems. We have money, but we only buy quality products. We don't buy shabby products." As shocking as that remark was, it dawned on him as the key to his country's problem.

Upon returning to Japan, the politician issued the call to "save the nation by quality," as part of a broader strategy to "base the nation on trade." He then took a series of steps to carry it out. Japanese products finally shed their inglorious images as cheap knock-offs and shabby products and assumed an aura of "high quality." In March 1970, as if seeking to proclaim its final salvation, Japan spent a whopping US$2 billion on an international fair in Osaka. The fair drew participants from 77 countries, and was a big success. In an article published in the *Chicago Tribune*, Herman Kahn, a founder of American futurism, proclaimed:

Japan has established itself among world economic powers, and the 21st century will belong to Japan.

Japan was the world's fastest growing economy throughout the 1970s. In the 1960s, China and Japan had been neck-and-neck in GDP, but by 1980, the Japanese had outstripped the Chinese by four times in this regard. Toward the end of 1980, Japan overtook the United States to become the number one automaker in the world. That year its auto output broke the 10 million mark to reach a world-record high of 11.04 million, accounting for over 30 percent of the world total. Because automobiles are a mark of industrial civilization and an indication of national competitiveness in the modern world, the media could not resist the story. In 1980, the American television network NBC aired a prime time program entitled "If Japan Can, Why Can't We?" to compare the auto industry of the United States with that of Japan. According to the narrator, Lloyd Dobyns, a little over ten years before, Japan had been notorious for its shoddy products and "Made in Japan" used to be synonymous with low quality. However, the label "Made in Japan" gradually became the world standard of quality. American youths were proud of driving a Japanese coupe. In the international market, Japanese products from electronic appliances, watches, cameras, automobiles to semiconductors were becoming best sellers. The Japanese mode of business management became an example for businessmen and politicians. Japan rapidly grew into an economic powerhouse, investing enormous resources in many foreign countries.

Japan's economic bonanza gave the Chinese people pause for thought. China and Japan were virtually at the same starting point in the 1960s, but after only a short time, China lagged far behind Japan. Why? While people were racking their brains for an answer to this puzzle, Deng decided to pay a personal visit to Japan.

Deng Goes to Japan to Get a Personal Feel for Modernization

In the fall of 1978, at the invitation of the Japanese government, Deng visited Japan as Vice Premier of China. This visit – the first ever to Japan by a top Chinese leader since the founding of the People's Republic – took place amidst the uninterrupted growth in Sino-Japanese relations that had been flourishing since the two nations normalized their diplomatic connections. The purpose

Deng in Tokyo, with Tanaka Kakuei, former Prime Minister of Japan, October 1978.

Chatting with local news reporters aboard a train on the Shinkansen, the 210-km/h Japanese high-speed railway, October 1978.

was to promote friendly bilateral relations at a time when the prevailing trend and good wishes of both peoples were behind it. Deng and his entourage were accorded a warm welcome and formal reception at both government and nongovernmental levels. One Japanese newspaper reported, "Deng's visit brought the Japan-China friendship into every household," and "a new age is dawning for China and Japan." The newspaper also proclaimed that the visit had whipped up a "Deng Cyclone" in Japan. Aside from the negotiations and meetings, Deng visited Japan's modern enterprises and high-tech facilities, and engaged in extensive contacts with business executives, veteran economists, and engineers and managers. He also toured three factories: Nissan's Zama Car Storage Facility in Kanagawa Prefecture, Nippon Steel Corporation Kimitsu Works in Chiba Prefecture, and Matsushita Electric Works' Ibaraki Factory in Osaka Prefecture. At the Zama factory, Deng rode an electric car for a tour of the factory's body workshop and assembly line. He got a personal feel for what modernization was all about when he was shown a robot-operated welding production line with a particularly high degree of automation. Deng said, "China is pursuing its own modernization. We are grateful to developed industrial countries, the Japanese industrial circles in particular, for their assistance in this regard."

On his way from Tokyo to Kyoto on October 26, Deng boarded the "Light No. 81" train for a ride on the Shinkansen, the 210-kilometer high-speed railway. When a Japanese reporter asked him how he felt, he replied that all he could feel was speed, as if someone was pushing him along. "I think this kind of train would really suit us in China," he said.

At the Nissan Auto Company, when Deng learned that the company's annual output averaged 94 vehicles per worker (whereas China's best auto manufacturer, First Auto Works, averaged one vehicle per worker), he said with a sigh, "Now I know what modernization means. I would like to welcome developed industrial countries, my friends in Japanese industry in particular, to work with us for China's modernization."

The Japanese public was able to get a taste of Deng's candid, pragmatic and extroverted personality during his visit. He was often heard saying:

I came here for no other purpose but to seek advice in Japan. We want to learn from every developed country, and we also want to draw on the good experience of our less well-off Third World friends. The world is advancing by leaps and bounds. It is hard to reach the levels that Japan and the European and North American countries have reached today, and will be even harder to attain their levels when the 20th century comes to an end 22 years from now. We are sober-minded in our estimation of the difficulties facing us, but we are eager, too, to bring about modernization. Toward that end, we need sound policies, and we must regard as our starting point for development the advanced technology and management know-how of the world today. But we must concede our backwardness in the first place, because we can only have hope by remaining honest about ourselves. Then we must be good at learning. We are very hopeful because of our attitude, policies and principles.

These remarks neatly summarized his Japan visit, and they also reflected his thoughtful views on the urgent need of China for reform and opening.

Deng Mentions the Opening-Up Policy to Foreign Guests

In October 1978, Deng met with a journalists' delegation from West Germany and had a deep discussion with his guests on opening China to the world and learning science and technology at an advanced world level. Speaking about the experience and lessons of Chinese history, he said his country had made its contributions to the world in the past but its development had also been stagnant for a long time. Now it is time for China to learn from the developed countries, he said. In answering his guests' questions, he used the term "opening up" in no uncertain terms for the first time. "As to your question about whether the policy of opening up that we are going to adopt runs counter to our tradition, my answer is that good traditions must be preserved, but we should also make new policies under new circumstances," he said. "We bring in advanced technology to develop productivity and improve our people's living standards. That is beneficial to our socialist country and socialist system."

In November 1978, Deng arrived in Singapore for a formal visit. Singapore had a population of 2.5 million and a territory of a little more than 600 square kilometers. From the 1960s onward, the country set great store by international economic relations and took an active part in global market competition. When developed countries began shifting traditional industries to other parts of the world, Singapore took the opportunity to bring in a steady stream of foreign funds and advanced technology. Thus it rose quickly to become one of Asia's New Rising Economies, or "Four Tigers." The Singaporean success in boosting economic growth with foreign capital made a deep and lasting impression on Deng. On a visit to Jurong Town on November 13, he heard a detailed report by the Town Council on the development of the Jurong Industrial Park. He told his hosts that he wanted to bring their experience to China and follow their practice to develop the Chinese economy. Later, in a speech entitled "Proposals on Economic Work," he made special mention of his Singapore visit:

> I went there to learn the way they used foreign capital. Singapore allows foreigners to run factories on their land, and benefits from it in at least three aspects. First, foreign enterprises must hand in 35 percent of their profit, which becomes government revenue; second, local workers get paid for their labor in these enterprises; and last, this way of doing things has boosted the local service industry and local revenue. We must make up our mind, weigh the advantages and disadvantages of it, and get the arithmetic clear. Then let us do it, even if it is slightly unfair to us because, after all, it will bring about production capacity in China and some of our enterprises can feed off it. In my opinion, when we study financial and economic issues now, our starting point should be how to make the most of foreign capital and be good at it. It would be a great pity if we failed to use foreign capital.

The Machine-Building Industry's "Western Pilgrimage"

To speed up the development of the machine-building industry, the First Ministry of Machine-Building Industry sent two delegations abroad between October and December 1978. One delegation, headed by Minister Zhou Zijian (with An Zhiwen as deputy head, and Jiang Zemin as secretary-general), visited Italy, Switzerland, Federal Germany, France, Romania and Yugoslavia. Japan was the destination for the other delegation, headed by Vice Minister Zhou Jiannan. Thanks to careful preparations and detailed fact-finding plans, both delegations returned home with a good harvest of facts and figures to demonstrate the disparity between the Chinese machine-building industry and its Western European and Japanese counterparts.

Their joint report, delivered to the State Council on January 25, 1979, presented these facts and figures along with suggestions on how to catch up with the developed countries. The report said that over the past 20 years or so, European and Japanese machine-building industries had made a lot of headway, attained considerable scales of production and high technological levels, and were versatile enough to meet domestic demand and become a mainstay in foreign trade. Both Europe and Japan were making large, high-speed, high-precision machines. Their production processes were highly automated, specialized and diversified, and their management was scientifically sound and rather sophisticated.

By comparison, the Chinese machine-building industry, the report said, was far less developed in production capacity and technological, organizational and managerial levels. It had a long way to go in the following aspects if it was to meet the demands of the modernization drive:

First, its production capacity was only one fifth that of Japan or Federal Germany. According to statistics, the total business volume of the First Ministry of Machine-Building Industry in 1977 (excluding the figures related to the electronics, shipbuilding and aviation industries), was 32.7 billion yuan (US$18 billion), compared with Japan at US$100 billion or Federal Germany at US$80 billion. Japan and Federal Germany possessed just a little more equipment, but their labor productivity was at least eight times higher than that of China.

Second, in terms of technology, the Chinese industry trailed behind Western Europe and Japan by at least twenty years. 1) Most of the machines that China was building at the end of the 1970s were the sort being built in the West in the 1940s and 1950s. In other words, the Chinese products were below the advanced world level by two to three technological generations. France, for instance, had raised the capacity of the thermal power-generating equipment it was building from 125,000 kilowatts (kw) in 1953 to 900,000–1.3 million kw in the 1970s, while China was batch-producing generators with capacities of 100,000 kw, 125,000 kw and 200,000 kw, and the Chinese technology for building 300,000-kilowatt sets was yet to attain maturity. 2) The automation level of Chinese-made machines was so low that most of them were basically manually operated. The Japanese-made blast furnaces (4,000 to 5,000 cubic meters in capacity) were entirely controlled with computers for a daily iron output of 9,000 to 11,000 tons, whereas the Chinese models, with a capacity of 1,513 cubic meters and a daily iron output of 1,800 tons, were yet to be automatically operated. 3) In terms of precision levels, the Chinese products were lower than their Western counterparts by one to two grades. For example, the super-heavy-duty horizontal lathes made in West Germany were 24 meters in length and 4.2 meters in gyration diameter and capable of working on components with a dead weight of 500 tons. China, by comparison, had just finished trial-producing a horizontal lathe 16 meters in length and 3.15 meters in gyration diameter. 4) The Chinese products were handicapped by high-energy consumption and low durability. The "Iron Bull" brand tractor made in China was 30 percent heavier and consumed 10 percent more fuel than its Fiat brand counterpart from Italy. 5) The technological processes were outdated and new processes in use were a rarity in the Chinese machine-building industry. This was particularly the case with the hot-working field, where the rate of mould-pressed and forged work pieces was more than 60 percent abroad and only 26 percent in China.

Third, China lagged behind other nations in terms of the industry's organizational and managerial levels. Large corporations in the West were already organizing large-scale collaboration along specialized lines of production, and were benefiting from scientific corporate management based on the wide use of computers and increasingly higher levels of automation. Production organized along specialized lines enabled them to turn out a variety of products and remain highly adaptable to market demand – not to mention the fact that these corporations had no lack of medium-sized and small companies to produce parts and accessories for them. By contrast, medium-sized and small firms in China were not in a position to supply large companies with parts and accessories because of their low technological capacities and lack of complete sets of equipment and effective testing facilities. Furthermore, most companies in the West had introduced computerized data processing to production links – from the placement of orders, design of products and technological processes, and management of production quotas, to preparations for production, production procedures, transportation in workshops and warehouse management. In China, only a few major factories were using small computers to compile operational plans and handle a few management tasks, leaving the lion's share of management work to low-efficiency manual labor.

The disparity between Chinese and foreign machine-building industries was manifold, the joint report said, but it all boiled down to labor productivity. All-worker labor productivity was equivalent to 40,000 yuan to 50,000 yuan in Romania and Yugoslavia and 80,000 yuan to 100,000 yuan in Western Europe and Japan. Barring certain incomparable factors, the labor productivity in the Chinese machine-building industry was three to four times lower than that in Romania and Yugoslavia, and seven to eight times lower than that of Western Europe and Japan.

The joint report to the State Council assessed the situation: "The Chinese machine-building industry must strive to catch up. Western Europe and Japan attained modernization in about 20 years. We can do the same if we work hard."

To attain that goal, the joint report urged the government to put a premium on the machine-building industry, and called on those in the industry to be bold and step up the introduction of new technology. Specifically, the joint report suggested the following "four combinations":

1. Building pace-setting factories and transforming old ones. This calls for importing workshops and production lines for major fields where China lacks the needed technology and is unlikely to develop them quickly on its own. Workers and staff of all the factories should be mobilized to pursue technological innovation and transformation based on the resources at hand; but at the same time foreign experts should be invited to help improve the technology, products and management of selected factories,

so that the experience gained can be employed to bring along other factories.

2. Importing complete sets of equipment and procuring the technologies for building such equipment. This will allow us to master advanced manufacturing technology more quickly and at a lower cost. For example, nuclear power plants should be imported along with the relevant technology, so that China, by means of a period of cooperative production, will be able to master the technology and develop it independently.

3. Importing main-engine manufacturing technology and importing technology for manufacturing key accessories. For instance, the import of automobile and tractor manufacturing technology is incomplete without the import of technology for manufacturing oil pumps and spray nozzles.

4. Importing technology for building major equipment and importing the technology needed to manufacture products calling for similar technology. For instance, when buying tractor-making factories and associated technology, we need to import technology for manufacturing farmland capital construction equipment, because mastery of the former makes it much easier to master the latter. Regarding international experience, we hope that the departments concerned will import equipment and related technology along with relevant blueprints and techno-logical processes, and engage in collaborative production with foreign partners. This will not only save foreign exchange, but also enable the domestic machine-building industry to absorb and master the manufacturing technology. Those key compo-nents and raw materials that China does not have the expertise to produce should also be imported to help foster domestic manufacturing capacities.

The joint report recommended the development of a well-defined strategy and overall planning, so that foreign technology could be imported in order of priority and urgency, and that priority should be given, in particular, to the purchase of complete sets of crucial equipment and accessories and general-purpose serial products. This would concentrate the limited resources on solving key problems. To facilitate joint ventures and cooperative production with Chinese and foreign investment, the joint report said, legislation should be enacted, red tape streamlined and work efficiency improved as soon as possible.

The joint report also proposed to: expand machinery exports; step up research and development; speed up technological upgrading and the cultivation of engineering and management personnel; and revamp administration over the machine-building industry.

Based on negotiations with a host of foreign corporations during their fact-finding tours, the two delegations came up with a tentative "shopping list" for 140 imports of equipment for iron and steel, power generating and other basic industries, as well as hot-working expertise and the essential technology for manufacturing heavy-duty vehicles and basic accessories. This included importing core technology from Italy (for building 80- to 150-horsepower wheeled tractors), from France (900,000-kilowatt nuclear power stations), from Switzerland (Swiss ABB, 300,000- and 600,000-kw thermal-power generating sets), and from Japan and West Germany (large steel rolling mills and related metallurgical equipment). Also on the list were the importation of a heavy-duty vehicle plant from General Motors of the United States, and the transformation of the First Auto Works with the help of a Japanese company.

The joint report drew enthusiasm from the central leadership and staff of the First Ministry of Machine-Building Industry; it both broadened their horizons and inspired them to boost the industry's resourcefulness at home, while quickening the pace of the opening-up process. Deng pointed out:

> For some time in the past, we had been accused of "worshiping foreign things and toadying to foreigners" simply because we wanted to draw on the advanced science and technology of developed countries. Today, everyone knows that was sheer nonsense. We have sent many people to see the world, which has enabled them at least to know what it looks like out there. We will never become a developed country if we dawdle behind closed doors, remain conservative, and get carried away with unfounded conceit.

China's increasing international outreach enabled the country to develop economic connections and trade with Western countries and particularly to import major technological projects. Sending delegations on carefully planned fact-finding tours abroad helped advance opening up efforts. Members of these delegations were required to take crash courses in diplomatic discipline and etiquette, and to make visit plans before they set off, and were asked to write detailed reports after they returned. According to the available statistics, during the three-year period from July 1, 1977 to June 30, 1980, the ministries and commissions of the State Council sent a total of 360 delegations abroad (not including the frequent foreign visits by top leaders), and the country's science and education institutions and trade departments sent 472 delegations. These tours enabled us to promote international economic cooperation, learn advanced foreign technology and management expertise, get a personal feel of the disparity between China and other countries in economic and technological development, and think of ways and means to catch up with the advanced world level. Of all these foreign visits, Deng's trips to Japan and Singapore, and Gu Mu's to Western Europe were the most crucial to launching China's effort to open up to the outer world.

This episode of Chinese history ran the gamut – from the debates over the criterion for judging truth and the drive to restore national order and to set things right in science and education, to redressing miscarriages of justice and other legacies of the Cultural Revolution, and dispatching delegation after delegation to see how things stood in foreign lands and to prepare for an open policy. These furnished the political, ideological and organizational conditions for the successful convocation of the Third Plenary Session of the 11th Party Central Committee, an historic turning point that heralded the age of reform, opening, and modernization.

A Historic Turning Point for China

In late 1978 (from November 10 to December 15), the Party held a meeting to prepare for the Third Plenary Session of the 11th Party Central Committee. Among the 212 delegates to this 36-day Central Working Conference were leaders from all provinces, autonomous regions and municipalities, and commanders of military zones. Presided over by Chairman Hua Guofeng and Politburo Standing Committee members Ye Jianying, Deng Xiaoping, Li Xiannian and Wang Dongxing, the conference heard reports by delegations from east, central south, southwest, northwest, north and northeast China. Agriculture was the central topic, but before it was put on the table, the delegates spent two days discussing Deng's proposal that the focus of Party work be shifted to the socialist modernization drive starting from 1979.

At the time, public demand for repudiating the Cultural Revolution was mounting; this was echoed by the discussions on "emancipating the mind" at the conference. The theory of "continuing the revolution under the proletarian dictatorship" had lost its rallying power. The delegates were in favor of a change in focus for the Party's agenda, but change could not be made without first addressing a number of major political issues. The discussions gradually gravitated toward what could be done to lift a host of political and ideological taboos. The conference, naturally, changed course as a result.

In his speech, Chen Yun shunned the conference's prescribed topics on the economy. Instead, he listed a number of Party veterans who had been wrongly convicted as traitors during the Cultural Revolution and called for overturning their verdicts. His demands were immediately echoed by Tan Zhenlin, Wan Li, Wang Shoudao and Kang Keqing. Tan Zhenlin even went out of his way to candidly criticize those who had committed mistakes under the influence of the erroneous concept of the "two whatevers." In his speech, Hu Yaobang proposed that conclusions be reached on all the major issues of principle left over by the Cultural Revolution. Thus the effort to solve all remaining historical problems was pushed forward to a new stage.

At the conference the participants agreed to address all the Cultural Revolution verdicts on major issues of principle, and made suggestions for major policy decisions. Some of those issues were addressed during the conference itself.

On December 13, Deng delivered his now well-known speech entitled "Emancipating the Mind, Seeking Truth From Facts, and Looking Toward the Future in Unity." His tone was somber and earnest, as he described China's critical political juncture and suggested a radical way forward:

> If a party, a country or a nation always puts dogma above everything else, follows close-minded ways of thinking and allows superstition

Deng (*second from left*) delivering his speech at the closing ceremony of the Central Working Conference, December 13,1978. The speech, entitled "Emancipating the Mind, Seeking Truth From Facts, and Looking Toward the Future in Unity," set the tone for the forthcoming Third Plenary Session of the 11th Party Central Committe.

to hold sway, then it will make no progress and will lose hope. The party, or the country, will be doomed. ... We should allow some areas, enterprises and workers and farmers to earn more and live a better life earlier than others through diligence and hard work. When some people become better off ahead of others, they are bound to have a tremendous demonstrative impact on their neighbors and will prompt them to follow their examples. In this way, the national economy as a whole will keep advancing wave upon wave, enabling people of all ethnic backgrounds throughout the country to become rich at a relatively faster rate.

These lines, which later became an important policy to stimulate the national economy, pointed the way for reforms in localities and industries. The entire speech answered a series of fundamental questions confronting the Party at an historical turning point, and defined the tasks and direction for the Party. It also set the tone for the Third Plenary Session of the 11th Party Central Committee, which convened five days later. This now-famous, important speech, based on an outline personally drafted by Deng, was prepared by Hu Yaobang, Hu Qiaomu, Yu Guangyuan and Lin Jianqing. The three-page outline, amounting to 400 words, raised the following topics:

1. "Emancipating the mind" and reviving up the "machine";
2. Giving full scope to democracy and tightening up the rule of law;
3. Looking back on the past for the purpose of looking toward the future;

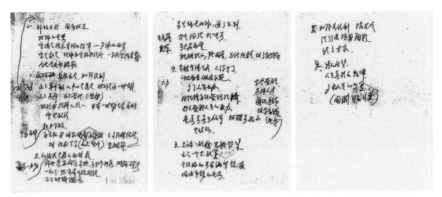

Outline of the speech "Emancipating the Mind, Seeking Truth From Facts, and Looking Toward the Future in Unity," in Deng's own handwriting.

4. Overcoming bureaucratism and over-staffing;
5. Allowing some places and people to get better off first;
6. Tightening up the responsibility system and setting quotas and rules; and
7. Some new issues.

With the addition of the line "Appraising the meeting" at the top of the first page, the outline listed eight topics altogether. In the course of preparing the speech, Deng often consulted the drafters and reviewed numerous drafts to deepen and flesh out his ideas.

The Third Plenary Session of the 11th Party Central Committee opened on December 18, 1978 in a snow-clad Beijing. The Plenary Session lasted only five days, but it was epoch-making, for its impact was monumental and far-reaching. The contents of Deng's December 13 speech became its central theme. The Plenary Session, by way of thorough discussions, systematically summarized past events and formulated a series of new principles and policies. None were more important than the policy decision to shift the Party's focus of work from "taking class struggle as the key link" to "developing the productive force," from seclusion to openness, and from rigorous dogmatism to reforms in all fields of endeavor. The Plenary Session also set the guidelines for work on international economic relations: "Be proactive in developing economic cooperation with all countries of the world on the basis of equality and mutual benefit, as well as self-reliance, with the goal of adopting technology and equipment at advanced world levels."

The Plenary Session marked a major watershed in the Party's political, ideological and organizational lines and heralded a new era of development for China. The meeting was a historic prologue to the reform and opening policy, which along with major changes on the homefront, caused immense global repercussions.

The "Deng Xiaoping Whirlwind" Sweeps America off Its Feet

The heroic notes of the National Anthem of the People's Republic of China reverberated in the air about the White House, in Washington, D.C. On January 29, 1979, Vice Premier Deng Xiaoping began his state visit, the first of its kind by a top Chinese leader, to the United States. That evening, President Jimmy Carter threw a state banquet in his honor.

At Lincoln Center in New York, his American hosts held a special performance. New Yorkers had gotten a previous glimpse of Deng's elegant poise and spontaneous sense of humor, having witnessed his 1972 participation in the UN General Assembly at the United Nations Headquarters (this was shortly after he had made his comeback to power during the Cultural Revolution). America was now swept off its feet once again by the "Deng Xiaoping Whirlwind." When he visited NASA's Johnson Space Center in Houston, and several times during interviews with American newspaper editors, Deng declared that "China could learn a lot from the United States," an attitude that was warmly and widely embraced by the US press, and gave Americans a positive impression of the Chinese leader.

On January 29, Deng and President Carter attended the above-mentioned special performance at Lincoln Center. Senator Paul Laxalt (Republican-Nevada) had been against establishing diplomatic relations with China, but after he attended the performance, he said in good humor, "They really beat us. Nobody can bring himself to vote against children singing Chinese songs."

At Deng's last meeting with President Carter during the tour, the two governments concluded agreements on consular relations, trade and exchanges in science and technology and culture. In China, extensive television coverage of Deng's visit gave the Chinese people a good chance to see and learn something about the outer world.

Almost everyone, from the top leaders to the man in the street, came to the same realization: "We have shut ourselves up for far too long."

In June 1981, the Sixth Plenary Session of the 11th Party Central Committee endorsed the *Resolution on Certain Questions in the History of Our Party Since the Founding of the People's Republic of China*, a 35,000-word document drafted under Deng's guidance. This resolution summed up the historical lessons and experience of China since the founding of the People's Republic and thoroughly repudiated the Cultural Revolution. Significantly, it also made a scientific assessment of Mao and resolutely defended his historical position and the importance of the scientific system of Mao Zedong Thought, thereby addressing a major strategic issue that had a close bearing on the destiny of the Party and the nation. This was another of Deng's major historical contributions in China's new age of development, reform and opening.

2

The Birth of Special Economic Zones

Our country, having no model upon which to pattern its opening-up policy, had to grope its way through trial and error. It all began in January 1979, when a Hong Kong businessman's letter asking for permission to open a factory in Guangdong Province was sent to Deng, who by then was the *de facto* top leader of China. Upon reading the letter, Deng wrote down the instruction, "As I see it, Guangdong should be given a free hand to give this sort of thing a try." Wang Quanguo, a former vice governor of Guangdong, recalled:

> After the Third Plenary Session of the 11th Party Central Committee, we had a strong sense that we stood no chance without reform and opening. Comrade Xiaoping's instruction came as a great inspiration and encouragement for us. Proceeding from reality and based on a study of the characteristics of Guangdong, we raised the proposal that Guangdong make the first step in the reform and opening.

Shekou, the Opening Salvo

Li Xiannian Pencils the Blueprint

Just a few months earlier, on October 9, 1978, the Ministry of Transport and Communications submitted to the central authorities the *Request for Instructions on Full Utilization of the Hong Kong Merchants*

Group. The *Request* suggested that the business of the Group should "base itself on Hong Kong and Macao, rely on the backing of the mainland, be oriented toward overseas, diversify its operations, lump purchases with sales, and combine industry and commerce." Furthermore, the document said, the group should do away with all unwarranted restraints and be given a free hand, so that it could quickly move ahead to adapt itself to the world market and step out the door to see how the rest of the world made things work and got business done. To ensure success, the *Request* urged the authorities to revamp the superstructure, simplify the red tape, and allow the Hong Kong Merchants Group the flexibility to handle issues on its own, including the power to take out local loans of no more than US$5 million for business purposes.

On October 12, Vice Premier Li Xiannian notified other state leaders of the *Request* with this instruction:

Chairman Hua, Vice Chairmen Ye, Deng and Wang, and Comrades Ji Dengkui, Yu Qiuli, Gu Mu and Kang Shi'en,

Please read and deliberate on this report. Approval is recommended. A lot more can be done than the report has suggested, provided we tighten up leadership and redouble our efforts to straighten things out among ourselves, loosen up a little bit and look a bit farther to the future in line with Chairman Hua's directive to "unshackle the mind a little more, be a little bolder, find more ways to get things done and step it up a bit faster." Please let me know if my suggestion is appropriate.

It did not take long for the leaders to finish reading the *Request*, and they granted it.

Why did the central authorities go to such lengths to back a company headquartered in Hong Kong? Established in 1872 by Li Hongzhang (1823-1901) with the endorsement of the Qing government, the China Merchants Steam Navigation Company was one of the three biggest government-run companies, along with the Kiangnan Arsenal and the New Textile Bureau in modern China, and played a unique role during the Modernization Movement. The group's function changed repeatedly from the time of the Revolution of 1911 led by Dr. Sun Yat-sen, which overthrew the Qing Dynasty, through the founding of the People's Republic. It was no longer the all-powerful organization it once had been. In 1951, its headquarters was renamed China People's General Shipping Corporation, but its Hong Kong branch retained the old name and came under the jurisdiction of the Ministry of Transport and Communications.

The Ministry of Transport and Communications appointed Yuan Geng Executive Vice Chairman of the 29th Board of Directors of the Merchants Group on October 28, 1978. The first thing Yuan did upon taking office was to brief his new colleagues on the directives of the central authorities and take steps to carry them out. While in Hong Kong, Yuan discovered that the ships of the Merchants Group could enter and leave the Hong Kong harbor free from inspection. The convenience this group's ships enjoyed in shuttling between Hong Kong and the mainland gave him the idea to set up an export zone somewhere on the mainland coast. After making investigations and comparisons, he decided that the Shekou People's Commune* in Bao'an County was the ideal place. This idea was backed by Ye Fei, Minister of Transport and Communications, and Liu Tianfu, Vice Governor of Guangdong Province. On January 6, 1979, the province and the ministry submitted the *Report on Establishing an Industrial Zone in Bao'an County of Guangdong Province by Hong Kong-Based Merchants Group* to Vice Premier Li Xiannian and the State Council. The report said that the Merchants Group had initially decided to set up an industrial zone in the Shekou People's Commune, so that inexpensive local land and labor resources could be fully utilized to bring in foreign capital, technology and raw materials.

Li Xiannian studied the report together with Gu Mu. Then the two vice premiers met with Vice Minister of Transport and Communications Peng Deqing and Yuan Geng for a discussion.

On January 31, when the four men gathered at Zhongnanhai in Beijing, Yuan Geng was the first to broach his idea to combine Hong Kong's abundant financial resources and advanced technology with the mainland's low-priced land and labor resources. "Yeah, you are right," Li said in response. "What

---

* "People's commune" was established in 1958 as an administrative district, equivalent to a township. It was abolished in 1983, and township was restored as the grass-roots administrative division in rural areas. (*Translator*)

we should do now is to put the strengths of Hong Kong and the mainland together, and make the most of foreign capital in our construction work. This should be done not just in Guangdong, but in Fujian, Shanghai and some other places as well." He told Yuan Geng, "Don't count on me for money to buy ships and build docks. You've got to get it done by yourselves. Live or die, that's your business."

Yuan unfolded a map of Hong Kong, and went on with his report. "We want, with the central authorities' full support of course, to fence off a piece of land for industrial use by the Merchants Group," he said. Li perused the map before he raised a pencil to draw two bold lines at the root of the southern peninsula, saying, "Why not? This peninsula is yours."

That generous offer caught Yuan by surprise. He was ill-prepared to "swallow" the whole peninsula, which amounted to several dozen square kilometers. All he could handle, he decided, was Shekou, a place of two square kilometers.

"What's your opinion about the request from the Merchants Group," Li asked Gu. Gu replied, "Just go ahead and write down your approval in principle. Then leave it to me to canvas the opinions of the departments concerned."

"All right, just let me put my stamp of approval on it," Li said as he wrote on the margin of the report. "Approval recommended. Comrade Gu Mu may discuss it with the comrades concerned and do it accordingly." The date was January 31, 1979.

Yuan Geng (*right*) reporting to Deng (*left*) on an inspection tour of Shekou, January 26, 1984.

Gu Mu Takes the Lead in Policy Studies

On February 2, 1979, Vice Premier Gu Mu called a meeting of the leaders of the relevant ministries – the State Planning Commission, the State Construction Commission, the Ministry of Foreign Trade, the People's Bank of China, the Ministry of Finance, and the Ministry of Transport and Communications – to discuss how Li's instructions should be implemented. "Now let's talk about the Hong Kong Merchants Group running factories in Shekou. They deserve some 'prerogatives' when they set up factories there. That is, while handling local administrative affairs according to domestic legislation, they should have the same entry-and-exit freedom they enjoy in Hong Kong," the vice premier said. He added, "According to what Comrade Xiaoping has said, Guangdong and Fujian can be more open than elsewhere. Comrade Xiannian has also written an instruction on a report from the Ministry of Transport and Communications." After Gu Mu related Li's instruction, he gave the floor to Yuan Geng, who spoke about the benefits of attracting foreign investment from the base of Guangdong:

> The price of land in central Hong Kong is second only to Tokyo's Ginza district in the world today... one square foot sells for HK$15,000, and the price of industrial land has topped HK$500 per square foot even in the outskirts. Wages there are high too. After studying all aspects of the issue, we have arrived at a consensus to use the land and labor of Guangdong in the vicinity of Hong Kong and Macao to attract money and technology from Hong Kong. If we can do this, no consortiums in Hong Kong will be able to beat us. The Ministry of Transport and Communications and Guangdong Province have drawn up an action plan. Only the export tax issue is inconclusive, pending the central authorities' decision.

Gu Mu added in, "We can use some incentives on that too."

Yuan went on to spell out his ideas on how to set up the industrial zone and factories. "The construction of this industrial zone will not cost the Ministry of Finance a single penny," he said, "provided you exempt us from tax for ten to 15 years. After that, we'll deliver all we earn to the state."

Minister of Finance Wang Bingqian said, "I have no comment on that, but as to taxation, we won't follow what's being done at home. We'll follow the practice of Hong Kong. That means you'll pay tax in Shekou the way you do it in Hong Kong."

Vice Minister of Foreign Trade Liu Xiwen said, "We will grant you preferential tax rates on imports and exports, but I will have to talk to the customs about the specifics."

Even though the topics discussed at the meeting were about specifics, the decisions made on that occasion were about to shake the world.

The construction of the much-deliberated Shekou Industrial Zone commenced with a boom of explosives on July 20, 1979. The blast was set off to cut into a mountain to make room for a dock. The eventual dock, 600 meters in length and large enough for 500-tonners, was completed in less than a year, enabling freighters and passenger ships to shuttle to and from Hong Kong, thereby addressing a nagging bottleneck on transportation.

China's first special economic zone thus took shape right below the Shekou Fort, where Chinese troops under the command of Lin Zexu and Guan Tianpei fired the first cannon against British invaders in the First Opium War of 1840.

Designating a piece of land in China on which a Hong Kong-based company would be allowed to run business the Hong Kong way was something no one had ever done, or even thought of before. Naturally, when the decision was made to do exactly that, it raised a lot of eyebrows at the Ministry of Transport and Communications. Some accused Yuan Geng of "monkey business," predicting that he would end up a loser. Some were categorically opposed to running the industrial zone. In sharp contrast to all the booing from the ministry, consortiums in Hong Kong expressed an appreciation bordering on envy. Li Ka-shing, Fung King Hey, Ying Sheung Wu and many other Hong Kong business moguls came to Yuan Geng. "Mr. Yuan," one of them asked, "why don't you give us a piece of that land of yours, and some of the power the central government has given you, so that we can do it together?"

Two years later, in December 1981, when Hong Kong Governor Murray MacLehose arrived in Shekou for a visit, he was stunned by the speed of construction, and congratulated local builders for having gone that far just in 28 months. He estimated that it would have taken 54 months to get the same amount of work done in Hong Kong.

Jiang Zemin Pitches In

The difficulties the builders of Shekou encountered in the early years were unimaginable to people today. Many of the problems were ideological or institutional. In one instance, after the construction of a seven-kilometer highway leading to the industrial zone, a construction company deliberately left a 200-meter section unpaved, right at the entrance to the industrial zone. As a result, the road was ridden with pebbly mud pools whenever it rained. Not only was it an eyesore, but it seriously affected traffic as well.

At the time, Shekou was just a sleepy fishing village where telephone service was sparse, not to mention the convenience of modern telecommunications. That is why the builders met with stubborn obstacles when they wanted to have a microwave telecommunications switchboard installed in the zone.

When Jiang Zemin, then Vice Minister of the State Import and Export Commission, accompanied Vice Premier Gu Mu on an inspection tour of Shekou on March 22, 1980, he was deeply impressed by the openness, reforms, development and changes that he had seen, but at the same time he felt deeply for the builders working under harsh conditions. When he visited Shekou again on August 8, he talked with Xu Zhiming and other zone leaders and spoke highly of the new progress the industrial zone had made in less than five months. "The construction rate of the Shekou Industrial Zone is very fast," he commented. "Everything here is so well organized, and the results are very good, too."

Speaking of the problems confronting the builders, Jiang pointed out, "It is true we are having many problems in the modernization drive. But in my opinion, some of the problems are a matter of understanding. The special zone is a new thing. Because most of us were isolated from the outer world for so long, we know little about the new things around the world. Therefore, what we think or do is often limited by old conventions. Of course, the influence of long years of embargo imposed on us by foreign countries also has something to do with this. The problems occurring in our thinking can be forgiven or changed through persuasion and education. But some of the problems are rooted in feudalism or even feudal secessionism. For example, some government departments, holding all the power to themselves, will not budge an inch if you do not follow their lines. We have got to do something about this form of feudal secessionism." Commenting on the telecommunications woes that were bothering the builders, he said:

> Telecommunications service is a big problem. We can't afford to let this problem hold us back when we are building factories in collaboration with foreign investors. It is said that telephones are common in Hong Kong, where there is one telephone to every four persons. Our country is lagging behind in this field. The scarcity of telephone lines makes it very hard for us even to apply for installing a telephone, not to mention the expense of getting one installed. To meet the needs of running joint ventures with foreign investors, the Shekou Industrial Zone is doing a good thing by raising money to build microwave telephone lines between Shekou and Hong Kong by way of Shenzhen. We have got to stand by you.

He asked Qin Wenjun, Deputy Director of the Guangdong Provincial Administration of Special Economic Zones, to talk to the postal and telecommunications authorities of Shenzhen and Guangdong about the Shekou builders' problem with the microwave telephone station. He himself promised to talk to Minister of Posts and Telecommunications Zhu Xuefan about the problem.

Before long, experts arrived from the Ministry and provincial and municipal post offices at Yuan Geng's invitation. They told him that the problem was technically solvable. Convinced, Yuan thought that he could get it done this time. To his surprise, however, the issue met a new snag. The posts and telecommunications authorities insisted that revenues from the future telephone service would belong to them, but that the costs incurred in building the facilities should be covered by the industrial zone itself. What is more, after the microwave telephone station was built, people in Shekou would have to dial long-distance and direct calls to Hong Kong through the local long-distance telephone bureau. Yuan had no choice but to report this and other problems to the central government.

On September 3, 1980, Party General Secretary Hu Yaobang read a confidential Xinhua report entitled "Several Bottlenecks Encountered in the Construction of the Shekou Industrial Zone." He immediately issued the directive:

Comrade Gu Mu,

The Central Committee is determined to oppose and stamp out all descriptions of bureaucraticism. My suggestion is for you to take the case of the said special zone and make a thorough investigation of it. I want you to see if it is true that bureaucrats are bent on making a determined effort, and whether there are bureaucrats who do nothing but waylaying. Whenever necessary, you have got to sanction some people (preferably with economic sanctions). Otherwise, not only will bureaucraticism prevail, but the Four Modernizations will be long in coming.

Gu Mu lost no time in asking the State Import and Export Commission to implement the general secretary's directive.

On September 12, 1980, Jiang Zemin chaired a special meeting to deal with the four "bottlenecking problems" in the construction of the Shekou Industrial Zone. For this he called together the Ministry of Post and Telecommunications, the Ministry of Foreign Trade, the General Administration of Customs, the General Labor Administration, and the State Administration of Science and Technology. The meeting produced an order that the Ministry of Post and Telecommunications loosen its control and make an exception for Shenzhen, so that a special switchboard providing direct-call service to Hong Kong could be bought and installed in the Shekou Industrial Zone while the municipality set about solving its longer-term telecommunications equipment installation problem. The switchboard was to start operation in March or April of 1981 under the Merchants Group. The meeting also worked out solutions to other problems, such as the deployment of technical workers and technicians and importation of engineering equipment.

When the discussion switched to the 200-meter stretch of road that had been left unfinished, the participants found that none of them were in a position to tackle the problem. It was only after

Governor Liu Tianfu of Guangdong arrived in the afternoon that they broke through the impasse when he promised that the provincial government would do all it could to help the industrial zone solve the problem.

Jiang Zemin repeatedly appealed to the participants during the discussion, "Everyone here, please back the industrial zone. Please give it a green light." A few days later, just 24 hours after the dismissal of the head of the construction department – who was charged with "getting at people by the throat, grabbing at whatever benefits came into sight and asking for favors" – the road section was paved with asphalt, turning the troublesome eyesore into part of the thoroughfare to and from the industrial zone.

In December 1980, Jiang made another trip to Shekou (his third visit that year), this time to tour Shenzhen and Zhuhai together with Vice Premier Gu Mu.

The Shekou Industrial Zone was established to bring in foreign investment to boost export-oriented industry. No industrial zone could function on its own, however, without residential quarters, shops and service facilities. In those years, domestic commodities were in such shortage that the newly founded Shekou Industrial Zone could not meet the daily needs of the many foreigners who had settled down to live and work there. The zone was in need of a shopping center that could sell imported goods and charge foreign exchange. Running this kind of shopping center in a fishing village was unprecedented for China. These kinds of shops were monopolized by government-designated departments. Sensing a business opportunity in it, a Hong Kong merchant surnamed Chen petitioned Yuan Geng for permission to open a joint-venture store there. Yuan, who saw the need for a shop there, but was uncertain about its business future, jokingly asked Chen what she would do if she could only sell one bottle of soda a day. "It's okay for me to sell one bottle a day for a little while," the woman answered, "but if I'm still selling one bottle a day six months later, then I'll have to call it quits and pull out." An agreement on the store was concluded between the two sides and submitted to the provincial authorities for approval. The authorities, not knowing how to proceed with no precedent to follow, passed the buck to one another, and the deal got bogged down.

The same thing happened to a contract on direct shipping between Shekou and Hong Kong. Yuan Geng, once again, had to do something to get the attention of the central authorities.

On October 16, 1981, the Xinhua News Agency ran an article for internal circulation entitled "Builders of the Shekou Special Zone in Shenzhen Encounter Two Problems." The article reported that red-tape and procrastination on the shopping center and on the Shekou-Hong Kong navigation arrangement were impeding the implementation of central and provincial directives on Shekou. Upon reading the article, Wan Li instructed: "Comrade Gu Mu, please do something about this." Gu replied: "Let's discuss it tomorrow."

When Jiang Zemin read this article, he did what he had done a year earlier on the "four bottlenecking problems." After talking to the relevant departments, on October 24 he presented his solutions to both issues in a report to Gu Mu:

Vice Premier Gu Mu,

Having consulted Wang Runsheng [Director General of the General Administration of Customs] and Wang Douguang [Deputy Director General of the General Administration of Customs] on the two cases reflected in the article in Issue No. 2492 of the Proofs of Domestic Trends, *and having queried the Shekou Construction Headquarters on the details, I would like to present my solutions as follows.*

First, the establishment of a shopping center in Shekou. Central Document [1981] 27 stipulates, "With the exception of cigarettes and alcoholic beverages on which tax is levied at half the minimum tax rate, and of a tiny number of articles on which tax is levied according to relevant stipulations, the other articles should be imported duty-free. The goods and articles to be shipped from the special economic zone to the hinterland should be handled in compliance with the legislation concerning conventional imports. In other words, before the boundary is erected around the zone, such shipments should be handled according to customs' provisional regulations. The Shekou Construction Headquarters has said that they are stepping up construction of the zone's second boundary. According to a report from the customs authority, over the last couple of years the workers and staff in Shekou have been buying imported television sets and other articles duty-free, and if people are allowed to use foreign currencies to buy imported goods at the shopping center in question, this will have the effect of increasing the number of recipients of the supplies. This could cause an uncontrollable influx of outsiders into Shekou. We agree with the customs authority's opinion that the shopping center should not be opened for business until the second boundary is erected, in keeping with the principles to "loosen control on outsiders and tighten it up on insiders," and to "loosen control at first and tighten it up later on." We have instructed the Shekou Construction Headquarters to finish erecting the second boundary of the industrial zone as soon as possible.

Second is the issue of opening the Shekou Port to passenger ships. Document 75, issued by the State Council General Office on September 26 of this year, approved the Shekou Port to accommodate passenger ships. The Shekou Construction Headquarters maintains that coordinated inspection facilities are in place at the port and can start work as soon as the customs people move in. Customs, for their part, have replied that they received the documents on short notice, and because the Kowloon Customs Office is already running short-handed, they do not have enough people to send to Shekou. It has been initially decided, through further consultations, that the customs people will be posted on November 15 and the Shekou Port will be opened no later than November 20.

That's all for this report. Please let us know if this is doable.

Jiang Zemin
October 24, 1981

With the intervention of Wan Li and Gu Mu, the path was cleared, and Jiang Zemin signed the *Proposals of the State Import and Export Commission on Handling the Shopping Center of the Shekou Industrial Zone and the Opening of the Shekou Port* and issued it to the Guangdong Provincial Administration of Special Economic Zones. Thus the two problems that had been weighing most heavily on Yuan Geng were finally resolved. On the morning of June 23, 1982, the long-anticipated first joint-venture shopping center in China was opened to several hundred shoppers queuing up at the front gate. The store, at the time a nondescript affair in comparison with the posh shopping centers we see today, reported fine returns before long and continued to rise in popularity as a major local tourist attraction. During one of my tours of Shenzhen, I went out of my way to see the shopping center which, with its endless array of commodities and bustling crowds, compared favorably with its Hong Kong and Western counterparts and stood in stark contrast to the hinterland stores where the stacks were virtually empty.

Zone's Trailblazing Shakes the Establishment

Despite the fact that its establishment was not listed in the state plan and got no government financing, the industrial zone thrived all the same, thanks to its authority, granted by the government, to endorse industrial projects of up to US$5 million in investment and to borrow from foreign banks. With these two government mandates, Yuan Geng visited businesses and banks all over Hong Kong. Within two years, his Merchants Group obtained 1.5 billion yuan in loans to level the land of Shekou, bring in tap water, electricity and cooking gas, and build the infrastructure and residential quarters. To get returns from the borrowed money, he simplified red tape to attract investors to the factory buildings that were already built in the zone. It usually took no more than a month for an investor to run through the negotiations, contracting and registration necessary to land a business certificate. All that was left thereafter was to ship in the equipment and have it installed to begin production. Businesspeople and professionals flocked into the zone as a result. In a little more than two years, some 100 enterprises had opened shop in Shekou.

The Shekou experiment was not simply an exercise in "emancipating people's minds," it was also a drastic transformation of central planning and the prevailing personnel and labor systems. In the process, Shekou scored a number of "firsts." It was the first in China to bring in investment and loans from outside of the mainland, to make its own decisions to examine and take on construction and industrial projects, and the first to allow businesses to make their own decisions and bear the responsibility for their own losses and gains. On March 28, 1980, Shekou was the first in China to introduce a new personnel system whereby staff members and workers had to compete for job vacancies. In 1983, with the go-ahead from Hu Yaobang, Shekou was the first to experiment with a system allowing the public to recommend candidates for local official posts and to appraise the performance of incumbent officials. On April 24, 1983, some 2,000 people gathered in Shekou, named candidates and cast votes, and finally elected 15 people to the first administrative committee of the industrial zone. All staff persons transferred to Shekou, regardless of their original salary grades, were carefully selected through a screening process in which their talent and competence were carefully measured; only those who survived the process could land the jobs they coveted. To get rid of the notorious "lifelong tenures," the Shekou government put local government officials' performances through democratic assessments once a year; those who failed to gain at least a 50 percent vote of confidence were immediately dismissed. Local workers, for their part, were asked to sign contracts to get the jobs they wanted.

High speed, high efficiency and high returns were the direct results of these reforms. This prompted Yuan Geng to come up with a catchphrase that immediately caught on nationwide: "Time is money, efficiency the lifeline." This phrase allowed the Merchants Group to grow from a small concern with 100 million yuan in assets in 1980, to a giant corporation with assets of 20 billion yuan in 1992, the same year in which Yuan retired.

Hu Yaobang (first row, center) inspecting the Shekou Industrial Zone in the company of Ren Zhongyi (behind Hu) and Yuan Geng (far left), February 9, 1983.

86

The early reforms and experiments of Shekou were a process of "fording the river by groping for stepping stones." At the time, few realized the fact that what the builders of the industrial zone achieved had already shaken the establishment to the core. As pathbreakers fighting their way out of the encirclements of traditional central planning, the Shekou builders' contributions were tremendous and historically significant.

Guangdong and Fujian Set the Pace

It was unrealistic – given the nation's vast territory and regional disparities in socioeconomic development and investment environments – for all the regions to jump on the opening-up bandwagon at the same time.

As early as 1977, a group of officials went to what was then Bao'an County in search of ways to stem massive illegal immigration to neighboring Hong Kong and to ensure supplies to Hong Kong and Macao markets. (The group included members of the State Council Office of Finance and Trade, the State Planning Commission, the Ministry of Foreign Trade, the Ministry of Finance and other departments of the State Council.) One of their decisions was to build Bao'an and Zhuhai into centers to produce perishables, livestock and poultry to supply to Hong Kong and Macao. Later, the government earmarked 4 million yuan from sea-sand sales revenues to bankroll the building of a number of vegetable, poultry and aquatic farms in Bao'an County.

In March 1978, the State Planning Commission and the Ministry of Foreign Trade dispatched a working group to Bao'an County. There the group, headed by Yang Wei, Director of the Administration of Production Bases under the Ministry of Foreign Trade, joined colleagues from Guangdong Province to study the prospects for building non-staple food producing and exporting bases in Bao'an and Zhuhai counties. On the basis of the study, the working group and county authorities signed an annual production and export plan and outlined three- and five-year programs.

The State Planning Commission and the Ministry of Foreign Trade then organized a fact-finding delegation headed by Duan Yun,

Vice Minister in charge of the State Planning Commission, for a tour of enterprises and markets in Hong Kong and Macao. During the tour (from April 10 to May 6), the delegates conversed with mainland organizations stationed in Hong Kong and local factory owners and businesspeople, and compared notes with colleagues from Guangdong. When they returned to Beijing they submitted a report on their findings about these two economies and analyzed the reasons behind their robust growth.

Both cities, according to the report, had ample financial sources and low-cost labor. Both were free ports, which made it very convenient for them to bring in needed raw materials and technology and equipment. Local factories were highly adaptive to the changing market by matching output with demand and by producing only what the market needed. Both cities spared no effort in developing export-processing industries and expanding exports by using external funds to import equipment, raw materials and semi-finished products to be processed or assembled by local labor forces. After summarizing the two cities' major approaches to economic development, the report recommended: developing Bao'an and Zhuhai into two production and exporting centers; going all out to develop non-staple food production and increasing exports of perishables, livestock and poultry; boosting local building materials and processing industries; opening up sightseeing and tourist zones and running commercial, services and entertainment facilities. The report also advised that in order to build up these two counties in the near future, it would be necessary to adopt certain special administrative measures, such elevating their administrative status from county- to prefecture-level municipalities directly under provincial administration, and dispatching capable officials to bolster local leadership. The report also suggested the following tactics: giving full scope to the role of mainland trade organizations stationed in Hong Kong and Macao; making the two cities instrumental in promoting export-processing and assembling businesses; heightening the mainland's economic presence in Hong Kong and Macao; and stepping up unified leadership over efforts to develop economic relations with Hong Kong and Macao.

On June 3, Hua Guofeng and other top leaders heard the delegation's report and issued this directive: "This report is approved in general. We have got to do what is certain to succeed, and do it right away and without fail." The State Council General Office immediately issued the *Report on an Economic Inspection Tour of Hong Kong and Macao* to the relevant localities and departments.

In early April 1978, Xi Zhongxun was appointed Second Secretary of Guangdong Provincial Party Committee to preside over the daily work of the province. Uppermost on his mind was how to do away with dogmatism and mobilize resources and advantages to bail the province out of its economic woes and put local development onto sound footing.

Two months later, in June, Xi convened a meeting to hear a report by Vice Governor Wang Quanguo on his tour of five Western European countries as a member of the delegation headed by Vice Premier Gu Mu. It was then decided that the report should be relayed to a meeting of local officials (at and above the department-head level) to be convened at Guangdong's Sun Yat-sen Memorial Hall. Those who participated in that meeting were elated by what they heard.

Xi followed up with a second meeting, on June 20, to study the central authorities' directive on the *Report on an Economic Inspection Tour of Hong Kong and Macao*, to work out ways to handle the construction tasks in Bao'an and Zhuhai, and to launch export-processing and assembling businesses in both places.

Early the next month, Xi arrived in Bao'an for a visit. The development disparity between the two sides of the Shenzhen River, with Shenzhen on one side and Hong Kong on the other, drove home to him that the only way to rejuvenate the local economy lay in developing the economy and opening up to the outer world.

On October 23, 1978, on the basis of repeated investigations, studies and discussions, Guangdong Province submitted to the State Council the *Report on a Tentative Plan for Building Foreign Trade Bases and Urban Development in Bao'an and Zhuhai Counties*. The report proposed, in addition to developing foreign trade as a means to consolidate the southern gateway to the motherland, turning Bao'an, within three to five years, into an exports manufacturing center that would combine industry with agriculture at a fairly high level, and would also include a sightseeing zone to attract tourists from Hong Kong and Macao. The report also suggested that the two counties be elevated to municipalities at the prefecture level.

Xi continued to call for more support and latitude for Guangdong. In a speech ("On How to Go All Out and Make Quick Progress in the Construction Work of Guangdong"), which he delivered to a central-south China panel session at the Central Working Conference (November 10 to December 15, 1978), he said:

> I hope that the central authorities will give Guangdong more help and the localities more leeway to handle their own problems. If we are allowed to absorb funds from Hong Kong and Macao and from among overseas Chinese, bring in a batch of advanced equipment and technology, buy electricity and import some feedstuffs from Hong Kong, then we can retool our state farms, animal farms and fresh-water aquatic breeding farms, and turn them into models where we can train people and gain experience. I also hope that Guangdong will be empowered to make its own decisions on economic matters such as the processing of materials supplied by foreign clients, and compensation trade, so we can streamline unnecessary procedures and red tape.

Delegates from Fujian Province said that they wanted to take advantage of the province's status as homeland to many Chinese nationals living overseas to attract investment from these people and the countries where they lived. They also wanted to be given a free hand to develop export-oriented trade and blaze a new trail for local economic development. They wanted the central authorities to grant them preferential policies, to raise the share of foreign trade revenues to be retained by local governments, and turn Fuzhou and Xiamen into open ports. These suggestions and opinions commanded the attention of the central authorities.

The session continued, and on December 11, the Central Committee appointed Xi First Secretary, and Yang Shangkun Second Secretary, of the Guangdong Provincial Party Committee.

On January 23, 1979, Bao'an County was renamed Shenzhen Municipality, with Zhang Xunfu as Municipal Party Committee

Secretary, and Zhuhai County became Zhuhai Municipality with Wu Jianmin as Municipal Party Committee Secretary. The State Council approved Guangdong Province's summary proposal for the zones at Bao-an and Zhuhai (*Report on a Tentative Plan for Building Foreign Trade Bases and Urban Development in Bao'an and Zhuhai Counties*) on February 14, and agreed to change the two counties to municipalities beginning on March 5.

Preparing for an Export Processing Industrial Zone

While Bao'an County (the predecessor of Shenzhen Municipality) began building itself into an export goods manufacturing center, Guangdong Province received a proposal for the establishment of an "export-oriented processing industrial zone" in Shantou.

In early 1979, when Wu Nansheng, Seretary of the Guangdong Provincial Party Committee, arrived in Shantou for a meeting, he was dismayed by the city's rundown streets and stagnant economy. Shantou is a famous homeland for millions of Chinese nationals living overseas, and used to be a thriving port city. After the founding of the People's Republic, despite the Western blockade on China, Shantou was one of the better developed cities in the country thanks to the backing of millions of Hong Kong and Macao people, including prominent figures, as well as natives living overseas who, out of a sense of loyalty or sentimental attachment, did what they could to help their homeland. As a result of the ultra-leftist trend of thought and the chaos of the ten-year Cultural Revolution, Shantou trailed far behind other seaboard cities in Guangdong. Wu considered whether, by assimilating some of the practices of foreign countries, Shantou could be turned into an export-processing industrial zone to attract foreign investors to open business there. "If it is unrealistic to turn the entire city into such a zone," he wondered, "can we just cordon off part of the city proper, pool local financial and material resources to build such a zone, and then build on the experience to expand it?

On the evening of February 21, the governor telegraphed the Guangdong provincial authorities to tell them about the outstanding problems he had seen in Shantou. He told them that the city was a good place for foreign trade and for processing materials or semi-finished products supplied by foreign investors. "If we can carry out policies to mobilize the resources and advantages at home and abroad, shake off outdated conventions, and decontrol some of the power in order to let the local people do what they need to do," he continued, "the city's dismal situation could be fundamentally changed in three to five years."

At a March 3 provincial leadership meeting, Wu proposed to designate a piece of land in Shantou in which to experiment with a package of incentive policies to try to attract foreign investment and other good things from abroad. All the leaders present were in favor of the proposal. Xi Zhongxun said, "This is something we should do, and the entire province should do." He asked his colleagues to draft a document on this proposal, so that he could bring it to a Central Working Conference to be convened in April.

"Why Don't We Call Them 'Special Zones'"

Participants at a provincial meeting, chaired by Yang Shangkun on April 1 to 2, 1979, deliberated over the draft of the report to the forthcoming Central Working Conference. Guangdong Province, they maintained, enjoyed two unique advantages: proximity to Hong Kong and Macao, and a large population of natives living and working overseas. If the central authorities would grant Guangdong with sufficient autonomy to adopt flexible steps and stimulus policies, these two advantages could stand the province in good stead for accelerating local economic development. It was decided to petition the central authorities to allow Guangdong to "take the first step ahead of other provinces."

Thus the government of Guangdong was set to establish export-oriented industrial zones by fencing off pieces of land in Shenzhen, Zhuhai and Shantou and by doing things in unconventional ways. They were hesitating, however, about how to designate the lands and how to name them. Wu recollected, "We were racking our brains for a name. In foreign countries they were commonly known as 'free trade zones' or 'free ports,' but as they knew that at the mention of the word 'free,' people would immediately think of national sovereignty and 'foreign concessions' and 'enclaves.'" He considered "export processing zone" as an option, but immediately thought better of it, for it was a familiar name from Taiwan. Everyone was thinking hard, but they could not come up with the best name for the new zones. Xi and Wu even consulted Ye Jianying on the matter, but Ye could only ask them to report the issue to Deng.

The Central Working Conference to discuss economic issues was held as scheduled in April 1979. The demands of Guangdong and Fujian for special policies to stimulate local economies were also considered. In his report to the conference, Xi Zhongxun expressed his hope that the central authorities would delegate Guangdong Province with the necessary decision-making power to deal with foreign economic relations and allow the province to set up export processing industrial zones in Shenzhen, Zhuhai and Shantou in the vicinity of Hong Kong and Macao. "We have discussed the issue at our provincial meeting," he continued. "At this meeting we just want to ask the central government to give us some power and let us in Guangdong make the most of favorable local conditions to take the first step in the nation's modernization drive."

The proposal drew a positive response from Deng. "Applying some special policies in Guangdong and Fujian, using the money and technology of overseas Chinese, and allowing them to run factories there won't turn us into capitalists," he said, "because the money we make won't go into the pockets of Comrade Hua Guofeng or others among us. Ours is ownership by all the people. I just can't see that things would go wrong if we allow the 80 million people of Guangdong and Fujian to get rich first." Deng was all too willing to grant Xi's petition on the proposed export processing zones. "Why don't we call them 'special zones,'" he said. "That was the name for the Shaanxi-Gansu-Ningxia Border Region in the beginning." On a previous occasion, Deng had said, "The central authorities do not have the money, but we can give you some policies to allow you to do it on your own and blaze a new trail."

This was the first time that Deng had mentioned the term "special zone," which was to become the origin and abbreviation of the official name "special economic zone," a name that represented a breakthrough and new path for the opening-up policy.

Deng's choice of the term was well-thought out. He believed that first, China could learn from similar actions taken in other countries and regions, and second, the term was evocative of the Party-led Shaanxi-Gansu-Ningxia Border Region of the 1935-1949 period. This was a "special zone," which differed from the Kuomintang-ruled regions in terms of political, economic and cultural systems and policies. Neither the foreign "special zones," nor the former border region, however, ever approached the same level of national significance as the special economic zones that would flourish in China during the new age. The plan to cordon off a few places, apply to them certain special policies and flexible steps for international economic activities, and to explore approaches to speed up socialist economic development – all under the preconditions of the Party leadership and the socialist system – was completely in accord with the reality of the country and the objective law governing economic development. The chain of events in due course proved Deng's farsighted decision to run the special economic zones.

During the working conference, Deng formally asked the central authorities to approve the demands of Guangdong and Fujian. The *Regulations on Issues Concerning Vigorous Development of Foreign Trade and Increase of Foreign Exchange Revenues*, which featured the passage "Running the Special Zones on a Trial Basis," was endorsed at the conference, along with the decision to run such zones in Shenzhen, Zhuhai, Shantou and Xiamen.

When the conference shifted its discussion to how to expand foreign trade, many participants felt that it was feasible to experiment with special export industrial zones in the above-mentioned four cities and to develop export manufacturing. The conference also determined that special policies and flexible steps be adopted in Guangdong and Fujian, so that the provinces would have ample leeway to develop foreign trade, augment foreign exchange revenues and speed up local economic growth. The impact of Deng's proposition for "special zones" was as positive and emphatic as a boulder tossed into the deep blue sea.

Decontrolling Power and Granting Incentive Policies

In May of 1979, Gu Mu, along with a dozen or so leaders of central ministries and commissions, went on a fact-finding tour of Guangdong and Fujian. They spent a week with local leaders amending the *Tentative Proposals on Running Special*

Export Zones on a Trial Basis in Shenzhen, Zhuhai and Shantou submitted by Guangdong Province on May 5, and in hammering out the details for the special zones with leaders and experts from both provinces. After much deliberation, they reached the consensus that in order to tap the economic potential of Guangdong and Fujian, it would be necessary to revamp the excessively centralized planned economy and get everyone involved in the grand undertaking. Accordingly, on June 6 Guangdong delivered to the State Council a report on giving full play to Guangdong's advantages to expand foreign trade and speed up economic development; three days later, Fujian sent in a report on using funds raised from overseas Chinese and foreigners to develop foreign trade and expedite socialist development.

Hua Guofeng acknowledged the reports and encouraged the Guangdong delegates at the Second Session of the Fifth National People's Congress on June 23, 1979. Addressing their discussion meeting, he said:

> The Party Central Committee and the State Council have resolved to grant Guangdong with some incentive policies and more decision-making power. Just as you comrades have proposed, and the central authorities have consented, we shall also set up special zones in Shenzhen and Zhuhai, because development in these special zones may be a lot faster. Because Guangdong is different from other provinces in that it is the motherland's southern gateway and is in close proximity to Hong Kong and Macao, it can develop a bit faster in the drive for the Four Modernizations. I sent Comrade Gu Mu there to do some investigation and studies and solicit the opinions of the provincial leaders and people from various quarters. After returning to Beijing, he has written a report for the central authorities.

The central authorities seriously and carefully considered the reports from Guangdong and Fujian. On July 17, Yao Yilin presented the galley proofs of their response (*Instructions of the Party Central Committee on Releasing Two Reports From Guangdong and Fujian Provincial Party Committees Concerning Implementation of Special Policies and Flexible Steps*) to Hu Yaobang for his instruction. The next day, after reading the provincial reports, Hu added the words "for international economic activities" to the titles of those reports and between the lines of both texts, and changed the word "special" in one of the subtitles "Introducing a Special Economic Management System" with the word "new." Then he wrote a short message to Hua:

Chairman Hua,

The spoken phrase "special policies" is a simplified term. It may cause misunderstanding within and outside of the Party if it is put verbatim in the central documents. Having discussed it with Gu Mu and (Yao) Yilin, I would like to suggest that we add the restrictive term "for international economic activities."

Shall we issue this document to other provinces and municipalities? It may also serve to encourage and enlighten them. Please consider my suggestion.

Hu Yaobang
July 18

PS: Comrade Gu Mu has asked that this document be dispatched as soon as possible.

It did not take long for Hua to go through the reports and give his approval to send copies to every province, municipality and autonomous region.

On July 20, the Party Central Committee issued Document [1979] 50, *Instructions of the Party Central Committee on Releasing Two Reports From Guangdong and Fujian Provincial Party Committees Concerning Implementation of Special Policies and Flexible Steps for International Economic Activities.*

This document pointed out that the Party Central Committee – taking into consideration the fact that Guangdong and Fujian were geographically close to Hong Kong and Macao; had many natives living overseas; were rich in resources and possessed many advantages for speeding up local economic growth – had decided to apply special policies and flexible steps for international economic activities in both provinces.

This would give them more autonomy, so that they could develop their competitive advantages, pursue the opportunities presented by the current world situation to step ahead of other provinces and build up their economies as soon as possible.

The Central Committee and the State Council agreed, in principle, to adopt on a trial basis the economic management system proposed in these two provinces' reports. The system was actually an all-round contract system under central leadership.

Central Document [1979] 50 stated clearly that this new management system was to come into effect in planning, foreign trade, finance, monetary affairs, materials, commerce, wages and prices in both provinces. Special export zones were to be set up on a trial basis in two municipalities, Shenzhen and Zhuhai; after experience had been gained from these two zones, consideration would be given to establishing such zones in Shantou and Xiamen.

The document also stressed that the adoption of special policies and flexible steps for international economic activities in the two provinces was a novel undertaking yet to be experienced in all fields. This was particularly the case with international economic activities, many of which were still empty blanks. The provincial authorities, it urged, should tighten up leadership, step up investigation and studies, become good at learning new things, and bring major changes to their work styles. It also made clear that the central authorities had high expectations for the development of both provinces. The tasks weighed heavily upon the shoulders of the local leaders, the document reminded, because future national development hinged on the pioneering work in these two provinces. The document called on various central departments, therefore, to adjust themselves to the new system, and urged those leaders who handled business activities on a daily basis to heighten their sense of responsibility.

An interesting glitch occurred with the printing of Central Document [1979] 50. The document was signed on July 15, when all the approval and signing procedures were not yet fulfilled. In the days that followed, however, the central leaders made major amendments to its title, contents and scope of circulation, and it was not until July 20 that the document was officially issued.

Thus July 20 was printed at the end of the document as the issuing date instead.

With this document sent out to the rest of the nation, work immediately got under way to establish the special export zones. In September 1979, Gu Mu visited Guangdong once more, where he met with Xi Zhongxun, Yang Shangkun, Liu Tianfu, Wang Quanguo and Wu Nansheng, urging them to develop these zones into models. Their experience, he said, should be continuously evaluated and their work constantly improved. "How should the special zones be run?" he asked, and then answered:

> In two ways. One is to enact legislation, and the other is to set a few fine examples. These places are supposed to make money, whether through joint ventures or wholly foreign-owned businesses. These are where the attractions lie, attractions that can become a stabilizing factor for Hong Kong and Macao. The economies of Hong Kong and Macao are booming, and now we are adding Guangdong to the fold. What's wrong with that? The processing of supplied materials, joint-venture factories, wholly owned factories … There are so many methods for getting things done. You may draw on the methods of Hong Kong and Macao, and give free rein to all your abilities.

Xi asked him how to proceed: Go small, medium-scale, or in a big way? Gu Mu answered:

During a meeting with Konosuke Matsushita on October 9, 1980, Deng said, "We are granting Guangdong and Fujian provinces some special treatment and will run a special economic zone in a place in Guangdong in close proximity to Hong Kong. These are just an experiment to us. Foreign capitalists are welcome to invest, open shop and compete there."

In my opinion, we have no choice but to resolve to go big and get it done quickly. The central authorities' intention is for Guangdong to take the first step and go all out to do it. You cannot become trailblazers if you walk like a woman with bound feet. Guangdong has got to ride whip-and-spur, and race to lead the way for the nation. You are building two special zones, carrying out special policies and flexible steps for international economic activities throughout the province, so you must have a little bit of "Monkey King" spirit. Old conventions and taboos will get us nowhere; they should definitely be left behind. You should take flexible measures, and make larger strides, while keeping pace with your city-planning efforts.

With these words, the curtain was lifted on the trailblazing phase of the opening-up initiative in China.

Setting Up a "Frontline General Staff"

In March 1979, the State Council established an import and export leading group to open up prospects for the opening policy and bolster up leadership over foreign economic relations and trade. Yu Qiuli was group leader, the deputy group leaders were Wang Renzhong, Wang Zhen, Fang Yi, Gu Mu, Kang Shi'en and Chen Muhua, and Gu Mu was in charge of day-to-day operations. After a few months' practice, the central authorities discovered that the new opening-up effort was essentially a systems-engineering project that involved many fields at home and abroad, and that only a strong leading group would be up to the major strategic mission of opening the nation up to the outer world.

In July, the Party Central Committee proposed the establishment of a "State Import and Export Commission" – to coordinate control over imports and exports, foreign exchange balance and technology transfers – as well as a "State Foreign Investment Commission" to strengthen control of foreign investment. The proposal, which was made to the Standing Committee of the National People's Congress, also recommended that Vice Premier Gu Mu serve as chairman of both commissions. This proposal was endorsed on July 30, 1979, at the Tenth Session of the Standing Committee of the Fifth National People's Congress.

The Party Central Committee and the State Council then followed up on August 23, 1979, with a paper spelling out the details. The *Circular on the Missions and Organizational Structures of the Import and Export Commission and the Foreign Investment Commission* clarified that the two names would come under a single organization, and laid down the organization's missions, organizational structure, agenda and work requirements.

The principal functions and missions of the two commissions were to:

1. join the relevant departments in drafting principles, policies, rules and regulations for imports and exports, technology transfers, the use of foreign investment and economic cooperation with foreign countries, to study and summarize experience, and reform the relevant management systems;

2. join the State Planning Commission in examining, deliberating, and drafting long-term and annual plans for imports and exports, technology transfers, economic cooperation, and foreign exchange revenue and expenditure, to coordinate work in the relevant fields, and monitor and supervise the execution of these plans;

3. organize the relevant departments and provinces, municipalities and autonomous regions to take effective steps to expand exports and augment foreign exchange revenue;

4. organize, in compliance with the *Law on Chinese-Foreign Equity Joint Ventures*, the drafting of procedures and related administrative acts on enforcing that law; and to organize the relevant departments to examine and endorse the agreements, contracts and constitutions concerning joint ventures;

5. bring the departments and localities under an umbrella administration to coordinate advanced technology imports, foreign capital utilization and equipment imports; to supervise and monitor the parties concerned with mastering, digesting and importing technology for the purpose of enhancing domestic manufacturing abilities; and

6. examine and deliberate long-term accords or agreements on economic cooperation or trade between Chinese and

foreign governments, and submit them to the State Council for endorsement.

In December of 1980, the State Council ruled: "In the days to come, all the work on economic cooperation between China and Western countries and on the aids provided to China by relevant mixed committees or countries, shall be managed, organized and coordinated uniformly by the State Import and Export Commission."

The central leadership appointed Vice Premier Gu Mu to become minister of the two commissions. The other members were:

- Full-time vice ministers – Wang Daohan, Zhou Jiannan, Ma Bin, Jiang Zemin, Wei Yuming, Zhou Xuancheng, Lu Xuzhang;
- Concurrent vice ministers – Gu Ming, Zheng Tuobin, Gan Ziyu, Jia Shi, Bu Ming, Qiu Chunfu, Xie Beiyi;
- Full-time committee members – Ji Chongwei and Li Hao;
- Jiang Zemin, as concurrent secretary-general; and
- Deputy secretary-generals – Li Hao, Luo Baoyi and Fang Xiao.

In September 1981, Chen Muhua was appointed first vice chairwoman.

Because opening to the outside world was uncharted territory for China, the two commissions accepted recommendations from all quarters and hired a host of prominent figures as special consultants, including Vice Premier Chen Muhua, Rong Yiren (chairman and general manager of CITIC), Lei Renmin (former first vice minister of Foreign Trade, vice chairman and deputy general manager of CITIC), Liu Ningyi, and some well-known industrialists and entrepreneurs. Letters of appointment signed by Vice Premier Gu Mu were conferred on each consultant. Advisors on special topics were also chosen from among experts and professors from at home and abroad. An advisors' office headed by Xie Shuangqiu was responsible for handling liaison and other services for the consultants. Xie – one of the two mainland journalists who had covered and witnessed the signing of an agreement on the return of Taiwan from Japan to Chinese sovereignty in 1945 – was himself a knowledgeable advisor. The advisors' office that he headed became a de facto "brain trust" that played a major role in the beginning of the opening effort.

The two commissions, with the approval of the central authorities, established a number of departments under their purview:

- General Office (in charge of personnel and liaison work) headed by Li Fakui, Li Youzhang, Fei Jiaji and Hu Guangbao;
- Integrated Administration Department headed by Luo Baoyi and Song Yifeng;
- Foreign Investment Administration, headed by Feng Tianshun and Shi Yumin;
- Export Administrative Bureau headed by Yang Wei;
- Technology Import Administration headed by Chen Yang and Pei Chao;
- Agreements and Legislation Bureau headed by Xing Lu;
- Research Office headed by Shi Qingye, Ma Meili, Zhao Jing, and Zhou Li;
- Advisors' Office headed by Xie Shuangqiu.

In July 1980, the State Council took a number of steps to further streamline and strengthen the oversight of international economic activities:

- It appointed the two commissions to minister to and coordinate work on development and assistance loans provided by the World Bank and foreign governments;
- established the Office for Government-Loan Projects, headed by Zhang Quan and Li Lanqing (this author);
- transferred to the State Import and Export Commission, the State Planning Commission's Processing and Trade Office (in charge of businesses involved in processing and assembly with foreign-supplied materials and components and compensation trade), with Zhao Yiwen and Cao Yunzhang as directors;
- established the Bureau of International Economic Cooperation headed by Bu Zhaomin; and
- set up the Preparatory Office for the College of International Business Management headed by Ma Jingfu and Han Yuanzuo.

The staff was small but highly efficient. There were 200 staff members in August 1979, when the two commissions were established; and by March 1982, the number grew with additional functions and tasks to reach 344.

Shortly after the Import and Export Commission was established, branches were set up in provinces, municipalities and autonomous regions. Thus a complete administrative system, from the central to local level, was brought into shape, which effectively guaranteed the implementation of the relevant government principles and policies. The Commission served as the State Council's "general staff" for pushing strategic arrangements for the opening-up policy.

Because its work had a close bearing on the inception and implementation of the top leadership's strategic policy decisions on the opening-up policy, the Import and Export Commission began its hectic work while simultaneously setting up its own organizational structure. It joined the State Planning Commission in:

- carrying out a technology import plan for the year and drawing up such plans for the next two years;
- formulating application and approval procedures and administrative regulations on such imports;
- organizing the drafting of relevant bylaws and guidelines on negotiations with foreign investors within the framework of the *Law on Chinese-Foreign Equity Joint Ventures*;
- studying approaches to the special policies and flexible steps granted to Guangdong and Fujian provinces, drafting procedural regulations concerning the running of special economic zones on a trial basis, and addressing the difficulties and problems that had occurred in the construction of the Shekou Industrial Zone and other special zones;
- studying the procedures for experiments with the reform of the foreign trade administrative system;
- convening a symposium on the work of exports in Beijing, Tianjin and Shanghai to study export-expansion plans and steps;

- urging various departments (the military industrial departments included) to ramp up foreign exchange revenues through imports;
- preparing for a national conference on import and export work;
- organizing the use of World Bank loans and government loans from Japan and other countries;
- working together with the United Nations Development Program on the establishment of an international economic management college;
- and taking steps to speed up personnel training for the opening-up endeavor.

In a little more than two years, the Commission organized the drafting of a series of policies, legislation, rules and regulations concerning foreign economic relations and trade, and convened a number of national or regional conferences on major issues, thereby playing an important role in paving the way for the launch of the opening-up policy.

The staff members of the Commission were selected from the State Planning Commission, the State Economic and Trade Commission, the State Construction Commission, the Ministry of Foreign Trade, the Ministry of Foreign Economic Relations and Trade, and a number of industrial departments. All those chosen went through strict screening, and only those who were politically and morally sound, had practical experience, were good at collaborating with others, and knew technology, the foreign trade business and foreign languages, could make it to the Commission.

When I first arrived in the office, Jiang Zemin had me quartered in a room on the top floor of the office building. It did not take long for me to make the acquaintance of a neighbor by the name of Duan Wei. Initially, I knew Duan only as a scholarly man, but later, I came to learn about his amazing life experience.

Duan was studying at Kyoto University when the War of Resistance Against Japan broke out, and he went all the way back to China, wanting to join the war efforts. In Chongqing, with the recommendation of the underground Party organization, he entered the Ministry of Foreign Affairs of the Kuomintang government and joined the Party after passing rigid screening procedures. Later, he was transferred to the Soong Ching Ling Foundation in Hong Kong to procure funds, medicine and other materials badly needed in the liberated areas in the mainland. After the war, the Party sent him to study at Cambridge University in England, Berlin University in Germany, and Moscow University in the Soviet Union.

Returning to China in 1952, he was treated as a ranking official as he worked in the law department of the Ministry of Foreign Trade. However, during the anti-Rightist campaign that began in 1957, he was branded as a "rightist" for his criticism of a higher-up and assigned to sweep the street along Beijing's East Chang'an Boulevard.

In the aftermath of the Kaloran Incident in Indonesia on September 30, 1965, local Chinese residents were persecuted, and hooligans attacked the Chinese embassy and consulates. The Indonesian government withdrew its embassy in Beijing and asked the Chinese government to close its embassy and consulates in Indonesia. Before the Indonesian ambassador left China, he ran into Duan, an old acquaintance, and said to him, "Mr. Duan, if you have the opportunity, please come to see me in Indonesia." A nonchalant Duan replied, "All right."

The ambassador did not leave China; instead, he resigned his post and stayed in Beijing to become general secretary of the Asian-African Journalist Association. Unbeknownst to him, his Chinese friend, Duan, paid a dear price for their brief encounter. Someone had overheard Duan's short reply to the ambassador and ratted on him. As a consequence, he was thrown behind bars, and then sent to a labor reform camp. His wife dumped him, leaving him alone in his misery. It was not until the nation began to open up that he was acquitted to become a staff member with the Import and Export Commission.

Duan was not known as "erudite" for nothing. He spoke Japanese, English, German and Russian – it was not until a singer showed up to take an Italian lesson from him one Sunday that I came to know he also spoke Italian. He was also well versed in international law and economics. He had translated a lot of much-needed foreign language reference materials into Chinese, and during our days together, he impressed me as a diligent man. He also taught young people foreign languages, passed on to them knowledge and experience, and on occasion became as much a friend as a mentor. I once jokingly told him he was an "unearthed cultural relic" – the Chinese synonym for "treasure." From Duan's appointment to the staff we could see that the Commission, under the leadership of Vice Premier Gu Mu, had done an exemplary job in discovering, recruiting and respecting talent.

As a staff member, I attribute the Commission's success and big role in the early years of the reform and opening policy to the trust and blessing of Deng and other central leaders, as well as to the efficiency of the leadership headed by Gu Mu.

In 1978, as a leader of the Third Auto Works' preparatory office for establishing a heavy-duty truck plant, I started negotiations with some of the world's major automakers on the import of complete sets of technology for building heavy-duty trucks. At the time the Import and Export Commission had not been established. Vice Premier Gu, who was in charge of key national construction projects, was interested in our work and dispatched Tang Hong to keep up with the progress of the negotiations. Whenever problems occurred during the negotiations, we consulted many leaders for advice. These included Wang Daohan, a leader of the Ministry of Foreign Economic Liaison; Gu Ming, Zhou Jiannan and Gan Ziyu, who headed the State Council Leading Group for New Technology Imports. Jiang Zemin, then a foreign affairs director from the First Ministry of Machine-Building Industry served as our immediate higher-up during the negotiations.

These people's unstinting support for the cause of reform and opening initiated by Deng Xiaoping, their strong sense of mission and responsibility, cordial personalities and their pragmatic work style, never failed to move anyone who had the good fortune to benefit from their effective counsel and help. To keep abreast of progress in the negotiations and to help us address issues that had been submitted for instruction, Zhou Jiannan sent Zhang Quan as liaison officer to attend all the negotiations. The report I wrote toward the end of 1978, asking for the high echelon's instruction on whether we should talk to foreign investors on joint ventures, won Deng and Gu's approval, and I owe it to Zhang Quan because it was he who submitted the report in the name of the "Office of the State Council Leading Group for New Technology Imports." On one occasion, when I called on Wang Daohan for his advice on joint ventures, a topic I knew very little about, he gave me a very enlightening lesson and then sent for Wei Yuming to find some reference materials for me. All the things Wei found for us, whether articles on joint ventures between East European and Western countries, or the legislation, contracts and constitutions associated with this field, were valuable references. My good feelings for these leaders were further deepened after I was transferred to the Import and Export Commission and worked under their direct leadership.

The Import and Export Commission was a new organization with staff members from all over the country. The leaders guided the staff by personal example and instruction. Under their guidance and following their requirements, the staff fostered a fine working style and good learning habits. They never allowed themselves to be content with half-baked knowledge. Rather than staying aloft and bossing people around, they were always ready to go down to the grass-roots level to see how things stood there. Disdaining bureaucratic buck-passing and wrangling over trifles, they championed unity and cooperation and strove to do things in innovative and pragmatic ways. Everybody worked to relieve those working at the forefront of controversy and help them to solve problems. Everyone observed the principles of honesty, industriousness, frugality, acting with impartiality and justice, and avoiding the temptation to misuse personal connections. The Commission's top leaders made a point of staying connected with each other and practicing criticism and self-criticism with equanimity. Sharing the harsh living conditions of the time, they queued up with the rank-and-file in the cafeteria during mealtimes. Jiang Zemin even worked for a time in the kitchen helping to straighten out cafeteria management, improve nutrition, and see to it that warm meals were served to those who came late to eat.

On September 1, 1981, the central authorities issued a document further refining the administration of the growing set of issues surrounding the opening-up policy. The *Decisions on Stepping Up Unified Leadership and Specialized Management of Foreign Economic Relations and Trade* spelled out the challenges and some changes designed to address them:

> Since the adoption of the opening-up policy at the Third Plenary
> Session of the 11th Party Central Committee, our nation's imports

and exports have registered considerable growth, the utilization of foreign investment and diverse forms of international economic cooperation and technological exchange have been proceeding step by step. The situation has been very good. Confronted with a complex and highly competitive world market, the work of foreign economic relations and trade is predicated on government policies and timeliness and what is being done at home. This calls for overall planning. Despite the improvements we have made in the last couple of years, our organizational and management work still falls short of the demands of the new situation due to such problems as overlapping organizational structures, confusion over functions and responsibilities, cumbersome red tape, and low efficiency. To do a better job in foreign economic relations and trade, we must take concrete actions, while further revamping the administrative system and bringing the initiative of various localities and departments into full play, to step up the work of the State Import and Export Commission and its Party Group and put the work on economic relations and trade under compatible administrative authorities. We must also, where necessary, further readjust and regroup the existing institutions handling foreign economic relations and trade, so as to guarantee the implementation of the Party's line, principles and policies and to raise work efficiency. For these purposes, the Party Central Committee and the State Council have made the following decisions:

The State Import and Export Commission is a comprehensive department that brings the work of economic relations and trade throughout the country under its jurisdiction. Its main tasks are: implementing the principles, policies and directives of the Party Central Committee and the State Council concerning the work of foreign economic relations and trade; organizing, promoting and supervising the relevant departments and urging them to be conscientious in their respective jobs in developing foreign economic relations and trade; coordinating with the implementation of our nations' foreign policy to better serve national economic readjustment and development and the effort to speed up the Four Modernizations.

The State Import and Export Commission, under the leadership of the Party Central Committee and the State Council, takes administrative charge of the following bodies: the State Foreign Investment Commission, the Ministry of Foreign Trade, the Ministry of Foreign Economic Relations and Trade, the State Administration of Foreign Exchange, the Bank of China (in joint administration with the People's Bank of China), the General Administration of Customs, the General Administration of Quality Supervision, Inspection and Quarantine, the International Trust and Investment Corporation, and the China Council for the Promotion of International Trade. It exercises unified administration over, and coordinates the foreign economic relation and trade work of, the other State Council departments, various provinces, municipalities and autonomous regions, and Chinese institutions stationed in foreign countries.

To enhance discipline inspection in the field of foreign economic relations and trade, it is decided to establish the Foreign Economic Relations Discipline Inspection Committee under the dual leadership of the Central Discipline Inspection Commission and the State Import and Export Commission.

Readjustments and regrouping shall be made to the existing foreign economic relations and trade organizations in accordance with the principles of enhancing unified leadership, separating government functions from corporate management, streamlining the institutions and downsizing the staff, practicing economy and ensuring efficiency. The State Import and Export Commission is therefore instructed to put forward readjustment and regrouping plans on the basis of meticulous investigations and thorough preparations, and submit them to the Party Central Committee and the State Council for examination and approval before they are carried out organizationally.

The decision to expand the power of the State Import and Export Commission reflected the central authorities' 100-percent vote of confidence. Six months later, in a State Council organizational reshuffle, the Import and Export Commission was merged with the State Foreign Capital Commission, the Ministry of Foreign Trade, and the Ministry of Foreign Economic Liaison, to form the Ministry of Foreign Economic Relations and Trade. Its functions were transferred to the relevant department in the new ministry. Before the merger took place, Wang Daohan had been appointed successively as Secretary of the Shanghai Municipal Party Committee, Vice Mayor and then Mayor. Zhou Jiannan had become Minister of Machine-Building Industry, Jiang Zemin, Minister of Electronics Industry, and Wei Yuming, Vice Minister of Foreign Economic Relations and Trade. I myself was promoted to become Director General of the Foreign Investment Administration under the new ministry.

During its service of more than two years, the State Import and Export Commission distinguished itself under the direct leadership of Gu Mu in fulfilling the missions entrusted by the central authorities. Its accomplishments in carrying out the opening-up policy fell into four categories: 1) Creating the special economic zones; 2) Developing foreign trade; 3) Bringing in and utilizing foreign investment; and 4) Introducing advanced foreign technology and management expertise. The Commission did a great deal of superlative pioneering work and served as the "general staff" for getting the opening-up policy off to a good start. That experience has become an indelible memory for all the members of the Commission.

From Special Export Zones to Special Economic Zones

It did not take long for Guangdong and Fujian to achieve striking results from applying incentive policies and flexible steps to the special export zones they had established on a trial basis. This drove home to the people in these two provinces that the special export zones, as instruments of the reform and opening policy, had good reason to make extensive use of foreign capital and introduce advanced manufacturing technology to develop production and energize local economies. On the other hand, it was also understood that these zones could not play a role as trailblazers for the opening- up initiative if they were limited to export processing. The special export zones were a mere drop in the bucket, compared with the nation's 9.6 million-square-kilometer territory. Even if they could deliver several billion yuan of foreign exchange revenues to the state, that amounted to very little for such a large country. These zones were doing their bit in creating jobs, but the one or two million jobs they created were negligible among the nation's 1.3 billion people. This prompted the people in Guangdong and Fujian to think that their special zones should not just become production bases – they should serve as "windows" and "testing grounds" through which China could observe changes in world economic situation, market supply and demand, and development in science and technology, could shift advanced foreign technology and management expertise to, and provide beneficial experience for the rest of the country. They believed that these zones could also become "big schools" for training and supplying competent professionals for the country.

Everyone felt that the term "special export zone" did not do justice to these zones' broad functions. It was suggested at a symposium on the work of the special export zones held in Guangdong on October 31, 1979 that they be renamed "special economic zones," a term which the participants believed was richer in meaning and more in keeping with the central authorities' intentions. They felt that the term entailed two connotations. First, it expressed that such zones are the grounds for conducting multiple economic experiments, and for applying special economic policies, management frameworks and flexible economic steps to international economic activities, and could serve as showcases to help promote economic cooperation and technological exchanges with other parts of the world. Second, the term suggests that the zones differ from Hong Kong and Macao in that their socialist nature will remain unchanged.

In late March 1980, Gu Mu arrived in Guangzhou to chair the Working Conference on Guangdong and Fujian Provinces, at which the execution of central directives was examined, and issues concerning the development of special export zones were further studied. At the conference, the vice premier accepted Guangdong's proposal to rename the special export zones as "special economic zones" and had the decision written into the *Summary of the Working Conference on Guangdong and Fujian*.

A few weeks later, on May 16, Central Document [1980] 41 was issued to transmit the Summary to the relevant departments with the following directive:

The practice of this year has attested to the soundness of the central authorities' decision to adopt special policies and flexible steps for foreign economic activities in Guangdong and Fujian. Both provinces have made big strides and achieved remarkable results. On the basis of the two provinces' advantages, the central authorities have decided to designate certain areas in Shenzhen, Zhuhai, Shantou of Guangdong Province and Xiamen of Fujian Province and run them as special economic zones on an experimental basis. In these special economic zones, the administration could adopt systems and policies that are different from those of the hinterland, provided the Four Cardinal Principles* are upheld and national sovereignty is not impaired. Pending major reforms in the national economic system, it is inevitable that problems will occur in the process of experimenting with a new system in Guangdong and Fujian provinces. This refers to conflicts of interest that will crop up on our road to progress. Our task is to conscientiously and timely summarize experience, study new situations and solve new problems. The central authorities maintain that the experience summarized and steps proposed at this conference are feasible and should be implemented in earnest. The economic restructuring to be conducted in Guangdong and Fujian will be conducive not only to economic growth in these two provinces, but also to nationwide economic restructuring.

The directive also pointed out that it was necessary to be at once aggressive and prudent in pushing the construction of the special economic zones:

It is necessary to change the name "special export zone" into the more meaningful "special economic zone." The administrative system and the policies to be adopted in the special economic zones shall differ from those for the hinterland in that the economies of these zones will be regulated by the market, and their income tax, land use fees and wages shall be slightly lower than in Hong Kong and Macao so as to attract foreign investment and the investment from among overseas Chinese.

---

* The Four Cardinal Principles were the four fundamental values outlined by Deng Xiaoping in 1979. These were to adhere to: the socialist path, the people's democratic dictatorship, the leadership of the Communist Party of China, and Marxist-Leninist-Mao Zedong thought. (*Translator*)

This directive clarified that the special economic zones were to be constructed mainly by incorporating foreign investment, and that their economies were to be regulated by market forces. The directive concluded by ordering Guangdong to be focused on running the Shenzhen Special Economic Zone without fail.

Making an Exception for Special Economic Zone Regulations

The running of special economic zones called for a legislation endorsed by the highest legislature to guide and standardize people's conduct. For that reason, the State Council entrusted Guangdong with drafting the *Regulations of Guangdong Province on Special Economic Zones*.

Guangdong approached the task in two ways. The first was to put the special economic zones in perspective from a theoretical point of view. Uppermost on the minds of the drafters of the Regulations was the question: Does the proposition, "Make capitalism serve socialism," hold water from the viewpoint of combining theory with practice? By widely consulting classic Marxist-Leninist canons, they compiled the booklet *Marx and Lenin on Foreign Economic Policy* to prove that in the course of historical development, no categorical demarcation line can be drawn between socialist and capitalist economies, because the former is built on the latter, which is fully developed. For that reason, socialism is fully capable of utilizing and assimilating the material wealth and management methodology created by capitalism to build and develop itself. The second way was to study and draw on the international experience. The drafters combed through various materials about free trade zones, free ports and export processing industrial zones in other countries and regions to find foreign ordinances, legislation and policies and measures for promoting economic development. Then they carefully studied these materials to gain valuable tips from them.

Practical questions kept cropping up in the process of drafting the Regulations. Should the special economic zones be granted complete decision-making power? The answer was that these zones could not play their role as "testing grounds," and reform and opening would become empty talk, if they were not freed from the established administrative and management systems. How preferentially should foreign investors be treated? Foreign investors would not come, and opening up would also become empty talk if these zones could not woo them with attractive tax, and labor and land use prices. At the time, controversy was buzzing about the special economic zones and the use of foreign investment. Some equated the zones with "colonies," "revived old foreign concessions," or a downright "restoration of capitalism." The drafters also had a hard time choosing the appropriate terminology. For instance, the term "land rent" is evocative of such unpleasantries as "foreign concessions," which literally means "rented land" in Chinese, and "rent collection" recalls the behavior of rapacious rural landowners in pre-Liberation China. Thus it was replaced with "land use fee." Would the position of the working class as masters of their country be in jeopardy if foreign-invested companies were allowed to sign labor contracts with employees? These and many other questions would have derailed the opening-up initiative had it not been for Deng's timely instruction: "Let's quit squabbling, and allow people to experiment and make mistakes."

The draft of the *Regulations of Guangdong Province on Special Economic Zones*, which was begun in August 1979, was completed after a little more than a month's frenzied work. After submitting it to provincial authorities for deliberation, the drafters held a series of hearings to solicit opinions from prominent Hong Kong figures. There was no lack of opposing voices. Most people pointed out that because the drafters had not been daring enough, an unnecessary wariness was all too revealing in the draft, as if the special zones would get out of hand with the arrival of foreign investors. The provisions abounded in words that asked people not to do this or that. This prompted someone to say that these regulations were not about welcoming and encouraging investors, but about how to restrict them. Such criticisms reminded the drafters that more than anything else, the Regulations should allow Hong Kong, Macao and Taiwan and overseas Chinese investors to make money. Patriotism should take a back seat, they realized, for it would not work to ask people if they were patriots or not before deciding whether they deserved the opportunity to come and make money. Only if people could "smell" and see money would they come in droves and the special economic zones stand a chance to make a profit. There is, indeed, a dialectical relationship in it.

Having straightened their thoughts, the drafters began their revisions under Gu Mu's personal guidance. Other national leaders also shared their views on the zones' direction of development, business principles, management system, and economic legislation. After the revised draft was endorsed (at the Second Session of the Fifth People's Congress of Guangdong Province on December 27, 1979), a second round of amendments began in compliance with the instructions of Gu Mu and a working group dispatched from the State Council. New opinions were sought in earnest as the draft went through more rounds, until the 13th draft was finally submitted, on April 14, 1980, to the Standing Committee of the Guangdong Provincial People's Congress.

According to established Chinese practice, local legislation comes into force right after the Provincial People's Congress endorses it. In the case of the *Regulations of Guangdong Province on Special Economic Zones*, however, the local authorities saw fit to put it further through the National People's Congress, the nation's top legislature. They believed that double endorsement would make the Regulations more authoritative, emphatic and easily enforced. After all, the opening-up policy and special economic zones were unprecedented in a socialist country, and, what with the lingering effect of the ten-year Cultural Revolution, granting privileged tax reductions to foreign investors tended to touch a sensitive nerve with those who did not like the new policy. Ye Jianying, Chairman of the Standing Committee of the National People's Congress, who happened to be visiting the province on an inspection tour, conveyed Guangdong's petition to Beijing. The General Office of the National People's Congress, however, dismissed the petition for the single reason that there was no precedent for the top legislature to deliberate and endorse local legislation. Undeterred, the Guangdong authority appealed to Ye once again. The special economic zones belong to the nation, they argued, and we would not dare to run such zones if the National People's Congress wants no part of the regulations. The request was eventually granted.

On August 21, 1980, the Fifth NPC Standing Committee, chaired by Ye Jianying, held its 15th session to hear explanations of the

Regulations and elaborations of the top leadership's decisions on setting up special economic zones in Guangdong and Fujian, by Jiang Zemin, vice minister of the State Foreign Investment Commission, on behalf of the State Council. Jiang pointed out that because running the special economic zones was a major step in national economic development, the *Regulations* was an important piece of legislation that should be deliberated and endorsed by the National People's Congress. He then spelled out the regulations in four aspects.

First, the foundations and nature of the special economic zones. In compliance with the tasks listed in the *Report on Government Work* adopted at the Second Session of the Fifth National People's Congress to "continue to do a good job in technology transfers, actively utilize foreign capital and strive to expand exports," by referring to the experience of some developing nations with running export processing industrial zones as a means for speeding up economic development – and for the purpose of developing foreign economic cooperation and technological exchanges, expanding exports and promoting the socialist modernization drive – the preparations for the special economic zones commenced in July of the previous year in certain designated areas of Shenzhen, Zhuhai and Shantou in Guangdong Province and Xiamen in Fujian Province. Shenzhen was the first to start building such a zone.

This type of special economic zone absorbs the wholesome ideas and the universal practices of some export processing industrial zones in the world and incorporates some Chinese characteristics. They represent a special approach to encouraging and using foreign capital and speeding up economic development in selected areas under the socialist system. The two provinces, Guangdong and Fujian, which are the homelands of many compatriots from nearby Hong Kong, Macao and Taiwan, as well as many natives residing overseas, hold special appeals to foreign investors and investors from among Chinese nationals living overseas, and are thus well endowed to establish special economic zones in certain designated areas.

The special economic zones shall adopt different systems and a more open policy than the hinterland. They shall make full use of foreign capital and technology to develop industry, agriculture, animal husbandry, aquatic breeding and poultry farming, tourism, housing, high-tech research and manufacturing. Because these zones are engaged in a comprehensive economic undertaking broader in scope than ordinary export manufacturing zones, they shall be called "special economic zones" to show the difference.

There are more than 70 export processing zones around the world today. Most of them are yielding fine economic returns. The Shenzhen Special Economic Zone is running smoothly since construction began. This is particularly the case with its Shekou Industrial District, which has shown some fine prospects.

Second, the fundamental principle for the organization and administration of special economic zones. The special economic zones must be administered to safeguard state sovereignty. The land belongs to the People's Republic of China. Enterprises and individuals in the Shenzhen Special Economic Zone shall observe Chinese laws, ordinances and relevant regulations in their activities. Foreigners shall be screened and granted permission to invest in the special economic zones; they shall obey the administration of the Chinese government.

An administrative committee shall be established in the two provinces to exercise, under the direct leadership of the provincial people's government, government functions and unified administration over the special economic zones. Dual customs offices shall be established there and will follow the principle of tightening up internal administration while loosening up administration over external activities.

Third, preferential policies toward enterprises in the special economic zones. Among the preferential clauses provided in the *Regulations*: Foreign investors shall be allowed to run wholly owned enterprises after passing approval formalities; foreign banks and insurance companies shall be allowed to set up affiliated institutions; import and export goods shall be exempt from customs duties; tax rates on enterprises in the zones shall be lower than in the hinterland and slightly lower than in Hong Kong and Macao; entry and exit formalities shall be streamlined for the convenience of departures and arrivals; foreign exchange control shall be relaxed to an appropriate degree; and foreign businesses, and foreign workers and staff members shall be permitted to transmit their lawful profits and wage incomes out of China through banks in the special economic zones, provided the relevant taxes are paid. According to this legislation, Sino-foreign joint ventures in the special economic zones shall be accorded more preferential treatment than their counterparts outside the zones.

All these stipulations take China's interests into consideration while taking full account of the interests of foreign investors, compatriots from Hong Kong, Macao and Taiwan, and overseas Chinese investors – all for the purpose of facilitating the absorption of foreign capital, advanced technology and management expertise to speed up the modernization drive.

Fourth, steps to be taken for construction of special economic zones. Because the endeavor to build special economic zones is surrounded by difficult economic and ideological struggles and limited by experience and financial and material resources, it is necessary to follow a principle of both boldness and prudence. We must be prepared to focus available resources on the building of the Shenzhen Special Economic Zone before commencing construction on the Zhuhai, Xiamen and Shantou special economic zones.*

Construction of these four special economic zones shall be carried out step-by-step under an overall plan. The first step is to level the land and build facilities for tap water, electricity, roads, telecommunications and other infrastructure needed to attract foreign investors. Certain barriers shall be erected to separate these zones from neighboring areas for effective administration. All the investment projects to be launched in these zones shall meet the requirements of the overall plan. It is imperative to make use of the existing infrastructure for projects that call for less investment but are quick to recoup costs and yield tangible economic returns. In that way, these zones can engage in production and develop themselves simultaneously.

For lack of experience in formulating a national law on special economic zones, we began by drawing up the *Regulations of Guangdong Province on Special Economic Zones*. Before the State Council deliberated and endorsed the *Regulations*, the State Import and Export Commission invited comrades from the relevant departments and from Guangdong Province to review the draft on several occasions,

---

* The speech went on to describe the geographical dimensions of the zones. (*Translator*)

and necessary amendments were made to it as a result. I hereby ask that this legislation be examined and debated at the current session.

On August 26, the 15th Session of the Standing Committee of the Fifth National People's Congress endorsed the *Regulations of Guangdong Province on Special Economic Zones*, which came into effect immediately, and announced the establishment of special economic zones in certain fenced-off areas in Shenzhen, Zhuhai and Shantou. Thus legislative procedures were completed for all three special economic zones in Guangdong Province. Even though the *Regulations* amounted to only 2,000 words, it took nearly a whole year – from drafting, canvassing opinions, deliberations at the provincial people's congress, and deliberations and amendments at the State Council to its endorsement by the National People's Congress. Every word of it had been carefully chosen and weighed.

The *Regulations* highlights the special economic zones' hospitable economic climate for foreign investment and their special approach to economic growth, which boil down to three points: first, encouraging foreign investment and ensuring the legitimate rights and interests of investors with the preconditions of equality and mutual benefit and protection of China's state sovereignty and interests; second, granting investors with preferential treatment; and third, adopting an administrative system in keeping with the nature and requirements of the special economic zones.

To define the geographical scope for each zone, the planners went through an uphill process beset with heated debates. For a time, no one knew exactly how such a zone should be run and how large it should be, but they were clear that the export processing zones and free trade zones in foreign countries were too small to be copied in China. Thus the State Foreign Investment Commission, together with Guangdong and Shenzhen authorities, put their heads together to find a solution.

Some proposed that a no-man's land near the New Territories of Hong Kong be fenced off or walled in to create a space in which to build factories, import materials and launch the processing industry. To facilitate management, some suggested that there should be no residents in the zone. Workers would report to work with their passes and leave right after they clocked out, and they would not be permitted to carry things in or out of the zone. Opponents of this idea countered: What if this tiny place is eventually filled to capacity with factory buildings? A special zone is not supposed to last for only two or three years. What would we do? Keep fencing off one piece of land after another? With the topography of Shenzhen in mind, they suggested that walls or wire fencing be installed along the ridge of a mountain range that runs east to west, to cordon off 100 square kilometers of flatland and rolling country for the zone. This would give the special zone ample space for development and could effectively stem smuggling, they argued. Critics of the suggestion claimed that nowhere in the world was there a special zone that large, for it would include all the 24,000 residents of the city proper of Shenzhen. If those living in Shatoujiao, Nantou and Shekou were also walled in, the entire zone could have a population of 100,000. Feeding this many people would call for a lot of energy and resources, they said, and there would be little to spare for pursuing development and bringing in foreign investment and seek development.

After much research and repeated debate, the planners arrived at a majority consensus that the area to be reserved for the special zone should be large enough to accommodate the simultaneous development of primary, secondary and tertiary industries, to allow all-round political, economic and cultural reforms, and to guarantee both the scale and momentum of the effort to procure foreign investment. A zone like that could have a great influence on the rest of the nation, could help foster China's reform efforts and image of openness to the world, and enable the drafting of overall and systematic plans for both urban planning and industrial construction without missteps and detours.

The leaders of Guangdong Province were in favor of a large special economic zone, but they also knew that large often meant trouble. If leadership was lax and management flawed, economic disorder would inevitably result. Thus they suggested situating the zone on the proposed irregular strip of land – 327.5 square kilometers extending east and west for 49 kilometers, with an average width of seven kilometers. It would become the world's largest special economic zone, and, if launched, an unparalleled feat in history. The central authorities immediately approved of the suggestion.

Firecrackers boomed in Shenzhen immediately after the arrival of news about the endorsement of the *Regulations*. People were elated that their small town would soon blossom into a metropolis. The impact of the festivity was instantly felt on the other side of the Shenzhen River. The Hong Kong people were caught by surprise. What the central authorities had approved a year ago was a "special export zone," but today it was designated, through legislative procedures, as a "special economic zone." It was definitely the first of its kind in China and, for that matter, throughout the world.

What Is Special About Special Economic Zones?

At a meeting held on April 23, 1980, the Guangdong Provincial People's Congress appointed Wu Nansheng Director of the the Guangdong Provincial Administration of Special Economic Zones. In Fujian, Governor Guo Chao became Director of the Administration of the Xiamen Special Economic Zone. Both provinces went about drawing up construction plans, setting up executive bodies, publicizing the zones and inviting foreign investors to visit them.

In winter 1980, Xi Zhongxun and Yang Shangkun were transferred to central leadership. Ren Zhongyi, former First Secretary of Liaoning Provincial Party Committe, and Liang Lingguang, former Minister of Light Industry, replaced them as governors of Guangdong Province. The first thing the two governors did upon taking office was to begin preparations for the establishment of the Shenzhen Special Economic Zone and filling its leading body with pragmatic and hardworking officials, shrewd administrators and talented professionals. In March 1981, Liang Xiang became Mayor of Shenzhen. Shortly afterward, the central authorities elevated the status of Mayor of Shenzhen to that of provincial vice governor, the same status granted to the Mayor of Guangzhou. Thus, in a little more than two years, Shenzhen accomplished a quantum leap from a tiny county in January 1979 to a municipality under a mayor with a vice governor portfolio in March 1981. This leap spoke volumes about Shenzhen's importance to the nation's reform and opening endeavor and the high hopes the central government placed upon it.

"We don't want money; we want state policy!" That was Shenzhen's demand. The Guangdong authorities did their best to grant incentive policies to the special economic zone. Whenever Governor Ren attended a meeting in Beijing, he missed no opportunity to seek central government backing and preferential policies.*

At first, the Shenzhen Special Economic Zone had few resources at hand. Its only attraction was land. At the time, however, the idea of wooing investors with the right to land use was heresy, as well as a cardinal matter of principle. Taking a careful approach, the leaders dug into the Marxist-Leninist classics for political and theoretical backing. In Vladimir Lenin's *The State and Revolution*, they found the quotation from Engels:

> ...the "working people" remain the collective owners of the houses, factories and instruments of labor, and will hardly permit their use, at least during a transitional period, by individuals or associations without compensation for the cost. In the same way, the abolition of property in land is not the abolition of ground rent but its transfer, if in a modified form, to society.

This lent legitimacy to exactly what the leaders of Shenzhen wanted to do. Because "land rent" was something of a taboo in public opinion and government policy, they changed the phrase to "land use fee."

Fundraising Experiments at Luohu District

The tiny 0.8-square-kilometer Luohu District was where the Shenzhen Special Economic Zone really got off to a good start.

All the zone could get from the central authorities were incentive policies. The zone was left to its own devices to raise

---

* Those were the years in which the nation had just begun to restore the rule of law across the land, and the existing body of legislation was falling short of the demand of a fast diversifying society. Sans applicable laws, the government had no alternative but to formulate policies to promote its reform and opening-up effort. The National People's Congress was later to write these policies into various state laws. (*Translator*)

the money it needed. No foreign investor, however, would want to open shop on barren and rugged land. To attract foreign investment, the Shenzhen authorities had to level the land and bring in a minimum of "amenities" such as electricity, tap water, roads and telephone service. But it cost 90 yuan per square meter, and the money was nowhere to be found. With the intervention of Vice Premier Gu Mu and Jiang Zemin, Vice Minister of the State Import and Export Commission, the central government granted a loan of 30 million yuan as startup money. Though not a substantial amount, the money was a godsend, and the leaders of the special economic zone were delighted.

They used the loan together with a little amount of local financial input as the "seed fund" to open up Luohu District.

But even that choice caused a lot of controversy, so much so that it became what was later known as the "Luohu Incident." Some wanted the money to be spent on Futian District in the vicinity of Hong Kong's New Territories. They suggested just opening up a few square kilometers to build a port at Huanggang (Lok Ma Chau, as Hong Kong people call it), because that was where some Hong Kong investors had promised to invest. That suggestion was turned down because the British authorities of Hong Kong were mute about opening the port, which would make it impossible to develop Futian District. Thus, attention was drawn back to the tiny Luohu District between Luohu and Man Kam To ports. The snag, however, was that the altitude of that district was just two meters above sea level. A heavy downpour of rain could turn it into swampland.

"You wouldn't want our Hong Kong compatriots and overseas Chinese to roll up their trousers and wade through the water to and from the local railway station, would you?" opponents asked rhetorically. "The Shangbu District or the area north of Liberation Street is a better place, where you can do a lot more things with the same amount of money."

Proponents of Luohu insisted that the district, which was close to the two ports and the railway, was the mainland's gateway to Hong Kong and could be sufficiently improved:

The appearance of Luohu District could leave a deep impression on those arriving from Hong Kong. The involvement of compatriots of

Hong Kong and Macao, patriotic Chinese nationals living overseas, and foreign entrepreneurs means a lot to the development of the Special Economic Zone.

They suggested that the low-lying part of the district be elevated with earth obtained by leveling the Luohu Hill beside the railway station. "That serves two purposes," they argued, "the raised altitude will make large-scale development possible, and leveling the Luohu Hill will remove an obstacle to the development of the railway station and the Luohu Port." Only after Gu Mu and Jiang Zemin gave their nod to this suggestion did the dispute about where to begin come to an end.

The construction of the Shenzhen Special Economic Zone began with a deafening boom of explosives on Luohu Hill. Less than a year later, the hill was gone, and with the 1.3 million cubic meters of earth thus obtained, the land of Luohu District was raised by 1.07 meters. The builders leveled the land, built roads, brought in electricity, tap water, cooking gas, and telephone service, and opened up a 2.3-square-kilometer land between the Luohu Railway Station and Man Kam To. According a speech by Wu Nansheng (delivered at a May 1981 Guangdong-Fujian working conference on special economic zones), the Shenzhen Special Economic Zone spent a total of 56 million yuan on the Luohu District and – with an infrastructure investment of 70 yuan per square meter – obtained 400,000 square meters of land for commercial use, not including the spaces taken up by roads, landscaping and public utilities. Sales of the right to the use of land of the Luohu District could bring in a revenue of HK$2 billion, or HK$5,000 per square meter. This indicated that by using a government startup loan as the "yeast" for the "fermentation" of fund accumulation, the special economic zone could manage without government investment in construction.

Hard-Won 30-Million-Yuan "Yeast"

There was a story behind the 30-million-yuan startup fund.

At first, financial problems plagued the builders of the Shenzhen Special Economic Zone. The problem came to the attention of those of us involved in the opening-up initiative. In March

1980, Gu Mu held a meeting in Guangzhou to review the way Central Document [1979] 50 was implemented in Guangdong and Fujian. Jiang Zemin and other central department leaders were present at the meeting along with the governors of both provinces. In response to Guangdong's request for a loan of 100 million yuan to be used in 1980 and 1981 for infrastructure construction at the Shenzhen Special Economic Zone, the *Summary of the Working Conference on Guangdong and Fujian* (issued on May 16 in Central Document [1980] 41) instructed: "Allocation of foreign exchange loans for the two provinces and the Renminbi loans needed for infrastructure construction of the Shenzhen Special Economic Zone shall be arranged by the People's Bank of China and the China Construction Bank." Later, the state approved a 50-million-yuan loan to be granted to Guangdong by the China Construction Bank. The first installment of the loan, in the amount of 20 million yuan, was issued by the bank in 1980. At the beginning of 1981, Guangdong submitted a request to the State Import and Export Commission for the remainder of the loan. On February 4, 1981, the Commission asked the China Construction Bank to solve the problem. But the bank replied that it had arranged for all the loan requests for the year and had no money to spare for Guangdong.

On March 31, 1981, Shenzhen Mayor Liang Xiang petitioned Zhou Jiannan, Vice Minister of the State Import and Export Commission, to grant the remaining amount of the loan as soon as possible. Zhou instructed:

> According to the stipulations in Central Document [1980] 41, the first batch of 20 million yuan of the 50-million-yuan loan for infrastructure construction of the special economic zone in Guangdong was granted last year, and the remaining sum is to be issued this year. I have talked to Wang Bingqian and Tian Yinong of the Ministry of Finance and decided to pay 10 million yuan as the first installment. Endorsements by Finance Ministers Wang and Tian and Ministers Chai and Gan of the State Planning Commission are therefore requested.

The request was quickly granted by top leaders of the ministry and the commission. The relevant departments under the State Planning Commission, however, thought otherwise. According to the stipulations of Central Document [1980] 41, they said, it is the responsibility of the People's Bank of China and the China Construction Bank to arrange foreign exchange loans for the two provinces and Renminbi loans for infrastructure construction of the Shenzhen Special Economic Zone. What is more, they added, the stipulations do not specify how much money should be granted to whom in 1980. They suggested that Guangdong Province follow the stipulations of the document and talk directly to both banks, a suggestion that was later approved by the leaders of the Commission.

In early May, Jiang Zemin consulted Zhou Jiannan, and both believed that Zhou's reply to Liang's letter should be followed, because, they said, "The responsible members concerned have read the letter and given their approval in writing."

At the request of the State Import and Export Commission, the China Construction Bank issued a document on June 12, asking its Guangdong branch to issue 10 million yuan to the Shenzhen Special Economic Zone. Thus, with a loan totaling 30 million yuan, infrastructure construction at the zone was finally begun.

Selling Preconstruction Apartments to Raise Development Money

On January 8, 1980, a property company was established in Shenzhen to develop international real estate business. Liu Tianjiu, Chairman of Hong Kong's Millie's Company sent a representative to deliver his proposal to work with the company on East Lake Garden, a luxury residential complex. Millie's promised to sell the preconstruction apartments of the complex, with the profit divided 4:6 between Millie's and the Shenzhen company partner. The Shenzhen company, however, wanted 80 percent of the profit. Liu replied immediately that he just wanted 15 percent of it. The Shenzhen side was puzzled as to why the man was so generous. It did not take long for them to find out. In February 1980, right after Shenzhen ratified the property company's investment agreement and its blueprints for the East Lake Garden, Millie's ran an advertisement in a Hong Kong newspaper to sell 266 apartments. The apartments were priced at HK$2,730 per square meter, averaging HK$100,000 per suite, only half the price of the same type of apartment in Hong Kong. The advertisement drew 5,000 aspiring buyers, and Millie's had to draw lots to select the eventual buyers. In this way Liu quickly collected all the money needed for building the East Lake Garden. The Shenzhen property company, for its part, earned several million yuan from the deal.

The staff of the Shenzhen property company was delighted by the "windfall." If Liu Tianjiu can make big money from the small cost of a single advertisement, they asked themselves, why can't we sell preconstructed homes to raise real estate development money on our own? With the approval of the municipal government, the company began work on another posh residential compound, Garden View Park, with Hong Kong's United Enterprise (Shenzhen) Company serving as the sales agency in Hong Kong, Macao and overseas on a 7 percent commission. Starting with a 3-million-yuan bank loan, the Shenzhen company completed the residential compound with an investment of HK$150 million, netting HK$100 million in profit.

The choice to raise development funds by selling homes before they were built was a wise one under the circumstances. All such plans, however, must be undertaken in the light of local reality. Later, some localities rushed to follow Shenzhen's example, but they failed to earn the necessary funds. As a result, many buildings were left unfinished, incurring heavy losses. It was, indeed, a typical bitter lesson.

By selling preconstruction housing, collecting land use fees and taking other innovative steps, the builders of the Shenzhen Special Economic Zone raised more money to level the land, build roads and bring in electricity, tap water and telecommunications facilities, thereby furnishing favorable conditions to attract foreign investment. In five years, from 1980 to 1985, Shenzhen utilized US$1.28 billion of foreign investment, or 20 percent of the nation's total foreign direct investment volume during the same period. The zone completed 7.63 billion yuan in aggregate capital construction investment. With energy, transport, telecommunications and other infrastructure projects built with both state funding and foreign investment, they established a framework of nine industrial subzones. Businessmen flocked from Hong Kong and overseas to invest in factories.

The Shenzhen phenomenon prompted some people to say that "state policy is money." What they did not know was that money was what the government lacked most. In those days, construction progress often became stuck at the mere mention of money. The dilemma, however, was that few people actually knew how to turn state policy into money.

Xiamen Multiplies Fundraising Channels for Development

Fujian Province started setting up the Xiamen Special Economic Zone right after the central authorities gave the green light. Xiamen was one of the earliest open ports in China, having established a customs office as early as 1683. For the more than 3 million Fujian natives living in other parts of the world, Xiamen is always the major gateway to their homeland. On December 17, 1979, the Fujian Provincial General Shipping Corporation's large passenger ship the *Gulangyu* completed its maiden voyage to Hong Kong, thereby inaugurating Fujian's first maritime passenger shipping line since Liberation in 1949. The relaxation of tension in the Taiwan Strait made it convenient for Taiwan compatriots and overseas Chinese to visit Xiamen. To speed up planning and preparation for the special economic zone, Fujian had a top engineering design institution in Beijing draw up a construction plan. After numerous revisions to the plan, they finally decided to build the zone in a 2.5-square-kilometer area in Huli District in northwest Xiamen.

I remember that on July 22, 1980, Jiang Zemin received two guests, Guo Chao, Governor of Fujian Province, and Lu Zifen, Mayor of Xiamen, who came to the State Import and Export Commission to brief us on their plans for the Xiamen Special Economic Zone. During the Working Conference on Guangdong and Fujian, which Gu Mu had chaired in Guangzhou some three months earlier, Jiang had an inspiration for the zone and asked local leaders to draw up a plan and prepare for it. From April 1 to 5, directly after the working conference, he headed a fact-finding group visiting Shantou, Xiamen and Fuzhou. While in Fujian, he surveyed Langqi Island in Fuzhou and Huli District in Xiamen. Because Langqi was a barren island without the apparent makings of a development zone, Huli was chosen as the site for the Xiamen Special Economic Zone.

In a July 28 letter to Vice Premier Gu Mu, Jiang said that he thought Xiamen's plan was workable, for the city had the infrastructure and other conditions well-suited to running a zone. He suggested that Xiamen be allowed to set up the zone in an area of 1.1 square kilometers, a proposal that was readily accepted. On October 7, 1980, the State Council issued the decision to locate the Xiamen Special Economic Zone in an area of 2.5 square kilometers in Huli District, and to start the first phase of development on 1.1 square kilometers.

Through Jiang's intervention, the People's Bank of China granted a low-interest loan of 50 million yuan, which, combined with a local 30-million-yuan government construction fund and a local 30-million-yuan low-interest loan grant, became the startup money for the Xiamen Special Economic Zone. On October 15, 1981, a ground-breaking ceremony was held to mark the beginning of construction.

The Xiamen Special Economic Zone came under construction at the same time as the Huli Industrial Zone and ancillary projects all over Xiamen. These included Xiamen International Airport, the first phase of Dongdu Harbor, and a 10,000-channel program-controlled telephone switchboard. Executive Secretary of the Fujian Provincial Party Committee Xiang Nan urged the builders to focus their efforts on infrastructure. Speaking at a meeting of the special economic zone's administrative committee, he said:

> Where there is no airport, there will be no special zone. We must determine to build an airport in Xiamen. Now that we've decided to build the special zone and to open our gates to the outside world, we have to take off from here.

With a preferential loan granted by the Kuwaiti Arab Foundation in 1981, Xiamen Airport made Chinese airport construction history when it opened to air traffic in 20 months – January 1982 to October 1983 – from scratch to finish, and reached its designed capacity three years later. Xiamen Airways, established on July 25, 1984, was the first local air company in China.

Dongdu Harbor, with an annual cargo handling capacity of 2.6 million tons, was one of the ten key harbors then under construction in the nation. When its first phase of construction was completed in 1983, Xiamen more than doubled its harbor shipping capacity.

Negotiations over a 10,000-channel program-controlled telephone switchboard began in 1981 and ended with a deal to import the necessary installations from Japan's Fuji company for a total investment of 20 million yuan. The switchboard was completed in January 1985, along with an imported 960-channel microwave telecommunications center. This advanced Xiamen's telecommunications service to a world-class level.

Jiang Zemin Goes Abroad in Search of a "Special Prescription"

By this point a question was lingering on people's minds. The economic zones are special, but in what ways? What stimulus policies and steps should be taken to run these zones well? The Shekou experience with running an industrial zone and a special export zone was not enough to provide all the answers. It was thus deemed necessary to draw on foreign experience and combine it with Chinese reality to formulate the necessary policies and measures.

From September to November 1980, with assistance from the United Nations Industrial Development Organization (UNIDO), Jiang Zemin led a nine-member Chinese delegation on an educational tour of eight export processing zones and free trade zones in Singapore, Sri Lanka, Malaysia, the Philippines, Mexico and Ireland. The members of the delegation included Qin Wenjun, Deputy Director of the Guangdong Provincial Administration of Special Economic Zones; Huang Shimin, Vice Mayor of Shenzhen; and Lu Zifen, Chairman of the Xiamen Municipal People's Congress.

Just before the delegation set off, a Sri Lankan opposition party member stationed in Beijing lodged a complaint with the delegation members. He charged that his country's ruling party was promoting a colonial economy and committing treason in his country's export processing zone, where workers were being exploited, and foreigners were wallowing in extraterritorial prerogatives. He wanted to dissuade the delegation from going to his country, saying that the visit could only boost the ruling party's "bloated arrogance." The Chinese side told him that China was not sending a government delegation but a non-government learning delegation at the invitation of the UNIDO. But the man was unconvinced, and he was still protesting even after the delegation returned to China.

The educational delegation set off from Beijing on September 26, and stayed in Thailand for a day before arriving at Colombo, where they were put up at Universal Hotel. Upon learning that the room rent was US$30 whereas the money given by UNIDO was US$47 a day for each member, which should also cover food and transportation, Jiang Zemin protested that it was too expensive and moved the delegation to Duro Hotel, where the rent per room was only US$11. During the six-nation tour the delegation collected large amounts of reference materials. On their way back to China, they stopped over in Geneva for two days of discussion with United Nations experts on special economic zones. During the discussions, the delegation summarized in five points its findings on the foreign experience:

1. The legislation was sound and mature and highly operational;
2. All the zones began small and gradually expanded according to general development plans;
3. The administrative systems were quite flexible, with local governments and enterprises enjoying maximum autonomy;
4. Due attention was paid to personnel training; and
5. All the zones were implementing incentive policies on imports and exports and on foreign investment.

Back in China, the delegation submitted four proposals:

First, judging from the situation at home, a consensus was what mattered for the smooth development of special economic zones in Guangdong and Fujian. Even though the National People's Congress had endorsed and promulgated the *Regulations of Guangdong Province on Special Economic Zones*, people must see eye to eye on why these zones should be established, what kind of zones they should be, and what was good and bad about them. The report then suggested that the central authorities organize economists and theoreticians to study and clarify these and other questions with a view to boosting the morale of the builders of these zones.

Second, it was imperative to clarify the nature of the four special economic zones and formulate well-defined principles and policies for them. With a view to these zones' different situations and locations, the Shenzhen Special Economic Zone should follow the examples of the Badan Export-Oriented Processing District of the Philippines and the Mexico-Texas Border Region Free Trade Zone of Mexico and build itself into a free trade zone, and Zhuhai, Shantou and Xiamen might become export processing zones in the main, while developing housing, tourism and other undertakings. Shenzhen's Luohu District and Shangbu Industrial Zone should be developed first, but a long-term plan should be drafted for the development of a designated 327-square-kilometer area. At the same time, the Shenzhen Customs and frontier inspection posts should gradually gear their services to a free trade type of special economic zone. The other three special economic zones should start planning according to prescribed targets.

Third, the administrative relationships and economic systems of the special economic zones should be further defined. The necessary power must be delegated to their administrative organs so that they could handle these zones' heavy tasks and large scales.

As to the economic systems for these zones, the report submitted the following suggestions:

1. Each zone might be registered as an independent accounting unit to control and deploy state investment in capital construction.

2. The repayment of capital construction bank loans should be the responsibility of the zones, which, in the first few years, might use their own revenues for local construction.

3. Special economic zones needed not to follow the country's current foreign exchange administrative rules, and the Bank of China should allow these zones to open their own foreign exchange accounts. Their foreign exchange savings deposits should carry interest and be freely withdrawn and used.

4. Enterprises in the zones should, in principle, recruit workers from among local residents, and select managers and engineers throughout the province and the nation

with the support of the State Labor Administration and departments concerned.

5. Foreign-invested enterprises in the zones should pay full wages to workers and staff according to their own rules, and abolish all the grain, non-staple food, medical service, housing and frontier residence allowances. The workers should pay individual income tax.

6. The Shenzhen Special Economic Zone might follow customs regulations to pay taxes or be granted tax reduction or exemption when importing consumer goods from Hong Kong to supply local residents. Such imports should be controlled by state-owned shops or the zone itself, and foreign investment should be generally disallowed in this field, while equity joint ventures in such imports might be established only when and where foreign investment is involved.

7. Prices in the special economic zones were to be mainly regulated by the market.

8. Basic salaries and wages should be issued as usual to government functionaries and workers and staff members in the special zone over and above a special zone allowance. Their housing, medical expenses and other fringe benefits should remain unchanged for the time being.

Fourth, it was necessary to speed up enacting economic legislation. The report suggested that the Guangdong Provincial Special Economic Zone Administrative Committee be requested to draft procedures for implementing the *Regulations of Guangdong Province on Special Economic Zones* as well as procedures on legislation governing customs, foreign exchange, border entry and exit, land use fees and labor and wages. It should submit these drafts to the State Council for deliberation and approval.

The central authorities spoke highly of the educational delegation's six-nation tour, because it provided important reference and backing for building the special economic zones and for formulating relevant state policies. They readily adopted some of the delegation's proposals.

Ten Special Policies

In December 1980, Governor Ren Zhongyi told Gu Mu and Jiang Zemin, who were visiting Guangdong Province, that the special economic zones needed a more open policy in international economic activities. "Building the special economic zones," he stated, "is not about earning some foreign exchange revenue for the country. It is more important for the zones to take the first step in special zone construction and gain a series of experience in economic restructuring, in combining central planning with the market to regulate the economy, and in exercising Party leadership over economic work." He added, "I believe the Shenzhen and Zhuhai special economic zones cannot succeed without policies that are more special than the 'special policies and flexible steps' already granted to Guangdong and Fujian."

"Ditto," said Gu Mu, adding jokingly:

> Yours is an "independent kingdom," or "semi-independent kingdom." And you are the "king." Look around the world, and you can see that wherever a special zone is set up, it comes inevitably under the personal care of the president, prime minister or king. In my opinion, we should involve government departments in building special zones and studying relevant issues at regular intervals. But what is most important is that you, the "king" or "president," should personally attend to the Shenzhen and Zhuhai special economic zones.

At the time there was a lot of public misunderstanding about the special zones. People were debating about whether such zones were socialist or capitalist. After consulting Marxist works, Governor Ren had his own take on the issue. "As I see it," he said, "the term 'national capitalist' applies to every enterprise, be it a joint venture or wholly foreign-owned company. However, in the case of our special economic zones, you can't say they are national capitalist, because they are under the leadership of a socialist country, practice special policies and take flexible steps. They are socialist special economic zones."

From May to June of 1981, Gu Mu presided over a working conference on Guangdong and Fujian and the special economic zones.

The governors of the two provinces, Ren Zhongyi, Wu Nansheng and Xiang Nan, attended the conference along with state department leaders and responsible members of special economic zones. Economists Qian Junrui, Xu Dixin, Xue Muqiao and Gu Nianliang were present as special guests. In preparation for the conference, Zhou Jiannan, Vice Minister of the State Import and Export Commission, spent 20 days investigating and studying in Shenzhen and Zhuhai, and acquired a wealth of first-hand data in the process. Participants from the provinces complained that because the central authorities had granted special policies and flexibility to Guangdong and Fujian, leaders of some State Council departments were worried that the zones might slip onto the capitalist road, mar the national economy, and commit other mistakes. The leaders, they said, were also apprehensive that granting the economic zones with more autonomy in the import and export business might rob national trading corporations of old clients and market channels and cause chaos, and that was why the sentence, "No exception shall be made for Guangdong and Fujian," appeared so frequently in the documents these departments issued. The governors of the two provinces wondered aloud why people should be so exasperated since the central authorities had hardly given the economic zones anything that was really special or flexible enough for them to make the first step.

Skeptics and supporters were widely divided in their opinions. To make peace, governors Ren and Xiang said in a joint speech:

> Why don't you give us certain do's and don'ts, such as: first, don't take the capitalist road; second, adhere to the Four Cardinal Principles; third, resolutely fulfill the tasks assigned by the central authorities; fourth, don't regard yourselves as special Party members; and fifth, carry out the nation's unified foreign policy. Under these principles, we would like to beg the central authorities not to keep such a tight rein on us. Please give us a free hand to chart a new path.

The governors' only demand was to be given a free rein and certain power to get things going.

During a private conversation at the conference, an official from one of the provinces was heard joking to people from the central ministries, "Please leave us alone now that the do's and don'ts have been drawn up. Please write no more 'Guangdong and Fujian are no exception' on documents." The conference was a success in that it put virtually all the participants on the same page about the special economic zones. Later, the central authorities endorsed the *Memorandum on the Conference on Work of Guangdong and Fujian Provinces and Special Economic Zones.*

The *Memorandum* stated:

> Practice over the past year and more has justified the central policy decision to grant special policies and flexible steps to both provinces and to establish special economic zones. In the short span of time since this experiment began, we have already achieved some remarkable results and gained some experience, thereby bringing hope to people and enhancing their confidence. The conference called for "emancipating the mind" and unifying understanding on certain issues, and maintained that running special economic zones on a trial basis is an important special policy for the two provinces, as well as a new way to carry out the opening-up policy and bring in foreign investment. The special zones are economic, rather than political, in nature, and state sovereignty is exercised in an all-round way. They are "special" in that they carry out state-mandated special economic policies and a special economic administrative system and are therefore essentially different from the "foreign concessions" of old China. Running the special economic zones has proven to be a relatively more practical way to expand exports, utilize foreign capital, import technology and develop the economy. To China, these zones are schools in which we learn to compete with foreign capital, follow economic norms and learn modern economic management; they are also bases for grooming skills for both provinces and even the entire country.

While setting forth new steps for the two provinces to push economic restructuring, the *Memorandum* also presented ten policy-related proposals:

> First, in both planning and construction the special economic zones should proceed from local circumstances and pay due

attention to results, and each of them shall have a distinct development focus. The Shenzhen and Zhuhai special economic zones shall be built into comprehensive zones that combine industry, commerce, agriculture and livestock breeding with housing and tourism. Export processing business shall be central to the Xiamen and Shantou special economic zones, where tourism shall also grow as a sideline. All the zones should lose no time in drafting all-round socioeconomic development plans. More than anything else, they must do a good job in infrastructure construction, and develop themselves in designated areas step-by-step and within their means.

Second, the customs shall grant preferential tax rates and duties on the goods and articles imported by the special economic zones.

Third, entry and exit formalities should be simplified to facilitate arrivals and departures. The special economic zones have the right to notify the visa authorities to sign entry visas for foreigners and overseas Chinese, and to grant multiple entry visas of no longer than one year to those who need to come and go repeatedly.

Fourth, the labor and wage system shall be reformed. In the special economic zones, all the workers and staff members shall come under a contract system whereby enterprises have the right to recruit people, put them on probation or dismiss them. The practice of "low wage supplemented with multiple allowances" shall be gradually phased out. Worker wages may comprise both basic and floating wages. The special economic zones shall also establish a retirement and social insurance system for workers and staff members.

Fifth, the special economic zones may place orders with relevant foreign trade companies for commodities needed on local markets, and settle the transactions in foreign exchange. Local commerce shall be predicated on state ownership, but the special economic zones may also run joint commercial enterprises with foreign investors and be allowed to import necessary commodities. These zones may run their own foreign trade under state policy guidance; they may also be entrusted by provinces, municipalities and autonomous regions to handle those import and export businesses that are not exclusively run by the Ministry of Foreign Trade.

Sixth, the Renminbi shall be the major currency in circulation in the special economic zones, but foreign currencies may be used in designated fields. Chinese banks registered in Hong Kong and Macao shall be allowed to set up branches in these zones, where steps will be taken to allow selected foreign banks to open branches. The two provinces should formulate their own foreign exchange administrative policies in light of actual situations. The State Administration of Foreign Exchange shall establish sub-administrations in these zones.

Seventh, striving to raise construction funds for the special economic zones. Foreign investment shall be the chief source for such funds, with as much as possible of this funding to be raised from overseas Chinese and Hong Kong and Macao compatriots. The banks in the special economic zones should be allowed to use savings accumulated from loan grants in the next few years and loosen up restrictions on such loan grants. It was originally decided that the municipalities of Shenzhen and Zhuhai may not hand in their financial revenues for three years, but now it has been decided to extend that deadline to 1985. All four special economic zones shall open independent accounts for foreign exchange revenues (including the portion of foreign exchange coupons to be withdrawn from circulation), and retain the increases over such revenues' 1978 base numbers for construction purposes over the next five years. The revenues from local land development shall be put at the disposal of local development companies.

Eighth, airports, harbors, railways, telecommunications and other enterprises and institutions shall be permitted to incorporate foreign investment in wholly owned businesses or joint ventures, and bear the responsibility for the losses or gains arising therefrom.

Ninth, it is necessary to formulate legislation governing construction projects that should be sped up in the special economic zones. It is thus proposed that the Standing Committee of the National People's Congress pass necessary bills to authorize the standing committees of the provincial people's congresses of Guangdong and Fujian to draft individual laws or regulations for the special economic zones under their respective jurisdiction, and submit them to the Standing Committee of the National People's Congress and the State Council for the record.

Tenth, the special economic zones shall establish administrative organs in line with the principles of streamlining institutions, downsizing staff and ensuring efficiency, and be amply empowered to handle issues and to coordinate relationships on their own.

The *Memorandum* also urged Guangdong and Fujian provinces to be aggressive in streamlining and downsizing administrative organs and staff and in overcoming such bureaucratic flaws as cumbersome organizational structures, overlapping institutions and dilatory work habits. In particular, these tasks should be handled without fail right from the beginning in the special economic zones. The *Memorandum* went further to call on the two provinces to persist in fostering good social mores, to tighten up public security, and to crack down on smuggling.

On the basis of the *Memorandum*, the planners worked out a complete package of more concrete incentive policies and flexible steps for the special economic zones.

Guangdong Governor Ren Zhongyi was one of those who zealously advocated for and carried out the top leadership's strategic arrangements for the reform and opening up to the outside world. In his concluding speech to a meeting of three levels of provincial officials on October 5, 1981, he pointed out:

> To carry out the special policies and flexible steps, we have to be bold in experimenting and innovating and persist in opening up to the outside world, and we must be more relaxed in handling internal affairs and more liberal in decentralizing power.

Addressing a meeting of departmental leaders at both the provincial and municipal levels on November 18, 1981, Ren stressed:

> We must adjust our minds to the new circumstances arising from the special policies and flexible steps that call for a more untrammeled mind. Special policies should be really special, the flexible steps really flexible, and the first step really taken. Otherwise, it will all be empty talk.

139

In a report to the Fifth Party Congress of Guangdong Province on February 24, 1983, the governor summarized the province's five-year experience with the special policies and flexible steps, and he mentioned once again the need to be more open and flexible in taking the first step:

First, to be more open to the outside world means we must loosen control on the power to approve the entry of foreign capital, transform the foreign trade system, implement government policies toward overseas Chinese and give full play to the major role of the overseas Chinese and Hong Kong and Macao compatriots in domestic economic development; second, to be more relaxed toward internal affairs means we must transform central planning, curtail mandatory planning and extend guidance planning, revamp the pricing, logistics, financial, tax, monetary and labor systems, and restructure agriculture; third, to be more liberal in decentralizing power means we must decontrol power for planning, capital construction, foreign economic relations and trade, pricing administration and personnel, finance and resources down to the county and enterprise levels, and diminish mandatory planning, adopt all kinds of economic responsibility systems and integrate responsibilities with power and interests.

At a conference on the work of the special economic zones in Fujian Province in September 1983, Xiang Nan said that to well manage the Xiamen Special Economic Zone, it would be necessary to tackle four "special" issues, that is, to clarify special tasks, carry out special policies, create a special environment and adopt special ways of doing things. "Special tasks" referred to bringing in foreign capital and technology, well managing the export processing zones and boosting tourism. "Special policies" entailed more preferential treatments for foreign investors and places where there were many natives living and working overseas. A "special environment" meant one with high efficiency, convenient transportation, social stability and public security, and comfortable living conditions. "Special ways of doing things" were those designed to improve efficiency, economic vitality and the leadership's rallying strength, to overcome bureaucratism, carry forward the pioneering spirit, reform inappropriate systems and make concerted efforts to succeed at everything that was being undertaken.

Delegating Legislative Power to Certain Departments

At a session of the Standing Committee of the National People's Congress in November 1981, Jiang Zemin, Vice Minister of the State Import and Export Commission, delivered a speech on behalf of the State Council to articulate the *Decisions to Authorize the People's Congresses and Their Standing Committees of Guangdong and Fujian Provinces to Draft Legislation on Specific Economic Fields.* Jiang gave a brief introduction to events since the establishment of the special economic zones:

> Since the *Regulations of Guangdong Province of the People's Republic of China on Special Economic Zones* was endorsed by the Standing Committee of the Fifth National People's Congress and promulgated by the two provinces on August 26, 1980, it has drawn strong responses and attention from industrialists and businesspeople from foreign countries and Hong Kong and Macao, who have been arriving in droves to see how things stand at the foreign economic zones and how to engage in business negotiations there. This has reenergized the foreign economic activities in these zones and yielded some heartening achievements and economic returns.
>
> Toward the end of June 1981, Shenzhen Municipality had signed 720 economic contracts, and 76 percent of those projects had come under construction or commenced production. Of these 720 contracts, 17 were for wholly foreign-owned projects, seven were equitable joint ventures with Chinese and foreign investment; and 623 were processing, assembling and compensation trade projects, totaling HK$2.458 billion in investment, and bringing in 6,000 sets of machinery and equipment. By the end of that month, HK$500 million had been put to use, the completed buildings had topped 500,000 square meters in floorspace, 17,500 people had landed new jobs, the fees paid for the finished projects and the profits shared between the parties concerned had totaled HK$161 million, and foreign investors had been reimbursed with a total of HK$13.65 million worth of equipment imports. The establishment of the special economic zones and the implementation of a more open economic policy have vastly boosted local industrial and agricultural production. In 1980, Shenzhen reported a total industrial and agricultural output value of 186 million yuan, up 20 percent from 1979, and its financial revenue

was 54 percent higher than in 1979. The livelihood of the people of Shenzhen has improved considerably; migration has diminished vastly, and more than 200 migrants have returned home.

The Shekou Industrial Zone, developed and managed by the Merchants Group of the Ministry of Transport and Communications, has been a pace-setter for the special economic zones under construction. In less than two years, it has finished capital construction in an area of one square kilometer and established 14 enterprises with a total investment of some HK$500 million, five of which will begin operation before the end of this year. It is expected that the industrial zone will collect a total revenue of around HK$20 million from land use fees, dock operations and sales of villas. Their experience boils down to two aspects. First, the Merchants Group has been given such autonomy that, instead of having to abide by the current administrative system and submit applications and petitions to layer upon layer of higher authorities, they make their own decisions, from engineering prospecting, planning, blueprinting, and bank credits to negotiating and signing contracts with foreign investors. Second, they do everything by following economic laws. The headquarters of the industrial zone make a routine practice of signing contracts with construction teams selected through public bidding; and every enterprise is held accountable for its board of directors and makes business decisions free from intervention by the Merchants Group. All the Merchants Group's executive departments in the industrial zone have dramatically raised their work efficiency and economic results by following the principle of separating government administration from business management, and establishing enterprise companies that function as independent accounting units and bear the responsibility for their own profits or losses. The Shekou mode of management has furnished valuable experience for transforming the current administrative system.

Speaking about the other three special economic zones, Jiang said:

After the Fujian Provincial People's Government ratified a general plan for the Special Economic Zone of Huli District, the government of Xiamen is organizing the relevant departments to examine the initial designs for the zone and requisitioning land to be leveled to bring in tap water and electricity and build roads, airport, telecommunications service and docks. Preparations are also in progress for the first phase of construction projects in the zone. The Zhuhai and Shantou special economic zones of Guangdong are also redoubling their efforts to draft general plans.

Jiang concluded:

Despite the good progress we have made so far, many foreign investors are still taking a wait-and-see attitude. This is because the ratified document, the *Regulations of Guangdong Province on Special Economic Zones,* has just laid the principles down on paper. Specific policies and ordinances, such as those on enterprise registration, wages, land use, and border entry and exit procedures, are yet to be announced. Moreover, we have yet to enact rules and regulations for individual fields. In the meantime, with no definite legislation and procedural regulations to go by, officials of these special economic zones often find themselves in an awkward position in foreign economic activities and in handling various issues, for they dare not act as freely as they want to. The result is that their decisions are often inconsistent or mutually conflicting. Therefore we can accept no delays in formulating specific economic regulations for the special economic zones. In order to adapt business management to the special economic zones as entities that deal with the world market and use foreign investment, we cannot afford not to have specific regulations. Given our lack of experience, things will be very tough for us if we start drafting unified national economic legislation for the special economic zones right away. It is therefore feasible to authorize Guangdong and Fujian provinces to formulate their own legislation in light of the realities of these zones. Then these laws can be amended and set the stage for the formulation of national legislation in the future.

Jiang Zemin set about working to bring the granting of special legal powers for the two provinces into harmony with the law at all levels. He proposed that the Standing Committee of the National People's Congress endorse the "Bill on the *Decisions to Authorize the People's Congresses and Their Standing Committees of Guangdong and Fujian Provinces to Draft Legislation on Specific Economic Fields*" in compliance with principles laid down in the Constitution." (In so doing, he was acting on the *Circular of the Party Central Committee and the State Council on the Memorandum on the Working Conference on Guangdong and Fujian Provinces and Special Economic Zones* issued in Central Document [1981] 27.) Of the wording "in compliance with principles laid down in the Constitution," he said:

> Because what we are talking about here is the establishment of special economic zones, when we draw up individual economic laws, we must follow the principles laid down in the Constitution, adhere to the Four Cardinal Principles, act in accord with the nature of our nation, and uphold the socialist orientation. The bill proposes that the drafting work should follow Article Seven in Chapter II of the *Organic Law of the Local People's Congresses and Local People's Governments of the People's Republic of China*: "The people's congresses of provinces, autonomous regions, and municipalities directly under the Central Government may, in the light of the specific conditions and actual needs of their respective administrative areas, formulate and promulgate local regulations, which must not contravene the Constitution, the law and administrative rules and regulations; they shall report such local regulations to the Standing Committee of the National People's Congress and the State Council for the record." This proposal is to urge Guangdong and Fujian provinces to consult the policies, laws and decrees, and administrative ordinances when they work out economic laws and regulations in keeping with the nature of the special economic zones. When Guangdong and Fujian provinces start to work on individual economic laws concerning their special economic zones, they should canvass the opinions of the leading departments of the State Council.

The bill, which was later endorsed by the Standing Committee of the National People's Congress, not only enabled the two provinces to draft specific local economic laws to guarantee smooth progress in the special economic zones, but also set in bold relief what is really "special" about these zones. From Jiang's explanations on behalf of the State Council, we could see the work of the special economic zones had already won the confirmation of the nation's top-echelon decision-makers.

Preferential Income Tax Rate at 15 Percent

When the special economic zones were still in infancy, the Guangdong government was hemmed in by rigid rules and regulations and outmoded conventions. The documents it drafted for the Shenzhen Special Economic Zone were loaded with prohibitions, limitations and sanctions, and said little about how to follow established international practices, grant foreign investors with benefits and preferential treatments or cultivate a sound investment environment.

For a time, the provincial government asked for a 30 percent income tax rate for enterprises in Shenzhen, which was almost twice as high as the Hong Kong rate at 17 percent. When opinions were solicited about it, everyone said it was too high to be attractive to anybody. Compatriots from Hong Kong and Macao said such a high tax rate would only discourage foreign investors, an opinion that was shared by such patriotic figures as Chuang Shih-ping.

A famous overseas Chinese leader and financer, Chuang had served as Vice Chairman of the All-China Federation of Returned Overseas Chinese, Vice President of the China Overseas Friendship Association, Delegate to the National People's Congress and Member of the Standing Committee of the Chinese People's Political Consultative Conference. In December 1949, he borrowed US$10,000 and opened the Nanyang Commercial Bank, hoisting up the five-star national flag on the inauguration day. He was also remembered for his special role in China's post-Liberation economic rehabilitation efforts. Once, entrusted by Marshall Ye Jianying, he secretly shipped HK$500 million in cash and an amount of US dollars to Hong Kong and deposited it in his bank to earn interests for the nation. He was the founder of the first Chinese-invested bank in Hong Kong and the first foreign-invested bank in the mainland. The Hong

Kong Special Administrative Region awarded him the Grand Bauhinia Medal, the highest of all honors and awards from the Hong Kong government, in recognition of his highly significant life-long contributions.

Chuang Shih-ping was the first man Wu Nansheng turned to, as early as February 1979, when he hit upon the idea to run an export processing zone in Shantou. The Hong Kong banker lost no time in collecting all the written materials on similar zones in the Taiwan region, the Philippines and Singapore and he rushed them to the governor. These materials provided major references for Guang-dong's initial opening-up policy blueprint.

In August 1979, the leaders of Guangdong encountered some tough questions in the course of drafting the *Regula-tions of Guangdong Province on Special Economic Zones*. For example, in which aspects were the "special policies" special? What enterprise income tax rate was appropriate? The effort to cut down on the tax rate came under fire from the relevant authorities, forcing the drafters to settle at 30 percent. Attending a meeting to deliberate over these questions, Chuang said candidly:

> Cheap labor and low factory building rents are all the advan-tages we have at hand to open the special economic zone, but these are not enough. Our legislation, especially where taxation is concerned, should be a lot more liberal and preferential than in the export processing zones of other Asian countries and regions. We need to make things as convenient as possible for those coming to invest in factories. Only thus can foreign investors sense the appeal and see the money. Otherwise, we have no hope of beating the competition. If we do not follow economic norms and established international practices, what good will come of this kind of regulations on the special economic zone? If you put regulations like this up for a vote at the National People's Congress, I, and all the other delegates of Hong Kong and Macao for that matter, will abstain.

His opinions were taken seriously. After comparing notes and frequently consulting reference materials, and after studying the central government's intended special policies and flexible steps, the Guangdong government concluded that the special economic zone ought to provide more incentives and conveniences for investors than many export processing zones in other countries and regions. A low enterprise income tax could lure investors into taking early action and running large factories, which would serve to speed up the development of the zone. The *Regulations of Guangdong Province on Special Economic Zones* was passed at the Second Session of the Fifth People's Congress of Guangdong Province on December 27, 1979. The enterprise income tax rate was finally set at 12 percent.

The controversy surrounding the enterprise income tax rate, however, was far from over. In fact, it was hotly debated at a March 1980 Guangzhou meeting on experiments with the special economic zones in Guangdong and Fujian, presided over by Vice Premier Gu Mu. Central government delegates were opposed to the 12 percent tax rate, arguing that a nation could only have one flat tax rate and the special economic zones should be no exception. A compromise was finally reached, as the memorandum of the meeting stated:

> The special economic zones may apply different economic system and policies from the other parts of the mainland provided the Four Cardinal Principles are upheld and state sovereignty is not impaired. To attract investment from overseas Chinese and foreigners, the income tax, land use fees and wages in these zones may be set slightly lower than those in Hong Kong and Macao. It is thus initially decided that the tax rate is set at 15 percent.

Jiang Zemin called a meeting to discuss his explanations to be delivered to the Standing Committee of the National People's Congress on the establishment of special economic zones in the two provinces and the draft *Regulations of Guangdong Province on Special Economic Zones*. On July 7, 1980, delegates from central government departments and the two provinces of Guangdong and Fujian met for this purpose in Beijing. The discussion eventually focused on the tax rate. The departments concerned insisted on a flat tax rate and argued that 15 percent was too low. Jiang said, "It is true that we need a flat tax rate but we must also be mindful of different priorities. The special economic zones are just one of the priority areas that deserve some incentive policies." The delegates were swayed by Jiang's argument and accepted the 15 percent tax rate, which was ratified by the Standing Committee of the National People's Congress along with the *Regulations of Guangdong Province on Special Economic Zones.*

In his April 18, 1984 report to a Beijing municipal meeting of veterans on the opening-up policy and the principles for the special economic zones, Gu Mu summed up the special nature of these zones in four aspects.

> First, the special economic zones depend mainly on absorbing and utilizing foreign capital and on exports for economic growth. Under the guidance of the socialist economy, the economies of these zones differ from other parts of the mainland, where the state-owned socialist economy holds sway, in that they are integral entities in which multiple economies coexist, and where joint ventures with Chinese and foreign investment, cooperative enterprises and wholly foreign-owned companies serve as the mainstay.
>
> Second, the economic activities in these zones are regulated in the main by the market. This is different from the hinterland, where economic activities are subject to central planning.
>
> Third, these zones offer special incentives and conveniences with regard to taxes, revenues and border entries and exits to foreign investors.
>
> Fourth, they exercise a different administrative system and enjoy greater decision-making power than the hinterland, or, to quote an old refrain of the time, these zones had "broken through the prevailing system.

Gu Mu repeated these points on several other occasions, including a current affairs report meeting held by the Publicity Department of the Party Central Committee on October 30, 1984. At the Ninth Session of the Sixth National People's Congress held on January 7, 1985, he gave another version in his report on the construction of special economic zones and the efforts of the 14 coastal cities to open further to the outside world. According to his new version, the special economic zones were "special in four respects": they live mainly on foreign capital; their economic activities are regulated in the main by the market; they offer investors special treatments and entry-and-exit convenience; and their decision-making power on economic activities is greater than what is delegated to certain provinces. At a discussion meeting in Shenzhen in February 1985, he set the goal to build the entire municipality into a comprehensive export-oriented special economic zone, with its main thrust on boosting industrial development and increasing foreign exchange revenue through export expansion.

Fording the River by Groping for Stones

Thanks to the relentless efforts of the second-generation central leadership, centered around Deng Xiaoping, China finally threw its gates wide open to the outside world, and established four special economic zones in Shenzhen, Zhuhai, Shantou and Xiamen in one sweep.

With no experience to draw from, these zones were brought into being basically by "fording the river by groping for stones." Relevant policies and legislation were being drafted for the first time, and it was only natural that problems of one kind or another would crop up while the zones were still in their infancy. What these zones, once began, had accomplished was not only the pride of people in the mainland. It also surprised our Hong Kong and Macao compatriots and even people from developed countries. To many, it was inconceivable.

Before Shenzhen became a special economic zone, it was where people migrated in droves to sneak their way into Hong Kong in hopes of a better life. According to 1978 statistics, an average farmer in Hong Kong's New Territories was making upwards of HK$13,000* a year, while the annual income for a Guangdong farmer just across the bay averaged a meager 7.4 yuan. In Bao'an, the mainland county closest to Hong Kong, a total of 70,000 people abandoned some 90,000 *mu* (6,000 hectares) of farmland and fled to Hong Kong during the period from 1951, the year the Hong Kong-Guangdong border was closed, until 1980, when the Shenzhen Special Economic Zone was established. Massive illegal immigration posed a serious social problem for both Guangdong

---

* According to Pacific Exchange Rate Service, one US dollar was worth HK$4.6837 in 1978. HK$13,000 was equivalent to US$2,776. (*Translator*)

and Hong Kong. Man Kam To Port alone received four truckloads of illegal immigrants repatriated from Hong Kong everyday in 1978. During summer holidays, local school buildings were requisitioned, with all the desks and benches fashioned into makeshift beds to accommodate these people. With the establishment of the special economic zone, the once rampant illegal immigration rush vanished almost immediately.

However, the special economic zones, born of a self-secluded China where the impact of ultra-leftistism lingered, were surrounded with doubt and reproach from the very start. Their harsh beginning could be ascribed to institutional impediments, but none were greater than ultra-leftist thoughts and smuggling.

Special Zones Are Socialist, Not Capitalist

Those who did not like the opening-up policy abhorred the special economic zones. They cast aspersions on them, labeling them as "enclaves of the international bourgeoisie," "mere copies of Hong Kong and capitalism," "colonies," and "tainted foreign concessions." Some, who could not bear the sight of the new things emerging in these zones, openly questioned whether these zones were capitalist or socialist. There were also people out to vent their spite because decentralization of power had robbed them of their prerogatives under decades of centralization of political power and monopoly over economic management. One disgruntled veteran was all tears when he visited Shenzhen, saying, "Here the only red thing left is this five-star flag in my hand." Some theoreticians argued, "Our government disposed of all foreign-invested firms back in 1952, so how can we justifiably turn around and offer land to foreign capitalists today? We accomplished the transformation of capitalist industry and commerce back in 1956, so how can we rationalize bringing in foreign capital to replace national capital?" A clamor of sarcasm, distress, bewilderment and disappointment brought invisible, yet heavy pressure to bear on the builders of the special economic zones.

At a May-June 1981 State Council conference, all the doubts burst loose, but no question was louder than whether these zones were just another version of "foreign concessions" or "colonies," rather than instruments of socialism. The conference emphasized the need to open people's minds and put them on the same page, but insisted that all the doubts were groundless. These are economic zones, not political zones, the conference stressed, in which state sovereignty is fully exercised. They could not be put on a par with the foreign concessions and colonies born of unequal treaties. For Guangdong and Fujian to adopt special policies and flexible steps in foreign economic activities and to run special economic zones on a trial basis involved major reforms that would inevitably come across complicated new situations. It was necessary to carry forward the revolutionary spirit and be bold to experiment and innovate. The conference called on people to do whatever was in accord with the Party's line, principles and policies and beneficial to economic readjustment and development in the two provinces and throughout the nation. The conference also urged the State Import and Export Commission to do a good coordinating and organizing job, and set up an efficient working body to handle the task.

The builders of the special economic zones bravely stood up to the pressure. "Different opinions about the special economic zones were already there from the beginning, and people worried about whether we were embracing capitalism," said Deng of the controversy, "but what has been accomplished in Shenzhen has given a definite answer to those who were worried. The special zones are socialist, not capitalist."

Laying Equal Stress on Material and Cultural Development

Smuggling, an illegal activity that sneaks around customs supervision and evades taxes, has long existed at home and abroad. The causes behind it are many, including price disparities between home and foreign markets, government control of import and export goods, domestic shortages of certain goods, high customs duties, and lax customs control. The bottom of the matter, however, is the smugglers' sheer desire for criminal profiteering. It is unfair to say that smuggling is an upshot of the opening-up policy.

Coastal regions are susceptible to smuggling activities. Hence the Chinese terms "walking on water," (smuggling), "walker-on-the-water," (smuggler) and "goods sold on the water" (smuggled goods). Shortly after Guangdong and Fujian provinces started implementing special economic policies and running the zones on a trial basis, smuggling became a serious problem. The involvement of some government officials in such activities threw local economies into serious disorder and spoiled the government's image. The lack of experience on the part of law-enforcement departments, plus the glaring commodity price differences between the mainland and the rest of the world, served to exacerbate the problem.

The central authorities, acting on the proposals by Deng and Chen Yun, issued an emergency circular on January 11, 1982, calling for a stern crackdown on breaches of discipline and criminal offenses in the economic field. Xi Zhongxun, Yu Qiuli, Peng Chong, and Wang Heshou were dispatched to Guangdong, Fujian, Zhejiang and Yunnan, where smuggling and sales of smuggled goods were most rampant, to convey the instructions of the central authorities and urge local governments to take emergency steps to tackle the problem.

However, some people who were either deeply influenced by ultra-leftist thinking or accustomed to the former rigid monopolizing system ascribed smuggling and some other problems to the opening-up policy and heaped abuse upon the authorities of Guangdong and Fujian and the special economic zones. Some of their castigations – calling smuggling "another blatant onslaught of capitalism" and branding special economic zones as "sources of smuggled goods" – sounded familiar. Some went so far as to predict that Guangdong would collapse in three months "if it is allowed to go on with what it is doing now." They demanded the repeal of all the decentralized power and the enactment of laws to contain what was going on in these zones, and asked the authorities to abolish the special policies and flexible steps and close the zones. The two provinces and the special economic zones were under enormous pressure.

From February 11 to 13, the Party convened a meeting to discuss the work of Guangdong and Fujian provinces to further understand and carry out the emergency circular, and to deal effectively with smuggling, corruption and bribery. Naturally, a major topic at the meeting was the relationship between the new anti-smuggling initiative on one hand, and the ongoing special policies and flexible steps implemented in Guangdong and Fujian and the special economic zones on the other.

On March 1, Central Document [1982] 17 was issued to circulate the resulting memorandum from this meeting to the localities, calling on people to be fully aware of the seriousness, harm and danger of economic offenses and to fully carry out the anti-smuggling campaign. At the same time, the notice suggested, they must strive to summarize the experience gained and put the government guideline in perspective, in order to promote the healthy development of international economic activities and to continue to run the special economic zones well.

At this critical moment, in a conversation on April 3, 1982 with Hu Qiaomu and Deng Liqun, Deng pointed out:

> The mission before us is two-sided, and we've got to grasp both sides with white-knuckled hands. On the one hand, we must persist in the policy of opening up to the outside world and invigorating the home economy, a policy that has been justified by practice and therefore tolerates not the slightest hesitancy on our part. However, we must improve this policy wherever necessary in practice. On the other hand, we must stay level-headed and heighten our vigilance as we strive to do a good job in curbing economic offenses over the long run. If we neglect this aspect of our mission, we are likely to deviate from socialism, and our modernization drive will be in jeopardy.

During this period, Deng repeated this idea on different occasions, from conversations with other top leaders to meetings with foreign visitors, from Politburo meetings to central working conferences. He emphasized, "We've got to uphold the opening-up policy. This cannot be changed. If we really want to change it, all we can do is to change it for the better."

The key document on this matter, the *Decisions of the Party Central Committee and the State Council on Cracking Down on Serious Criminal Activities in the Economic Field*, which was issued on April 13, 1982, stated:

The work to execute the Party policy to open up to the outside world and rejuvenate the economy at home runs in parallel with the crackdown on serious economic offenses. Opening up to the outside world and invigorating the home economy are pragmatic and unswerving policies our Party has adopted in light of the needs of the socialist modernization drive. These policies will never be changed or shaken by our effort to clamp down on criminals who have seriously infringed upon the economy.

Vice Premier Gu Mu inspected Guangdong and its special economic zones from March 27 to April 3, 1982. After hearing a report of Shenzhen municipal leaders, he said:

In a little more than a couple of years, with a little money given by the state and the province, and by relying only on central principles and policies, you have started from scratch and produced all this today – that's no easy task. I believe you have accomplished a lot.

He added that practice had proved the sensibility of the central authorities in deciding to experiment with the special economic zones.

To this day, we have found not a single case in which the nation was humiliated or state sovereignty was surrendered. Nobody has gotten a big raw deal or been badly double-crossed at the hands of foreign investors. Nor have we taken on anything that we cannot carry through to the end. Therefore, there is no question that we are on the right road. Doubts about whether the special economic zones can continue are simply groundless.

He urged people to evaluate their experience, saying, "We must summarize what we have done for the purpose of moving forward."

Another of the vice premier's missions during this Guangdong tour was to organize anti-smuggling efforts. The central authorities accepted his proposal to take steps to strengthen anti-smuggling agencies at the national and provincial levels and to set up a working framework for coordinating the relevant parties – including customs, public security organs, border inspecting troops and industrial and commercial departments – against smuggling. Acting on his proposal, local authorities regrouped and re-tooled their anti-smuggling forces, tightened up their monitoring of offshore fishing activities, brought to justice those individuals and organizations seriously involved in smuggling, and sternly punished smuggling kingpins. All this helped to effectively curb smuggling and other economic offenses in a little more than six months' time.

The top leaders' insistence on laying equal emphasis on both aspects of the nation's endeavor served to put both the modernization and opening-up efforts on one hand, and the anti-smuggling drive on the other on track. Criminal offenses in the economics field were put down while the nation continued to open up. Both Guangdong and Fujian provinces and their special economic zones steered clear of the road to retrogression and sped up their economic growth along a road of healthy development. As Guangdong's Governor Liang Lingguang remarked, "It is unfair for some people to link criminal offenses with the opening-up policy. In fact, the opening-up policy has set higher requirements on business administration."

Economic restructuring at the national level beginning in 1979 caused a lot of difficulties for the experimental special economic zones at the initial stage of the opening-up efforts. That round of economic restructuring was a contingency policy created to deal with grave economic overheating and inflation. Its measures included: trimming capital construction; closing, suspending or merging some factories; scaling down production in some factories or shifting them to other fields; and curtailing defense expenditures and corporate and institutional administrative upkeep. Because of the difficult economic situation at home and problems arising during the course of building the special economic zones, some of which were unavoidable byproducts of the process of development, fault-finding of the special economic zones continued to mount. This, coupled with the abolishment in early 1982 of the State Import and Export Commission (which had been in charge of the special economic zones), brought more pressure to those working on these zones. As Gu Mu recalled during a 1998 conversation, "The situation then, especially in the first six months of 1982, was like 'the sighing winds of frosty autumn.'"

Gu Mu, however, was unfazed by the adversity. He said:

Opening up to the outside world is the top leadership's fundamental strategic policy for the modernization drive. The establishment of the special economic zones was initiated by Comrade Deng Xiaoping, decided by the Party Central Committee, written into law by the Standing Committee of the National People's Congress, and executed under the guidance of the State Council. All these remain unchanged, and, what's more, no top leader has ever said we are doing something wrong. People have misgivings about capitalism because China had its fill of imperialist invasions in modern history. Some people, having been influenced by the "leftist" influence for so long, are questioning the wisdom of the special economic zones and the opening-up policy. This is understandable, but for our part, we have to prevent and overcome the side effects of what we are doing now.

As to his own personal feelings, he said, "I am not bothered by anything people are saying about me, but I must direct myself to the mission the central authorities have entrusted to me, which is to push the work on the special economic zones."

During a conversation in Zhongshan, Guangdong Province, Ye Jianying asked Gu Mu in a solicitous tone, "There are so many different opinions about the special economic zones. Can you stand it?" Gu replied, "You bet I can."

Special Economic Zones Must Go On

Deng and the other top leaders had been concerned with the progress of the special economic zones from Day One, even during the difficult days of the national economic restructuring. Addressing the Central Working Conference in December 1980, he made the resolute, timely statement:

The decision to set up a few special economic zones in Guangdong and Fujian must be carried on. ... Under the precondition of national independence and self-reliance, we must go on with the series of economic policies that serve to open up to the outside world. At the same time we have got to size up our experience and improve our work.

"The special economic zones should stick to the established principles, but the pace of development can slow down a little bit," Deng said, chiding leaders of Guangdong during the conference. "We want you to slow down a little bit out of our consideration for the temporary difficulties facing the national economy right now. However, the established principles cannot be changed. The special economic zones should move on resolutely. That's what matters most."

Speaking at a Party Central Committee meeting in early January 1982 on dealing with the outbreak of smuggling along the coasts of Guangdong and Fujian provinces, Deng said that on no account should people falter in carrying out the opening-up policy. He stressed once again that the policies to open up, invigorate the domestic economy and improve the management of the special economic zones should be further carried out. On December 20 and again on the 31st, Zhang Yun, former deputy secretary of the Central Discipline Inspection Commission and member of the Central Advisory Commission, wrote twice to Hu Yaobang and Deng to affirm the approaches and activities of Guangdong and the special economic zones, and to demand that efforts be continued to eradicate the influence of "leftist" ideology and maintain the stability of practical policies. Since 1982, she reminded, the amount of revenue Guangdong turned over to the state treasury had grown over and again, "but the number of restrictions imposed on the province have been rising as well, and the leeway provided by the flexible policies and steps keeps shrinking."

Deng, highly mindful of the way the special policies and flexible steps were put into effect in Guangdong and Fujian, instructed on Zhang's first letter, "This letter can be reprinted and delivered to the comrades on the Political Bureau and the Secretariat of the Party Central Committee," and on the second letter, "This situation needs attention. I would like to ask the State Council and the State Finance and Economic Leading Group to discuss it." Upon hearing a report from Guangdong Governor Ren Zhongyi on the construction of the Shenzhen Special Economic Zone, he said, "You've got to keep it going." When the governor told him that the Shekou Industrial Zone was under fire for its plan to hire foreigners as corporate managers, he pointed out, "There is nothing wrong with hiring foreign managers. This is by no means treason."

In February 1983, Hu Yaobang, General Secretary of the Party Central Committee, went on an inspection tour of Shenzhen. While there, to voice his support for Shenzhen, he wrote the inscription, "Special things should be done in special ways; new things should be done in new ways. Your stance should not be changed, but your approaches should be entirely new."

On October 30, 1982, Chen Yun, upon reading the *Initial Summary of Guangdong Province on Running Special Economic Zones on a Trial Basis*, responded, "I have read this initial summary submitted to me on October 22. It is very good indeed. ... The special economic zones must be run, and run better by continually evaluating experience."

In March 1983, Wang Zhen arrived in Guangzhou to see what was going on there. When told that some people were accusing the special economic zones of developing capitalism, he said angrily:

Hu Yaobang (*front right*) on a tour of Shenzhen, May 23-24, 1984. Liang Lingguang stands at the far right.

These people are more outdated than those of the 1861–1894 Foreign Affairs Movement, and no better than Zheng Guanying*. They are saying there are more smugglers today than before and that people's minds are corrupted by bourgeois ideas. Would smugglers disappear if we did not open up? They would still be there. The key lies in how you handle such things. We have to open up. To shut ourselves behind closed doors can only result in backwardness.

While visiting Shenzhen in October 1981, Vice Premier Bo Yibo pointed out that it was necessary to understand the significance of running the special economic zones:

> You must be highly conscious of it. In my opinion, all these things can be done – joint ventures, cooperative management, wholly foreign-owned companies. You don't have to be afraid of them. You have launched tourism and the real estate industry, but it is not enough. You have to launch large-scale industry to build up a special economic zone in the true sense of the term – and it cannot do without industry. The central policies for the special economic zones will not be changed. You've got to be confident in this. You've got to make a success of it.

The support voiced by Deng and the other top leaders came as a spark of inspiration for the builders of the special economic zones, and further boosted their confidence and resolve to manage the zones well.

The majority of economists and theoreticians at the time were in favor of the opening-up policy and the special economic zones. Most of them did not view the zones as a contradiction. They saw them as places where state, collective and private sectors coexisted, but where the processing industry – based on foreign-supplied materials, compensation trade, cooperative enterprises, and equity joint ventures – took up the lion's share of the local economies. However, the entities were subject

---

*   Zheng Guanying (1842–1922), a native of Xiangshan County, present-day Zhongshan, Guangdong, author of the celebrated book *Warnings to a Prosperous Age*, and a modern Chinese thinker known for his complete system of reformist theory. (*Translator*)

to socialist legislation and government supervision, and even wholly foreign-owned companies were no exception. The special economic zones, they argued, could not be equated with "colonies" or "foreign concessions" of the past. Proponents of the special economic zones went so far as to delve into Marxist-Leninist works in search of theories to justify their beliefs.

On November 15, 1982, with Gu Mu's blessing, a report on the status of the zones (*Outline Report to the Secretariat of the Party Central Committee on Implementing Special Policies and Flexible Steps and Experimenting With Special Economic Zones in Guangdong and Fujian Provinces*) was composed. The report contained two chapters: one on the zones and the other on the two provinces where they were located.

The *Outline Report* gave a general overview of the origin of the special economic zones and what they had accomplished and what remained to be done after three years of experimental existence. It stated:

> The special economic zones we are running on a trial basis are administrative areas under the people's democratic rule. They adhere politically, ideologically and culturally to the socialist orientation. In the economic field, they uphold the leadership of the socialist economy, allow multiple economic sectors to coexist, and, following a more open policy in economic dealings with foreign investors, they bring in foreign capital and technology, develop production, expand exports, improve the livelihood of the people, and safeguard stability and order in the border regions. Over the last three years these zones have done a great deal of work, got off to a good start in absorbing foreign investment, imported advanced technology and equipment in batches, developed industrial and agricultural production quickly, and made much headway in infrastructure construction and cultural development. Massive illegal immigration no longer exists. The local people wholeheartedly stand for the central policy decision to run these zones on a trial basis. However, some drawbacks and problems have occurred in the day-to-day work of the special economic zones. For instance, some contracts on the introduction of foreign capital or technology have left something to be desired. The Shenzhen Special

Economic Zone has gone a bit too far in expanding its development scale, and for a time they were panic-buying farm and sideline
products at higher prices and importing luxury consumer goods for
sales in the hinterland, but they have stopped these behaviors now.

The *Outline Report* then listed three issues to be tackled in
order to improve the management of the special economic zones.

First, the leadership and administrative system of the special
economic zones should gradually break through the nation's
prevailing system. To facilitate experimentation with the breakthrough, the State Council shall take control of relevant principle
and policy issues, and major problems arising from it shall be
promptly reported to the premier for immediate decisions. The
two provinces should further tighten up day-to-day leadership
over the special economic zones and address the problems that
should be solved under their jurisdiction in a timely fashion.

Second, the special economic zones shall be given more
decision-making power. State leadership over these zones should
be limited mainly to principles and policies, to affairs that need to
be handled uniformly by the central authorities (such as foreign
affairs, public security, border inspection, customs, taxation),
and to the examination and approval of general development
plans and major construction projects. Except for these fields,
the special economic zones should be allowed to act according
to actual circumstances. The relevant central departments, when
formulating regulations concerning these zones, shall take their
distinctiveness into consideration and refrain from seeking
uniformity with the rest of the country.

Third, with regard to the materials needed for the construction
of the special economic zones – particularly those for state-invested
projects, projects financed with domestic loans, infrastructure development, and the building materials needed for the ancillary facilities
of foreign-invested projects – the central government should assist
these zones as best it can, by listing these projects in independent
accounts so that the necessary materials can be dispatched exclusively
to these zones.

The report also presented proposals on speeding up the improvement of legislation for the special economic zones and assisting them in addressing their shortages of government functionaries and professionals.

Regarding Guangdong and Fujian provinces, the *Outline Report* stated that the existing problems had been basically solved, that both provinces should go on with the special policies and flexible steps and strive to become vanguards for the modernization drive. The report also sought support from the relevant departments for proposals on financial contracting arrangements, management under central planning, the use of foreign capital and import of foreign technology, foreign trade business power and market materials.

On the same day (November 15), a report was written based on discussions between the relevant State Council departments and leaders of both provinces. The *Memorandum on Issues Concerning the Running of Special Economic Zones on a Trial Basis* echoed the *Outline Report* of the Secretariat in many aspects. A few weeks later, on December 3, 1982, the central authorities transmitted the *Memorandum* to localities in the form of Central Document [1982] 50, pointing out, among other things, "Running the special economic zones on a trial basis is a major step in carrying out our national foreign policy in the new period of historical development." The *Memorandum* stated again: "The Secretariat and the State Council have decided that Comrade Gu Mu shall take charge of this field of work."

In March 1982, I was appointed Director General of the Foreign Capital Administrative Bureau of the Ministry of Foreign Economic Relations and Trade. My responsibilities included equity joint ventures with Chinese and foreign investment, government loans and special economic zones. My first action on taking up office was to inspect the construction work and enterprises in the Shenzhen Special Economic Zone. I wanted to do something to counter the widespread rumor that "with the exception of the five-star red flag, everything in Shenzhen has gone capitalist."

During my previous visit to Guangdong in 1979, Shenzhen had struck me as a tiny town studded with foreign trade depots, while Zhuhai had looked every bit like a typical Chinese village. I was surprised by what I saw three years later. Shekou reminded me of a small city in a developed country, while Shenzhen was bustling with construction activity and, judging from the general level of the time, had taken on the initial look of a modern metropolis with sophisticated industry and services. The same people I had seen three years earlier had changed so much in their attitude toward work and service. Many local companies with investments from Hong Kong businesses – in such fields as processing work with client-supplied materials, designs or components, compensation trade, equity joint ventures and cooperative enterprises – were already in batch production. The quality and sophistication of much of the equipment and products there simply couldn't be found anywhere else in the mainland. Zhuhai, although lacking new industrial projects, was a lot more beautiful than before. In the city's Gongbei District, I saw some modern tourist facilities, where the service was much better than in other cities in the country.

Before I wrapped up my tour, I invited some of the zone's builders and Chinese managers of foreign-invested firms to a discussion meeting at the Guangming Overseas Chinese Farm. I wanted to hear their experiences, the difficulties and problems they had encountered in their work, and what they wanted from the central government. The farm had just made a name for itself for its winning partnership with foreign investors. With the go-ahead from Secretary of Guangdong Provincial Party Committee Ren Zhongyi, the farm's experience was being promoted in Guangdong Province, and as a result, the province was making great progress in international business cooperation. The problem was that some central government departments did not appreciate it.

At the meeting, Wei Nanjin, Director of the Guangdong Provincial Economic Work Commission, spoke about the development in his province of cooperative businesses with foreign investors, citing the Guangming Farm as an example. At one point in his talk, I hastened to say to the participants that this type of business was a wonderful way of doing things.

The meeting lasted a whole day. Every speaker poured out his or her feelings. Some become emotional as they related what had really happened to them and their companies. All of them defended the wisdom of the central authorities' policy decision to run the special economic zones and to use foreign capital. When talking about their experiences, they were full of confidence and determination. Much of what they said, however, was negative, dwelling on difficulties. Some reeled off a string of examples and vented their grievances. One speaker said that he felt as if he were "homeless," or like a "monster" coming out of nowhere whenever the government departments he visited cold-shouldered him for his requests for help or instruction to get things done. Most of the speakers citing problems said they found it difficult to carry out relevant central policies and measures. Expressing their wishes, they said they would like to see central policies unchanged – such as the policy to "do special things in special ways" in the special economic zones – but to decentralize power and give those working at the grass-roots level a free hand.

The differences between what I saw and heard in the special economic zones and the harsh criticisms that were making the rounds in the country then were so stark that they often made me lose sleep. Immediately after the day-long discussion meeting was over, I spent the entire evening putting together a list of all that I had seen and heard during that trip in a report to be delivered to the central authorities. Many days later, I heard that the top leaders had taken my report very seriously and sent people to Shenzhen for further investigations and studies.

In January 1983, to further promote the use of foreign investment, I held a meeting in Guangdong of representatives from eight southern provinces. Zeng Dingshi, Vice Governor of Guangdong, delivered a well-received speech to the meeting, as did Wei Nanjin and the leader of the Guangming Overseas Chinese Farm of Shenzhen.

After the meeting, I visited Shenzhen again. My findings during that visit convinced me once again that the policy decision to open up our nation and run the special economic zones was 100-percent correct.

Public Bidding: No More Dragged-out Construction

The competition-proof egalitarian system often left construction projects to drag on for years. The "Five-O'clock-Shadow Projects," as they were called in the Chinese vernacular, were eyesores in many cities across China at the time. While

I marveled at the amazing construction speed in Shenzhen, I also tried to find out the secret to it. Thus I went to see a 20-story building that was almost completed after a construction period of 18 months. The International Commerce Plaza, with a floorspace of 52,000 square meters, was a joint-venture project between the Shenzhen Real Estate Corporation and the Zhongfa Datong Real Estate Corporation. The two partners had signed an agreement on this project in September 1980, with the Shenzhen side providing 12,000 square meters of land and the Hong Kong side HK$60.27 million.

When the agreement had been drafted, the building company designated by Shenzhen government's capital construction department sent in a price proposal for 590 yuan per square meter and a technical proposal for a two-year construction period. The Hong Kong side found both proposals unacceptable, and the construction contract was delayed as a result. It happened that the general managers of the Shenzhen Real Estate Corporation had just returned from a visit to Hong Kong. Having observed the sophisticated corporate management there, they felt that the system whereby the government arbitrarily allocated building teams to construction projects was a grave impediment to the development of the special economic zone. This way of doing things was liable to high costs, low construction quality, long construction periods, long delays and low economic returns. It was high time, they believed, that this system was phased out. By referring to foreign construction contracting conventions, the corporation drafted the *Provisional Procedures Concerning Public Bidding for Construction Projects*, which the municipal government immediately endorsed.

In August 1981, the Shenzhen Real Estate Corporation held a public bidding on the International Commerce Plaza project. Eight bidders attended. The government-designated building company was one of them, but it refused to amend its price and technical proposals. Finally, the construction contract was awarded to the China First Metallurgical Construction Corporation with proposals of 398 yuan per square meter and an 18-month construction period. Because many issues of principle had been tackled during the bidding, it took just two-and-a-half days for the construction contract to be finalized after a delay of nearly 12 months. The contract stipulated that the construction corporation was to bear all responsibilities for labor, supplies, construction period, building quality and the total construction cost. It was to be fined 300,000 yuan for each month of construction delayed and awarded 300,000 yuan per month for completing the construction ahead of schedule.

As this was the first public bidding ever held for a building project in the mainland, the local government raised some eyebrows by allowing the bidding to take place in the first place. The government-designated building company took the case to higher authorities everywhere. Sympathizers said the bidding was like "internecine strife" or a "sabotage of the state plan in the interests of the capitalists." A local leader argued that the contract should be awarded to a local company. To solve the problem, the Shenzhen Municipal Government convened a meeting of leaders of state and provincial construction commissions and leaders of Shenzhen. The debate at the meeting was heated, but the municipal government was adamant that it was sensible to award the contract to the highest bidder, and that the old system that spawned indolence and backwardness should be replaced with competition. Representatives of the State Construction Commission listened to the discussion and ruled that steps for reform should be taken in the capital construction field, with public bidding being one such step. The case was settled.

After being awarded the contract, the First Metallurgical Construction Corporation streamlined its management and put its funds to rational use. For instance, it earned HK$1 million in interest from its bank deposits of prepaid construction fees. The construction speed rose steadily, until the corporation could finish one floor every seven days on the main building of the complex. In 1983, the International Trade Building was completed two months ahead of schedule, or eight months faster than the government-designated building company's proposed deadline. The engineering quality was rated "excellent," with 9.46 million yuan of investment saved. The construction corporation netted a profit that accounted for five percent of the total project cost, over and above an award of HK$800,000.

Shenzhen Speed: Three Floors a Day

With the establishment of the special economic zone and its ever-increasing imports and exports, Shenzhen rose to become a showcase for China's newly adopted opening-up policy. In 1980, many provinces, municipalities, autonomous regions, ministries and commissions of the State Council insisted on setting up branch offices in Shenzhen to serve as tentacles for feeling out the outside world. They wanted a piece of land on which to erect their own office buildings. This prompted Shenzhen to raise money for the construction of a large building to house all the branch offices. A blueprint was produced for the 53-floor International Trade Building, which was to become the tallest structure in the mainland in the 1980s.

Stakes were driven into the ground at Luohu Street in downtown Shenzhen in May 1982, and the construction of the foundation for the trade tower was completed five months later. In August 1983, construction of the standard floor of the tower began. After repeated studies, the builders adopted the newly invented sliding shuttering technology for construction. At first it took them seven days to finish one floor in the main building. Later, the structure went up by one floor every five days, and then every four days. Beginning from the 13th floor skyward, the speed reached one floor every three days, and two days at the fastest. By contrast, the world's top construction speed at the time – as recorded by a 32-floor apartment building in Honolulu and the 64-floor Hopewell Center and the 50-floor China Resources Building in Hong Kong – stood at four days per floor. In comparison with the traditional shuttering erection technology, the sliding shuttering technology shortened the construction period of the Shenzhen International Trade Building by 113 days and saved 1,200 cubic meters of timber, 250 tons of steel pipes, and more than 300,000 yuan in construction fees. The construction corporation achieved fine economic returns. In addition to repaying one million yuan in loans, it also added 3.97 million yuan worth of fixed assets.

On March 15, 1984, Xinhua News Agency reported that the builders of the Shenzhen International Trade Building had chalked up a new world-record for construction speed at the rate of three floors per day. This impressive rate was dubbed the "Shenzhen Speed." Later, the three keys to this speed – selecting the blueprints through comparisons and appraisals, choosing the building team by public bidding, and contracting out the construction work – were adopted by building companies throughout the nation.

As the Song-dynasty poet Lu You said in his poem *Visiting a Village West of the Mountains*, "Where hills bend, streams wind and the pathway seems to end, / Past dark willows and flowers in bloom, lies another village." Having gone through a period of twists and turns, the young special economic zone eventually embarked on a road of rapid development.

The Policy for Special Economic Zones Is Sound

After a few years of development through trial and error, questions about the experiment with special economic zones remained. How were the zones faring? Did any of the rumors, accusations and doubts about them hold water? Was the opening-up policy right or wrong? Should they be allowed to continue? As these questions had an important bearing on the opening-up endeavor, Deng decided to go and see for himself. In addition to investigating the answers, he wanted to hear what the zones' builders were saying. From January 22 to February 16, 1984, in the company of Politburo members Wang Zhen and Yang Shangkun, he inspected Guangzhou, Shenzhen, Zhuhai, Xiamen and Shanghai.

On January 24, when the train carrying Deng and his entourage pulled up at Guangzhou Railway Station, Governor Liang Lingguang of Guangdong Province stepped aboard the train to greet him. Without so much as an exchange of pleasantries, Deng said in a somber tone, "I proposed the establishment of the special economic zones and the Party Central Committee decided on it. I came here because I want to know if my idea worked or not."

It was natural for Deng to choose Shenzhen as the first stop on his itinerary, because it was the best known of the four special economic zones. When the train entered Shenzhen Railway Station at noon, he disembarked to shake hands with local leaders waiting on the platform. In the afternoon, after taking a nap in the hotel, he began hearing Mayor Liang Xiang's work report. When the mayor told him that, thanks to rapid development since the birth of the special economic zone, the city's industrial output value had reached 360 million yuan in 1982 and jumped to 720 million yuan in 1983, Deng interrupted, "Doubled in one year's time?" That was exactly one of the promises he had made when he presented his proposal on the special economic zones to the Central Working Conference on April 5, 1979. The mayor confirmed it, adding, "That figure is over ten times what it was in 1978, the year before the establishment of the zone. Our financial revenue has also multiplied by ten times." Deng was all ears throughout the mayor's 40-minute report, chipping in occasionally. Liang concluded his report, and said, "Comrade Xiaoping, instruction please." Deng answered, "I've just taken it all in, so I won't say anything for now. Let's go out and see how things are out there."

Wherever he visited, Deng had the habit of going to the top of the tallest building to take in the whole view. At the Luohu Shopping District, he saw the International Trade Building standing in a forest of tall buildings and was impressed by the prosperity of the district. He listened with rapt attention when

Deng (*center*) visiting the Shenzhen International Trade Building, under construction in January 1984.

the mayor, pointing to a construction site across the street, told him that the 53-story building was being built by the same builders who held the world record for erecting one floor every three days. He was delighted when the mayor told him that Luohu District, already home to the mainland's largest cluster of tall buildings, had planned to add more than one hundred more buildings.

People might wonder (young people especially) why all this talk about tall buildings and fast construction, which seem like no big deal today, should make Deng so happy. In order to understand this, you would have to know that back then, when Shenzhen's neighbor Hong Kong had long since become an immense forest of tall buildings, the tallest building in the entire mainland for half a century was a 24-floor building in Shanghai. Moreover, outside of the special economic zones, the egalitarian practice of "everybody eating from the same big pot, regardless of one's share of the workload" was still holding sway, and the construction authorities had their hands full just dealing with the "Five-O'clock-Shadow Projects" and striving to promote a "proper construction period." With those facts in mind, one can understand why Deng was so happy.

Deng and his entourage began the second day of their Shenzhen inspection tour at the Shangbu Industrial Zone for a visit to the Shenzhen Industrial and Trading Center under the China National Aero-Technology Import & Export Corporation. This 17-month-old corporation was the first in Shenzhen to import and develop computer technology and provide relevant services. When he arrived at a workshop, Deng took a look at the equipment, heard a detailed introduction to computer technology and software, and took in a chess game between a player and a computer. "A Chinese-American scholar told me that software designers in the United States are mostly young students," Deng said to his hosts. "With so many youngsters and students all over China, we have loads of potential talent to develop our own computer software." Later, on February 16, he said in Shanghai, "The popularization of computers should start with kids."

Deng's next stop was Guangdong's richest fishing village. Nestled by the Shenzhen River in a comfortable environment, the village comprised 32 two-story houses, each with six bed rooms and two sitting rooms, with a floorspace of 180 square meters. In one of the houses, the host, Wu Bosen, told Deng that his village had a net income of 470,000 yuan the previous year, averaging 5,970 yuan a year or 439 yuan a month per villager. "That is higher than my salary," Deng said. "It will take a long time, one hundred years at least, for all the rural areas in our nation to attain this living standard." Mayor Liang said, "Actually, I doubt it will take that long." Deng responded, "Seventy years at least, that is, from now until the end of this century, and we've got to add another 50 years, because we have so many people."

On the morning of February 26, Deng's motorcade left the hotel and drove in the direction of Shekou. On their way, the mayor pointed at a barren expanse of land and told Deng it was where Shenzhen was to build its first university, Shenzhen University, and the students would start the new school year in the coming September. Everyone regarded the empty space with bewilderment. "Can you make it, in such a short time span?" Deng asked. "No problem," came the answer. True to the mayor's words, Shenzhen University welcomed its first batch of students seven months later that year.

After Deng reached the office building of the Merchants Group's Shekou Industrial Zone, he went to a meeting room on the seventh floor, where Yuan Geng, chairman of the industrial

Deng on an inspection tour of the Shekou Industrial Zone, January 26, 1984. (*First row, from left to right:* Liang Lingguang, Yuan Geng, Deng, Yang Shangkun, Wang Zhen.)

Deng (*center*), Yang Shangkun (*second from left*), Wang Zhen (*fourth from left*) and Liang Lingguang (*third from right*) posing for a photo with Henry Fok Ying-tung (*second from right*), Ma Man-kei (*third from left*) and his wife.

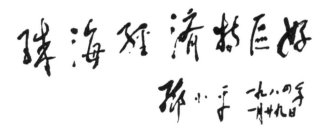

On a visit to the Zhuhai Special Economic Zone on January 29, 1984, Deng wrote the inscription, "The Zhuhai Special Economic Zone is good."

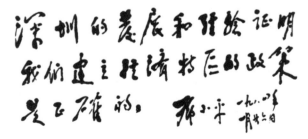

Deng wrote an inscription for the Shenzhen Special Economic Zone, February 1, 1984. The inscription reads, "The development and experience of Shenzhen prove that our policy to establish special economic zones is correct. Deng Xiaoping, January 26, 1984."

zone, briefed him on the development of the zone. When the report was over, Deng paced the floor and stopped by a window. Pointing at the busy Shekou Harbor, he asked Yuan, "When were the docks built? What kind of ships can it accommodate?" After Yuan answered his questions, Deng said appreciatively, "It's wonderful that you have built such a harbor."

Yuan then took Deng and his companions to Sea World Plaza in the town center of Shekou. This was a complex of shops, hotels and restaurants built in 1983 by converting the rooms of the ex-*Ancerville*, a French-built passenger ship launched by French president Charles de Gaulle on April 5, 1962. The China Ocean Shipping (Group) Corporation bought it in April 1973, and renamed it *Minghua*. Deng went aboard the ship – the name "Minghua" remaining in gold painted letters in both English and Chinese characters on the bow and stern – and climbed to the top deck to look at the scenery of the industrial zone and the Shenzhen Bay. He was so happy with what he had seen that day that during lunch he drank three cups of *maotai*.

Deng Speaks Highly of Special Economic Zones

On the afternoon of January 26, Deng wound up the Shenzhen leg of his South China tour and set off for the Zhuhai Special Economic Zone on board a Navy gunboat. While there, he inspected the Xiangzhou Woolen Textile Mill, the Shishan Electronics Factory, the Jiuzhou Harbor, and the Shijingshan Tourist Center.

On the morning of January 28, Deng climbed up the Mountain of Third Sister Luo to the north of the Hot Spring Hotel, where he was staying. On his way back his bodyguard suggested that he follow the same road he had just taken. Deng said, "I never take the same road." When meeting with Henry Fok Ying-tung of Hong Kong and Ma Man-kei of Macao that night, he said, "I am the man who proposed the special economic zones. Looks like I made a good choice."

At noon on January 29 (his last day in Zhuhai), Deng wrote the inscription: "The Zhuhai Special Economic Zone is good." In the afternoon, he left for Guangzhou by way of the city of Shunde.

Upon learning that Deng had written an inscription for Zhuhai, the mayor of Shenzhen rushed his men to Guangzhou to ask for his calligraphy. Deng wrote, "The development and experience of Shenzhen prove that our policy for setting up special economic zones is correct. – Deng Xiaoping, January 26, 1984." The day he wrote the inscription was February 1, but Deng deliberately put the date of his departure from Shenzhen on the inscription. The day he arrived in Shenzhen he had said, "I am not ready to say anything about it just now." Evidently, two days of in-depth investigations in Shenzhen plus a few more days of deliberation were enough to convince him that he had indeed made a sound policy decision for the nation.

On February 7, Deng arrived in Xiamen. The following day, in a meeting arranged by Wang Zhen, First Secretary of Fujian Provincial Party Committe Xiang Nan and Deng discussed the Xiamen Special Economic Zone. Xiang had three requests to convey: first, because the 2.5 square kilometers that had been designated for the zone was too small, he hoped that the zone could be broadened to the entire 131 square kilometers of Xiamen Island; second, he hoped the central government could give the special economic zone more power to get things done better and faster; and third, because developing the Xiamen Special Economic Zone alone was not enough to help the people of Fujian Province to beat poverty and become rich, the governor requested that the Southern Fujian Delta embracing Xiamen, Zhangzhou and Quanzhou be designated as an open region. Deng nodded approval time and again when he listened.

During his stay in Xiamen, Deng inspected the Dongdu Harbor, the Gaoqi Airport, the Huli Industrial Zone and Xiamen University, and took part in a local tree-planting function in the rain. On February 9, he wrote an inscription in honor of the Xiamen Special Economic Zone: "Run the Special Economic Zone better and faster." By writing this and the other two previous inscriptions, Deng gave his reaffirmation of the policy decision and the practice of running the special economic zones; by expressing his expectation for the zones to do better in the future, he also signaled his estimation that there was much room for improvement.

While talking with local leaders in Shanghai on February 14, Deng said:

> During this tour I have seen a number of special economic zones and hotels. The Hot Spring Hotel is entirely owned by Henry Fok, who makes 20 million yuan a year from it, but he will hand it over to us a few years from now. This is something you can do too. As I see it, the problem with the opening-up policy is not that we should close down, but that we are still not open enough.
>
> ...
>
> Our current building industry, housing construction, and houses built for sale, in particular, cannot be changed overnight. Our construction speed is slow, as slow as a snail's pace, but in Shekou and Shenzhen, construction is a lot faster – they can finish an entire floor of a building in a few days – because they have adopted the contracting system. They are the same old bunch of builders, but they can do it a lot faster simply because the method has been changed. Some of our systems have got to be changed. The "big pot" practice never worked and never will.

Wang Zhen, who accompanied Deng during the whole trip, wrote in his *Report on Accompanying Comrade Deng Xiaoping on His Inspection Tour of Guangdong, Fujian and Shanghai*:

> In December 1979, when I was still Vice Premier, I had led a number of State Council ministers on a visit to Shekou, for the purpose of finalizing a plan on how to support and help the Merchants Group of the Ministry of Transport and Communications to develop the Shekou Industrial Zone. At the time, Shekou was just a seashore with some barren hills. The roads were rugged. There were no toilets, and no washing water. This time around, when I arrived with Comrade Xiaoping on his inspection tour, Shenzhen and Shekou had changed dramatically. High-rise buildings are now everywhere. Roads stretch in every direction. The docks for 10,000-tonners and the helicopter airport have all come into operation. Telecommunications, tap water, electricity, flood control, gas, waste-water disposal, and other pieces of the infrastructure have taken shape. A modern industrial city has emerged

by the South China Sea. I was really happy to see all this. It reminds me of the old saying, "After three days of absence, we have got to see the 'man' in a new light."*

On February 24, 1984, Deng called Hu Yaobang and some other top leaders together for a conversation about the special economic zones. He said:

I have recently gone to Guangdong and Fujian to see three special economic zones. And I also went to Shanghai to see the Baoshan Iron and Steel Company. These visits gave me some perceptual knowledge. Today I wanted you to come for a chat about how to run the special economic zones and open more cities to foreign investors. In order to set up the special economic zones and carry out the opening-up policy, we have got to define our guideline, which is, instead of abolishing the policy, we must loosen up on it. Shenzhen gave me the impression of a booming city. The Shenzhen speed of construction is really fast. When they build houses they can finish a whole floor in a few days' time, so that it does not take long for them to complete a big building. Their building teams are from other parts of the country. They are efficient because they have adopted a contracting system with well-defined rewards and penalties. Shenzhen's Shekou Industrial Zone is growing even faster, for the single reason that we have given them a little power to make their own decisions on expenditures below the 5 million dollar mark. Their slogan is, "Time is money, efficiency is life." The special economic zones are windows – windows onto foreign technology and new knowledge, and windows for showcasing the policy of openness. These zones can bring in technology, and help us refresh our knowledge and learn management, for management is also a kind of knowledge. Turning the special economic zones into open bases can be very beneficial to us, not

---

* According to the classical Chinese novel *Romance of the Three Kingdoms*, this remark was made by Lu Su, Commander-in-Chief of the Kingdom of Wu, to Gneral Lu Meng, upon finding that, following the King of Wu's admonition, the general had fostered a reading habit and quickly turned himself from a boorish warrior into a wise man. Here, the author personifies Shekou as he cites this saying to show how surprised he was by the city's dramatic changes. (*Translator*)

just in developing our economy and cultivating skills – it can also enhance our nation's global impact. I learned that public order in Shenzhen has been much better than before, and that people who ran to Hong Kong have begun to return. One reason for this is that plenty of jobs are available out there [in Shenzhen] and people are making a lot more money. From this you can see that in the final analysis, spiritual contentment comes from material civilization.

During the conversation Deng also said:

> The area designated for the Xiamen Special Economic Zone is too small, and we have got to turn all of Xiamen into a special economic zone. In this way, we can absorb large amounts of capital from overseas Chinese and Hong Kong and Macao compatriots, and many foreigners will also come to invest. This can also bring along the neighboring areas and bring the entire Fujian economy to life. We may not call the Xiamen Special Economic Zone a free port, but we can carry out some free port policies there, because there is precedent for it in the world. Foreigners are willing to come and invest so long as we allow capital to come and go freely. I don't see this as a losing cause. A lot of good will come of it. Apart from the special economic zones we have now, we may consider opening up some port cities, such as Dalian and Qingdao. These places will not be called "special economic zones," but can apply some of the policies that are being applied to special economic zones. We have to open up Hainan Island too. It will be a huge accomplishment if we can quickly boost the economy on that island.

Every leader present was in favor of what Deng had said.

Deng's remarks can be seen as the central leadership's renewed affirmation of the work of the special economic zones and a new assessment of that period of work. The General Office of the Party Central Committee issued a transcript of this conversation (on paper with no letterhead) to central departments and local governments. These remarks also played an historic role in bringing forth a common understanding of the opening-up policy and in validating confidence for it throughout the nation. The first quarter of 1984 has, therefore, gone down in history as the "springtime" of China's opening-up endeavor.

In 1985, new problems occurred and the special economic zones once again came under fire at home and abroad. Deng was the first to make his stand clear. On August 1, 1985, during a meeting with members of the 13th Delegation of the Komeito Party of Japan, he said:

> Not long ago I told a foreign guest that what we have been doing in Shenzhen is an experiment. This has caused some people abroad to speculate whether China will change its policy once again and whether I have gone back on my judgment on the special economic zones. For that reason, here I want to share my two opinions with you. The first is that the policy to establish the special economic zones is correct; the second is that the special economic zones are still experimental in nature. These two opinions do not contradict each other. Our opening-up policy as a whole is also an experiment, a large experiment from a global point of view. Overall, reform and opening is an unswerving policy for China, but we have to be cautious in the course of opening up. We have scored some good marks, but we have to be modest about it.

In June 1987, he proclaimed to some foreign guests, "Now I can let myself go to say that our decision to establish the special economic zones is not only correct but also successful. All the doubts about it have disappeared." This is Deng's historical assessment of, and conclusion on the special economic zones in line with the idea that practice is the sole criterion for testing truth.

Later, Jiang Zemin also pointed out:

> As we look at it now, our effort to run the special economic zones in those years played an important role in our reform and opening endeavor as a whole. The special economic zones were a nascent phenomenon in our socialist construction, a great pioneering undertaking, and something that had never happened in the past. Some people were full of hope for it, and some people doubted it, but under Comrade Deng Xiaoping's guidance, and through our

own efforts, we gradually clarified some major issues, such as the guideline for building these zones, their nature, function, status, role and management approaches. For nearly 30 years, the special economic zones have served as both windows and vanguards for the reform and opening policy. They have played a major role in leading the efforts toward opening up, institutional innovation, and industrial upgrading, and in spreading these efforts to the entire country. Practice has amply proved that the decision to create these zones is entirely correct.

Designing a Framework for Opening Up Coastal Regions

Following Deng's instruction to open some coastal port cities to the outside world and to carry out certain special economic zone policies there, the central authorities decided to call a meeting of provincial governors to make the arrangements. In March 1984, Vice Premier Gu Mu was given the mission to prepare for the meeting, and he began by going on a fact-finding tour of Tianjin and Dalian, which were on a list of the cities to be opened up. He went back to Beijing with the following ideas:

- First, the opening of the port cities should be closely combined with the technical transformation of local enterprises, that is, improvements to the quality of their products, technological levels and business practices.
- Second, these are old "centrally planned economy" cities that cannot offer a fertile investment environment anytime soon because they are way behind in infrastructure and urban development; some of them, however, could develop a "microclimate" for foreign investment by opening up small areas and equipping them with running water, electricity and telecommunications, roads and other facilities and good services. These areas could then become economic and technological development zones.
- Third, because an umbrella state policy will not work, given the idiosyncrasies of these cities, it is imperative to provide guidance and examine their opening-up plans on an individual basis.

- Fourth, more than anything else, local officials should be trained to enhance their awareness and refresh their understanding and perspectives.

The meeting took place in Zhongnanhai in Beijing on March 26, 1984, with Gu Mu and Hu Qili presiding. It was attended by the mayors of Shanghai and Tianjin and the governors of Shandong, Jiangsu, Zhejiang, Liaoning, Fujian, Guangdong and Guangxi, the leaders of some cities directly under provincial jurisdiction and of special economic zones. Responsible members from 40 or so departments of the State Council were also present. Gu Mu began the meeting by conveying Deng's February 24, 1984 remarks on the work of special economic zones and on opening up a number of coastal cities, including Shanghai, Tianjin, Dalian, Qingdao, Yantai, Ningbo, Wenzhou and Beihai. He asked participants to study and take in these remarks. After reviewing developments under the opening policy, he stressed

The central authorities convened a meeting of leaders of relevant provinces and municipalities to deliberate a proposal to further open up Dalian, Tianjin and 12 other seaboard habor cities to the outside world (March 26-April 6, 1984). Here, Deng was meeting with the participants at Zhongnanhai, where the meeting was held, April 6.

the need to resolutely carry out Deng's instructions and step up efforts to utilize foreign capital and bring in foreign technology. He urged everyone to be bolder in pursuing reforms and to adopt more liberal policies to motivate localities and enterprises to utilize foreign capital, import technology, transform old factories, upgrade traditional products and develop new products. The central authorities' decision to open up these cities, he stressed, could only be made to work with great resolve and enthusiasm, methodical approaches, proactive and pragmatic steps, and painstaking efforts, because it involved a wide spectrum of fields, was closely associated with state policies and could have a major international impact.

Addressing the questions raised by local leaders at the meeting, Gu Mu made the following points:

> First, no more special economic zones are to be established for the time being; second, local authorities should raise the needed funds from all quarters, rather than pin their hope on generous state appropriations; third, localities should proceed from reality and open gradually wider to the outside world while overcoming the bandwagon mentality; fourth, the special economic zones should meet Deng's requirements and assert themselves to become pace-setters for national economic growth; fifth, due importance should be attached to personnel training; and sixth, it is imperative to promote character-building and cultural development.

These instructions dispelled some people's misgivings about premature openness to the outside world and unbridled increases in the number of open cities.

During the 12-day meeting, the provincial leaders had animated and wide-ranging discussions about Deng's directives and Gu's speech. Everyone was in high spirits as they shared their personal understandings of Deng's instructions, talked about local plans, and offered suggestions to the central leadership. Because the meeting was held at Huairen Hall inside Zhongnanhai, the seat of the central government, it drew the attention of many top leaders, who often came by to listen and speak their minds during the discussions.

When the name "development zone" was discussed, the participants suggested that it be changed into "economic development zone." Then someone argued that the purpose of such a zone should not be limited to creating a "micro-environment" to procure foreign investment and speed up economic growth, but should also stress the introduction of advanced technology from abroad. Thus the term "economic and technological development zone" was unanimously accepted.

As to which coastal cities should be opened, a list had been drawn up during Deng's February 24 conversation with a number of central leaders. In the course of the meeting, however, Gu Xiulian, Governor of Jiangsu Province, rushed to the scene with a proposal that was approved by the State Council. As a result, two Jiangsu cities, Nantong and Lianyungang, were added to the list. Then the leaders of Guangdong and Fujian asked why the list did not include any coastal cities in their provinces. They were told that it was definitely not an oversight: the two provinces did not have cities on the list because they had already opened their gates to the outside world with state-mandated incentive policies and flexible steps. Finally, a compromise was reached on their protests, and Guangzhou and Zhanjiang of Guangdong Province, and Fuzhou of Fujian Province were added to the list. In the end, a total of 14 coastal port cities were slated to open up to the outside world.

During the photography session after the meeting was over, Deng told the participants, "The key to making the opening policy a success lies in employing people who know what they are doing. That is why we should work hard to train our cadres." The meeting was by far the most intensive and high-level of all the work conferences that had been held concerning the policy of opening up.

On April 23, after hearing a progress report from Gu Mu on the plans to open up the coastal cities, and on local leaders' responses to it, Chen Yun said that he was all for the decision and stressed the importance of summing up the experience as the work went along. A subsequent Politburo meeting discussed and endorsed the *Summary of the Discussion Meeting of Some Coastal Cities*, and transmitted it nationwide on May 4 in Central Document [1984] 13 with the note:

The implementation of the policy of opening up in this country during the historic period calls for progressive development. The coastal port cities must make the first step with a view to their fine locations, economic foundation and managerial and technological capabilities. While utilizing foreign capital, technology and markets, these cities should, as a priority, strive to transform old enterprises and launch a number of medium-sized and small projects that call for less investment, have quick capital turnover and yield fine returns. By doing so, they can quickly become a great deal stronger, and better position themselves to support the rest of the nation with their financial, material and human resources and to disseminate their experience in internal and foreign exchanges.

The *Summary* said:

The central authorities are opening up coastal port cities and urging the special economic zones to do a better job by giving them not money, but incentives in two categories:

Deng, Li Xiannian and other state leaders reading over newspaper coverage of special economic zones on April 6, 1984, right after meeting with participants of the meeting to deliberate opening up 14 seaboard cities to the outside world.

1. Low tax rates and a portion of the domestic market as an economic incentive to foreigners who invest or provide advanced technology; and
2. More autonomy for coastal port cities so that they may have more leeway in foreign economic activities. This policy calls for reshuffling the current economic administrative system. The relevant departments at the central and provincial levels should act on Comrade Deng Xiaoping's remarks and the spirit of the memorandum, formulate a series of procedural regulations, strengthen their leading bodies and staff and step up guidance and supervision to ensure the implementation of this policy. ... The Party Central Committee and the State Council entrust Comrade Gu Mu to supervise and monitor the implementation of this policy and coordinate or arbitrate any conflicts that may occur in this regard.

The *Summary* also set forth a number of other important policies. These included speeding up the use of foreign capital and introducing advanced technology; better managing the special economic zones and speeding up their development; extending the Xiamen Special Economic Zone to all of Xiamen Island; and developing and building up Hainan Island "without fail."

The *Summary* stressed the need to further open up the coastal port cities, to revitalize the cities, and local enterprises involved in international economic activities, by decontrolling certain policies and revamping some administrative systems, and to align foreign resources (including capital, materials, technology, expertise and personnel), plus the expansion of the Chinese share of the world market, closely with industrial restructuring, corporate technical transformation, and administrative reforms in these cities.

If all these endeavors would work, the *Summary* stated, economic growth would pick up speed, and regions, enterprises and people were bound to get rich more quickly. When the coastal cities and the four special economic zones are connected along the coast from north to south to form a frontline for the opening-up policy, they will inevitably spur on the development of their respective regions of the country and boost national economic construction by developing science and technology, disseminating management expertise, bringing prosperity to the home market, expanding foreign trade, transmitting economic information and cultivating and supplying competent professionals.

According to the *Summary*, the 14 coastal port cities to be opened further to the outside world were: Tianjin, Shanghai, Dalian, Qinhuangdao, Yantai, Qingdao, Lianyungang, Nantong, Ningbo, Wenzhou, Fuzhou, Guangzhou, Zhanjiang and Beihai.

The *Summary* prescribed ten policies for these cities:

1. Broadening their autonomy with regard to approving construction projects with foreign investment;
2. Increasing the foreign exchange quotas and loan grants at their own disposal;
3. Supporting them to use foreign capital and bring in the advanced technology necessary to transform old factories;
4. Granting certain preferential treatment to equity joint ventures, cooperative enterprises and wholly foreign-owned enterprises;
5. Setting up economic and technological development zones step by step;
6. Vigorously developing export processing with materials supplied by foreign partners;
7. Re-categorizing certain open cities;
8. Stepping up infrastructure construction;
9. Stepping up government guidance on the use of foreign capital; and
10. Urging these cities to become pace-setters in the reform effort.

The *Summary* stated that some of these cities might designate certain areas for establishing economic and technological development zones with well-defined boundaries. No efforts should be spared in these zones, it said, to bring in the advanced technologies badly needed in China, and to run "clusters of research institutes" in the form of joint ventures, cooperative firms, wholly foreign-owned enterprises or Sino-foreign cooperation. These zones should also promote cooperative production, research and design for developing new technology and up-market products; boost foreign exchange revenues through exports; provide the country with new materials and key components and accessories; and promote new technological processes, new technology and scientific management expertise. Some economic and technological development zones should also be developed into international transit trade centers. All these zones should have roughly the same decision-making power to endorse foreign-invested projects as the special economic zones.

Mayor Li Ruihuan and I represented Tianjin at this discussion meeting. We left the meeting feeling at once elated and inspired. The entire city of Tianjin took on a festive mood after we reported our findings and feelings to the municipal government and local officials. Everybody wanted to do their bit to carry out the central policies and stipulations for establishing the economic and technological development zones. After a hectic round of study and planning, we lost no time in preparing to set up the Tianjin Economic and Technological Development Zone, which we planned to locate on an expanse of abandoned salt pans and saline-alkali land on the beaches of the seaside Tanggu District.

Tianjin Harbor: Dysfunction Is the Mother of Invention

At the time a common problem confronting coastal port cities in their opening-up efforts was their lack of freight-handling capacities due to outdated infrastructure. In the beginning of the 1980s, freighter holdups and backlogs at these harbors were already troubling the State Council, even though the nation's import and export volume was rather small. In March 1981, for example, the nation's coastal harbors received an average of 340 foreign trade freighters a day, or 200 more than in the same month of 1980. However, some 90 of these ships were loading or unloading, while about 240 others were waiting to load or unload, and more than 2.5 million tons of cargo were stacked up on the docks, waiting to be shipped out. It became an annual routine for the State Council to issue a notice urging local governments to organize emergency operations to unload imported materials, speed up dispatches of export commodities, and do what they could to tackle the backlog problem. By 1984, backlogging at the harbors had grown to such an extent that it threatened to derail the opening-up initiative. Tianjin was one of the harbors most seriously bogged down by this problem.

In March 1983, the municipal government of Tianjin was regrouped. I was appointed Vice Mayor in charge of foreign relations, and my portfolio also included liaison work with the local harbor, customs and banks that were stationed in Tianjin but directly under the central government. One day, Mayor Li Ruihuan was chairing a meeting of members of the new leading body when his secretary came to say that Vice Premier Wan Li wanted to talk to him on the phone. When the phone call was over, the mayor returned to relate to us what was going on. "Comrade Wan Li asked me what we were doing. I told him we municipal leaders were discussing the division of responsibilities among us. He got very impatient, and told me that more than 100 freighters were being held up in our anchorage ground [in the sea near Tianjin], waiting to enter the harbor for unloading. 'How can you sit there holding an office meeting?!' the vice premier asked in disbelief."

When the mayor explained that the harbor was under the jurisdiction of the Ministry of Transport and Communications, not the municipality of Tianjin, the vice premier said, "You are the man I talk to now, since the harbor is located in Tianjin."

Mayor Li then said to me, "You are in charge of liaison with the harbor, but you are a newcomer. Let's go there together." He called off the meeting, and the two of us rushed off to the harbor. After spending some time investigating the situation we discovered some of what was holding up the harbor operations. The main problems were as follows.

First, there was a grave shortage of cargo handling capacity. The Tianjin Harbor, the history of which went back nearly 200 years, was a major international trading port for China and the marine gateway to Beijing. A support for the economic growth of Tianjin, it was also a major commodities distribution and maritime trading center for northeast, north and northwest China. The "New Harbor," so-called to distinguish it from the old inland Tianjin Harbor on the Haihe River, was built in the Bohai Bay in 1952. It was only after the inland harbor disappeared that the seaport was renamed Tianjin Harbor. It began with an annual cargo handling capacity of 740,000 tons, which reached 5.22 million tons in 1960, thanks to nine years of expansion efforts. In the early 1980s, it could handle 10 million tons of freight, but fell way short of the maritime shipping demand that was snowballing with the adoption of the opening-up policy. Serious traffic jams and backlogging became commonplace. One day, when the problems came to a head, 190-plus freighters were waiting to be unloaded at the anchorage ground, incurring, among other losses, a compensation fee of US$8,000 per day.

The second problem was an unwieldy administrative setup. Harbor affairs, highway and railway transportation, customs red tape, commodities inspection, animal and plant quarantine, health checkups, harbor supervision, shipping commissioning, cargo agency service, and whatnot – these are the links on the chain of a harbor's day-to-day operations. The loading and unloading processes could be adversely affected if any one of these links in the chain went awry. These links, controlled by different authorities, not surprisingly often fell out of sync, which was a major factor affecting efficiency.

The third issue was the disarray in harbor management. The root cause behind the harbor malfunctioning was the lack of effective incentives and restraints, stemming from the practice of "everyone eating from the same big pot" – no matter what their contribution to the work, or how well they performed their jobs. In other words, there was neither motivation nor pressure on the workers. Moreover, the harbor was asked to hand in all of its revenues and counted on the Ministry of Transport and Communications for maintenance and expansion outlay. A lack of government investment was another bottleneck in the development of the harbor.

To solve these problems, something had to be done with the harbor's administrative and operational systems. Tianjin Municipality proposed to the State Council that the harbor come under the dual leadership of central and local governments, with the local government mainly responsible, and that the harbor be allowed to sustain itself and to use its revenues to offset its expenses. Specifically, the proposal called for setting up a leading group and an office under the municipality to unify the administration of Tianjin Harbor, to coordinate loading and unloading operations, and to raise work efficiency. The proposal, if granted, would mean that the harbor would no longer hand in all its earnings, and the Ministry of Transport and Communications would stop investing in it, so that the harbor would be left to survive on its own and pay for its own development under a unified state plan. On the surface of this proposal, the harbor would seem to be getting the worse end of the deal, given that the harbor at the time was receiving more money from the ministry than it was delivering. As we saw it, however, it was well worth the financial "loss" to "buy" a better system. Under the proposal, the harbor and the district of Tanggu surrounding it would each stop minding their own affairs. Rather, the district could depend on the harbor to develop itself, while better serving the harbor. The proposal gained the support of Li Peng (then Vice Premier in charge of the national transportation network) during his inspection tour of Tianjin in November 1983.

On May 7, 1984, after nearly a year of feasibility studies and experiments, the central government officially endorsed our proposal on the Tianjin Harbor on a five-year, experimental basis. A major breakthrough in revamping the Chinese harbor administrative system was thus on the horizon. By the end of 1986, just a little more than two years after the proposal was endorsed, unexpected results were already emerging, at least in the following respects:

First, with loading and unloading operations better coordinated and the work force highly motivated, the harbor saw marked improvements in both work efficiency and economic returns. During the three years from 1984 to 1986, the harbor, on its own, raised more than 660 million yuan to invest in development, more than double the 270 million yuan the harbor had received from the state in the previous three years from 1981 to 1983. Acting on Mayor Li's instruction to "save a life before treating the disease," the harbor sped up loading and unloading by using the most sophisticated machines (bought for the grand sum of 200 million yuan) and by carrying out technical transformation.

Second, the district of Tanggu had come a long way in urban development, and had embarked on a road to prosperity. History offers proof that many big cities have grown up with the backing of harbors. Tianjin was no exception, having become a big metropolis largely on the strength of its inland river harbor. Due to institutional impediments, however, for a long time after its inauguration in 1952, the New Harbor did little to boost the development of

Tanggu District, which, in return, did little to help the harbor. While the harbor had to function like a society unto itself, the residential quarters of the Tanggu District dwindled to shanty towns. The administrative reshuffle brought the district and the harbor together in a relationship of mutual support. A new modern harbor city was born as a result.

Third, in 1984, just at the time when the Tanggu Economic and Technological Development Zone was established on land dotted with abandoned salt pans, one of China's first containerized docks came under construction at Tianjin Harbor. Unprecedented changes were taking place in both the harbor and Tanggu District, and a thriving harbor town was rising.

The results of institutional restructuring won recognition from all quarters. During his September 1985 tour of Tianjin, Vice Premier Wan Li was so happy about what he saw that he asked the central government to extend the experiment with the new system for another five years. Shortly afterward, the Ministry of Transport and Communications began promoting the experience of Tianjin Harbor, in an attempt to adapt the nation's harbor administrative system to the requirements of the opening policy. Practice later showed that those harbors that had transformed their management had all scored rapid development, and those that had not were still muddling along at a snail's pace.

Under a new, streamlined administration, Tianjin Harbor never slackened its progress in reforms. It went on to strip its government functions from business management and to readjust its management structure. To raise funds, the harbor launched itself on the capital market by turning its storage and transportation branch into a listed company and established an equity joint shipping company. After nearly 15 years of hard work, it has become a world-class harbor with digitalized container docks, a well-equipped bonded area and an export processing zone. The once bleak Tanggu District took on a new look and set the pace for the development of Tianjin's coastal areas.

It had taken Tianjin Harbor 22 years to raise its freight handling capacity from 740,000 tons (in 1952) to 10 million tons (in 1974). Under the reform and the opening policy, however, within only 14 years (from 1974 to 1988), that capacity exceeded 20 million tons. Five years later, the figure topped 30 million tons. Since then, the freight handling capacity of Tianjin Harbor has kept to an annual growth of 10 million tons, an achievement rarely experienced in China's coastal harbor development history. In 2001, Tianjin became the first harbor in north China to have handled more than 100 million tons of cargo in 12 months. In 2007, the harbor, with an annual freight handling capacity of 309 million tons, ranked fourth in the nation and sixth in the world. With its loading and unloading capacity of 7.1 million standard containers a year, it is among the top 20 of the world's busiest containerized harbors.

The opening of the 14 coastal cities and the establishment of the first batch of "economic and technological development zones" marked the beginning of the nation's all-round openness to the world. As Deng said at a Central Military Commission discussion meeting on November 1, 1984:

> We are doing two things. One is to open up to the outside economic world, and the other is to invigorate our home economy. The reforms are meant to invigorate the home economy, and invigorating the home economy means opening up on the home front. Both are part of the policy of opening up. Some of us are still not clear about what opening up is all about – they tend to mistake it for opening up to the Western world only. Actually our opening-up policy is three-dimensional. One dimension is to open up to the advanced Western countries to help bring in the foreign capital and technology we need. Another dimension of the policy is to open up to the former Soviet Union and other Eastern European countries. Even though our relationships with them are not the same as they used to be, we can still engage them in businesses and technological exchanges and partnerships. We can even let them join us in joint ventures and technology transfer projects – for example, they can do their share in our 156 technology transfer projects. A third dimension of our policy is to open up to other Third World countries – we can draw a lot from their specialties and strong points. That is why I say opening up to the outside world is not one-dimensional, but three-dimensional.

Those two ideas – that invigorating the domestic economy is equivalent to opening up the home front and that the opening-up policy is three-dimensional – are integral components of Deng Xiaoping Theory and have been major guidelines for the nation's reform and opening. It is true that we learned many aspects of reform through the opening-up process, but we also feel that our day-to-day work simply pressured or "squeezed" steps toward reform out of us. All the while, reform has paved the way for the opening-up policy and has promoted it. China, with Deng's guidance, has been able to adopt the opening-up policy and a series of steps to keep up with economic globalization and the changing Chinese reality, and to gradually bring about an all-round openness that has spread from the coastal regions to the hinterland.

Development Zones Hold Great Promise

On January 4, 1985, Deng summoned Gu Mu for a conversation. "I want to talk to you about Ningbo," he told the vice premier, "but before that, I want you to tell me about everything." The vice premier informed him of the last eight months' progress surrounding the opening up of the 14 coastal port cities. Satisfied with what he heard, Deng said, "It looks like these cities hold great promise."

In August 1986, Deng arrived in Tianjian for an inspection tour. On the evening of August 19, he said to Mayor Li Ruihuan, "During this visit I want to see your development zone and the sights of your city. I also want to take a look at the harbor."

Visiting Tianjin Harbor on the morning of August 21, Deng learned that the harbor had grown vastly under the dual leadership of the Ministry of Transport and Communications and the Tianjin Municipality (with the latter bearing the greater share of responsibility), and through a series of steps toward reform, including the policy of "allowing the harbor to cover its own expenses and to feed itself," the initiatives of both central and local authorities were brought into full play. Over the last two years and more, the harbor's economic returns had risen by 60 percent and its cargo handling capacity by 22 percent, and the longstanding problem of freighter congestion had been solved, to the satisfaction of foreign businesses. At this Deng said with a sigh:

It's the same group of people, with the same piece of land, but reforms have made such a difference in efficiency since they began. All this has happened for the simple reason that we have given them some power, not the least of which is the power to use human resources.

This was the second time Deng had mentioned reforms during the tour. On a previous occasion, when inspecting Tianjin's Middle Ring Road, he had said:

It's true, isn't it, that the reason you finished building this road so quickly was because you used the new contract system. We must carry out reforms and adopt the contract system – so we have a responsibility system in which work is contracted out section by section and from one level to another.

That philosophical remark struck a deep chord with all those who heard it. It reminded me of the case of a 60-kilometer-long highway that was being built a few years earlier to disperse

▲ Deng (*left*) took a look at the newly built Central Ring Road in Tianjin in the company of Li Ruihuan (*right*), August 20, 1986.

◄ Deng (*second from left*) inspecting the container berth of Tianjin Harbor along with Li Ruihuan (*first left*) and the author (*behind*), August 1986.

traffic from the harbor at Tanggu to downtown Tianjin. With only 14 kilometers to go before completion, construction slowed to a standstill, because the building team that had been formed for this project was biding its time for the next job to come along. If they finished the highway, the workers would be idle and the team would make no money. A few years had passed, but the stalemate remained. All the while, traffic in the harbor kept worsening. The harbor people were chagrined, but there was nothing they could do about it. The problem was solved only after Vice Premier Wan Li ordered the completion of the highway within three months. Procrastination of this sort would have been unimaginable in the subsequent years of reform and opening.

On the same day as the harbor tour, Deng toured the Tianjin Economic and Technological Development Zone in high spirits. He heard a report from the zone's administrative board, and met with the foreign partners of some local joint ventures. With the establishment of the 33-square-kilometer zone on December 6, 1984, the once bleak and desolate salt marshland was no more. In less than two years, the first phase of construction was well under way in an area of 4.2 square kilometers – three square kilometers for the industrial zone and 1.2 square kilometers for residential quarters. Roads, running water and electricity facilities were being built in an orderly fashion, factory buildings were springing up one after another, and the entire construction site was bustling with activity. In early 1986, the catchphrase for the builders had been "make things convenient for investors and help them make money," but in the middle of the year, it was switched to "simulate an ideal international investment environment." Every construction project at the site shifted up a gear as a result. "With your instructions in mind, we worked hard and got off to a good start," the leader of the administrative board told Deng. "With a government loan of 370 million yuan, we focus our development plan on one piece of land at a time. Once we start to make money out of it we move on to the next piece of land. We also start inviting foreign investors when construction is still going on, just to get development rolling." The zone had signed 35 contracts with investors from 11 countries and regions, he reported, and 20 factories were to start production before the end of that year.

Delighted with the zone's fast accomplishments, Deng told his hosts, "You've done a great job with the Tianjian Development Zone. Now that you have established a brand name for yourselves and improved your investment environment, foreigners will feel comfortable and confident about coming to invest."

Then he told the foreigners on the scene, "We still want to give a free hand to people in their opening-up efforts. People won't be motivated unless they are left free to do what they want to do. There is no way at this point for us to call it quits." Committing his writing brush to paper, he wrote the inscription: "The development zone holds great promise." This line gave expression to his convictions about the opening policy and the economic and technological zones, and embodied his earnest hope for the builders. Under his solicitous guidance, the Tianjin Economic and Technological Development Zone became a pace-setter in national economic growth through the years.

3

Bringing in Advanced
Technology and Equipment

China was 15 to 20 years behind advanced world levels in science and technology by the time the Cultural Revolution collapsed, and the gap was even wider in some specific fields. When we came to the realization that backwardness in science and technology was a major hindrance to economic development, we knew we must draw on advanced technology throughout the world to boost our economy. We stood no chance of catching up with the advanced world level, let alone surpassing it, if we turned a blind eye to the global trends and level in science and technology development.

At the time, expectations were running high throughout the country for the achievements of economic development and the Four Modernizations. The central leadership reached the consensus that we should accelerate economic development by tapping all promising factors, including learning and incorporating advanced foreign technology and equipment. Back in 1975, when Deng was running the day-to-day operations of the Party Central Committee and the State Council, he was strongly behind importing new technology and equipment that were pivotal to the development of certain fields, and declared it a cardinal government policy to do so.

Uninterrupted Learning Is the Key to Progress

A nation's greatness lies in its readiness and ability to learn from other nations' advanced cultures and technologies. There is no limit to the development of science and technology; if you stop making progress, you will definitely start to slip back into mediocrity. The adoption of ancient China's "Four Inventions" (the compass, paper, printmaking and gunpowder) by the Western countries was a case in point. When the Western imperialists bombed open our nation's doors 150 years ago with the gunpowder our ancestors had invented, Wei Yuan (1794-1857), a prominent Qing-Dynasty thinker, famously said we should "learn what the foreigners are good at to beat them." He thus became the first Chinese person credited with the idea of learning and incorporating advanced foreign technology.

Science and technology advanced a long way over the course of the 20th century throughout the world. Statistics indicate that technological progress accounted for 5 to 20 percent of economic growth in the early period of that century, but the figure grew to 50 percent in the mid-20th century and 60 to 80 percent in the 1980s. After World War II, the United States enlisted talent from all over the world and brought in advanced technology, thereby scaling the apex of world technology. The Soviet Union recruited 20,000 economists and technicians from all corners of the globe in 1932; people in the West believed this was why the Soviets were able to obtain, in just three years' time, the technology that other countries had taken 30 years to develop. In the 30-year span between 1950 and 1979, Japan, to accomplish its takeoff, purchased 33,800 foreign technologies to the tune of US$10.1 billion. It was estimated that it would have taken Japan more than 100 years and US$200 billion to invent these technologies and put them to industrial use.

The Chinese Communist Party has advocated learning and introducing advanced foreign technology ever since Mao took over the helm. In the early days of the People's Republic, despite the boycotts imposed by the West, the country fulfilled its First Five-Year Plan for socioeconomic development by importing some 400 technological projects from Eastern Europe, with 156 major ones from the Soviet Union alone. During that period, we built three iron and steel works in Anshan, Wuhan and Baotou, three chemical industrial bases in Jilin, Lanzhou and Taiyuan and a series of mainstay machine-building factories such as the First Auto Works of Changchun, the Measuring and Cutting Tools Factory of Harbin, the First Machine Tools Works of Shenyang and the Tractor Plant of Luoyang. These projects enabled China to dramatically narrow the gap between its former technology level and the advanced level of the industrialized world and to lay the groundwork for industrialization in less than a decade.

In 1960, China's relationship with the Soviet Union soured, and the nation turned to the West for technology imports. The purchase of a Japanese vinylon plant in 1962 was followed by imports of complete sets of equipment from Britain, the United States, West Germany, Austria, Sweden, Italy and Holland. This helped fill in some of the country's technological blanks.

By the time China was restored to its lawful seat in the United Nations in 1971, and normalized diplomatic relations with the United States and Japan, the outside world had become a lot friendlier. Mao, Zhou Enlai and other veteran top leaders seized the opportunity to purchase large chemical fiber and fertilizer plants from the West to help clothe and feed the population.

At the time, the developed countries were pushing exports at low prices to beat economic woes at home. In January 1972, acting on Premier Zhou's instruction, Yu Qiuli, Minister of the State Planning Commission, called a meeting of the Ministry of Light Industry and the Ministry of Foreign Trade to discuss how to seize the opportunity to bring in complete sets of technology and equipment for the production of chemical fibers and chemical fertilizers, which were in big demand in the nation. On January 22, Li Xiannian, Hua Guofeng and Yu Qiuli submitted to the premier the State Planning Commission's report on the matter (*Report on the Import of Complete Sets of Technology and Equipment for the Production of Chemical Fibers and Fertilizers*). The report called for importing four chemical fiber plants and two synthetic ammonia installations from France and Japan. The four plants, estimated to cost US$270 million, were to be installed in Sichuan, Liaoning, Shanghai and Tianjin for a combined annual production capacity of 240,000 tons of synthetic fiber (equivalent to 250 million kilograms of cotton, enough to weave 1.33 billion meters of cloth). The two synthetic ammonia installations, each with an annual output of 300,000 tons, were to be built in Sichuan and the city of Daqing in Liaoning. On February 5, the premier approved the *Report* and sent it to Mao for review. Two days later, Li Xiannian returned it to Yu Qiuli, Qian Zhiguang and Bai Xiangguo for official implementation. After this precedent, the metallurgical, machine-building, telecommunications, civil aviation, railway and other departments sent in requests for importing foreign technology and equipment, including continuous 1.7-meter-wide steel plate rolling mills and chemical installations.

Encouraged by smooth progress in technology and equipment importation, the State Planning Commission submitted another wish list to Li Xiannian, Ji Dengkui, Hua Guofeng and Zhou Enlai. The *Report on Increasing Equipment Imports and Extending Foreign Economic Exchanges* (of January 2, 1973) included a shopping list of large installations and equipment in 26 categories in support of agriculture, infrastructure construction, basic industries and the manufacturing industry. The items on this list, to be purchased within three to five years, included 13 chemical fertilizer plants, four synthetic fiber installations, three petrochemical plants, ten hydrocarbon mills, 43 composite coal mining machine sets, and three power-generating plants. All these would cost a total of US$430 million, hence the name "Project 43."* Deng was very much concerned with these projects. In June 1973, shortly after his previous comeback to power, he went on an inspection tour of the Jinshan General Petrochemical Works, then under construction in Shanghai. On a rainy summer day two years later, he visited Jinshan for a second time after seeing off some foreign visitors in Shanghai. While there, he inquired about the progress of the nine imported installations one by one, what they were intended for, where they had come from, and how much foreign exchange had been spent on them. Seeing that some of the giant installations stood as tall as a three- to four-story building, he wondered how they had been transported to the site. The construction leader told him that, in the absence of large trucks, the veteran bamboo-raft workers of the Shanghai Municipal Transportation Bureau had

---

* In the Chinese language number system, the number "430 million" can be referred to as 43 "one hundred ten thousands."

mapped out a clever plan to ship the assortment of huge tanks and derricks from a dock on the Huangpu River to the site by way of the Yangtze River. An amazed Deng was profuse in his praise of the workers. Back in Beijing, he sent Gu Mu to call an on-the-spot meeting at Jinshan to educate all those responsible for "Project 43." That action unleashed a wave of massive technology and equipment imports in the nation.

The effort, in the waning years of the Cultural Revolution, to bring in advanced foreign technology and equipment, presented a valuable opportunity for China to learn from the outside world, laid the foundation for building an industrial and economic system, and set the stage for the birth of the opening-up policy.

Braving Interference to Make Foreign Things Serve China

The implementation of "Project 43" met with interference and sabotage by the Gang of Four and their local followers. As Deng pointed out, the Gang did their damage to the economy and other fields of endeavor by "partially understanding" Mao's ideas and policies and quoting him out of context. This was exactly what happened during the early stage of construction of the Second Auto Works, where I was working as a factory director. Under the central leadership headed by Deng, however, we braved the Gang's interference, and combined self-reliance with the introduction of foreign technology, which allowed us to move ahead at a faster pace with our plant construction work.

Second Auto Works Pools Resources and Brings in Foreign Technology

The Second Auto Works was a strategic project designated by Mao and the central leadership to develop and produce automobiles for civilian and military purposes, with a premium on military vehicles. Mao was personally concerned with the progress of the factory, one of the "Third-Line Defense Projects" being built in the hinterland and away from the vulnerable coastal and border provinces, in a campaign to "prepare against war, against famine and serve the people." The factory came under construction in 1969 and began batch production in 1975, a period that coincided with the most intense stage in the struggle against the Gang of Four.

Self-reliance was the major principle for building the Second Auto Works, as the authorities pooled what good equipment and technology the nation could offer to buoy it up.

The principle was a sensible one. The Gang, however, carried it to extremes. First, they demanded that the auto plant be built entirely with domestic resources – doing it otherwise would mean "worshiping foreign things and fawning over foreigners," a "comprador philosophy" or even "treason." The result was that although over 90 percent of the technology and equipment employed on the project were domestically developed, the lack of certain key elements made it impossible for the Second Auto Works to start normal production. We were forced to make do with hastily trial-produced home equipment. For instance, the engine, which is to a vehicle what the heart is to a human being, was rushed into batch production even before its design had been improved. As director of the engine factory of the Second Auto Works, I had my hands full just dealing with quality problems on a daily basis.

Second, the Gang refused to follow normal ways of doing things. Before the overall design was completed, they wanted the builders to draw the blueprints, install the equipment, build the factory, and start production all at once. When the factory buildings were still under construction, they asked us to research and develop new products in makeshift reed-mat shacks. While the vehicle was still being trial produced, they instructed us to put together a model and send it to Wuhan for display amidst pomp and pageantry. Since this was a "political task of paramount importance," we were told to focus our daily work on its fulfillment. As one of the side effects of all the rush, the construction work on the auto plant was seriously delayed.

Third, the Gang did all they could to make things difficult for the builders. They forbade the use of bricks in factory buildings, demanding that rammed-earth walls be erected instead. They ruled that heavy-duty rolled steel was too thick for load-bearing roof structures and should be replaced with lighter materials. Under the pretext of fostering "affinity" between workers and the farmers living nearby, they had us build un-partitioned, open latrines rather than flush toilets in the factory, which drew local folks to the workshops and dormitories every day to collect night soil for manure for the fields. Old-fashioned latrines represented Marxism, they felt, whereas toilets with modern sanitation facilities symbolized the reactionary bourgeoisie. They even forbade building factory walls, in the belief that such walls would only alienate the workers from their peasant brothers. Thus stray cattle and donkeys became an everyday spectacle on the construction site, and thefts of appliances and materials were a common occurrence.

Telephone service was another headache in those days. While the world had entered the age of coded telecommunications, all we had in China were telephones with hand-cranked generators (the type the Empress Dowager Cixi was using in the early 20th century), or step-by-step or crossbar telephones. It happened that a factory in Shaanxi Province had just developed a kind of coded telephone. The Second Auto Works was the first in the nation to use it on a trial basis. The telephone service, however, often got the phone numbers mixed up, so that a call meant for Mr. Zhang was often linked to Mr. Li. With all the mishaps, we did not feel we were building a modern factory at all.

These obstacles made the going increasingly tough for us. Factory leaders, engineers and workers often came under fire for openly challenging the wrongdoings under the Gang's misguidance.

In July 1973, we were at our wit's end as to how to go on with our construction work. We were compelled to report directly to the central authorities, to say that if things were allowed to go unchecked like this, the Second Auto Works would have no good future, and we could let the entire nation down. On July 19, Vice Premier Li Xiannian held a hearing on the auto plant in Zhongnanhai in Beijing. I was one of those who attended the meeting to voice our concerns. Addressing the hearing, the vice premier affirmed the builders' hard-working spirit. He pointed out that while it was a good idea to pool the nation's resources for the construction of the auto plant, but it was absolutely wrong to carry the idea to extremes. According to the law of dialectics, he said, if you overdo something, you will achieve the opposite of your aim. Speaking of the toilets, the vice premier commented that in his long revolutionary career he had never heard of a trivial issue like that being blown up to such political proportions. Joking about the telephone service, he said, "What would happen to me if a phone call meant for Mao connected me to Chiang Kai-shek?"

During the hearing, Li summoned the Minister of Post and Telecommunications, asking him to solve the telephone problem within three months. As a result, the crossbar telephone service was brought back to our factory. Li urged us to solve product quality problems, demanding that mistakes be corrected without delay. That would involve solving key technical problems, bringing all substandard products up to standard, phasing out all the appliances that did not work, and rebuilding all the factory buildings that could not be used. He went on to say that we should import the equipment that we could not make by ourselves, and that we should invite foreign experts to help solve those product quality problems that we were not capable of solving. We were all touched by the vice premier's bold attitude and pragmatic approach.

This Beijing hearing, at which solutions were found to a number of irritating problems, became a turning point in the annals of the Second Auto Works. It was with Vice Premier Li's strong encouragement that our factory began bringing in advanced technology from foreign countries.

My colleagues were so happy about the outcome of the hearing that when the meeting was drawing to an end, they asked me to do them a favor. Knowing that I was an old acquaintance of Wang Shuming, the State Council Chief Adjutant on Duty, they wanted me to ask him for permission to take in a movie in Zhongnanhai. Not wanting to disappoint my colleagues, I emboldened myself and went directly to Vice Premier Li with the request. To my pleasant surprise, he said, "Why not? You may have supper here too, then you can go to the cinema after you have finished eating."

Later, the central leadership sent Gu Mu to our factory to help speed things up. In 1975, after Deng took charge of the routine work of the Party Central Committee and the State Council, he began setting things right and restoring order to the nation. Tangible results were achieved before long. The construction of our factory started anew in the scientific and practical fashion advocated by Deng. With considerable effort, we overcame the arrogance of the Gang's cohorts, who were out to spoil things, and began systematically to set our work on track.

First, we restored the workshop for the production of power takeoff gearboxes. This kind of gearbox is an essential component in a cross-country vehicle, as it allows for four-wheel drive and can also deactivate the four-wheel drive by applying power to the two rear wheels. The two-wheel drive does the job under normal circumstances, but the four-wheel drive must be used when the vehicle is moving along rugged roads, in the desert or under other harsh road conditions. The early models of military vehicles made in our country were without the power takeoff gearbox. That was why the auto works' initial designs did not involve a gearbox-making workshop, and the progress of the factory was held up as a result. When the decision was made to restore the workshop, we took a scientific approach that enabled us to complete the construction of a quality workshop in 56 days – a record construction speed. The workshop is still in use today.

Second, we remedied the drawbacks in the engine design. With no mature products available at home, we had to make do with a model trial produced by the First Auto Works. But problems occurred in our newly assembled vehicles, such as torn cylinder interlayers, worn tappets, pistons pulling at the cylinders, wheel break lock-ups, and gasket combustion. We worked out some solutions but the engines we had built still left a lot to be desired. Later, with government approval, we turned to the Ricardo Company – a world-leading British provider of engineering solutions and strategic consulting to automotive and other industries – for technical advice. Through repeated consultations, the China National Technical Import and Export Corporation entered into an agreement with Ricardo in November 1977. Under the agreement, Ricardo tested and studied the samples we had sent them, and raised scores of questions. Then a contract on improving the engine was concluded between the two parties, with the Chinese side demanding that the improved model be viable and durable enough to pass a 1,200-hour bench test. The British side said that it could guarantee 2,000-hour durability on the improved model, a promise that was duly delivered.

Taking advantage of the opportunity, we sent a group of engineers to join the Ricardo engineers in experimenting with, testing and improving the engine. These people returned from Britain with enough expertise to design China's own engines.

That experience with Ricardo and the British auto industry deeply impressed our engineers in a number of ways: 1) Whenever Ricardo designed components and assemblages, they did it based on accurate calculations on the computer. My colleagues remembered that, after calculating the specifications of the piston we had sent them, they decided that the cylinder interlayer was too thin, a decision that tallied with the degree of wear and tear on the interlayers in our Chinese model. 2) Whenever Ricardo finished designing a mono-cylinder engine, they would improve on it repeatedly before applying it to multi-cylinder engines. 3) British auto-makers offered excellent, speedy after-sale service, and saw to it that the accessories were delivered on demand within 24 hours inside the country or within a week anywhere in the world. It was also discovered that new cars in Britain had to have their marketing prospects assessed by experienced accountants, and only those models that were certain of a profit could be commissioned for batch production.

Third, we were able to produce standard-quality automobiles by combining imported advanced foreign equipment with reliable, domestically produced equipment. None of these imports were dispensable, even though they made up only a small percentage of our production line. We could not turn out flawless vehicles if any part of the equipment was flawed. The sophisticated equipment, purchased with a government allocation of US$450 million, played no small part in ensuring the smooth operation of the Second Auto Works.

Those of us working at the grassroots level wholeheartedly supported and deeply appreciated Deng for what he accomplished in returning the country to normalcy during those precarious years. Had it not been for his leadership over the rectification effort, the nation could have gone astray once more, and the Second Auto Works would not have become the giant company it is today. Even today, however, there are still people who pit self-reliance against technology imports, champion

100-percent domestic products, and find the mere mention of technology imports intolerable. Remnants of ossified ways of thinking and doing things can still be seen today. As early as 1975, Deng said, "Countries are attaching a lot of importance to the introduction of new technologies and advanced equipment. Take apart one of their products, and you will see that many components were made in foreign countries." If 99 percent of the components required are available at home, we can come up with a perfect product by making up for the 1 percent deficiency with imports. If someone insists on 100-percent domestic production, the missing 1 percent could lead to total production failure. There is no lack of bitter lessons in this context.

Almost all the contracts under "Project 43" were signed in 1973. Toward the beginning of the following year, the Gang of Four called a mass meeting to whip up a campaign to "criticize Lin Biao and Confucius." While nominally a rally against the late, disgraced Lin Biao and Confucian thinking, it also went further to criticize the "modern-day Confucian surnamed Zhou," "No. 1 Inner-Party Confucian," "Lord Zhou" and "Prime Minister" – all barbs against Premier Zhou Enlai and those of his policies that could potentially undermine the legacy of the Cultural Revolution.

As if all this was not enough, Jiang Qing went so far as to instigate the "Crystal Snails Incident" and the "Fengqing Freighter Incident," and denounced the importation of a chemical fertilizer plant for the Daqing Chemical Factory. The nation's plan to import complete sets of technology and equipment came to a standstill as a result of her Gang's rampage.

The Crystal Snails Incident

The Crystal Snails Incident, which revolved around the importation of color television picture tubes from the United States, was one peculiar episode in the string of attempts by Jiang Qing to thwart progress in the name of Mao. At the time, China was developing color television sets, but was having technical problems with picture tubes. The Fourth Ministry of Machine-Building Industry sent a delegation of corporate managers from Xianyang and other places on a tour of the United States toward the end of 1973, with the intention of importing a color television kinescope production line from Corning Incorporated, a leading glass tube manufacturer. Toward the end of the tour, the American corporation gave each delegation member a crystal snail, made by Corning, as a souvenir. When she got word of it, Jiang Qing went berserk. Speaking at a meeting of the Fourth Ministry of Machine-Building Industry, she said that the Americans were using the gift to "call us names, insult us and imply that we are moving at a snail's pace." She also said that importing Corning's production line would be tantamount to "succumbing to the pressure of the imperialists" and "worshiping foreign things and currying favor upon a foreign country." She went on to accuse the State Council of committing "treason" and following a "slavish comprador philosophy." She demanded that the Ministry return the crystal snails to the US Liaison Office in Beijing and lodge a protest against it. "We cannot accept the production line from the United States," she said.

Reacting to Jiang Qing's outburst, Premier Zhou had the Chinese Liaison Office in Washington make a thorough investigation of the incident and the American customs and habits concerning the snail. The liaison office came back with the information that the Americans use the crystal snail as a gift because it is a token of happiness and auspiciousness, and reported to the premier that Corning Incorporated harbored no ill will at all when it presented the souvenirs to its Chinese guests. With this, the Political Bureau revoked Jiang's speech. However, the damage had already been done by then. In the aftermath of the "Crystal Snails Incident," the import of the color TV kinescope production line was delayed for years, causing a ripple effect on the progress of other technology import projects.

The Fengqing Freighter Incident

In 1964, with Chairman Mao's consent, Premiere Zhou issued the instruction to build and buy ships to boost the nation's maritime shipping industry. In 1970, the premier ordered that the nation should, within a few years' time, end its heavy reliance on chartered foreign freighters and begin building its own ships. "Only when and where the domestic shipbuilding capacity falls short of the demand can we buy some ships from other countries," the premier said, "so that our country's shipping industry can always keep the initiative in its own hands." The freighter Fengqing was one of nine 10,000-tonners built by the Shanghai Jiangnan Shipyard for the Shanghai Oceangoing Shipping Company under the Ministry of Transport and Communications.

A light-duty shipping test conducted shortly after the freighter's completion toward the end of 1973 revealed a degree of abrasive wear on the first cylinder of the main diesel engine. The Oceangoing Shipping Bureau of the Ministry of Transport and Communications, ruling that this degree of engine wear was an indication that the freighter was not up to the design standard, instructed the Shanghai Oceangoing Shipping Company to limit the Fengqing to short shipping missions as a precaution. Perturbed by the ruling, the authorities of Shanghai under the control of the Gang of Four called a public meeting on March 22, 1974 to denounce the shipping company for "worshiping foreign things and toadying to foreign countries." Under the Gang's instigation, some Jiangnan Shipyard workers and Fengqing crew members put up the slogan in a wall poster, "We need revolution! The freighter Fengqing needs long voyages!" On May 4, ignoring the ministry's warning, the freighter set off from Shanghai on a maiden voyage to Romania. The ministry had no alternative but to dispatch Li Guotang and Gu Wenguang to help ensure safety on the voyage. After the Fengqing returned safely to Shanghai on September 30, the local newspapers *Wenhui Daily* and *Liberation Daily* ran articles to take the ministry to task, using the success of the freighter's voyage as a pretext. The local authorities even detained Li and Gu as targets for public denunciation, and threatened to ferret out the two men's behind-the-scenes backers.

Not to be outdone by her Shanghai co-conspirators, Jiang Qing took the opportunity to charge the Ministry of Transport and Communications and the State Council with sheltering "slavish compradors." She said, "Now we are certain there are a handful of people in the Ministry of Transport and Communications who worship foreign things and curry favor upon foreign countries, people who are guilty of treason. They are exercising dictatorship over us with their bourgeois ideas." The real targets of her invective were none other than Premier Zhou Enlai and Deng Xiaoping. During an October 17 Politburo meeting, she challenged Deng to clarify his stand on the Fengqing issue, only to meet with a resounding rejection. Afterward, she spread the rumor that Deng, after being rendered speechless by her questioning, walked away from the meeting before anyone could stop him.

At the time, Mao was staying in Changsha in Hunan Province. Unbeknownst to Zhou and the other Politburo members, Jiang Qing had sent Gang member Wang Hongwen to see Mao to speak ill of Zhou and Deng. Wang told Mao that at the recent Politburo meeting, Jiang and Deng had fallen out with each other over the Fengqing. "It seems that Deng was sticking to his idea that it is better to buy ships than to build them on our own, and still better to rent ships than to buy them," he told the chairman. Mao scolded Wang for stabbing people in the back rather than talking face-to-face, and warned him not to hang around with Jiang any more.

When word about the conversation between Mao and Wang reached Zhou, who was hospitalized at the time, he summoned Ji Dengkui, Hua Guofeng, Li Xiannian and Deng Xiaoping to his bedside to inquire about the Politburo meeting and the Fengqing incident. He then asked someone to pass the message to Mao that, according to some of those who had attended the meeting, Deng had not walked out on her, as Jiang Qing had charged, but left the meeting on the advice of Li Xiannian. After Deng had left the meeting, so the message went, Zhang Chunqiao said he had anticipated that Deng would make a scene under the circumstances, and Jiang chimed in, saying that she had challenged Deng on purpose. It was thus evident that the Gang's offensive outburst at Deng during the meeting was premeditated. In response to Zhou's message, Mao reassured him of his backing for Deng. The farcical Fengqing Incident thus came to an end.

However, the Gang continued to sling mud at Deng for his insistence on the benefits of technology and equipment imports and compensation trade. In February 1970, during a meeting of provincial governors, Zhang Chunqiao, in conversation with Ma Tianshui, a leader of Shanghai and Gang cohort, maligned Deng as a member of the "comprador bourgeoisie" and, using Deng's approval of the import of ethylene-cracking installations and export of crude oil as pretexts, charged him with "pursuing revisionism at home and capitulationism abroad." Addressing an unauthorized conference of 12 provinces and autonomous regions on March 2, Jiang Qing equated sales of crude oil, coal and cotton to Western countries with "traitor's behavior," and once again dragged up the Fengqing Incident as an excuse to brand Deng an "agent of international capitalists." In his speeches on April 25 and May 24, Yao Wenyuan, another Gang member, alleged that exporting crude oil and coal and import technological installations was tantamount to "shifting the oil crisis from capitalist countries" to China and "surrendering to imperialism," "wholesale treachery" and a "policy to colonizing China." The Gang also acted up at other Politburo meetings to pour more scorn on Deng.

When the Political Bureau met on March 16 and June 25 respectively to hear a State Planning Commission report on industrial production and the execution of the national economic plan, Jiang and company once again vilified crude oil exports and the importation of chemical fertilizer and chemical fiber production installations as behaviors of "foreigners' flunkeys, quislings and renegades." "There is a mob of quislings in the Ministry of Foreign Trade," they said, adding, "There are also members of the bourgeoisie and comprador bourgeoisie in the Political Bureau." As if all this calumny were not enough, she let herself go further. "You are infatuated with foreign things and given to licking the boots of foreigners," she said cruelly, referring to her political opponents. "That's why you've bought so much garbage from them. Who knows how much the Lockheed Corporation has paid you!" At one point, the Gang also claimed that the establishment of a coal-exporting center was equivalent to ceding a piece of Chinese territory to foreign countries.

When a national planning conference was held at Beijing's Jingxi Hotel in July 1976, Wang Hongwen went there on four occasions to prompt his followers from Shanghai to raise difficult questions before the State Council. "We have to be relentless when it comes to condemning slavish comprador philosophy and foreign worship and cracking down on sham foreigners," he said.

Defying the obstructions, pressures, and excesses of the Cultural Revolution, the justice-upholding leaders and masses of people waged a relentless struggle against the Gang. Under the circumstances, they managed to import a number of major technological projects under the "Project 43" framework. Progress in this regard was particularly pronounced during the 1973 to 1977 period, when Zhou and Deng were presiding over the State Council, as the nation brought in a total of 250 packages of technology and equipment to the tune of US$4 billion. However, the Gang's sabotage did lead to the slashing of some major strategic imports, and the nation was robbed of a golden chance to speed up development much sooner. Fifteen years later, Deng recalled of that period of adversity with emotion:

> It won't do to shut the country off from the outside world. I remember arguing with the Gang of Four on the Fengqing Incident during the Cultural Revolution. It was just a 10,000-tonner. Now that we have opened up to the outside world, we are building ships with 100,000- or even 200,000-ton capacities. Without the opening-up policy, we might still have been building cars with hammers. Things today are so different from what they used to be. It is an essential change.

Boosting Technology Importation Becomes a Major State Policy

After Deng returned to power for the second time in his official career in 1973, he assisted Premier Zhou in orchestrating the nation's day-to-day work. In 1975, he began chairing the Party Central Committee and the State Council. In January 1975, he followed Mao's instruction and consolidated the army. Summarizing past and present experience, he sorted through the complicated aftermath of the Cultural Revolution and began setting things right nationwide. The thrust of his effort, however, was always on repudiating ultra-leftist mistakes.

On March 8, 1975, Deng told Ye Fei, Minister of Transport and Communications, "I am busy with priority areas such as railways, the iron and steel, coal mining and defense industries, and education. But as far as the rectification work on transport and communications is concerned, you'd better not wait and let a good opportunity slip through your fingers. Now that the principle for rectification has been set, you have a free hand to carry it out." Before long, he set about reorganizing and transforming industry and agriculture, commerce, culture and education, and science and technology.

During a State Council meeting to deliberate over the *Report on Issues Concerning Accelerating Industrial Development* on August 18, 1975, Deng stated that it was an essential state policy to bring in advanced foreign technology. He issued seven instructions, the second of which encapsulated the strategy:

> It is imperative to introduce new technology and equipment and expand imports and exports. We may consider signing long-term contracts with countries on buying their coal mining technology and equipment, and compensate them with coal. This is going to be a major policy for us. In short, we have to export more goods in return for some high-grade, precision and advanced technology and equipment, so that we can speed up the transformation of our industrial technology and raise labor productivity.

Thus he not only set the essential policy but also initiated the new idea of using compensation trade to jumpstart the effort to bring in advanced technology and equipment from outside the country. Due to the Gang's obstructions and sabotage, however, this brilliant idea was shelved shortly afterward.

It was not until Deng accomplished his comeback to power in July 1977 that he was able to promote technology imports with justification from a policy and political point of view. On September 14, he said while meeting some Japanese visitors:

> It is both natural and necessary for us to engage in international exchanges. The Gang of Four distorted Chairman Mao Zedong's instruction on self-reliance and did a stupid thing by condemning as "slavish comprador philosophy" some of the world's most sophisticated achievements. Every advanced achievement is a result of the concerted effort of all humanity. This is common sense even for the bourgeoisie, who are ready to assimilate whatever things are advanced in the world. You Japanese are a case in point. Self-reliance stresses the importance of relying on one's own effort and resources, but on no account should we exclude the advanced fruits in the world.

On September 29, when he joined Deng Yingchao in a meeting with British-Chinese writer Han Suyin, he pointed out:

We Chinese are intelligent. Taking this fact into consideration, we can be hopeful if we can also refrain from shutting ourselves up behind closed doors, can take as our starting point the most advanced scientific research results, make foreign things serve our nation, absorb all the good things from foreign countries, and innovate on the basis of learning to master them. I am afraid we will be hopeless if we fail to take the world's latest research results as our starting point and thus place ourselves in a better position to strive for progress. We must also draw on the world's most advanced industrial management expertise to develop scientific research and automation.

The same day, Deng met with a delegation of overseas Chinese and patriots from Taiwan, Hong Kong and Macao who had arrived for the 28th anniversary of the founding of the People's Republic. During the meeting, Deng stressed:

There's hope for us if we frankly acknowledge that we are lagging behind. The reason is rather simple: We must have a good intention to begin with, that is, the intention to do something. Only then can we hit upon sound principles, policies and methods for getting things done. We must learn whatever sophisticated achievements in this world are available to us, and bring them in as our foundation, regardless of whether people label us as "slavish compradors." Our philosophy is to take what we can take and put it to good use.

Addressing the opening ceremony of the National Science Conference on March 18, 1978, Deng once again underscored the importance of introducing foreign technology. He said:

The key to the Four Modernizations is the modernization of science and technology. Without modern science and technology, it is impossible to build modern agriculture, modern industry or modern national defense. Without the rapid development of science and technology, there can be no rapid development of the economy. ...

Backwardness must be recognized before it can be changed. You must learn from those who are more advanced before you can catch up with and surpass them. Of course, in order to raise China's scientific and technological level we must rely on our own efforts, develop our own creativity and persist in the policy of independence and self-reliance. But independence does not mean shutting the door on the world, nor does self-reliance mean blind opposition to everything foreign. Science and technology are part of the wealth created in common by all mankind. Every country or people should learn from the advanced science and technology of others. It is not just today, when we are scientifically and technologically backward, that we need to learn from others. Even after we catch up with the most advanced countries, we will still need to learn from them in areas where they are particularly strong.

A brainstorming meeting held by the State Council on July 6 to September 9 summarized the lessons and experience in economic construction and studied the successes of foreign economies, but its focus was on imports, particularly on how to step up technology transfers and expand exports and on the flexible steps to be adopted to utilize foreign capital. In his concluding report, Vice Premier Li Xiannian reiterated the need to do a good job in technology importation and to strive to expand exports. No resolutions were passed at the meeting, but the participants were able to see eye to eye with each other on the need to adhere to self-reliance while importing technology and equipment, to open the doors still wider, and to proceed with the modernization drive on a larger scale and at a faster speed.

The National Planning Conference that was convened shortly afterward called for three major changes on the economic forefront. One of the changes called for a "switch from a state of self-imposed insularity or semi-insularity that barred economic and technological exchanges with capitalist countries to actively bringing in advanced foreign technology, utilizing foreign capital, and making bold strides into the global market."

On November 3, 1978, the *People's Daily* ran an editorial entitled "Learning and Utilizing Advanced Experience of Foreign Countries." It said, among other things:

The socialist modernization drive amounts to a revolution that has an important bearing on the country's future and destiny. To accomplish this historical task at an early date, it is imperative to learn from and draw on experience and be good at absorbing all the good foreign things that we can use. In the meantime, we must combine learning from foreign countries with original innovations.

Every nation in the world has its strengths and weaknesses. Only by learning from each other and employing each other's strengths to make up for one another's deficiencies can progress be made to last. This is a truth borne out by the practice of many countries in modern times. As anti-revolutionary double-dealers donning ultra-leftist cloaks, Lin Biao and the Gang of Four were adamantly opposed to learning from other countries. They maligned our effort to draw on advanced foreign experience and introduce sophisticated foreign technology and equipment as acts of "comprador philosophy" and "treason." This was downright nonsense. ...

As is known to all, nations in the world have always been exchanging with and learning from each other in science and technology. Western countries obtained the four inventions of ancient China through imports from the Arabs; the exploration of the American continent and the Meiji Restoration of Japan were made possible mainly through the introduction of European technology. Don't forget, corn, potatoes and tomatoes were native to American Indians. This being the case, everybody in the world must be guilty of servility and treason according to the logic of Lin Biao and the Gang of Four. By their logic, the Chinese should only ride donkeys because trains belong only to foreigners, and they must stick to the abacus because computers can only be used by foreigners – only thus can people be deemed "patriotic." By disparaging learning from foreign countries as an action of "comprador philosophy," the Gang of Four concocted anti-revolutionary propaganda in a bid to usurp Party and state power. Science and technology are common wealth created by people across the world through long years of production and scientific experimentation, a wealth that knows no class, national or ethnic boundary and can be used by both the bourgeoisie and capitalist countries and the working class and socialist countries. To import selective advanced foreign technology and equipment on the basis of equality and mutual benefit and with a view to our needs, in order to bolster up the national economy and shore up the material foundation of the proletarian dictatorship – this is a sensible thing for us to do. What is wrong with it? On no account should we allow ourselves to be hoodwinked by Lin Biao and the Gang of Four and commit such folly as putting a halter around our own necks.

With underdeveloped industry and agriculture and low-level science and technology, plus grave interference and sabotage by Lin Biao and the Gang of Four, our nation remains in the economic backwaters to this day in terms of productivity and per capita income. But the aspiring Chinese people will never take backwardness lying down. We have bravely admitted our backwardness and coined the slogan "Learn from the strengths of all countries" because we want to catch up with advanced world level. Such bravery reflects exactly our firm confidence and firm conviction of the superiority of the socialist system, and the fact that we are patriots in the true sense of the term. The reactionary policy of closed-doorism and obscurantism pursued by Lin Biao and the Gang of Four was synonymous with retrogression; it served nothing but to push the people back to the semi-feudal, semi-colonial abyss.

At a working conference held (from November 10 to December 15) in preparation for the Third Plenary Session of the 11th Party Central Committee, the Party began, under the guidance of Deng Xiaoping, Chen Yun and other veteran top leaders, to correct ultra-leftist mistakes in its guideline. The opening-up policy and importation of technology and equipment became topics of heated discussions. Some participants hailed the central authorities' determination to bring in advanced foreign technology and equipment and capital as a major policy decision. A representative of the State Planning Commission told of a two-year economic development plan to shift from self-imposed seclusion to the progressive importation of foreign technology and capital and a bold entry onto the world market. Believing that such a plan could make things happen dramatically faster than if the nation continued to attempt to do everything from scratch behind closed doors, the participants urged the central leadership to take bolder and quicker steps to boost the modernization drive.

During the discussions, Li Xiannian and others accepted Deng Yingchao's proposal to distribute a number of reference materials among the participants just to give them some food for thought. These included *How the Soviet Union Boosted Its Economy With Foreign Capital and Technology in the 1920s and 1930s, How Japan, West Germany and France Achieved Quick Economic Growth After World War II* and *How Hong Kong, Singapore, South Korea and Taiwan Rose to Become Newly Industrialized Economies.* Some remarked that China could borrow some of the Soviet Union's opening-up steps in the 1920s and 1930s, such as the lease and transfer system, joint ventures, foreign loans, technological aid agreement with foreign companies, foreign experts and engineers, and machines and equipment imports. One participant summarized in three points the secret to Japan's successful rise – beginning in the 1960s and in only 13 years – to become the world's second largest economy: 1) making up for a shortage of domestic funds with massive borrowing of foreign capital; 2) introducing advanced technology and equipment from other countries; and 3) sparing no effort to groom talents in all fields. A Japanese friend, he said, had once told him that China should follow the Japanese example, but he had worried aloud that doing so might jeopardize China's state sovereignty. "My Japanese friend could not understand my worries," the participant said. "He said 'Foreigners have to observe your laws when they help you run factories. Will you lose your state sovereignty when you become rich and strong with their help? Did we Japanese infringe upon the state sovereignty of the United States when we ran factories on their territory?' The participant said this remark came as an eye-opener to him. "This reminded me that for so many years, rather than going abroad to see how things were out there, we created a bunch of taboos to bind ourselves hand-and-foot," he said. "Today, the central government is determined to adopt all the established business conventions in the world. This is indeed good news for the entire nation."

After a heated discussion at the Party's working conference, the adoption of advanced technology and equipment from the outside world was eventually put in writing as a long-term state policy in the communiqué of the Third Plenary Session of the 11th Party Central Committee at its closing session on December 22, 1978. The communiqué stated:

> While we have achieved political stability and unity and are restoring and adhering to the economic policies that proved effective over a long time, we are, in light of the new historical conditions and practical experience, adopting a number of major new economic measures, conscientiously transforming the system and methods of economic management, actively broadening economic cooperation on terms of equality and mutual benefit with other countries on the basis of self-reliance, striving to adopt the world's advanced technologies and equipment and greatly strengthening scientific and educational work to meet the needs of modernization.

Opening Up More Avenues to Bring in Technology

China stepped up technology importation about the time of the Third Plenary Session of the 11th Party Central Committee.

Abroad, opportunities already presented themselves. In the first half of the 1970s, the Western countries, coming off a postwar "golden age," were caught in the lowest economic ebb since the end of World War II. The United States, Japan, West Germany, Great Britain, France and Italy registered negative GDP growths during the 1974-75 period. While inflation soared, their economies teetered on the verge of further recession. To pull themselves from the mire, enterprises in these countries saw the potential of the Chinese market and showed a willingness to foster economic and technological partnership with China.

At home, more and more people were aware of the need to expedite the modernization drive by taking advantage of the world economic situation to incorporate as much advanced foreign technology, equipment and managerial expertise as possible.

Being inexperienced in technology imports, however, we knew little about what advanced technologies to bring in and how to convert them into real production capacities. To learn established Western practice and to seek international cooperation, the industrial departments sent one delegation after another abroad on fact-finding tours. These visits enabled us to blaze a new trail for the transfer, assimilation, incorporation and innovation of Western technology.

The State Council set up a leadership group on May 17, 1978 to unify leadership over new technology imports, with Yu Qiuli as Group Chief, and Gu Ming as Deputy Chief. The group's major tasks were:

1. with a view to the Ten-Year Outline Program for National Economic Development and the goal of realizing the Four Modernizations by the end of the 20th century – and on the basis of studies of domestic and world situation – to determine the direction and focus of technology transfers in the next three, eight or more years, and to map out an overall plan to strike an overall balance in importing technology and complete sets of equipment;
2. to study the principles, policies and proposals to be endorsed by central authorities concerning the introduction of new technology and set equipment, including guidelines for technological processes and policies for dealing with different countries in this field;
3. to organize, supervise and inspect the execution of import plans and summarize the experience gained in the process; and
4. to organize the research, assimilation and development of newly introduced technology.

For China, 1978 was a year of brisk development in technology imports. A total of 1,230 contracts amounting to US$7.8 billion in total contractual volume were signed with a dozen or so countries, including Japan, West Germany, Britain and the United States. Both figures surpassed the totals the nation had concluded with foreign countries in the previous 29 post-Liberation years. Over 90 percent of this contractual volume was committed to 22 key projects, including the first-phase construction of Shanghai Baosteel, four 300,000-tons/year ethylene-cracking plants with auxiliary equipment, three petroleum-based plants each with an annual output of 300,000 tons of synthetic ammonia and 520,000 tons of carbamide, and a coal-based 3,000,000-tons/year synthetic ammonia plant, phenol-acetone and m-cresol plants for the Beijing Yanshan Petrochemical Works.

The completion of these projects generated a variety of annual production capacities, including:

- 3 million tons of iron;
- 3 million tons of steel;
- 500,000 tons of seamless steel pipes;
- 90,000 tons of blister copper;
- 80,000 tons of aluminum;
- 1.2 million tons of synthetic ammonia;
- 1.56 million tons of carbamide;
- 900,000 tons of nitrophosphate;
- 1.2 million tons of ethane;
- 1.28 million tons of plastics;
- 1.77 million tons of organic chemical material;
- 730,000 tons of chemical fiber;
- 40 million tons of raw coal;
- 4 million tons of dressed coal;
- 703,000 kilowatts of electricity; and
- 960,000 color TV kinescopes.

By now the importation of technology and equipment had become the call of the day for Chinese industry. Impatience for quick economic growth, however, led to a rush on imports that the government could ill afford. For example, the contracts for most of these 22 import projects called for cash settlement in foreign exchange, not to mention an additional 60-billion-yuan investment in ancillary installations. With not enough foreign exchange reserve to cover the payments, the government had to borrow cash from the international financial market, where the interests were settled twice a year at an annual interest rate as high as 15 percent. This meant the principal and interest payments would be doubled in five years. The heavy payment obligation compelled the nation to postpone or revoke the 30-odd contracts signed with Japan to the tune of US$2.6 billion. The nation's credit standing was greatly impaired as a result.

To cope with the situation, some localities, while buying foreign technology with spot exchange, adopted a "three-plus-one" trade pattern – export processing with client-supplied materials, samples or components, plus compensation trade – to upgrade their technical level, promote production, and ramp up foreign exchange revenues to sustain spot-exchange payment for foreign technology imports.

During his September 20, 1978 inspection tour of Tianjin, Deng Xiaoping emphasized:

> We have got to process foreign-supplied materials and import foreign technology on a large scale. ... Let's get it started in Shanghai, Tianjin and Guangdong, and launch these projects by the hundreds or thousands, for this is the only way for people to get rich and for the economy to get energized. I wonder why everybody is waiting. We are doomed if we take a wait-and-see attitude.

The "three-plus-one" trade pattern, born of special government policies, was, for China, an unconventional way to bring in foreign technology. In the early days, this pattern referred to the practice in which foreign businesses supplied designs, raw materials and equipment to factories in China to be processed into commodities for exporting to the world market. Chinese factories and local governments drew a certain amount of processing and administrative fees from the profits, with ownership of the imported equipment to revert to the Chinese side after a period of time. Enterprises of this type first emerged in the Pearl River Delta in 1978. These included the Dajin Garment Manufacturing Factory in Shunde, the Taiping Handbag Plant in Dongguan, and the Xiangzhou Wool Spinning Factory in Zhuhai.

The State Council paid high attention to this novel trade pattern, believing that in the presence of abundant labor and available manufacturing facilities, it was an effective way to develop industrial production, upgrade technology, extend internal and external exchanges and ramp up foreign exchange

First page of the *Provisional Procedures Governing Export-Oriented Processing and Assembling Businesses* issued by the State Council, July 15, 1978.

First page of the *Interim Procedures on Supporting Exports With Imports* issued by the State Council, March 26, 1979.

First page of the *State Council Notice on Developing Export-Oriented Processing and Assembling Industry and Promoting Compensation Trade on Medium and Small Scales*, September 3, 1979.

earnings, provided that imported materials, capital, technology and equipment were put to optimal use.

However, obstacles abounded in both people's conception and the established economic system. Unless these problems were duly addressed, the new trade pattern could not last long. Thus the State Planning Commission, the State Economic Commission and the Ministry of Foreign Trade convened a meeting of leaders of various provinces and representatives from the grassroots level, and drew up the *Provisional Procedures Governing Export-Oriented Processing and Assembling Businesses*. Issued in State Council Document [1978] 139 on July 15, 1978, this legislation prescribed 22 feasible procedures for standardizing and promoting the development of this type of export processing and assembling industry. The State Council called on the relevant localities and departments, their leaders in particular, to rally their efforts, feed off each other, be strict with work efficiency and mindful of the overall situation, to lose no time and go all out to launch this industry as soon as possible.

To facilitate the export of the products of the "three-plus-one" processing and assembling industry in return for foreign exchange earnings, the State Council published the *Interim Procedures on Supporting Exports With Imports* on March 26, 1979 to address conflicts between this industry and the government foreign trade system. This step, in a sense, was an initial attempt to reform the traditional state monopoly over foreign trade. In view of the achievements, lessons and problems in the year-long experimentation with the "three-plus-one" trade pattern, the newly established State Import and Export Commission expanded and amended the 1978 *Provisional Procedures* of the State Council on the basis of the investigations, studies and discussions conducted alongside the State Planning Commission and the State Economic Commission in the relevant provinces and municipalities. The new version, promulgated on September 3, 1979, affirmed the achievements of the "three-plus-one" trade pattern, and further pointed out:

All that matters is to be aggressive in developing the export processing and assembling industry, promoting compensation trade on medium and small scales, and increasing foreign exchange revenue to back the socialist modernization drive. To do a good job in this respect, we should adhere to the principle of tapping the potential of our enterprises and bring their role into full play through renovation and transformation, develop as many more labor-intensive products as possible, and refrain from the single-minded pursuit of automation. Meanwhile, we must also insist on the principle of establishing direct links between producers and sellers, fixing production quotas according to sales, and integrating production with marketing. We must stress investigation and studies, stay well informed of the situation, and be well prepared for negotiations with foreign partners. The industrial, transport and communications, railway, foreign trade, financial, materials and banking departments, localities and enterprises should rally and coordinate their efforts to ensure that a good job is done.

Coal-for-Equipment Compensation Trade

To expedite growth in the "three-plus-one" trade pattern, leaders of the State Import and Export Commission personally attended to a number of major projects. A case in point was the expansion, through compensation trade, of the coal mining production capacity of Anhui Province. A major coal mining center in east China, the province could not supply the state quota of 22.06 million tons of coal in 1980 without revamping its outdated production equipment. The needed state investment, however, was hard to come by. To solve the problem, the province reached a compensation trade agreement with Nicheman Corporation of Japan, whereby the Japanese party was to supply US$15 million worth of coal mining apparatuses, equipment and other materials, and the Chinese side would compensate the Japanese side with 300,000 tons of anthracitic coal within two years. This deal was beneficial to both parties. The supplies from Nicheman were to be used exclusively to expand coal mines in Anhui. The centralized state control of coal supply, however, barred the province from using its own coal to compensate the Japanese company. Repeated appeals to the authorities came to naught. With Wan Li's support, the province and the Ministry of Coal Mining Industry jointly brought the case to the State Import and Export Commission and Vice Premier Gu Mu in April 1980. Basing himself on the findings of an investigation by the commission's export administrative bureau, Jiang Zemin, secretary-general of the commission, wrote to Gu Mu on May 28 with the suggestion that Anhui's petition be granted. The vice premier approved the suggestion the same day. The resolution of the coal compensation issue represented a significant breakthrough for compensation trade as well as this major coal mine expansion project.

Cutting Red Tape Down to a Single Stamp

The "three-plus-one" trade pattern was quick to catch on in the Pearl River Delta due to its prompt results in increasing output and revenue and soaking up unemployment with little investment. To speed things up, the Dongguan county government set up an ad hoc office to handle export processing and assembling projects. By cutting the otherwise cumbersome approval procedures down to the affixation of a single stamp, the office accomplished what was unimaginable in China at the time: businessmen from Hong Kong could anticipate sealing a deal in no more than one hour's time. As a result, the number of factories snowballed in Dongguan on a yearly basis. The county acquired US$1.7 billion of foreign investment during the 1978-1991 period.

In early 1982, I went on an inspection tour of the Pearl River Delta in my capacity as the newly appointed Director General of the Foreign Investment Administration under the Ministry of Foreign Economic Relations and Trade. When the local officials told me of their unconventional ways of doing business, I quipped, "So you are promoting efficiency just by hanging your office seals on your belts!" Some people might question this response, coming as it did from someone who was schooled in business management and thus knew the importance of conventions. From today's perspective, something did seem wrong in the business climate of Dongguan County. But in those days it was the only way to get things done; otherwise breakthroughs would have been out of the question, and people would still have been standing by watching with their arms folded as massive illegal immigration to Hong Kong went from bad to worse in Dongguan. Moreover, new things tend to thrive where there are no specific rules to govern them, not to mention the fact that many of the prevailing rules and regulations had completely lost touch with reality and were thus in urgent need of transformation. This was why demands for "decontrolling and decentralization" were mounting in coastal cities and among grassroots-level leaders in the early years of the reform and opening.

Enterprises engaged in the "three-plus-one" trade pattern played a special role in the economic development of the coastal areas. It is fair to say that the growing percentage of foreign-invested enterprises (for example, equity joint ventures, cooperative enterprises and wholly foreign-owned enterprises) in the Chinese economy in the 1990s and the subsequent advent of the high-tech industry would have been out of the question if not for the emergence of a legion of export processing and assembling firms in the 1980s. Even in the 1990s, such firms continued to carry considerable weight in the economy. The "three-plus-one" trade pattern – as a major avenue for bringing in technology, equipment and capital to generate foreign exchange revenues and new jobs – was consonant with the nation's notable rise in productivity level at the time.

Take Shenzhen for example. In the years after 1982, there was an impressive growth in that city's number of foreign-invested enterprises, most of which were transformed export processing and assembling firms. These included Konka Group, Zhonghua Bicycle Group, Goodyear Enterprise, Jiale Furniture and Huaqiang Sanyo. The rising export-oriented economy of Shenzhen was ascribed first of all to the robust development of these firms, which accumulated funds and trained the local labor force to the stage for further economic growth. These firms also created large numbers of jobs, to the great benefit of the people. Having hit paydirt from running such firms in Shenzhen, business owners from Hong Kong were able to dispel their doubts about the reform and opening policy and give up the "grab-the-money-and-run" mentality. On the basis of building or renting more factory buildings to upgrade production installations and paving roads to improve transportation, they went on to develop foreign-invested enterprises, thereby bringing about a situation in which export processing and assembling firms flourished alongside foreign-invested enterprises.

In retrospect, the "three-plus-one" trade pattern was instrumental in helping the reform and opening up effort to get off to a good start, improving technology, upgrading product quality and increasing product diversity. It expanded production by way of imported technology, equipment and capital, and played a vital role for China by opening up the world market, developing foreign trade, creating job opportunities and improving the people's livelihood.

Striving for Innovation and Transcendence

In 1979, the state began to adjust the work of technology transfers. In 1980, the State Import and Export Commission submitted a draft of the *Interim Provisions on Technology Introduction and Equipment Importation* to the State Council, and pointed out in the attached report:

> The purpose of introducing advanced and applicable technology and equipment from foreign countries is to enhance economic self-reliance. However, in practice, we are spending hefty sums of foreign exchange on the import of complete sets of equipment. Such imports often overlap, to the neglect of imports of equipment-building technology and the need to foster domestic manufacturing capacities. It is high time that this situation was changed. In particular, the introduction of foreign technology and import of foreign equipment should be immediately followed up with research, design and other technical efforts so as to assimilate, master and develop them.

On January 21, 1981, the State Council issued both the *Interim Provisions* and the report, specifying that the introduction of technology and equipment imports were designed to enhance the country's economic self-reliance and upgrade its science and technology to hasten the realization of the Four Modernizations. For this purpose, it was imperative to put imports of complete sets of equipment under tight control, and shift the focus onto the design and manufacturing technology and technological processes that were needed to boost domestic technological level and manufacturing capacity, particularly in the manufacture of machine tools, electric appliances, electronics, and instruments and apparatuses. All the equipment available at home, and all the prospecting and designing work that could be undertaken domestically or jointly with foreign partners, should be settled in China so that foreign exchange could be spared to meet crucial needs. The *Interim Provisions* was the first piece of Chinese legislation to define "technology introduction" and "equipment import" – meaning that the technology and equipment necessary for developing the national economy and raising the technological level could be acquired from foreign countries through trade or other forms of contracts. Thus a line of demarcation was drawn between "technology introduction" and "equipment import." The *Interim Provisions* further laid down the basic principle for technology introduction: Priority shall be given to the introduction of "software" technology needed to enhance domestic research and development, designing and innovation capabilities; in introducing foreign technology and importing foreign equipment, we shall be mindful of economic results, observe economic laws, and be conscientious about feasibility studies. It is also necessary to make full use of old factories by tapping their potential, adapting their technology and transforming their management, and to build as few new factories as possible, so as to economize on investment and human and material resources. Repetitive introduction and imports must be avoided, and the focus should be put on the introduction of individual technologies that were entirely new to the country.

According to incomplete statistics, the nation introduced or imported a total of 16,000 packages of technology and equipment to the tune of some US$12 billion during the 1980-1984 period. These included 113 color TV production lines, 70 refrigerator production lines, 15 duplicator production lines, 35 aluminium section-bar processing lines, 22 integrated circuit production lines, seven silicon steel sheet cutting lines, six float glass production lines, and a large number of assembly lines for foodstuff processing and light manufacturing industries. These introductions and imports filled in many domestic gaps, and greatly contributed to the technological reform of enterprises and the development of the national economy. Meanwhile, by assimilating and innovating upon imported technology and equipment, the domestically designed Chinese-character laser phototypesetting system, color television sets, digital-control telephones, and container inspection system surpassed the advanced world level.

Transcendence Through Technology Transfer: The Case of the Chinese-Character Laser Phototypesetting System

A major event on the Chinese technology scene in the early 1980s was the successful development of a Chinese-character laser phototypesetting system. It was an excellent example of what could be accomplished through the introduction and assimilation of, and innovation upon imported foreign technology and equipment. Up to that point, Chinese printing technology had been fairly outdated. Printing houses across the land were stuck in a "lead and fire" age, in which types were cast and set manually. In the State Import and Export Commission, as in so many other government institutions, companies and schools in the country, typists routinely sat before a cumbersome Chinese typewriter, selecting one key at a time – which, in turn, picked up the required Chinese characters from a tray containing several thousand such characters – and then striking it against a stencil to be fixed onto a mimeograph to produce copies of documents, reference materials and so on. Wang Xuan and other scientists, hoping to change this situation, began research in 1976 to develop China's first Chinese-character laser photo-typesetting system for practical use. Some positive results were yielded, but progress was held up due to a lack of coordination between researchers, designers and manufacturers, and also a lack of key components and equipment.

In 1980, the British Monotype Corporation invented a Chinese-character laser phototypesetter and put it on display at an exhibition in Beijing. This caused an argument between our home printers and researchers. While the former insisted on importing the equipment, the latter demanded government funding for domestic research and development efforts. When the argument came to a deadlock, the two sides went to the State Import and Export Commission for arbitration.

On January 1980, while the exhibition was still on, the Commission acted upon Jiang Zemin's suggestion and, after much deliberation, submitted six proposals in the *Report on the "Chinese-Character Laser Phototypesetting" Project* to Vice Premiers Yu Qiuli, Wang Zhen, Fang Yi and Gu Mu:

First, it is imperative to adopt the laser phototypesetting technology. The State Publishing Administration should purchase the Monotype machine on display in China to address urgent domestic publishing needs, on the condition that the British company bring the machine to a functioning level within two to six months.

Second, due support should be given to domestic innovation and invention efforts. This includes Peking University's endeavor to establish China's own laser phototypesetting system by incorporating the university's designing and researching results. For this purpose, it is suggested that 1) Peking University improve the model it has developed for a reliability test, to make sure that it can start normal operation eight hours a day before June 1980; 2) The government provide US$400,000 to import advanced large-scale integrated circuits, components and testing instruments to be used alongside Chinese software to improve the existing model's stability, minimize its size, and turn it into an internationally competitive laser phototypesetting system with Chinese characteristics.

Third, institutions that have already started laser phototypesetting research – including Peking University, Tsinghua University, the First Ministry of Machine-Building Industry, the State General Administration of Apparatuses and Instruments, the Fourth Ministry of Machine-Building Industry, the State General Administration of Electronic Computers, the State Publishing Administration, the Shanghai Municipal Publishing Administration, the People's Daily Press, and the Xinhua News Agency – work out a division of labor between them and coordinate their research and development efforts for the trial production of relevant Chinese-language telecommunications, indexing, photo-setting and automatic control systems.

Fourth, researchers and manufacturers should join efforts in applying domestic laser phototypesetting research results to industrial production. Once they have completed an industrial sample machine, they should deliver a technical and economic feasibility research report on it and designate the main and auxiliary manufacturers to foster production capacity and prepare the machine for the world market.

Fifth, manufacturers and users should be brought together to determine the output according to demand. The printing industry should work out a modernization plan that features annual printing quotas and annual demand for laser phototype-setting machines.

Sixth, the Japanese and South Asian markets should be studied as soon as possible to determine the market, production scale, and cooperative production prospects for the homemade Chinese-character laser photosetting machine, so that the new machine can contribute more to the modernization of the Chinese printing industry.

Jiang Zemin, following up on State Council instructions and repeated consultations with the relevant departments, wrote a report which was examined by Wang Daohan and Zhou Jiannan before it was sent to Vice Premier Gu Mu on February 22, 1980. Among other things, the report noted:

Peking University and other institutions have achieved notable results in research and development of the Chinese-character laser phototypesetting equipment, and the technology is near maturity. ... This project deserves active support, and we may grant a small amount of foreign exchange (say, US$200, 000) for them to import small-scale electronic computers, major peripheral equipment, integrated circuits, etc., so that they can go on with their experiments and bring the equipment to near perfection. ... The relevant departments should collaborate with Peking University and pool their efforts to bring the best possible results out of the project.

On February 27, Gu Mu instructed on Jiang's report: "In the beginning the departments concerned were somewhat divided on this issue, but having consulted them repeatedly, I am convinced that this plan is feasible. Please send the report to Comrades (Yu) Qiuli, Wang Zhen, Fang Yi, (Yao) Yilin, and (Ji) Pengfei for examination and approval."

With the backing of the State Import and Export Commission, and through painstaking research and development efforts, a task force headed by Wang Xuan finally succeeded in launching the first domestically designed and produced Chinese-character laser phototypesetting system.

In October 1980, Vice Premier Fang Yi, in charge of science and technology work, delivered a laser-photoset sample copy of the new book *No. 5's Sword** to Deng Xiaoping along with a letter from Peking University appealing for government help for the further development and promotion of the laser phototypesetting technology. Deng wrote on the letter, "You deserve our support." Under his personal care, the laser phototypesetting system began batch production without a hitch and gradually rose to become a new industry in its own right. Today, the system is widely used in the Chinese press and publishing industry. It has revolutionized the printing technology, delivered the printing industry from its "lead and fire" age, and ushered it into the age of computers and laser technology.

Jiang Zemin (*far left*) and Li Peng (*second from left*) visiting Founder Electronics, May 1992.

---

*   *No.5's Sword* is a novel that depicts the death-defying heroism of the underground Communist Party's central security and intelligence department in Shanghai during the Kuomintang rule in the 1920s. The department was headed by Zhou Enlai, whose code name was "No.5." (*Translator*)

The product has also entered Japan and other foreign markets. By the end of 2007, the "Founder" brand laser phototypesetting system had taken up 85 percent of the domestic market and 90 percent of the international market.

Baosteel, a World-Class Enterprise Born of Imported Technology

Iron and steel production had all along been at the top of New China's industrialization agenda. The embargo imposed by the West, however, resulted in a yawning gap between China and the world in this industry. In 1960, the Chinese steel output was 18.66 million tons, compared with 22 million tons in Japan. The tables were turned by 1973, however, when Japanese steel output more than quadrupled to reach 119 million tons, whereas the figure for China was only one fifth that of Japan, not to mention the huge disparity in product quality between the two nations. The labor productivity of the Japanese iron and steel industry was more than ten times that of its Chinese counterpart, and it consumed less than half as much energy to achieve it. The fast-growing steel and iron industry gave Japan a competitive edge in the machine-building, shipbuilding and automobile industries. However, in the aftermath of the 1973 world oil crisis, major Japanese iron and steel factories were forced to run under capacity while seeking the way out by putting their technology and equipment on sale. A China Metals Association delegation, headed by Vice Minister of Metallurgical Industry Ye Zhiqiang, visited Japan in September 1977, and returned to China convinced that there was a good opportunity to bring in some essential new technology and equipment from Japan.

In late November, the Ministry of Foreign Trade, the State Planning Commission, and the Ministry of Metallurgical Industry submitted to the State Council the joint *Report on Introducing New Technology and Equipment to Expedite Development of the Iron and Steel Industry.* Their suggestion: Let's lose no time in building the Shanghai Steel Rolling Works. The State Council immediately approved the suggestion.

On November 29, Li Xiannian met with Yoshihiro , Chairman of the Japan-China Long-Term Trade Committee and President of Nippon Steel Corporation (NSC). Yoshihiro, who had signed a Sino-Japanese agreement on cooperation for the iron and steel industry as early as 1958, was an old-timer in Sino-Japanese trade and a champion of friendship between the two countries. During the Cultural Revolution, his company worked on the construction of a 1.7-meter-wide steel plate rolling mill at the Wuhan Iron and Steel Works. At the time, intense confrontation between political factions in Wuhan seriously affected the project. Yoshihiro could never forget the enormous pressure on him from at home and abroad during those years. This time around, however, when Vice Premier Li talked with him to propose bilateral cooperation on the new steel factory in Shanghai, he accepted it without hesitation.

A NSC team from Japan arrived in Beijing for technical consultation. In December 1977, a planning team formed by relevant state departments and the Shanghai Municipal Government worked out a plan for the Shanghai Iron and Steel Works. Later, the Ministry of Metallurgical Industry, along with the State Planning Commission, the State Economic Commission, the State Construction Commission and the Shanghai Municipal Government, submitted a joint report, which became the subject of discussion at a State Council meeting chaired by Vice Premier Li Xiannian and attended by Vice Premiers Yu Qiuli, Gu Mu, Fang Yi and Kang Shi'en and a number of State Council ministers. Vice Premier Li urged those concerned to "be a little more enthusiastic, stay prudent, discreet, conscientious, modest and cautious, and commit as few mistakes as possible – but the bottom line is to make this project happen without fail."

The Shanghai Iron and Steel Works was modelled on the NSC Kimitsu Works, and the idea came from Deng Xiaoping. During a visit to that factory during his October 1978 tour of Japan, he told his Japanese hosts, NSC Chairman Yoshihiro Inayama and Director Saito Hiroshi, "I would like you to help us build a factory just like this."

On October 31, 1978, Li Xiannian arrived in Shanghai to inspect the preparations for the factory. He asked the builders to be economical as best they could and urged local leaders to speed up the training of workers and technicians. "Do work hard," he urged his hosts. "The hopes of the nation are in your hands!"

On December 21, 1978, the China National Technical Import and Export Corporation and the Nippon Steel Corporation

Gu Mu (*center*) cutting the ribbon for Baosteel, December 23, 1978.

concluded a general agreement on the purchase of complete sets of equipment for the project, now renamed "Shanghai Baoshan Iron and Steel Complex" (Baosteel).

Baosteel came under construction the day after the closing of the Third Plenary Session of the 11th Party Central Committee.

Nevertheless, by early 1979 the implementation of the general agreement between Baosteel and NSC had been postponed due to temporary financial difficulties on the Chinese side. This caused a lot of gossip within China. The central authorities sent Chen Yun to Shanghai for a reappraisal of the project. After repeated comparisons and deliberation, he concluded that the construction of Baosteel was entirely necessary. "Baosteel is the priority project for the modernization drive," he said, "and you've got to set a good example for us all."

At a June 16 meeting of the Commission of Finance and Economy of the State Council on the steel complex, both Li Xiannian and Chen Yun acknowledged in their speeches that, given the sheer size of the project, it had taken more time than anticipated to make a decision about it. Now that the project was underway and making good progress, they stressed, it had to be carried out through to the end. They urged the builders to see to it that every piece of the necessary equipment be included on the purchase list, that all the equipment be purchased together with the corresponding patents, and that the workforce be trained in advance.

When Wang Zhen inspected the construction site on July 4, 1979, he said, "We are pushing modernization, and Baosteel is a symbol of that. Stop throwing cold water on Baosteel! We have to have the guts to pursue modernization."

On July 21, Deng, who was visiting Shanghai to see how things stood there, said of the steel complex:

> Let me remind those of you in the municipal government that, first, you've got to build it, and second, you've got to do a good job of it. True, there is plenty of talk about the Baoshan Steel Works, but we don't regret our decision on it. What's at stake is that we must make it a success.

On another occasion, he proclaimed: "History will vindicate the construction of Baosteel."

That proclamation alone was not enough, however, to put public doubts to rest. Baosteel was destined to go through its share of twists and turns in its infancy. In November 1980, discussions held at a State Council meeting of provincial governors and a national working conference on planning led to a decision to cancel its construction. Further discussions that took place at a December 23 meeting of the Central Finance and Economy Leading Panel were inconclusive, and the meeting ended with a request to conduct another feasibility study on it. A week later, on December 30, Vice Mayor of Shanghai Chen Jinhua wrote to the State Council, suggesting that instead of cancelling it, the construction work be downscaled and slowed down enough so that authorities could wait for an opportune time to go full throttle again. In middle and late January 1981, a group of experts, including Jin Xiying from the State Planning Commission, Li Jingzhao from the State Construction Commission and Ma Hong from the Chinese Academy of Social Sciences, gathered at the construction site of Baoshan with leaders of the relevant ministries for a feasibility study meeting. At a February 10 State Council hearing on the feasibility study, Ma Chengde, Deputy Chief Executive of the Baosteel Construction Headquarters and Vice Minister of Metallurgical Industry, had this to say: "If we scrap the project, we still need 1.5 billion yuan to recoup the domestic investment. If we go on with it, we only need 2.5 billion yuan." At this, someone interjected, "Are you saying that one more billion yuan can save 10 billion yuan (the value of the Baosteel project), or else, 10 million yuan will go down the drain?" Ma answered, "That's exactly what I mean."

After the meeting, Yao Yilin, Gu Mu, Bo Yibo and Peng Chong inspected the construction site one after another. On August 7, a joint document of the State Planning Commission and the State Construction Commission (transmitted by the Ministry of Metallurgical Industry) endorsed the decision to continue with the first-phase project.

Thanks to the support of Deng and other top leaders, particularly to the grit and resolve of Baosteel workers in their tens of thousands, the first-phase project was completed on schedule and started production on September 15, 1985.

After hearing a report on the current economic situation from the relevant departments on December 22, 1983, Deng remarked:

> What really matters is developing energy, transportation, rolled steel, cement and timber. We should launch projects in these fields as soon as we can, or our economy will get bogged down. ... As I see it, we should begin the second-phase construction of Baosteel. The question now is, can we get it underway ahead of schedule? Can we make a decision on it? It will be no mean feat if we can attain an annual rolled steel output of 3 million tons.

On February 15, 1984, Deng arrived at Baoshan to gain some idea about the second-phase construction of Baosteel. Talking with some central leaders on February 24 before winding up his visit, he noted:

> The second-phase construction of Baosteel is scheduled for the Seventh Five-Year Plan (1976-1980). That is why today we are still importing 10 million tons of steel on a yearly basis. Can we do something to change the situation? If the second-phase project of Baosteel starts production ahead of schedule, we can cut the imports by 3 million tons a year and save more than US$300 for every ton of rolled steel imported. Can we take a long-term point of view and get the second-phase construction started sooner? It will put us at a disadvantage if we start the project by the Seventh Five-Year Plan, which would mean a waste of two years.

He continued with a note of urgency in his voice:

> We must get the project going right away. Don't wait until the Seventh Five-Year Plan. Let's do it this year. It would be a waste of time if we don't start doing it this year. We have got to race against time. It's no problem for China to borrow US$20 to US$30 billion of foreign exchange for this project – we can certainly afford the repayment.

As if all this were not enough, he repeated once again to make his point: "Let's make a decision, that is, start the project this year to save time!" With that declaration, the second phase of construction of Baosteel kicked off two years ahead of schedule. In 1991, the year the new project started production, the national steel output topped 70 million tons. Then the third phase of construction started immediately. By the end of 2000, when all of the 28 projects involved were completed and commissioned, Baosteel had raised its annual steel production capacity to 10 million tons. It became a Fortune Global 500 company in 2003, and paid off the principal and interests of all its debts eight years ahead of schedule in 2004.

Revisiting Baoshan in February 1984, Deng wrote an inscription in honor of the nation's number one steel complex: "To master new technology, we must be good at study, and even more so, we must be good at innovation." That is exactly what the Baosteel staff and workers did from the onset. By introducing, assimilating and innovating upon the new technology and equipment imported from Japan and other countries, they have come up with a thousand scientific and technological results and developed some 100 new products. As winner of a national gold medal for construction quality and a special national award for progress in science and technology, Baosteel today is tooled with world-class production technology, and is doing its share in bridging the technological and managerial gap between the Chinese iron and steel industry and its counterparts in developed countries. In 1996, China's iron and steel output both exceeded the 100 million-ton mark. In the world history of iron and steel industry, it took only 45 years for China to raise its annual steel output from 1 million tons to 100 million tons, as compared with 73 years for the United States, 71 years for the Soviet Union, and 49 years for Japan. In 2003, China led the world with an iron and steel output of 200 million tons.

Our experience with steel production proved that importation and innovation are mutually complementary, rather than conflicting. This importation, learning and assimilation – against a particularly conducive environment of global openness and competition – combined to become a major wellspring of, and impetus behind independent innovation.

4

Lessons for the Opening-Up Policy

A t a State Council brainstorming meeting in the latter half
of 1978, central government leaders decided it was better
to attract foreign investment through running equity joint
ventures than to procure foreign loans, on the ground that such
ventures could effectively forestall debts by way of joint investment
and management, which allowed both partners to share the interests
and risks. They instructed that preparations be made to transplant
this form of business to China. On January 17, 1979, during a talk
with Hu Juewen, Hu Zi'ang, Rong Yiren and other leaders of industrial and commercial circles, Deng Xiaoping, chief architect of the
reform and opening policy, made the remark that was to become a
major part of his strategy for national development:

> As things stand at present, it is necessary to develop the
> economy in multiple ways. We can utilize foreign funds and
> technology, and allow overseas Chinese and foreign citizens
> of Chinese origin to run factories in China. To absorb foreign
> capital, we may either employ compensatory trade or establish
> Sino-foreign joint ventures.

"We may... establish Sino-foreign joint ventures." That terse statement represents a judicious, far-seeing strategic decision that was to
add a new dimension to the effort to open the nation to the outside
world and draw foreign direct investment. The subsequent achievements in this effort were to rivet world attention on China. By the end

of 2007, the number of registered foreign-funded enterprises in China had exceeded 632,000, including 280,000 joint ventures with Chinese and foreign capital. In 2007, the volume of paid-up foreign direct investment into China totaled US$74.8 billion, with joint ventures accounting for 29 percent of the nation's aggregate tax revenue. In a short span of 29 years, China had started from scratch to become a major depository for foreign direct investment from across the globe. Attracting investment from abroad and establishing joint ventures not only helped China to get more funds, but also played no small role in spheres ranging from introducing advanced technology and management expertise, and training human resources, to developing domestic and overseas markets, and promoting reforms of state-owned enterprises to build a socialist market economy.

Joint Ventures, a Pragmatic Choice

The term "joint ventures with Chinese and foreign investment" is taken for granted nowadays in this country. But back in the late 1970s, when people were just beginning to shatter the mental shackles of the Cultural Revolution, the concept was still something outlandish and off limits in the economic sphere. Few people could understand it, let alone give it a try.

I was perhaps one of the few who ventured into this "forbidden zone" in the very beginning.

Deng Gives the Go-Ahead

In 1978, as director of a preparatory office for the building of a heavy-duty vehicle plant for the Third Auto Works, I was involved in negotiations on the transfer of heavy-duty automobile technology with a 17-member General Motors delegation headed by Thomas Murphy, chairman and CEO of the world's largest automaker. The week-long negotiations were held in the Beijing Hotel from October 21 to 28. Our American guests began the talks by acquainting us with different approaches to collaboration with foreign companies:

1. Sales of finished products and parts, rather than technology, which is the most common way of doing business.
2. Licensing of assembly work, whereby General Motors ships automobile parts, in complete knockdown or semi-knockdown fashion, to an overseas partner to be assembled into vehicles for sale on the local market.
3. Payable technology transfer, whereby General Motors would enter into an agreement with a foreign partner on a certain product for compensated transfer of technology and relevant personnel training.
4. Gradual increase in the proportion of self-manufacturing, whereby a partner may import auto parts from General Motors while gradually increasing its ability to produce such parts in the process of assembly work.
5. Transfer of manufacturing licenses.
6. Partners selling each other's products or parts, with the intention to maintain trade balance between both sides.
7. Establishing wholly owned subsidiaries in a foreign country.
8. Product buybacks, whereby a foreign partner uses technical expertise offered by General Motors and manufactures products to be sold back to General Motors to cover its foreign exchange expenses. This method never worked out, however, because both partners had difficulty seeing eye to eye on issues occurring during the manufacturing process, such as product quality, prices, and technical improvement.
9. Contractual building of a factory, also known as "turnkey factory," a method that, for lack of success, General Motors did not see fit for long-term cooperation.
10. Newly established joint ventures, whereby General Motors joins its partners directly with its capital, technology and management expertise.

During the negotiations, our American guests used a technical term we had never heard of before – "joint venture." We all spoke a little English and knew that "joint" means "together" or "sharing," and that "venture" stands for "risk." But when these two words were put together, it sounded like "risk sharing" to us. Since we were baffled by this strange phrase, it seemed to us that Murphy was rubbing it in when he said, "Why did you only talk about the import and transfer of technology, but didn't say anything about 'joint ventures' – by that I mean where both sides can invest in and run it together?"

At our request, during the negotiations on October 25 Murphy let one of his managers in charge of international cooperation give us an orientation on the "joint venture." By citing the experience of General Motors in such countries as the United Kingdom, Poland and Yugoslavia, the man told us of the advantages of this form of business:

1. It helps foster a sense of responsibility on both sides for long-term cooperation and investment returns and prompts them to do their level best to run the business well.
2. It provides an avenue for bringing General Motors' management expertise and sales know-how into full play.
3. It enables General Motors to keep improving its products and to transfer the latest manufacturing technology promptly.
4. It helps facilitate exports.
5. It enables General Motors to assist in technological training and business management.

▲ Chen Muhua (*right*) meeting with Thomas Murphy (*left*), who headed a GM delegation to China, October 26, 1978.

◄ GM Chairman and CEO Thomas Murphy on the Great Wall, 1978.

In short, a well-run joint venture means for General Motors an entry ticket to the local market, which is beneficial to its own growth as well.

Later that day, in response to our questions on the prospects of joint ventures in China, Weitz, manager of General Motors' joint venture in Britain, made the following explanations:

1. Investment ratio: General Motors found a ratio ranging from 10 to 90 percent acceptable, but was glad to leave the decision to the Chinese side.
2. Leading body: A board of directors comprising members from both sides, at percentages agreed upon by both parties through consultation. For instance, the board of directors of General Motors' joint venture in Yugoslavia consisted of five members from Yugoslavia and four from the American side, with the chairman appointed by the Yugoslavian side.
3. Composition of the management team varies by country. For example, the aforementioned joint venture in Yugoslavia had only a consultant and not a single manager from General Motors.
4. China may set up joint ventures with the General Motors headquarters in the United States or subsidiaries in Germany, Britain or Australia.

Joint ventures were an effective way to handle local government restrictions on exports, according to our American guests. They also advocated long-term collaboration and joint investment to counter trade protectionism in various countries, to meet the ever-increasing demand for product quality and to deal with the volatile foreign exchange rate. When the manager had finished his explanations, Murphy took the floor. He compared the joint venture to marriage, saying the two sides would put their money together, and make or lose money together like a couple. To the manager's elucidation Murphy added something to the effect that to run a joint venture means both sides pool money and efforts and share profits and losses. This form of cooperation is based on mutual benefit. To put it more simply, he added, a joint venture was like "a family bound together by marriage."

My colleagues and I found the information provided by our American guests at once fascinating, refreshing and educational, but at the same time, as persuasive as their arguments were, we were skeptical about the feasibility of joint ventures in China. You are capitalists and we are communists, I thought. How could we set up and run a business together? I found Murphy's comparison of the joint venture to marriage and family even more unthinkable. How could a communist marry a capitalist?

Our American guests were totally oblivious to their Chinese hosts' mental turmoil over the joint venture. During their stay in China, they invited us time and again to visit their companies in America, Britain, West Germany, Australia, Canada, and Brazil.

This was the first China visit by General Motors, which also became the first major transnational corporation to extend an official offer to China for long-term partnership in the form of joint ventures. On many occasions Murphy and his entourage expressed their willingness to work out a cooperation model in light of the reality of the Chinese automobile industry. The rules of the time in China were that negotiations with foreigners on important projects must be promptly reported in writing to the State Council Office of the Leading Group for New Technology Imports. As our negotiations with General Motors belonged in that category in terms of importance, I wrote a report and had it delivered to the Leading Group. Unexpectedly, this report came to the notice of the central leadership. Vice Premier Gu Mu, then in charge of this field of work, immediately had it circulated among other Politburo members for deliberation and endorsement.

Upon reading the report, Deng Xiaoping not only put his mark of approval on it, but also wrote down an instruction on General Motors' suggestion to establish a joint venture with China: "Joint ventures are workable." The pivotal importance of this line was soon borne out by the chain of events that followed.

Zhang Quan, a colleague from the State Council Office of the Leading Group for New Technology Imports, who was with us throughout our negotiations with General Motors, later recalled:

> The Office submitted the report, written by Li Lanqing, to the higher-ups and stressed the necessity and significance of establishing

joint ventures, which quickly drew the attention of the central authorities. What is particularly worth noting was Deng Xiaoping's instruction, "Joint Ventures are workable," which pointed the way toward opening up and utilizing foreign capital. A new form of economic entity was thus born in this country.

When leaders of the First Ministry of Machine-Building Industry showed us a copy of the report with Deng's directive on it, we were all elated, and our misgivings immediately evaporated into thin air. The minister lost no time in issuing a notice to the effect that our plans – the import of heavy-duty vehicle technology, the Beijing Jeep Corporation, and the Shanghai Car Technology Import Project – could proceed in the form of joint ventures.

When Deng's instruction reached those in charge of the Shanghai Car Technology Import Project, with whom we were in close contact, they were just as excited. Later, I happened to see one of their telephone records that read:

> **November 9, 1978, 4:06 pm.** A responsible member of the First Ministry of Machine-Building Industry called Weng Jianxin, who was responsible for negotiations on the Shanghai Car Technology Import Project, to say that Gu Ming, Vice Minister of the State Planning Commission, asked Vice Chairman Deng whether a joint venture was acceptable for a car project like theirs. Deng Xiaoping answered that, of course it was, and emphasized that it was suitable for the heavy-duty vehicle project as well. Deng also told Gu about the benefits of running joint ventures. As Gu Ming recalled that Deng, in the days leading to the Third Plenary Session of the 11th Party Central Committee, was already considering strategies and specific methods and procedures for opening up to the outside world.

After receiving Deng's instruction, we, together with the First Ministry of Machine-Building Industry, drafted a second brief report in which we proposed that preparations begin immediately for a visit to the United States for further negotiations with General Motors on the establishment of a joint venture. This report, again, came to the notice of the State

The second *Brief Report on New Technology Imports*, submitted by the Office of the Leading Group for New Technology Imports, with comments by Deng Xiaoping and other leaders, January 1978.

Council. On January 26, 1979, Vice Premier Gu Mu wrote on the report, "Approval is recommended. Please send it to (Yu) Qiuli, Geng Biao, Fang Yi, Wang Zhen, (Kang) Shi'en, and (Chen) Muhua for further instruction." Vice Premier Kang Shi'en reviewed the report the following day and, noting its importance, suggested that the report be submitted to Chairman Hua Guofeng and all the other vice premiers for deliberation and instruction. On February 11, Deng Xiaoping signed his approval on the report. Upon receipt of these instructions from the central leaders, the Ministry immediately began preparing for the US visit for further negotiations with General Motors.

On March 21, 1979, I joined a delegation headed by Rao Bin, Vice Minister of the First Ministry of Machine-Building Industry, on a fact-finding tour of the United States, Germany and France, where we were to talk to General Motors, Volkswagen, Mercedes-Benz, and Citroën about joint ventures. While we were being shown around the General Motors factory in the United States, I test-drove one of its new models; this

The author test-driving a new model during his visit to GM, 1979.

deepened my feeling about the disparity between the Chinese auto industry and that of the Western world, especially in the field of research and development. Running joint ventures was apparently a good way to quickly narrow the gap.

In the end, the negotiations with General Motors failed, due to internal reasons on the part of General Motors and to policy changes concerning the heavy-duty vehicle project back home. Nonetheless, that experience paved the way for negotiations with other foreign automakers on joint ventures and other projects. It took years before General Motors landed its first joint venture in Shanghai, but Thomas Murphy, a world-calibre entrepreneur and the supreme leader of the number one of Fortune Global 500 corporations, was the first man to broach the idea to China in 1978. He should be remembered for his optimistic foresight and strategic thoughts on the prospects of our country's reform and opening.

On February 21, 1979, the First Ministry of Machine-Building Industry and the Beijing municipal government submitted their *Report on a Jeep-Producing Joint Venture Between Beijing Auto Works and American Motors Corporation (AMC)* to the State Council. Among other things, the report stated:

In view of the brisk sales of Beijing Jeep 212 in the world market, we deem it necessary to revamp the Jeep assembly line of Beijing Auto Works by utilizing foreign investment and importing new technology so as to expedite the modernization of the jeep manufacturing industry in our country. Therefore, we negotiated with American Motors Corporation (AMC) from January 16 to 26 in Beijing on establishing a joint venture to manufacture jeeps. Initial agreement has been reached on major principles, and a memorandum of understanding has been signed.

Further negotiations were held between the two sides. In May 1983, or four years after the State Council approved the report, an agreement was concluded for the establishment of the Sino-US Beijing Jeep Corporation, the first joint venture with Chinese and foreign investment. In Shanghai, six years of negotiations between the Shanghai Auto Industrial Corporation and Volkswagen of Germany culminated in the signing of a contract on a joint venture to produce Santana sedans in November 1984.

Coca-Cola's Return to China

Apart from General Motors, Coca-Cola was another American multinational corporation that became aware of the tremendous business opportunities offered by China at the dawn of the opening-up era. Coca-Cola was no stranger to the Chinese. It was already catching on in the Chinese market before the birth of New China in 1949. When the normalization of Sino-US diplomatic relations was still in the air in the 1970s, Coca-Cola had already opened an interim resident office at Beijing Hotel. John Hunter, who was in charge of the company's affairs in China at the time, said that if every Chinese drank one can of cola a year, it would mean a huge market of several hundred million dollars. However, a Coca-Cola comeback in China was easier said than done. The Chinese were worried that if it was allowed to happen, it could mean the undoing of the fragile Chinese soft drink industry. What is more, to the Chinese Coca-Cola was laden with symbolic baggage – to some, the mere mention of the brand name would summon the image of a "master exploiter."

I remember reading an English article during my boyhood, and I can still retell the gist of the story:

> Once upon a time there was an old American woman, lonely and dying. She stood shakily at the door, as her physical strength was failing her, searching for something or someone with a look of expectation in her dim eyes. When a boy happened to walk by on his way home after school, the old woman hastened to ask him for help. She wanted him to write down her will for her. The boy consented. Handing him a pen and a piece of paper, she dictated, "I don't have much money left. The only things I have are a Bible and a cross necklace. I would like to leave them to my daughter after my death. Her name and address are..." The boy did not know how to spell the words "Bible" and "necklace," but he did not want to disappoint the old woman either. When he searched his mind for the correct spellings, he spotted a big billboard beyond the open window. On it was the picture of a beautiful girl with a bottle of Coca-Cola in her hand, and she was saying, "Coca-Cola, drink Coca-Cola please!" So the boy scribbled that sentence down and, palming it off as what the old woman had dictated, told her that he had finished. She replied feebly, "Thanks. You may go now." Then she lay down on her bed and passed away in silence. At that juncture, a gust of wind came, whirling her written will into the air and out of the window. It turned out that she was the beautiful woman pictured on the billboard. She had advertised for Coca-Cola all her life, but was left penniless in her evening years. The irony was that, inadvertently, she had advertised one more time for Coca-Cola, free of charge, before breathing her last.

John Hunter was undeterred. He plodded on against the odds. Arguing that foreigners coming to China would want the drink, he entered negotiations with the China Cereals, Oils and Foods Import and Export Company (COFCO), which was already importing Coca-Cola to supply foreigners working or traveling in China. Citing the fact that China was opening up, and the demand from foreigners coming in droves to this country, he wanted to have Coca-Cola bottled in China. His perseverance paid off: on January 2, 1979, the day after China and the

First batch of Coca-Cola being sold at the Beijing Hotel by China Cereals, Oils and Foods Import and Export Company through consignment, January 1979.

United States proclaimed the normalization of diplomatic ties, an agreement was signed with COFCO allowing Coca-Cola to provide bottling facilities in major Chinese cities and tourist centers in the form of compensation trade. The company was also permitted to open factories in China to bottle and can the drink locally for sales in designated areas. In the period before a bottling factory was established, COFCO would be commissioned to sell Coca-Cola products in the country, in compliance with a Ministry of Foreign Trade ruling that these products were "only for sale in hotels and shops that accommodate foreigners." Despite this strict limitation, the Coca-Cola headquarters was nonetheless pleased, knowing that once the floodgate was opened, it could not be closed again. What happened later bore out Coca-Cola's farsightedness. Contrary to critics' prediction, Coca-Cola's return to China greatly boosted the national soft drink industry, which not only dominated the domestic market, but also found its way into international market.

Overseas Chinese Taking the Lead

Even before the Third Plenary Session of the 11th Party Central Committee, Deng and other state leaders were already sending signals to the outside world about the country's opening-up effort. However, many Westerners were slow in detecting such signals, let alone react properly. Compatriots in Taiwan, Hong Kong, Macao and overseas, on the contrary, knew better. In fact, they had long been looking forward to this day. They took the lead to invest in the mainland, open up new avenues for development, and provide advice, thereby playing a positive role in advancing the cause of reform and opening.

Deng Xiaoping met with Hong Kong, Macao and Taiwan compatriots, and overseas Chinese on many occasions. During a meeting with Richard Charles Lee and his wife on October 2, 1977, Deng said:

> The saying that "overseas Chinese have too complicated a background to be trusted" is reactionary. It is not that we have too many friends with overseas backgrounds, but that we have too few. Overseas relationships are a good thing. They can open up contacts in all fields.

In the early days of the reform and opening, both central and local government leaders made a point of meeting business-people from Hong Kong and Macao to hear them out. Taiwan, Hong Kong and Macao compatriots, and Chinese nationals residing in foreign countries offered candid suggestions on the economic development of their motherland, and they were also active donors to, and investors in China. Quite a few of them have become household names in China. Some have become my personal friends, including Kuang-piu Chao, K. C. Wong, Ma Man-kei, Henry Fok Ying-tung, Li Ka-shing and Run Run Shaw, to name just a few.

Even before Zhuhai was turned into a special economic zone, Kuang-piu Chao, chairman of Hong Kong Novel Enterprises and Macao Textile, had already visited the city seeking opportunities for cooperation. Many of us in foreign trade knew him as a long-time client. Not only was he a well-known legend himself, but the story about how he brought up his daughter, Susana Chou, the incumbent president of the Legislative Assembly of the Macao Special Administrative Region, was making the rounds in the country. To encourage Susana to help develop the family's textile business in Macao, for instance, he gave her a camera and sent her on a global tour to survey the international market, asking her to take snapshots of fashions and designs, so that she could return to design her own products for the world market.

Father and daughter thus became accomplished entrepreneurs in the textile industry. In 1978, they arrived in Zhuhai with a proposal for collaboration with the local government. Their company, Macao Textile, offered to buy sophisticated equipment and construction materials from Britain, West Germany, Japan, and America for HK$7.4 million for the establishment of a textile joint venture in Zhuhai, the Xiangzhou Woolen Textile Mill. All the local government was asked to do was to pay for the land use right and materials for factory buildings for a total of 550,000 yuan. The joint venture was to process materials supplied by clients, with Macao Textile providing technical guidance and selling the products overseas. Chao was to recoup, within five years, the principal and interest of his investment from the mill's processing earnings, at which point ownership of the mill would revert to the Zhuhai government. This model of cooperation, representing China's first experiment with overseas investment in running a factory under the opening-up policy, was later dubbed "compensation trade." Thanks to the sincere intentions of both sides and the backing of the relevant authorities, the green light was given to the project – all the way from the planning, red tape and the signing of a contract in August 1978, to the start of construction in November of the same year. One year later, the factory was completed and the equipment installed with a total floorspace of 6,000 square meters. Pilot production started in September and batch production began two months later. Over 500 business people and media people, and guests from a dozen or so countries attended the inauguration ceremony. Newspapers in several dozen countries hailed it as the first product of the opening-up policy and the earliest fruit of its special economic zones.

Of course, the joint venture was not without its problems in its early days. For instance, workers' skills and management fell short of the requirements; wages were not linked to the quality and quantity of work done; and the joint venture lacked sufficient autonomy to run its business. These problems were gradually addressed, however, through training and the introduction of advanced managerial expertise from foreign enterprises.

Chao's confidence in investing in the mainland increased as time went on. After the *Law on Chinese-Foreign Equity Joint Ventures* was promulgated, he went on to co-establish Tianshan Wool Textile in Xinjiang, which soon rose to become another successful joint venture in the nation's early years of reform and opening.

On September 13, 1980, Vice Premier Gu Mu and Zhou Jiannan met with four renowned patriotic entrepreneurs from Hong Kong and Macao on the opening-up policy. K. C. Wong (1907-1986), former president of the Hong Kong Chinese General Chamber of Commerce, had masterminded a massive influx of overseas Chinese capital to the new-born People's Republic, and donated a plane and other materials to the War to Resist US Aggression and Aid Korea (1950-1953). Apart from donations to the construction of many schools in the mainland, he set up a US$100 million education fund in 1985 to support Chinese students sent to study in foreign countries. Ma Man-kei, the long-time president of the Macao Chamber of Commerce, has been a motive force behind industrial and commercial collaboration between Macao and the mainland. He himself has set up enterprises and invested in or donated to the construction of hotels, highways, bridges, and schools in the mainland. A one-time president of the Chinese General Chamber of Commerce of Hong Kong, Henry Fok Ying-tung (1923-2006) pioneered Hong Kong's inland investment in the early years of reform and opening. His contributions included the White Swan Hotel in Guangzhou, the Hot Spring Resort in Zhongshan, the construction of many highways and bridges, the Fok Ying-tung Sports and Physical Education Foundation (a welfare foundation for the disabled), Jinan University in Guangzhou, and Ying-tung Natatorium (Swimming Center) in Beijing. Li Ka-shing was nicknamed "Superman" in the business world. In 1979, his Cheung Kong Holdings acquired the time-honored Hutchison-Whampoa, thus establishing him as the first Chinese ever to acquire a British consortium. Up to now, Li's contributions to the mainland, Shantou University included, have totaled several billions of HK dollars, and his investment has amounted to several dozen billions of HK dollars.

During the September 13 meeting, the four magnates put forward many good suggestions. K. C. Wong suggested that the mainland maximize the use of foreign investment and advanced technology, adding that it could be done in a cost-effective way through compensation trade. In utilizing foreign investment, he added, public bidding was preferable to private channels. According to him, an interest rate of 12 to 15 percent on foreign investment, which would allow the country to recoup the investment by the end of the contract term, was appropriate. This approach, which could also provide effective personnel training, should be popularized nationwide.

Gu Mu asked:

You've just said that the more foreign capital we get, the better off we become. But we're concerned that if we start too many projects all at once, we'll have a hard time following up with peripheral investment. If the energy supply and transportation cannot meet the demand, it will be hard to guarantee good economic returns. How can we square that with what you've told us about maximizing the use of foreign capital?

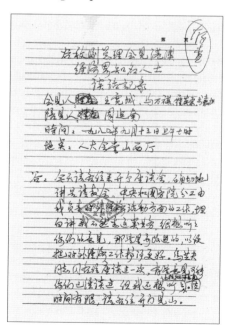

Memo of the conversations between Gu Mu, K. C. Wong, Ma Man-kei, Henry Fok Ying-tung, and Li Ka-shing, September 13, 1980.

To this Wong replied:

> We should channel as many resources as possible to four areas: docks, transportation, electricity and telecommunications. For example, when a good job is done in road construction, the enhanced transportation efficiency will make things a lot easier for us.

Gu Mu asked whether it would be feasible to use foreign funds for projects in Guizhou and Yunnan provinces, which were rich in coal but lacked transportation service. Li Ka-shing assured him that it would certainly work if coal mining rights were contracted to foreigners for a few years before they were taken back. "The more profits they make, the more returns we'll get. Those of us in Hong Kong can invite people who are interested. Then we can hold public bidding and award the contracts to the best bidders. We can call off the bidding if we cannot land good bidders," he said. Ma Man-kei suggested that a detailed plan be drawn up for the coal mining industry in Guizhou under the framework of an overall national plan. He added that if railroads could reach Guangdong Province, the local power industry would be greatly boosted.

In his speech, Henry Fok Ying-tung stressed the need to pay careful attention to institutional issues and human resources, and that if issues such as long-term planning, cumbersome bureaucracy, and business mismanagement were not handled properly, investment could be in jeopardy. Therefore, he said, "The state should avoid making impulsive investments. We have to maintain political stability and unity, and develop our economy in a steady manner. Panicky and 'swarm-mentality' investment simply gets nowhere."

In his concluding speech at the meeting with the four Hong Kong and Macao moguls, Gu Mu said:

> We should build up our country mainly by our own bootstraps, but if we fail to avail ourselves of the opportunities offered by the international community, success will be long in coming. What we expect of you is not investment, but your suggestions, and your obligations to the country.

When talking about the contributors to China's opening-up effort, we should not forget Run Run Shaw. I came to know him many years ago and admire him deeply for his patriotism and devotion to education. A celebrated filmmaker in Hong Kong, he has produced over 1,000 movies, including *Golden Dragon*, the first sound motion picture in China. He is particularly devoted to education, having donated more than 3 billion yuan to some 5,000 schools and educational projects in the mainland. School buildings, libraries and science museums named after him can be seen all over China. When asked about his passion for education, Shaw answered, "National rejuvenation hinges on talent, and talent can be groomed only through education. The cultivation of talents is in our country's fundamental interest." In 1990, the Chinese Academy of Sciences named Planetoid No. 2899, discovered by China, "Planet Run Run Shaw" in recognition of the man's contribution to public welfare.

I mention these people to show that China's reform and opening program has had the support of Taiwan, Hong Kong and Macao compatriots and overseas Chinese right from the beginning.

The First Law on Foreign Investment Is Born

Upon Deng Xiaoping's approval of a report on establishing joint ventures with Chinese and foreign capital, the State Council asked the First Ministry of Machine-Building Industry to make an initial and swift feasibility study of a number of auto-making projects then under negotiation, and to prepare for the drafting of a constitution and a contract for joint ventures. Vice Minister Rao Bin, then in charge of both missions, immediately brought the negotiators and drafters together under the same roof at the Ministry's guesthouse at Suzhou Hutong in Beijing.

By that time, the developed countries had already developed more or less the same legislation on investment. The legislation was so comprehensive that there was no need to enact a special law on transnational joint ventures. Neither could such laws be found in developing countries. Chinese lawmakers, therefore, had nothing to go by when asked to draft the constitution and a standard contract for joint ventures in China. The General Motors people had told us about their crankshaft-making joint venture in Yugoslavia, which, to our knowledge, was the only one of its kind between a socialist country and a capitalist country. But our study of the relevant documents, obtained with the help of the Chinese Embassy to Yugoslavia, yielded little information of value. Thus our preparation for drafting the Chinese joint venture constitution and contract could only be based on issues arising from negotiations and on the circumstances of our country. Some of us went out of our way to attend foreign professors' lectures on international laws at Peking University. We also consulted veteran industrialists and entrepreneurs. Jerome Cohen, Professor of Law from the University of Washington, and Liu Yiu-chu, a patriotic barrister from Hong Kong were invited as consultants for the drafting of the constitution and contract for joint ventures.

Barrister Liu told us that the constitution and contract were not enough to cover joint ventures with Chinese and foreign capital. The nation needed a "law bank," she suggested, which meant that we should formulate a law on Sino-foreign equity joint ventures to serve as the legal basis for the constitution and contract to be drafted. Her proposal drew positive response from leaders of the central government.

Gu Ming, then Vice Minister of the State Planning Commission and Vice Chairman of the Legislative Committee of the National People's Congress, recalled: About the time of the Third Plenary Session of the 11th Party Central Committee, toward the end of 1978, Deng pointed out time and again that the rule of law should be guaranteed in socialist construction, especially where the use of foreign capital and import of equipment and technology were concerned. On no account should decisions be left in the hands of a few individuals, he said, and no time should be lost in enacting economic statutes. Acting on Deng's instruction, Ye Jianying, Chairman of the Standing Committee of the National People's Congress, issued the order that legislation work be started immediately with Peng Zhen, Vice Chairman of the NPC Standing Committee, in full charge, and Gu Ming presiding over the drafting work. The team of drafters consisted of experienced experts from the industrial and business circles, law specialists and consultants from Hong Kong, as well as those of us involved with foreign companies. Telegrams were transmitted to 20 or so Chinese embassies abroad, asking them to assist by gathering useful information. Peng Zhen and Gu Ming chaired a number of hearings, and joined the team of drafters in discussions.

While the drafters agreed on granting foreign investors with preferential treatment, it took many rounds of discussion to work out the specifics. For example, the corporate income tax rate was eventually set at 30 percent plus a 3 percent local surtax rate, over and above a certain mitigation or exemption period. It turned out that the 33 percent tax rate was slightly lower than in most Southeast Asian countries and regions.

Another focus of discussion was whether the duration of a joint venture should be limited, and if so, how long it should be. If the term was too short, would it prompt short-sighted behavior on the part of foreign investors?

A third focus of discussion was the proper percentage of foreign capital in a joint venture. The question was whether there should be a ceiling or a floor on it. Some drafters favored a ceiling at 51 percent, while the others chose a floor of 25 percent. Rong Yiren determined that a ceiling was unnecessary because the nation's goal was to obtain as much foreign investment as possible, but a floor was definitely needed. When Ye Jianying got word of the discussion, he saw no reason why foreign capital in a joint venture should be kept below 51 percent, but he saw fit to set the base number at 25 percent. Thus the issue was settled. Later, when the draft of the law on joint ventures with Chinese and foreign capital was submitted to the National People's Congress for approval, Ye emphasized that the right to amend this law belonged to the National People's Congress and asked that this stipulation be written into the law.

Deng Xiaoping was personally concerned with the drafting work. During a meeting with Takeiri Yoshikatsu, leader of the Komei Party of Japan, on June 28, 1979, he said of the law pending the endorsement by the NPC:

This law still leaves something to be desired, owing to our lack of experience. We would rather it be taken as a statement of our political intention than a piece of legislation.

Given our limited understanding and actual conditions at the time, the best we could do with the *Law of the People's Republic of China on Chinese-Foreign Equity Joint Ventures (draft)* was to prescribe general principles on certain issues before we delivered it for deliberation and endorsement. The Second Session of the Fifth National People's Congress endorsed it on July 1, 1979 and promulgated it on July 8, 1979.

The promulgation of the *Law on Chinese-Foreign Equity Joint Ventures* was a milestone in the nation's effort to execute Deng's strategic plan for absorbing foreign investment and setting up joint ventures. Despite its imperfections, which required later amendments, the law furnished the legal backing for that effort and was instrumental in the rapid, healthy growth of joint ventures in China.

Owing to the deep-rooted influence of ultra-leftist ideology, however, it was natural for people to take different attitudes toward such major issues as the country's collaboration with foreign capitalists in running joint ventures. In came Deng Xiaoping, who was adamant in his political and moral support of it. During an inspection tour to Tianjin in August 1979, he told leaders of the municipal government:

What I'm going to say is still the same – "emancipate the mind." To emancipate the mind is to stick to dialectical materialism. Government departments should be released from outmoded ideas. Local governments should do the same. The energy released from an emancipated mind can be enormous. We won't be able to develop productivity without emancipating the mind. ... In the past, whoever dared to undertake the Four Modernizations or joint ventures would have been weighed down by the all-too-serious labels "believer of slavish comprador philosophy" or "renegade." Even today some people are still accusing us of going in for capitalism instead of socialism or class struggle. Our rationale is quite simple: If we are to demonstrate the superiority of the socialist system, the key lies in developing productivity and boosting people's incomes. Empty talk, however smooth, will only leave everybody in poverty. Then could there be any superiority to speak of?

These remarks struck a deep chord in everyone present, and inspired heartfelt admiration for Deng, the great proletarian revolutionist and statesman who was able to pinpoint, from a multitude of things, the decisive link and to return the nation to normalcy by rectifying the guidelines.

CITIC: A New Channel for Foreign Investment

Another event that hit the headlines in 1979 was the inauguration of the China International Trust and Investment Corporation (CITIC). Inspired by his conversation with Deng on January 17, Rong Yiren brainstormed with some colleagues and submitted the proposal, which was approved by the central government in June. The State Council then set up a preparatory group for it on July 8, the day the *Law on Chinese-Foreign Equity Joint Ventures* was promulgated. According to the CITIC constitution and the relevant state legislation, the mission of the corporation was to channel, absorb and utilize foreign investment, to import advanced technology and equipment, and to invest in construction projects, for the purpose of spurring socialist development. In the meantime, the Fujian Foreign Investment Enterprise Corporation (predecessor of the Fujian International Trust and Investment Corporation) was founded in Fujian Province to procure overseas Chinese capital to run enterprises or joint ventures in China.

Deng Xiaoping closely followed the progress of CITIC. Whenever he met Rong Yiren, he always inquired about the preparations for it. According to Rong, Deng once told him, "It all rests on you to recruit staff and handle things. You are the man in charge." Time and again, Deng urged him to "defy interference and not to worry about interventions from government departments. At the same time, don't get bogged down by red tape and bureaucracy." These remarks already contained the embryo of the idea that Deng was soon to broach: to separate government administration from business management.

After a few months' preparation, CITIC was officially established on October 4, 1979 directly under the administration of the State Council. It met with quite a few snags in its operations due to institutional impediments and lack of experience. Thanks

Deng Xiaoping meeting with Rong Yiren (*first left*) and some members of the Rong family, including those in the mainland and overseas relatives on a sightseeing tour from the US, Canada, Australia, as well as Hong Kong and Macao, June 16, 1986.

to the support of Deng and other state leaders, the company eventually took root and gathered momentum with the completion of its dark brown office building – the tallest of its kind in Beijing at the time – with its bronze nameplate graced with an inscription in NPC Chairman Ye Jianying's own handwriting. The rise of CITIC evoked positive responses both at home and abroad, for it played no small role in China's effort to solicit the much-needed foreign investment. In 1981, the Jiangsu Yizheng Chemical Fiber Plant, one of the 22 major state construction projects, was about to collapse for lack of follow-up money. When Rong learned of the situation, he petitioned the State Council to save the plant by issuing bonds overseas. Many found the proposal outrageous. They said, "Imagine socialism wanting to borrow from capitalism! What will become of our economy if that is allowed to happen? What are the CITIC people up to?" Braving the opposition, the State Council granted Rong's petition. In January 1982, CITIC issued 10 billion yen of private placement bonds in Japan, which were purchased by 30 financial institutions at an 8.7 percent interest rate for a term of 12 years. With the money thus raised, the Yizheng Chemical Fiber Plant completed its first phase of construction and went into operation.

Over the years, by drawing upon the successful economic experience of Western countries, CITIC has carried out extensive economic and technological cooperation at home and abroad. At home, it has set up industrial enterprises in such fields as finance, technology, trade, real estate, and economic consultation. Abroad, it has invested and issued bonds whenever opportunities presented themselves, and never stopped exploring uncharted territory in the business world. In a relatively short period of time, it has grown into a world-renowned conglomerate and served as a new window on China's opening-up endeavor, thus making its due contributions to the socialist modernization drive.

The First Group of Joint Ventures

On June 26, 1979, Vice Chairman of the NPC Standing Committee, Peng Zhen, in his briefing on the *Law on Chinese-Foreign Equity Joint Ventures (draft)* at the Second Session of the Fifth National People's Congress, pointed out, "For this law to be enforced without a hitch, we should make procedural regulations

Report on *Procedural Regulations for the Law on Chinese-Foreign Equity Joint Ventures (draft)*, submitted by the State Import and Export Commission, December 1981.

and relevant economic laws in the near future." Taking the cue, the State Foreign Investment Commission, established in August 1979, lost no time drafting procedural regulations while aggressively pushing the negotiations that would lead to the birth of the first batch of joint ventures in China.

At the time, negotiations were taking place on a number of joint ventures. Because of differences in social systems, Chinese and foreign negotiators found it difficult to see eye to eye on specific issues. This situation was not lost on central government leaders. They encouraged those of us at the negotiation table to keep an open mind. Now that we are cooperating with capitalist enterprises, they said, we cannot keep rigidly to central planning practices. While other enterprises continued to operate in the Chinese way, joint ventures should be geared up to international conventions. This situation called for special regulations to "disconnect" the joint ventures from the planned economy, and the opening of a "second battlefield" to accommodate them.

However, this was easier said than done. The negotiations could hardly move forward with ideological and administrative obstacles in the way. At my wit's end, I decided to turn to Deng for inspiration. I wrote a letter to him about the snags we had encountered, in which I said:

Acting on central government directives, we started negotiations on the heavy-duty vehicle project with General Motors of the United States and some other foreign companies toward the end of last year (1978). But we have found it very difficult to move the negotiations forward due to a host of unsettled issues of principle concerning planning, finance, price, tax, foreign exchange, credit, labor, wages, foreign investment, and logistics. We have petitioned the relevant authorities for solutions, but received no definite answers. Things have become rather tough for us negotiators during the past ten months. In name, we are under the leadership of the General Bureau for Automobile Production of the First Ministry of Machine-Building Industry, but in practice, the Bureau does not have the final say on a lot of things under the current multipolar bureaucracy, in which authorities invested with the veto power are entangled vertically and horizontally. Every time we want to get things done, we cannot budge an inch under this intricate bureaucracy, and we have the feeling we are being hogtied by numerous ropes descending out of nowhere.

Our work on joint ventures has all along received the solicitous care of the central authorities. We also have the backing
of the State Council Office of the Leading Group for New
Technology Imports, which is now the State Foreign Investment
Commission. Those of us directly involved in the negotiations
are resolved to do things faster and better and change the situation where our country spends hundreds of millions of US dollars
every year importing heavy-duty vehicles. However, despite our
effort and time, little progress has been made due to administrative obstacles. Central government leaders have instructed
us to open up a "second battlefield" and to "disconnect"
from the planned economy. Gu Ming, Vice Minister of the State
Planning Commission, has also encouraged us to "disconnect"
our heavy-duty vehicle project. When we seek instructions from
relevant authorities about how to do it, however, some of them
respond, "We don't know a thing about 'disconnection'" or
"Go ask those who told you so." Others just want no part of it
at all, as if they themselves have already "disconnected" from
us and our project. Price is another issue of great concern to our
foreign investors, who want us to provide relevant information so
they can prepare their plans. We prepared the needed materials
and suggestions months ago, but we want the State Commodity
Price Administration to review them for us. Wang Daohan and
Ma Bin, both leaders of the State Foreign Investment Commission, even called a meeting to urge the Administration to come

Manuscript of the author's letter to Deng in August 1979 about bottlenecks in joint
venture negotiations, and an abstract of the letter (*first page from left*) prepared by the
Letters and Calls Bureau of the General Office of the Party Central Committee.

up with a solution. But so far we have received no feedback at all. These are not the only cases in point. We are totally at a loss as to what to do next. The foreign investors, as they learn more about the situation, are growing increasingly anxious about the prospects of cooperation with us. This is perhaps one of the main reasons why the Japanese, who have had the most contact with us so far, are hesitant to launch a joint venture with us.

So it is our hope that the State Council will convene a meeting of leaders from the departments concerned to unify thoughts and decide what is to be done with joint ventures in terms of planning, finance, price, tax, foreign currency, credit, labor, wages, foreign investment, and materials. Perhaps it would be best to launch some pilot projects as soon as possible with the support of those departments.

The above ideas may sound half-formed. I write this letter for your reference only.

Deng's office considered what I had said in my letter to be no laughing matter. After Deng read and commented on it, Wang Ruilin, his secretary, sent it to Vice Premier Gu Mu with the note: "I am sending a letter to Vice Premier Gu, with the suggestion that he read it and issue an instruction on it. – Wang Ruilin, August 29."

Upon reading my letter the vice premier wrote in the margins of it: "(Wang) Daohan and (Zhou) Jiannan: Please consider the issues this letter has mentioned, and directly tell Li Lanqing, with whom you must be familiar, what you think about it. – Gu Mu, September 13."

By that time the State Foreign Investment Commission had already started drafting procedural regulations for the *Law on Chinese-Foreign Equity Joint Ventures*. However, the wide range of topics to be covered and their complicated relations with state policy, the time-consuming lawmaking process, plus the lack of experience, made it difficult for the Commission to finish the task anytime soon. So the Commission decided to prepare an initial directive, to tackle the urgent issues that had arisen from the negotiations.

After six months of research, coordination and drafting, the State Foreign Investment Commission submitted to the central government the *Request for Instructions on Issues Concerning Chinese-Foreign Joint Ventures* on January 14, 1980. Its main points were that:

1) A joint venture shall have a board of directors, to be chaired by a Chinese, who shall not decide everything on his own. Major issues, particularly those concerning fundamental rights and interests of the two parties, should be decided through consultation on the principle of equality and mutual benefit. Other issues should be settled by a majority or two thirds of the directors, pursuant to provisions of the agreement and constitution of the joint venture.

2) A joint venture shall be under the responsibility of a general manager. The office of the general manager shall be assumed flexibly – it may be held by the two sides to the joint venture by turns, by the Chinese side, or by the foreign side in the first years after the contract comes into force. The deputy general manager shall supervise the general manager in addition to assisting him. The general manager's important decisions and instructions shall also be signed by the deputy general manager to set both parties to the joint venture at ease.

3) To allay foreign investors' doubts, the Chinese government shall not confiscate or requisition the assets of the foreign partner to a joint venture. The foreign partner shall be duly compensated if circumstances (as in time of war) necessitate such requisitioning. It is implied in the provision of the *Law on Chinese-Foreign Equity Joint Ventures* that the Chinese government shall protect the lawful rights and interests of foreign partners to joint ventures.

4) A joint venture shall employ or dismiss workers and staff members according to its own needs, and fire those who have seriously violated labor disciplines. Such autonomy, and the concrete conditions attached to it, shall be provided for in a labor contract signed between the management and the trade union.

5) Some countries collect the corporate income tax at a certain rate after deducting from the gross profit a reserve fund, a venture expansion fund, and a bonus and welfare fund for workers and staff members. Our suggestion is that the corporate income tax shall be levied before the aforementioned deductions

are made, thus at the same tax rate, the amount levied shall be higher. So we see fit to set the tax rate at 35 percent, about 11 percent lower than in the United States, 15 percent lower than in Britain, France and West Germany, 20 percent lower than in Japan, and by and large the same as in the other developing countries. There shall also be a local surtax to cover urban development and other fees, to be collected by the central government and reallocated to localities; its rate shall be fixed later through consultation. To prevent excessive profits for foreign partners, an additional 50 percent income tax shall be imposed on a profit rate that goes beyond 20 percent after the regular corporate income tax is paid and the above-mentioned funds deducted.

6) A foreign partner can remit its profit abroad by using the foreign currency reserve of the joint venture, provided a 10 percent income tax is paid. However, that tax will be waived if no profit is remitted abroad, so as to encourage consumption and reinvestment in China.

7) The salaries and wages of workers and staff members will take as the standard the average of advanced piece-rate wages in China, with time-rate wages converted from labor productivity. At present, joint venture employees may be granted a 20 to 50 percent allowance based on the wage-and-bonus level for the same technical level in the same area or same type of business or production work. Labor insurance, medical insurance, state subsidy to employees (at an estimated 104 percent of the average pay), and housing construction fees (at an estimated 64 percent of their average pay) shall be spent under trade union supervision or submitted to the state.

8) To prevent joint ventures from excessive requisitioning and waste of land, a 15-year land-use fee of 200,000 yuan to 3 million yuan per *mu* (one *mu* equals one-fifteenth of a hectare) shall be collected. The exact standard for this fee shall be set by provinces, autonomous regions and municipalities in the light of the current level of local urban construction and demolition and resettlement expenses. Joint ventures may apply for a reduction of the land-use fee under special circumstances. Under the principle of equality and mutual benefit, and without compromising state sovereignty, the standard for this fee shall be handled flexibly to allow a profit for foreign investors, and be generous enough to maximize the influx of foreign investment.

Li Xiannian and Peng Zhen gave their consent in writing the day they received the *Request*. No time should be wasted to effect all the points listed in this document, they stated, and to speed things up, the approaches should be as flexible as possible. Both leaders suggested that the *Request* be transmitted to provinces, autonomous regions, municipalities and State Council ministries and commissions, so that it could serve as internal guideline for negotiations on joint ventures.

The central authorities transmitted the *Request* accordingly on February 6, 1980, along with the letter of consent from Li and Peng and the instruction:

> Running joint ventures with the international bourgeoisie is an extremely complex task, and something yet to be experienced by us all. It is thus difficult to handle every aspect perfectly. If we are too rigid, no one will come to us, and if we are too generous, our interests will be impaired. We must proceed seriously and never let down our guard. Localities and industries shall proceed realistically to hammer out the specifics of the principles and approaches listed in the *Request* through consultations with foreign investors. Only after a few contracts are signed can we sum up the experience and lessons and formulate relevant laws and regulations.

The dissemination of the *Request* in the form of an official central document with Deng's backing, the promulgation of the *Law on Chinese-Foreign Equity Joint Ventures*, and the adoption of a series of follow-up rules and regulations, paved the way for negotiations on a number of joint ventures and the initiation of talks on more projects.

Meanwhile, government leaders used the appropriate occasions to publicize the opening-up policy and the steps the nation had adopted for foreign investment utilization, which helped bolster foreign investors' confidence in China.

Vice Premier Yu Qiuli, when talking about joint ventures with Chinese and foreign capital at an April 10, 1980 press conference during his visit to Japan, stated on behalf of the Chinese government: "Our policy for this field of endeavor is clear: We are committed to honoring the joint venture contracts we sign with our foreign partners." Telling his hosts that more specific laws were yet to be enacted, such as corporate, tax and labor laws, the vice premier said:

> I can assure you of the following in no uncertain terms. First, in compliance with the *Law on Chinese-Foreign Equity Joint Ventures*, the Chinese government shall not confiscate or requisition the foreign investors' properties. Only under very unusual circumstances may the state demand the use of such properties with due compensation. Second, joint ventures shall operate within a system in which the general manager takes full responsibility under the board of directors, and either side to such a joint venture can appoint the general manager. Third, joint ventures shall be vested with autonomy to employ or dismiss workers and staff members according to business needs, or fire those who have seriously violated labor disciplines. Fourth, joint ventures are encouraged to purchase raw materials, fuels and parts from the Chinese market in the first place, but their foreign partners may also buy from international markets with their own foreign currency reserves. Fifth, when setting the rate of corporate income taxes for joint ventures, due consideration shall be given to guaranteeing foreign investors' reasonable profits and lawful rights and interests.

No Substituting Contracts for State Law

Back then, legislation work on foreign investment had just got off to a start, and the joint venture law was the only statute we had. In the absence of procedural regulations, legal blanks had yet to be filled in to handle many practical problems. People's awareness of the rule of law needed to be raised, too. As a result, the economic and trade contracts concluded with foreign partners often included clauses that put Chinese interests at risk.

In June 1980, the Guangzhou Legal Advisory Office reported two contracts that contained articles detrimental to state sovereignty and national economic interests. One was the draft *Contract on Establishing and Operating a Radial Rubber Tire Joint Venture in Guangzhou* between the Guangzhou Municipal

Rubber Industry Bureau and the French Sino-French Rubber Holdings. The draft contract stipulated: "This contract shall be subject to laws of the state of New York. ... Arbitration shall be carried out, in response to either party's request, by three arbitrators appointed by the American Arbitration Association in accordance with the regulations of the association." Also stipulated was the joint venture's right to issue and deal bills and securities, and to operate movable or fixed assets. The other was the draft of the *Compensation Trade Contract on Construction of a Twin-Tower Office Building in Guangzhou* between the Guangzhou Sci-Tech Exchange Museum and an American partner. It stipulated that the American party to the contract could terminate the contract without seeking agreement from the Chinese party and demand a refund for its paid-up investment and interests. Both contracts demanded that Chinese ownership of land be reverted to the joint ventures. In both cases the foreign party sought to sign the contract with the Chinese government as the other party, and requested that the Chinese party give up defense of sovereign immunity. Both draft contracts included clauses on taxation, customs, foreign exchange, salaries and wages, entry and exit visas that transcended the Chinese economic legislation – the intention of the foreign investors to substitute contracts for Chinese state law was all too revealing. The American consultants to the two contracts wanted to talk the Chinese side into accepting these clauses under the pretext that China did not have its own civil laws.

Upon learning of the cases, the Ministry of Justice immediately reported to Vice Premiers Gu Mu and Yao Yilin, suggesting that Chinese lawyers be hired whenever Chinese companies negotiated and entered into contracts with foreign investors. On June 10, Gu Mu forwarded to the State Foreign Investment Commission the Xinhua News Agency's note on an internal-reference report on the issue: "Wang (Daohan), Jiang (Zemin) and Zhou (Jiannan), please take a look at the problem." Two days later, the vice premier wrote down the instruction on the ministry's report, "This is a good idea. (Wang) Daohan, please do some research and prescribe some rules to be executed by the relevant localities and ministries and commissions."

With Wang Daohan, Zhou Jiannan, Jiang Zemin, and Zhou Xuancheng playing a coordinating role, the State Foreign Investment Commission issued the *Provisions on Negotiations and Contracts Concerning Chinese-Foreign Joint Ventures* on August 3, 1980. The *Provisions* asked governments and departments at all levels to tighten supervision over negotiations and contracts with foreign investors; to safeguard state sovereignty and interests while ensuring mutual benefit; to organize negotiation teams consisting of experts in policies, technology, law, and finance; to bring together negotiators for a study of relevant policies, laws and regulations, and make thorough planning; to take the initiative in setting forth the contract to be negotiated while making it a point to carefully analyze the contract proposed by the foreign side and consulting competent authorities before signing it; to operate within their bounds of authority to examine and approve joint ventures; to develop a pool of lawyers and accountants and to establish legal consultancy offices and accounting firms where possible. These provisions were stopgap measures in the absence of comprehensive laws concerning foreign investment.

The State Foreign Investment Commission (and later, the Ministry of Foreign Economic Relations and Trade) followed up with a series of draft foreign trade laws and regulations based on research and foreign experience. These included the drafts of the *Procedural Regulations for the Law on Chinese-Foreign Equity Joint Ventures* and the *Law of the People's Republic of China on Foreign-Capital Enterprises*. Rudimentary as they were, these laws formed a sound framework and groundwork for a much-improved legal system concerning foreign economic relations.

The Chinese practice in utilizing foreign investment in the early years of the opening-up policy also helped to improve the nation's arbitration system where foreign economic relations and trade were concerned. The Foreign Trade Arbitration Commission was already in place in April 1956, but its functions were restricted to matters of foreign trade. When it came to protecting the rights and interests of Chinese enterprises in making use of foreign investment, arbitration work had to be entrusted to Switzerland- or Hong Kong-based international arbitration organizations, a practice that was prescribed by state requirement in contracts signed with foreign investors in those years.

To plug up this loophole, the Foreign Trade Arbitration Commission was, with State Council approval, renamed the "Foreign Economic and Trade Arbitration Commission" in February 1980, and again in 1988, the "China International Economic and Trade Arbitration Commission." As its new names indicated, the commission's functions were extended from foreign trade to investment, and from national to international disputes. It became the first Chinese arbitration organization to which Chinese enterprises could turn for assistance in case of international disputes.

To prepare Chinese negotiators for foreign investors' queries about Chinese policies, and to regulate contract terms, the State Foreign Investment Commission compiled a collection of extracts of relevant articles and speeches by Chinese leaders. With approval by Wang Daohan and Jiang Zemin, copies of the collection were distributed among those in negotiations with foreign investors.

These steps made joint venture negotiations a lot more convenient. From the day the idea was broached until the end of June 1981, a total of 29 joint ventures with Chinese and foreign capital were established for a total investment of US$240 million, with US$197 million committed by foreign investors. Fifteen of these joint ventures were already in operation with fairly good economic results, and five were under construction. And a host of new joint ventures were being initiated or under negotiation.

To further relieve foreign investors of concerns about investing in China and to ensure the healthy operation of joint ventures that had already been established, it became necessary to draft procedural regulations for the *Law on Chinese-Foreign Equity Joint Ventures*. The State Foreign Investment Commission began the drafting work toward the end of 1979 and solicited opinions during the national import and export work conferences in 1979 and 1980. In November 1980, a symposium on Chinese-foreign joint ventures was held to deliberate and amend the draft. In January 1981, opinions on the revised draft were canvassed from the relevant State Council departments, some provincial and municipal import and export commissions or offices, law schools and institutions, and joint ventures. Law experts of the United Nations Center on Transnational

Corporations (UNCTC) and foreign law experts in Beijing were also consulted twice. In September 1981, over 110 participants from over 90 organizations – including 32 State Council departments, 15 provincial import and export commissions, and law schools, law firms and joint ventures – gathered at a forum and discussed the fourth draft chapter by chapter and article by article. A fifth draft was produced and submitted to the State Council thereafter for further deliberation, criticism and amendment in the principle of making the regulations conducive to attracting as much foreign investment as possible. Under the prerequisite of safeguarding state sovereignty, equality and mutual benefit, the regulations should be flexible enough to adapt to specific circumstances and enable incentive measures to be faithfully implemented. Where it was premature to lay down specific stipulations, problems could be handled through consultations by negotiators.

On September 20, 1983, the State Council approved and issued the *Procedural Regulations for the Law on Chinese-Foreign Equity Joint Ventures*, and authorized the State Foreign Investment Commission to interpret it and to recommend necessary amendments or additions to the State Council. The *Procedural Regulations* signified a quantum leap in Chinese legislation concerning Sino-foreign joint ventures.

Nothing is easy at the beginning, as the Chinese saying goes. The success or failure of the first batch of joint ventures could make or break this strategic arrangement. To guarantee success, the State Foreign Investment Commission made a point of providing Chinese negotiators with guidance and assistance and helping them solve practical problems occurring from negotiation processes.

The Birth of the First Three Joint Ventures

Through careful and minutely detailed negotiations on the basis of equality and mutual benefit, contracts of three joint ventures in China were inked on April 10, 1980 with the approval of the State Foreign Investment Commission. These were Beijing Air Catering, the Beijing Jianguo Hotel Corporation and the Beijing Great Wall Sheraton Hotel Corporation. The applications of the trio were sent in at the same time, but on April 21, China's number one joint venture certificate was granted to Beijing Air Catering for the single reason that it was the only productive company of the three.

In early May, 1980, Vice Minister Jiang Zemin, in charge of the State Foreign Investment Commission, was one of those who saw history in the making with the inauguration of the first joint venture in China, Beijing Air Catering. Before long, the other two joint ventures were born in succession.

These and others among the earliest joint ventures in China shared three salient features in common. First, they were small in scale, investment, and number, a fact that made sense at a time when most foreign investors were watching on with a wait-and-see attitude while a few "daredevils" tested the water. Second, most foreign parties to such joint ventures came from Hong Kong, which was natural because these compatriots knew China better than foreigners. Third, most of these joint ventures were in fields where China was utterly underdeveloped, or yet to get started, and many of their products had fine export prospects, something the Chinese government was only too happy to accept, provided they could maintain their own foreign exchange balances.

Notice of the State Foreign Investment Commission, approving establishment of Beijing Air Catering.

Jiang Zemin (*far right*), Shen Tu (*second from left*) and James Tak Wu (*far left*) at the inauguration of Beijing Air Catering.

Beijing Air Catering – The Very First Joint Venture

In times of food shortages, the quality and variety of air food naturally failed to meet the passengers' demand. Overseas planes coming in and out of the country had to supply food from Hong Kong or other places outside China. James Tak Wu, a well-known Hong Kong entrepreneur in the food processing industry, proposed to Shen Tu, director of the Civil Aviation Administration of China (CAAC), the idea of setting up a joint air catering venture. According to the eventual contract, of the total 5.88 million yuan investment, CAAC made up 51 percent and the Hong Kong side 49 percent. The joint venture, which officially went into operation on May 1, 1980, soon improved air food supply in China with advanced technology, equipment and international standard services. It also had a much higher output, from 640 meals a day under the original CAAC company to 60,000 meals daily by the end of 2007.

The new ways of a joint venture also brought dramatic ideological conflicts among the employees, who were used to the "big-pot" system – that is, payment disconnected from individual performance. The concept of "joint investment" made them excited and curious, and at the same shocked. Were the workers also owners of the joint venture, as they had been of state-owned enterprises? How were they going to interact with the foreigners who were now their bosses? Before, they had only seen foreigners at a distance in busy downtown areas. Would all the producing and managing methods of the original state-owned enterprise be thrown out? Could the Hong Kong concepts and regulations of management work smoothly in the mainland?

Before the joint venture came into being, the CAAC company would provide whatever meals they could prepare without considering the real needs of passengers. For example, the bread was as hard as cold steamed buns, with crumbs dropping at a touch. By contrast, the joint venture imported raw materials from abroad and baked bread with modern equipment, which was both pleasing to the eye and soft and tasty. This surprised the workers, who were accustomed to the traditional bread-baking process. More surprising things were yet to happen.

One day, a batch of food ingredients arrived in Beijing from Hong Kong, the contents of which were to be prepared for meals for foreign airlines. It included salmon, beef fillets and special sauces, and many other ingredients that were unknown to the mainlanders. Moreover, these half-prepared products and garnishes needed to be cooked with such new and special methods that the workers were simply dumbfounded.

For the veteran chefs, who were used to the clinking and clanking of traditional pots, bowls and woks, the new cooking utensils made of shining stainless steel suddenly turned them into new hands. They had to learn everything from the beginning and follow instructions given by their foreign foremen, who were appointed by the Hong Kong side and who spoke alien tongues. Naturally, they felt lost, uncertain and awkward.

At the early stage of the joint venture, mainland workers had to adapt quickly to the advanced international skills and ideas of food preparation while going through drastic cultural and ideological changes, such as punching in and out at work. Although this is now as common as wearing uniforms at work, it was a rare practice in the early 1980s.

Workers of the time were accustomed to the "big pot" system and "management by man" instead of "management by rules." They carried on endless talks about the "punching the clock" issue. Some felt perplexed, and others angry. Some remarked that they were the owners of the enterprise and now were required to punch in and out, supervised and inspected by machines; it was an insult! Others said that punching in and out was not a guarantee of work discipline, but a way for capitalists to "manage, controll and oppress" the workers. Still others made more vehement comments: punching in was like brandishing a whip over the head of the working people. Some even accused Hong Kong managers of being unfriendly and insulting, when the latter were simply reminding them to punch in. From the Hong Kong side, they could not understand the fierce opposition from the workers: punching in and out at work was one of the basic regulations for Hong Kong and international companies, and there was no need to make any explanations.

Punching in and similar practices that are now commonplace caused a so-called "fierce proletarian and capitalist ideological confrontation." Some were even reported to top CAAC authorities for consideration.

However, enterprises are enterprises. Once established, the joint venture embarked on the normal track of production and operation, and strict management was carried out. It served as a platform for people to gain a broader vision of the outside world, to understand what international standards were, and to learn the new demands and standards required of them. Having gone through complex emotional turmoil – from admiration and perplexity, to eventual adaptation – Beijing Air Catering gradually grew up to become an industry leader in China.

The first group of joint venture hotels catered to international guests also experienced hardships.

After the Third Plenary Session of the 11th Party Central Committee, China opened its doors to the outside world. Compatriots from Hong Kong and Macao, and overseas Chinese, as well as foreign travelers, flooded into this long-isolated land. The year 1978 saw the entry of up to 1.8 million visitors, exceeding the total over the previous two decades, and the number increased to 4.2 million in 1979. At the time only 1,000 beds were available in hotels that met the standards for accommodating overseas visitors. To make matters worse, infrastructure, service, food, and management all fell far short of those of star hotels abroad. To resolve the shortage of beds, in June 1978, the Beijing municipality set up a special group to arrange rooms for overseas Chinese and foreigners. The Beijing Hotel, Xinqiao Hotel, Minzu Hotel, Qianmen Hotel, Friendship Hotel, Prime Hotel, and Overseas Chinese Hotel were designated by the group to receive these guests exclusively. They were allowed to accommodate domestic meetings only in slack tourist seasons. In April 1979, the State Council approved the *Report on Hotels to Accommodate Foreign Visitors* submitted by the Beijing municipality and the China Tourism Administration. The report required the relevant departments and organizations to contact the Beijing No.1 Service Bureau to confirm room accommodations before starting invitation procedures for overseas visitors. No invitation would be approved without a room confirmation from the Bureau. The ministries even had to send staff to queue at the Beijing Hotel early in the morning for booking rooms and they were often unsuccessful. So they sometimes had to ask their guests to spend the night in the lobby while waiting for vacant rooms. Many visitors could not be accommodated immediately after a long flight; they would then be driven to scenic spots for sightseeing, or asked to wait in hotel lobbies or at the airport until rooms became available. Sometimes hotel rooms were so scarce that visitors had to be driven to Tianjin, or flown to Nanjing and Shanghai. In Guilin, a tourist city in the Guangxi Zhuang Autonomous Region, some visitors had the experience of sleeping on makeshift beds on the floor. So someone improvised a line of doggerel: "The scenery of Guilin is the best in the land / But I spent my night in Guilin sleeping on the ground."

The shortage of hotels had started to mar the image of China as an open country, and this caught the attention of the central government. Deng Xiaoping talked about the issue on October 9, 1978, saying, "It should be workable to use foreign investment in hotel construction. We should start in a number of places, such as Kunming, Guilin and Chengdu, and prepare one or two thousand beds in each place." He went further to make a calculation: If a foreign visitor spent US$1,000 in China, and if China received 10 million visitors in a year, that would bring in US$10 billion. Even if the number of arrivals was cut in half, it would still mean a profit of US$5 billion in profit.

To resolve the hotel issue, the State Council set up a leading group in charge of procuring overseas Chinese and foreign investment to build tourist hotels. The group was headed by Vice Premiers Gu Mu and Chen Muhua, and Liao Chengzhi, Director of the Overseas Chinese Affairs Office of the State Council. The leading group established its office in the China Tourism Administration, which was established in August 1978 and later renamed the State Tourism Administration. Lu Xuzhang, Director of the Administration, served as Chief of the office and Zhuang Yanlin, Deputy Director of the Administration, served as Deputy Executive Chief in charge of day-to-day work. Liao Chengzhi told Zhuang that his job was to procure outside investment to build hotels, an important condition for reform and opening. He emphasized, "Making use of overseas funds to build hotels is something new. For sure, there will be unexpected obstacles.

You should be prepared for all sorts of storms and waves lashing at you. Most importantly, you must stand firm and not be brought down by winds or waves. Be the first crab-eater*!" Gu Mu and Liao Chengzhi hosted a meeting at the Jingxi Hotel in Beijing from September 12 to 15 on how to effectively attract overseas funds. The memos of the meeting were submitted to the central government.

During a discussion on economic development with Yu Qiuli, Fang Yi and Gu Mu on January 6, 1979, Deng Xiaoping pointed out:

> To develop the tourism industry, hotels must be built quickly. For the first batch, we can use outside investment, and then we can build more hotels by ourselves. Once policies are made, we must carry them out. First of all, we must put the right people in charge; otherwise, implementation will be a problem.

Jianguo Hotel – The First Joint-Venture Hotel

To construct hotels with joint investment, the first and foremost thing was to find appropriate partners for cooperation, followed by negotiations, a feasibility analysis and the signing of contracts. Within a year, the Tourism Administration contacted and held talks with more than 120 overseas Chinese or foreign business people from more than 20 countries and regions, and made in-depth analysis about cooperative modes, the heights of potential hotels, building materials and furnishing, management, and debt-repaying ability.

It was then shortly after the end of the Cultural Revolution and the ultra-leftist trend of thought was yet to be completely eliminated. While the talks on cooperation were going on, critical voices quickly circulated. "They've been negotiating with one group after another of foreigners, and have treated the foreigners to so many roast ducks that if stacked up, they would be as high as a high-rise hotel. What on earth do they want to do?" "We have sent satellites into the sky; how come we can't

---

* This phrase refers to the vision and bravery that must have been involved when the first person undertook to catch and eat a crab and found it delicious. (*Translator*)

build and manage hotels by ourselves? Shouldn't we Chinese be ashamed to ask for help from foreigners?" During the negotiations, some potential partners recommended a type of building to be constructed with simple, prefabricated components. As soon as the foundation was laid, building parts would be transported immediately to the site for quick assembly, complete with furniture, and the hotel was ready for business! This interested people at the negotiation table, and even Deng Xiaoping and Gu Mu. Actually, this kind of structure had been used to house Japanese experts in a Sino-Japanese joint oil-drilling project in Bohai Bay. Yet when the negotiation got underway, criticism spread. "Isn't it blind worship of foreign things to import even sand and stone from abroad?" Such remarks were not the worst. More stringent was the accusation: "Building hotels with joint investment? Making money out of the Chinese people, together with foreign capitalists? This is a matter of class stand! Can't we build hotels by ourselves? Why should we ask foreign capitalists to do this? It's sheer treason!"

In the face of fierce opposition, Gu Mu, Liao Chengzhi and leaders of the State Foreign Investment Commission remained steady in their support of the Jianguo Hotel project. Actually, it was Liao Chengzhi who introduced Clement Chen, Jr., a Chinese American, a hotel manager and architect, to the Tourism Administration. In his youth Chen attended the St. John's High School in Shanghai. He later moved to the United States, where he had designed, built and managed hotels, and owned four hotels and an architecture firm in San Francisco. Experienced in hotel construction and management, Chen was willing to be of service to his home country.

Negotiations with Chen went smoothly. When he learned that previous negotiations had failed to reach an agreement because some people were afraid of being taken advantage of, Chen said, "Let's settle it this way. We shall draft a plan acceptable to all parties involved on the Chinese side. My only purpose is to set up the first joint hotel in China."

The two sides finally reached an agreement: Each would invest US$10 million to jointly build the 528-bed Jianguo Hotel, with the Chinese side taking up 51 percent of the shares and Chen 49 percent. After ten years' cooperation, the Chinese side could buy out all of Chen's shares for only one US dollar. Obviously, this was in favor of the Chinese side. Moreover, the US$10 million contributed by the Chinese side was low-interest loans from Hong Kong and Shanghai Banking Corporation, Citibank, and some other foreign banks, which saw this as a promising project and offered to provide loans.

On June 7, 1979, the Tourism Administration reported the result to the State Council. As there were neither laws or regulations nor previous cases to follow, the State Council found it difficult to make a decision at its work meeting. So the report was submitted to the 17 top leaders of the central government, who either read or wrote comments on the report. Deng Xiaoping was clear-cut in his attitude: To develop tourism, we must build enough high-grade hotels. After careful analysis, all the leaders gave their approval to start the project right away. Hua Guofeng, Chairman of the Party Central Committee and Premier of the State Council, concluded on the report: "Launch it as a pilot project and try to sum up experience."

After making a careful comparison, the hotel site was chosen on Jianguomenwai Street in downtown Beijing. According to the plan, the hotel would cover around 10,000 square meters with more than 20 stories. However, the residents behind the forthcoming hotel, who were staff of a State Council department, complained about the height of the building, saying it would block the sun from reaching their apartments. After rounds of negotiations, it was agreed that to guarantee the first-floor residents would be able to enjoy sunshine even on the Winter Solstice, the part of the hotel next to the residential building would be four-and-half-story high and the other part would not exceed nine stories. However, after ground-breaking in June 1980, some residents tried all sorts of means to sabotage the project, on the excuse that the construction disturbed the residents and affected the *fengshui* of the area. In the disguise of the night, they would come to uproot the fence set up during the day and even overthrow the concrete mixer. The project could not go on.

Zhuang Yanlin, who was in charge of the project, held several discussions with the residents but to no avail. Then Liao Chengzhi told him, "Yanlin, write a report and I'll submit it

(*From left to right*) Jiang Zemin, Wei Yuming, Zhou Jiannan, and the author at the Jianguo Hotel, May 8, 1985.

to the Party Central Committee; nobody is allowed to make trouble in this case!" When the report reached Deng Xiaoping, he wrote on it: "No trouble-making is allowed even for good reason, let alone for no reason!" He told his secretary to pass on the message immediately. Only then did the project proceed smoothly.

Completed in April 1982, the hotel introduced advanced international management experience and followed the practice of "vertical leadership, each level with its own responsibility, and clear division of work with emphasis on cooperation." The hotel was also the first in China to require its attendants to serve on their feet instead of in their seats. In July 1984, the State Council issued a document to popularize the hotel's management nationwide. All investment was recouped within three years of operation. At the end of the contract period, Clement Chen, Jr. transferred the hotel to the Chinese side for free. He even donated an indoor tennis court to the Beijing Xiannongtan Stadium in 1988. In the past 26 years, the hotel has won 28 international hotel management awards, including the International Gold Hotel Award and International Gold Award for Quality.

Chen Muhua (*with headscarf*) and George Michel (*center*), US Under Secretary of Commerce, at the ground-breaking ceremony of the Great Wall Sheraton Hotel, March 10, 1981.

Deng Xiaoping (*second from left*) meets with Henry Fok Ying-tung (*far left*) at the White Swan Hotel, February 1985.

Great Wall Sheraton Hotel Beijing

This is another luxury hotel built with a joint investment of over US$70 million shared by the Beijing branch of China International Travel Service and the E-S Pacific Development and Construction Company of the United States. The hotel incorporates the theme of the Great Wall in its modern-style architecture. For such a huge project, it was natural for the US company to hesitate at the beginning due to their lack of knowledge about China. Thanks to the effective coordination by C. B. Sung, a Chinese American, the project proceeded smoothly.

White Swan Hotel – The First BOT Project

The White Swan Hotel was built with the BOT model by the celebrated Hong Kong entrepreneur Henry Fok Ying-tung. In January 1979, on learning that the mainland was going to open up to the outside world, an excited Fok contacted the Guangdong Provincial Government, proposing to build a luxury hotel in Guangzhou. He promised to invest US$135 million and borrow US$6.31 million in bank loans in the name of the hotel. The BOT model was adopted for the first time on the Chinese mainland. BOT stands for "build – operate – transfer," which means that the mainland provided land while the Hong Kong side was responsible for raising funds and building and operating the hotel for a certain number of years before transferring it to the former. In the case of the White Swan Hotel, it was agreed that the Hong Kong side would operate the hotel for 15 years, with an extension of five years later on.

Fok Ying-tung is an old friend of mine. He once recalled:

Policy was what we were concerned about most when we made investments in the mainland at the time. In one of those early years, a fresco featuring a festive scene of different ethnic groups was painted at the Beijing Capital Airport, and among the cheerful crowd was a nude girl. This led to a fierce debate on the mainland. Each time I arrived in Beijing I would make sure to see whether the fresco was still there. Its presence was a reassurance for me.

He also recalled the difficulties caused by the short supply of materials under the planned economy back then.

> A large hotel needs thousands of different materials to build and furnish, but it was hard to get almost anything in the mainland, even bathtub corks. We had to use corks for thermo bottles as substitutes. Worse still, to import even small items we had to go through a dozen or so government departments for approval.

He later hit upon a good idea: he issued invitations for the hotel opening ceremony to celebrities in Beijing, Guangdong, Hong Kong and Macao, fixing the opening date way beforehand. Fok would then show the invitation to the relevant government departments when he went through various procedures. The tactic worked and greatly sped up the construction process. When the White Swan Hotel opened for business on February 7, 1983, more than 10,000 Guangzhou residents swarmed in to witness the grand event.

Grand Dragon Hotel in Beijing – A Weather Vane for Opening Up

In the autumn of 1978, Pao Yue-kong, a well-known patriotic entrepreneur from Hong Kong, visited Beijing for the first time. Nicknamed "King of Ships," Pao was the founder of World-Wide Shipping Group in Hong Kong and a controlling shareholder of Wharf (Holdings) Limited, two consortiums with a huge influence on the Hong Kong economy. Before leaving Hong Kong, he asked his townsman Lu Xuzhang (from Ningbo, Zhejiang Province), director of the State Tourism Administration, to reserve rooms for him at the Beijing Hotel, because he had heard that hotel rooms were hard to come by. Only when he arrived at the hotel did Pao find out that there was only one suite reserved for him and his wife, but none for his staff. The next day, Bao paid a visit to Lu Xuzhang in his office. When he saw the crowded offices of the Administration, usually with several people in a ten-square-meter room, he said to Lu, "Even the director of the State Tourism Administration could not reserve rooms for me. Hotels in Beijing are really in short supply. How could you develop tourism without hotels? I hope to donate 10 million US dollars to build a hotel and an office building for your Administration." He also made a very personal request that the hotel be named after his father, (Pao) Siu-loong (meaning "Grand Dragon").

Accepting overseas donations was, at the time, still a sensitive issue. There were different opinions, and the State Tourism Administration did not give an immediate answer.

More than one year after Pao made the proposal, he came to Beijing a second time on March 15, 1980, to discuss ordering ships and joint operation with the Sixth Ministry of Machine-Building Industry. After the joint operation agreement was signed on March 21, Hua Guofeng, Wang Zhen, Gu Mu, and Yao Yilin met with Pao, who again expressed his wish of donation. Hua Guofeng spoke highly of his enthusiasm for the construction of the country, and agreed to accept his donation of US$10 million. Pao wrote a letter to Hua on the same day to confirm the donation.

Even after the senior leaders had agreed to accept the donation, some people were still opposed to it, saying that we "must not accept gifts from capitalists" and "nor should we build up monuments for them." Inside the State Tourism Administration, there were different voices, too. On April 4, 1980, the Administration submitted to the State Council the *Application for Approval of a Donation by Pao Yue-kong for the Building of a Hotel and an Office Building*. The State Council approved the report within a few days and, on July 2, designated the State Tourism Administration to be responsible for choosing the construction sites.

With support from Wan Li and the effort of relevant organizations, Baijiazhuang in Chaoyang District of Beijing was chosen as the site of the hotel. On March 13, 1981, the project was listed in the construction plan for ministries and commissions under the State Council. The hotel was named Grand Dragon, after Pao's father. On July 4, 1981, Vice Premier Chen Muhua joined Pao Yue-kong and his father at the ground-breaking ceremony. Following the event, Pao wrote a check for the equivalent of US$10 million, but he could not find the right person to accept it.

When Deng Xiaoping learned of the situation, he decided to accept the donation by himself as a gesture of support. On the morning of July 6, 1981, Deng and Wang Zhen met with Pao and his father at the Great Hall of the People. Pao handed the check to Deng, together with a letter expressing his intention to donate another US$10 million for the construction of a library for the Shanghai Jiaotong University. Acceptance of Pao's donations became a weather vane, demonstrating to the world a gradually opening up China.

The meeting with Deng gave Pao Yue-kong greater confidence in taking part in the opening up and construction of the mainland. He initiated the establishment of the International United Shipping and Investment Company, a joint venture between Hong Kong and the mainland, at a time when the latter's export of ships was almost zero. Within two years the new company purchased six cargo ships from shipyards on the Chinese mainland, making a breakthrough in China's ship export. Pao also donated to many other projects in his hometown, including the Ningbo University.

Deng Xiaoping, Ye Jianying and Wang Zhen all gave strong support to the first two projects donated by Pao. It was decided at the very beginning that the Grand Dragon Hotel would be designed, constructed and managed by Chinese architects, workers and staff. However, low efficiency of some government departments in the early 1980s resulted in the delay of the project. It was not until February 13, 1983 that the construction began. By then, Pao's father had passed away a year earlier, and, naturally, he was disappointed. Deng was displeased when he got word of it. On September 3, 1983, he gave instructions in writing to urge the construction process and calligraphed the Chinese name of the hotel.

In the early 1980s, the construction industry and management in the country were still backward. Although relevant organizations attached great importance to this "Deng Xiaoping Project," quality problems still occurred from time to time. Deng twice sent his staff to the construction site to investigate, and demanded speedy solution to the problems.

Upon completion of the hotel on October 25, 1985, Deng Xiaoping, Yang Shangkun, Wan Li, Xi Zhongxun, Gu Mu, and 20-plus ministerial officials, together with Pao Yue-kong and his family, attended the inauguration ceremony. On the previous evening more than 60 ministerial officials in Beijing attended the opening banquet, which was a rare gathering to demonstrate the central government's determination to open up and appreciation of patriotic compatriots' contributions to the motherland.

Deng Xiaoping (*center, left*), Wan Li (*far left*), Xi Zhongxun (*second from right*), Gu Mu (*far right*), and Pao Yue-kong (*third from left*) at the inauguration ceremony of the Grand Dragon Hotel, October 25, 1985.

After attending the ceremony, Deng Xiaoping continued to keep an eye on the quality problems, demanding a report on the situation before 12 o'clock on October 29. On November 1, Deng wrote his comments on the report submitted by the State Tourism Administration:

> If quality problems like these should occur in buildings, who would dare to invest in Beijing in the future? The problems must be seriously investigated and dealt with. The construction industry in Beijing must be straightened out. No revenge (of those who disclosed and dealt with the problems) shall be tolerated.

On the following day, the Beijing Municipal Government held a meeting to relay Deng's instructions and arrange for the rectification of the construction industry of Beijing. Repair work on problematic parts of the hotel ensued, thereby launching the rectification campaign.

On February 8, 1986, following Deng's instructions on the quality problems of the Grand Dragon Hotel, Kang Keqing headed a third inspection group from the National People's Congress to visit the hotel to oversee the repair process. This was soon followed by a nationwide drive to rectify the construction industry.

In May 1982, Wang Zhen wrote a letter to leaders of the Shanghai Municipal Government, demanding that a good job be done in building the Pao Siu-loong Library for Shanghai Jiaotong University, and Ye Jianying calligraphed the name of the library to show his support. At the inauguration ceremony on December 27, 1985, attended by Wang Zhen and Shanghai municipal leaders Jiang Zemin and Wang Daohang, Jiang spoke highly of Pao's contributions: "Pao Siu-loong Library stands for the lofty philanthropic spirit of Mr. Pao Yue-kong and his family in support of the Four Modernizations, the cause of education, and the cultivation of talent for the country."

These early jointly funded hotels not only eased up the acute shortage of hotel rooms for foreign visitors, but also brought in sophisticated expertise to help improve the country's hotel management and service.

Joint Venture Revives Rattan Works Industry

The West Lake Rattan Works in Hangzhou, Zhejiang Province, had been saddled with backward technology, outdated designs, poor product quality, and lack of raw materials before it opened a joint venture with a Hong Kong company. Combining traditional processing methods with the new technology and high-quality materials provided by the Hong Kong partner, the company came up with more than 1,000 varieties of furniture using materials such as wood, bamboo and steel in addition to rattan. These newly designed products soon attracted overseas clients. At an exhibition of the products, a Japanese client placed an order of more than 100 types, totaling HK$100,000, and within a month, he placed another order of the same value. Soon, these products were selling well in countries and regions such as Japan, the United States, and Hong Kong. In its first year, the joint venture recorded an export turnover of HK$3 million, 1.5 times the joint investment. In 1982, the export turnover reached HK$5 million, an increase of 56 percent over that of

1981. During that two-year span, the joint venture netted a total profit of HK$600,000. The company set up 12 production bases at the beginning of 1982, enabling rattan works manufacturing in Zhejiang Province to switch from decline to prosperity.

Dynasty – China-Made "Western Wine"

Dynasty, a famous wine brand in China, is produced by the Dynasty Winery, a joint venture between the Tianjin Municipal Grape Garden and First Bureau of Light Industry, and Remy Martin of Bordeaux in France. The purpose of establishing the joint venture was to produce wines popular with foreigners, such as dry and medium-dry white wines, and dry and medium-dry red wines. After China adopted the opening-up policy, foreign visitors were arriving in droves. To meet their demand for wines, the nation had to import wines with hard-won foreign currency. So I came up with the idea of a joint venture with France. The idea coincided with Tianjin's aspiration to produce a brand-name wine. Since the famous brands of Chinese spirits all took many years to build, some suggested that we produce a "Western wine." So we started negotiations with Remy Martin. The two sides agreed on a registered capital of 800,000 yuan, with the Chinese side making up 62 percent, and the overseas side 38 percent (33 percent from Remy Martin and 5 percent from the Hong Kong International Trade and Technology Investigation Organization) in the form of imported equipment. The Tianjin Municipal Foreign Investment Commission and the State Foreign Investment Commission approved the project in principle in May 1980, and its contract and corporate constitution in 1981. Trial production began in August 1981 and 124,000 bottles were produced in October. Such efficiency and speed were rare in the country, and comparable with the "Shenzhen speed." The venture hired only 15 staff members and workers (plus a French expert, Pierre Delair, and his wife) to begin with, thanks to its highly automated equipment and operation. When the French couple had a baby later, I joked with them that we now had one more staff member.

Traditionally, the Chinese had been using the thermovinification method to make wines, which usually takes three years.

The author (*front row, third from left*), the Delairs (*front row, third and fourth from right*) and their baby, and Chinese workers at the Dynasty Winery.

The low-temperature fermentation know-how from France shortened the period to two to three months. The grape presses, also imported, were the best in the world at that time, and could produce juice at different grades, making full use of peels and seeds in addition to pulp. The fermenting buckets were made of stainless steel, a type not seen in China before. The first expert from Remy Martin was a hard-working and warm-hearted man. He soon helped the Chinese workers grasp the advanced wine-making technology imported from France. In October 1980, the French expert took three wines of the joint venture to Hong Kong. The samplers there, unaware of the origin of the wines, unanimously agreed that they were better than Australian products. In June 1981, the wines, officially branded Dynasty, entered the International Wine and Beverage Expo held in France and won acclaim from all the samplers. Some business people offered to be the first importers of Dynasty wines in their respective countries. A French television station broadcast a special report on the story of Dynasty. A Chinese restaurateur in France claimed that the Dynasty wines at his tables would make his business more prosperous.

There is a story behind the brand name. When we signed the joint venture agreement, the Chinese side insisted that the French be responsible for exporting 90 percent of the output. Therefore the naming became an important issue that had to take the international market into consideration. It so happened that at the time *Dynasty*, a long-running American television series, was being shown in Hong Kong, and was very popular with the audience. So we named the wine "Dynasty," believing that it would easily catch consumer attention. As expected, Dynasty wines found a ready market in Hong Kong and Macao, and later in the United States. For the first batch of wines, the production cost was 2.53 yuan per bottle, and its whole-sale price was HK$3.14 in Hong Kong, while in the United States the retail price was US$8.00. Naturally, the joint venture netted a profit in the first year of its operation.

Dynasty wines have won 14 international gold medals since they won the first one at the 1984 Leipziger Fruhjahrsmesse (Leipzig Spring Fair), including five from Monde Selection based in Brussels (1988 to 1992). For its achievements, Monde Selection also awarded the Trophy of International High Quality to the Dynasty Winery.

Following the success of Dynasty, China Great Wall Wine Company, another joint venture established by the China Cereals, Oils and Foods Import and Export Company, Great Wall Brewery in Hebei Province and Yuan Da Wine Industries in Hong Kong, made successful debuts on the market.

With the two joint ventures, China began to produce its own Western-style wines and gradually won a share of the international market. To a certain extent, these products also helped to change the Chinese habit of drinking strong spirits.

Joint Ventures Stimulate Domestic Industries

While color television sets were already a common household appliance in the United States in the 1960s, China produced its first color TV set as late as 1970 with imported tubes, and its quality and quantity left a lot to be desired. It was not until the 1980s that 12- or 14-inch black-and-white TV sets became one of the "three new major household appliances" in China, the other two being the refrigerator and washing machine. Color TV sets then were luxury items beyond the reach of the average Chinese. To add a little color to the black-and-white screen, people used to cover it with a transparent yellow plastic sheet. Establishment of the Fujian Hitachi TV Fittings greatly boosted the popularity of color television in our country. For a while, people worried that importing color TV sets would push domestic manufacturers to the brink of bankruptcy. But they were soon relieved to see a home market filled with China-made TV sets and an international market penetrated by Chinese exports.

The Cherokee Jeeps, produced by the Beijing Jeep Corporation, a Sino-US joint venture in Beijing, and Santana cars, made by Shanghai Volkswagen, a Sino-German joint venture, have changed China's automobile industry and opened up a new road for its development. Unlike the assembly plants in some other developing countries, China made definite demands on the rate of domestically manufactured parts in a vehicle from Day One. Other hard and fast rules for the automobile industry were laid down later, effectively improving the country's capability in manufacturing parts and whole vehicles, and laying a solid foundation for self-reliant innovation.

The first joint venture to produce shampoo and hair conditioner was the Sino-German Wella company. Shampoo used to be a novelty, and hair conditioner a rarity in China, where urban people had been washing their hair with laundry soap or toilet soap. Rural residents even could not afford laundry soap. Before making an investment in China, the Wella company made a sample survey of Chinese people's hair, which was found to be dry and rough. On the basis of the survey, the company worked out a tailored recipe for Chinese consumers. Wella products caught on in no time. Soon afterward, an increasing number of foreign and domestic hair-care manufacturers emerged, turning shampoo and conditioners into daily necessities in the country.

Another example was the Jinhua Watch Dials Plant, a small venture jointly invested by the Tianjin Watch Factory and a Hong Kong company. In the years of the planned economy, several watch factories in Shanghai, Beijing, Tianjin, and Guangzhou monopolized watch manufacturing in the country. Although the retail price of a watch ran as high as 60 to 70 yuan in spite of a meager production cost of nine yuan, supply still fell short of demand. However, the factories had to hand their profits over to the state. With little or no funding for production expansion, they had to make do with out-of-date technology and equipment to turn out old-fashioned watches.

Government control over the economy began to relax after the Third Plenary Session of the 11th Central Committee in late 1978. This change, plus the huge market demand and potential profits, triggered the rise of a large number of small watch factories. They produced watches of "miscellaneous brands," and sold them at flexible prices decided by local governments. The profits were immediately funneled back into production. Meanwhile, with the pricing and capital construction still under the tight control of the central government, the large state-owned watch factories gradually lost their competitive edge in the market. The Tianjin Watch Factory, a comprehensive manufacturer of parts and whole watches, was under enormous pressure. It was slow, having to take at least two years to come up with a new product, and was in dire need for investment. It so happened that Xie Hua, a Hong Kong businessman who was engaged in watch production for his entire career, wanted to move his factory to the mainland. Negotiations between the two parties went smoothly and soon an agreement was reached. In May 1980, the joint venture got approval from the State Foreign Investment Commission. The Hong Kong side could produce more than 300 types of watch hands and dial plates, which meant a great variety of new products for Tianjin. The Tianjin side focused on the inner workings of watches. This mode of specialized production was later promoted in other parts of the country, and was responsible for the long leap in development of watch manufacturing that enabled China to become a large exporter.

The success of the first array of Sino-foreign joint ventures testified to the wisdom of Deng Xiaoping in making the relevant strategic policies. They helped encourage more overseas investors to set up enterprises or joint ventures in the Chinese mainland. The State Foreign Investment Commission (and later, the Ministry of Foreign Economic Relations and Trade) provided great support to the early joint ventures. They followed every phase of their development, from early negotiation and agreement drafting to finding solutions to problems in their operations later on.

Overcoming Obstacles to Success

At that time, setting up joint ventures was still Greek to people in China, with so many things yet to be improved, such as conservative minds to be freed, rigid systems to be reformed and complicated work procedures to be simplified. For example, some people regarded negotiations with foreigners as a kind of class struggle, and the bargaining table as the battlefield. They were cautious with what they said or did, for fear of being taken advantage of or getting labeled as "compradors or agents for foreigners." Some organizations even had a "frontline political commissar" appointed among their negotiators to monitor the negotiation process. Under such circumstances, it was naturally difficult for negotiations to make progress.

Equality and Mutual Benefit – A Simple Principle

A typical example of a joint venture negotiation in the early days was the one with Renault of France in 1979. When asked about our expectations, we bombarded our French friends with requirements: 1) You should provide the latest models and manufacturing technologies, and transfer to us any new ones you will develop in the future; 2) Technology transfer must be made at a competitively low price; 3) You should be responsible for training our people to master the technologies; 4) You should be responsible for selling 80 percent of the automobiles produced by the joint venture in the international market with guaranteed profits; 5) As part of the joint venture, we shall only contribute land, factory buildings and what usable equipment we have. You should invest the capital needed; and 6) The Chinese side will hold the positions of the chair of the board and the general manager. Actually, we had still more conditions in mind, but thought it better to hear their response first.

The French side replied: In principle, the first three terms are sensible. As for the fourth condition, it should be the responsibility of the joint venture to sell all the autos produced, both at home and abroad; but we are aware that you do not yet have an international sales network. So at the early stage we could take more responsibility and leave the issue open for later negotiations. The fifth point is also understandable but there should be an evaluation of the factory buildings and usable equipment. As for the sixth term, we have no other choice but to accept it because your laws state so, despite the fact that the international practice is for the chair of the board to be appointed by the bigger shareholder. But frankly speaking, we can't see the point of your appointing the general manager. Anyway, we understand your concerns. But may we ask a question? After we nodded yes, they went on: You have reeled off a list of requirements, but why didn't you mention what good the joint venture can do us? Indeed, we had not mentioned a word of that. Actually, we had not thought about it at all. Just as we were too embarrassed to respond, they continued: A joint venture works for the benefits of both parties, who should share responsibilities and profits, and losses as well.

I found what they said made sense. The term "mutual benefit" always danced on our lips. How come we clean forgot it in practice? I guess it was because we did not really understand its true meaning. Only after more and more people learned to be mindful of the interests of our partners was China able to achieve so much in procuring foreign investment.

There were other concerns for the Chinese employed in joint ventures in the early days. For example, it was common for a Chinese employee to find an excuse to leave the office whenever he found out that he was alone with his foreign colleagues, for fear of being suspected of having an "illicit relationship" with foreigners.

Spare the Cows, Please

The "better leftist than rightist" thought still prevailing at the time almost caused a great loss in one case of recruiting foreign capital. In 1980, the Shenzhen Guangming Overseas Chinese Farm, with the help of foreign investment, imported 1,639 Holstein cows from New Zealand and Denmark. When the first 1,239 cows from New Zealand arrived at the Shenzhen Harbor, the Chinese quarantine department found 689 had running noses, which was seen as a sign of hoof-and-mouth disease. With these cows in danger of being annihilated on the spot, both the importing and exporting parties raised strong opposition, since all of the cows had been strictly examined and stamped okay before boarding in New Zealand. Moreover, there was no possibility of their being infected in a closed environment during the sea journey. The long, cold trip, they argued, might account for the running noses. The symptom would disappear in a few days.

Each side held fast to their argument. But the quarantine department was legally authorized to implement the decision they saw fit. At the time there was no sound arbitrary system to appeal to, so the animal farm turned to the State Foreign Investment Commission for help.

The situation put the Commission in a quandary because they had to consider the negative consequences, though the importing company's assertion might prove true. But if it did not turn out to be hoof-and-mouth disease, the "better dead than missed" principle would cause a great loss. After taking all factors into consideration, they finally came up with a solution: The cows should be kept in isolation and under close observation. Should any further signs of the disease appear, all the cows were to be disposed of right away; if no such signs appeared, the cows would be released from custody and returned to the farm. Both parties accepted the solution.

Fortunately, the cows showed no more symptoms during the next few days. After a thorough examination by experts, they were diagnosed with tracheitis. After this incident, the cows lived happy lives in China and paid back their rescuer by producing high-grade milk under the Guangming brand. The product soon entered the Hong Kong market in 1981 and seized a large market share. By 1983, Guangming Milk maintained its leading position with 70 percent of the Hong Kong dairy market. From 1983 on, as an alternative to importing cows, the Guangming Farm started to raise their own dairy cows, using the frozen sperm of fine breed cows. By 2007, the farm had 15,000 cows, with an annual milk output of 40,000 tons.

The story of these cows taught us the lesson that, while maintaining national interests, we should adopt a scientific attitude. Being overly cautious and inflexible can do more harm than good.

A Ridiculous Dividing Line

In the early 1980s, when the reform and opening-up policy was just being implemented, foreigners coming to China for business negotiations found an obvious dividing line between themselves and the local people. They just could not understand why they had to pay higher prices than their Chinese friends when checking into hotels, taking buses, and visiting museums, places of interest and parks. What's more, they could not use the Renminbi, but had to exchange their foreign currencies for special notes known as "Foreign Exchange Certificates," or FEC, which were issued as a foreign exchange control measure. Foreigners could use them to make payments, especially for goods inaccessible to locals. Because of this, the FEC gradually acquired a black-market value.

To draw a clear dividing line between "us" and "them," the simplest method was checking passports, but that was not workable on many occasions. For example, we once received a business delegation from the United States. A Chinese American who spoke fluent Putonghua worked as the liaison person. By the rules at that time, we were supposed to send a car to pick him up whenever we were having a meeting. But each time he would turn down our offer and come on his own. With no regular taxi service at the time, how could he manage? I could not help asking him how he made it to our place. "By bus," he replied. "Do you pay for your ticket with FEC?" "No. They don't accept FEC on buses," he said. I was shocked, "Did you play ticket-dodging? It's no joke to be caught!" "How could I steal a ride!?" he protested. Taking out a handful of coins from his pocket, he continued, "Look! I buy my tickets with these. Five cents for a ticket; is there any better deal for a foreigner?"

Then he told me the story of his group's visit to the Forbidden City. He went to the ticket office and got nine tickets for his party, for two yuan apiece. But at the entrance, the other eight people in his party were stopped behind him. Pointing to their fellow countryman, the baffled Americans asked the ticket inspector (in English of course), "We are all Americans. Why do you let him in?" The ticket inspector could not understand them and asked his fellow Chinese, "What are these foreigners mumbling about?" Knowing he would have to pay extra if he revealed his true identity, the Chinese American translated the English sentence as "They asked how come the Chinese guy can get in, but they can't." The ticket clerk answered, "The ticket price for Chinese visitors is two yuan each and for foreigners it's 20 yuan. I can't let them in unless they go buy the right tickets." Since a literal translation of the answer would only have further confused his American colleagues, the liaison person joked, "Because I have black hair, just like them. But you have blond hair. You look different." But his colleagues did not appreciate his joke and went on asking, "What if we dye our hair black?" "That won't work. You've got blue eyes; but mine are black." Seeing his colleagues shrugging in disbelief, the Chinese American told them to wait there while he went to have a talk with the person in charge. Actually he went to the ticket office and bought nine tickets with FEC, at the price for foreigners, and thus managed to lead the delegation inside the largest ancient palace complex in the world.

Experiences like those were quite common in the early opening-up era. While they may have seemed small to Chinese people, they were actually difficult for foreigners (most of whom were encountering China for the first time) to understand or accept. During some negotiations, our foreign counterparts would question the rationality of those regulations. The more explanations we made, the more irritated they became, even to the extent of blaming us for breaching the national treatment principle. We tried to find a solution to the problem of the two-tiered currency and pricing system, but with little success. If my memory serves me right, it was not until 1996 when the dividing line was finally abandoned.

Awkward "No Entry" Signs

During those days, signs like "No Passing for Foreigners" or "No Entry for Foreigners" were common in many places, some of which were well guarded while others were just left open. I myself knew of several places like this in Tianjin. One was the Jinhua Watch Dials Plant, a joint venture guarded against foreigners for no apparent reason. Another site with a "No Entry for Foreigners" signpost was the Dagu Fort, which had been long-since abandoned after being dismantled at the demand of the Eight-Power Allied Forces in 1900, and was now only a site for education on that period of national humiliation. One more example was the Dagukou Military Zone south of the Donggu Fishing Ship Lock. Within this forbidden zone were the drilling, oil exploration, transportation, and geological prospecting bases of the Offshore Oil Exploration Bureau, all of which had signed service contracts with Japanese or French companies. Foreigners needed to enter the zone almost every day; but on each entry they had to go through a complicated procedure, applying for permits approved by the Tianjin Foreign Affairs Office, Tianjin Public Security Bureau, the Garrison Command of the Zone, and so on. When the Exploration Bureau asked to remove the "No Entry" sign, the Garrison Command responded, "The sign was erected by approval of the Central Military Commission in 1953. It should not be removed without permission from the Commission."

Another extreme example was the experience of an inspector working for the American Bureau of Shipping (ABS). He often went to Shanggulin in Dagang (a suburban district of Tianjin) to inspect the pipe racks of the Fourth Construction Company of the Ministry of Petroleum Industry. The place was only a one-and-a-half-hour drive away from Tanggu District by way of some salt fields. But it became a six-hour nightmare for the American inspector because that shortcut was off limits to foreigners and he had to take the highway through Tianjin. He kept complaining about this, "I am supposed to work eight hours a day but actually I can do work for only two hours. That's a low efficiency rate!"

Some of those security regulations, the relevant departments reported, were completely unnecessary. In one case, some Japanese journalists asked for permission to take photos of an office building in which their experts worked, but they were refused. Upon reflection, we realized that no buildings could escape satellites above our heads; trying to keep these things a secret was no use. To make things worse, the regulations on what was to be kept confidential, and where, were not consistent. Every administrative department went its own way and unpredictable changes often happened overnight. It was under such a chaotic circumstance that the Offshore Oil Exploration Bureau and some other departments raised the request to revise the outdated regulations on the basis of the opening-up policy.

Back then, there was no reliable system for identifying foreigners. Since passports were not a common ID document among the Chinese, people would usually judge a person by his looks. Once in Beijing, a director general in charge of the military industry went with several others to a "No Entry for Foreigners" zone in a suburb. Because of an ammunition experiment accident during the War of Resistance Against Japan, his appearance had suffered great change, his skin whitened and his hair yellowed. The director general, having forgotten to bring any identity documents, was stopped at the entrance. Despite all the explanations from his companions, the guard would not let the director general enter. Things like this caused huge inconvenience to foreign business people. In sharp contrast with China, the United States adopted a fairly different approach. For example, at the US naval base in Hawaii, which was open to the public, visitors were routinely informed of the warships in service, but were denied access to military secrets. In China, everything seemed well guarded; actually there were loopholes for axe-grinders.

It was on September 16, 1982 – when a journalist published in the Xinhua internal reference a report titled "Problems to Be Studied and Addressed Concerning the Work and Life of Foreign Experts with the Offshore Oil Exploration Bureau" – that the issue drew the attention of Hu Yaobang, General Secretary of the Party Central Committee. He immediately wrote a long comment on it:

> The report reveals some ridiculous phenomena in our work. It is well recognized within our Party that the most urgent task at present is to open up a new prospect and improve the economic performance of our country. But how can we achieve the goals with so many irritating obstacles deeply rooted in our system? As far as I am concerned, many of our regulations and practices still fall short of the needs of new development. Worse still, some people have their minds set on harming rather than building

socialism. We must determine to eliminate those malpractices. Otherwise, we won't be able to achieve anything.

The State Council was also alerted, whereupon it organized a five-day meeting in Beijing in October, with representatives from more than ten relevant departments. Participants came up with some guiding principles for dealing with outdated or inappropriate regulations and practices. A memorandum including these principles was then forwarded to the related organizations, and this eventually helped to improve the situation.

An Impractical Requirement

One of the most talked about issues concerning joint ventures was whether the products should be sold abroad or at home. Take the Sino-French joint venture Dynasty Winery for example. The French side insisted on selling the wine on the domestic market as substitution for large amounts of imported wine. But domestic wine producers and the wine importer, China Cereals, Oils and Foods Import and Export Company, thought otherwise: They would not cut the volume of imports because of an increase of wine produced at home. So the Chinese side insisted on exporting all the wine produced by the joint venture to earn foreign exchange. The French side could not accept our point. Thus the negotiation came to a deadlock. After several rounds of further discussions, the French side made a concession as they saw more potential in the export market. The two sides finally decided to set up a small joint venture with an annual production of 100,000 bottles. The French side committed to selling 90 percent of the wine on the international market. The joint venture's Dynasty wine turned out to be highly popular, thanks to the fact that its quality was on a par with French wines. Foreign agents rushed in. New markets in Hong Kong and North America opened up. To the delight of all, the output kept increasing. For a time, we even had to ask the French side to lower the export portion so as to meet the rocketing domestic demand. However, when the Dynasty wine was sent to a national wine competition, it was refused for being a "foreign" product. It was not until 1984, when the Dynasty wine won a

Gold Medal at the Leipziger Fruhjahrsmesse (Leipzig Spring Fair) that the China wine authority awarded a prize to it. Today, not only is Dynasty a famous brand at home and abroad, but the joint venture has also entered the ranks of world-renowned large wineries.

A Special Tax Payer

Before Schindler China Elevator was set up, elevators produced by China had been notorious for their poor quality. Patriotic Hong Kong business people and friendly countries such as Pakistan did import elevators from us, but had to give them up because of the poor quality and lack of after-sale service.

I experienced two accidents with our elevators during a visit to Pakistan. Once, I got trapped in the carriage and could not get out. Another time, when I was stepping into the carriage, the doors suddenly closed and my arm got squeezed between the greasy rubber seal bands on the doors. Seeing the two black stripes on my sleeve, I felt rather embarrassed and ashamed of the poor quality of our products.

In 1980, negotiations began for the first set of joint ventures. As the quality of elevators had become a sore point for China, the Schindler negotiation was of special importance to us. But it got stuck from the very beginning by a question raised by the Swiss company about corporate income tax. Answering the question was like "making a silk purse out of a sow's ear," because at that time we did not even have a corporate income tax law for joint ventures, not to mention a standard rate. We told them the truth and promised to act according to the law when we had one. The *Law of the People's Republic of China on Chinese-Foreign Equity Joint Ventures* provides that joint ventures enjoy tax exemption for the first two years. For the next three years, they only needed to pay half of the tax. They would pay the tax in full five years later. We assured the Swiss company that with a long time still to go, they would not suffer any loss. But they were not convinced at all and insisted on getting a solid answer before signing the contract, because without knowing the tax rate for certain, they would not be able to make a medium-to-long-term estimate of the output of their investment, nor could they evaluate the feasibility of the project. Since the project played an important role in both clearing the way for more joint ventures in the future, and for improving the quality of made-in-China elevators, the State Foreign Investment Commission asked the Legislative Affairs Commission of the Standing Committee of the National People's Congress for permission to set at 24 percent the corporate income tax rate for the joint venture. The State Foreign Investment Commission had worked out the rate in consultation with the relevant departments. Upon approval of the contract by the Chinese government, our Swiss partner was reassured that Schindler would pay a corporate income tax at 24 percent, even if the future law prescribed a higher rate. If the future official rate turned out to be lower than 24 percent, Schindler would be taxed at the lower rate. Therefore, Schindler has remained a special tax payer, even though the corporate income tax rate on Chinese-foreign equity joint ventures was eventually set at 33 percent.

After the two elevator joint ventures, Schindler and Otis Elevator Investment (China), in Tianjin, went into operation, it seemed that the advanced design and manufacturing technologies would certainly result in elevators of excellent quality; but new problems occurred. In developed countries, elevators, especially those of standard models, were all made, assembled and tested in the factory. It was the responsibility of the manufacturer to send technicians to install elevators and provide after-sale services. Things were completely different in China. The factory only produced the parts and sold them to construction teams, which, knowing nothing about elevator manufacturing, would assemble and install elevators after finishing the building work. When problems occurred, the client could not directly contact the manufacturer for after-sale service. The poor quality of our elevators was not only the result of backward technology, but also the outcome of the irresponsible installation system. The old practice created a dilemma for the two joint ventures. After much coordination, they adopted the practice of their home countries and eventually led the whole industry in China to improve product quality and after-sale services.

Shortages of Almost Everything

At their early stage of operation, joint ventures were constantly troubled by the lack of materials and the coupon-based rationing system. Take a plywood company for example. Due to the lack of a central heating system, it had to buy boilers to provide the steam needed for production. At a time when only state-owned enterprises had access to ration quotas of coal, the joint venture had to use leftover bits of wood to fuel the boilers, but was told later by relevant authorities that it was not allowed to use wood as fuel. As summer approached, the factory planned to buy some electric fans for the workshops and offices but was unable to do so for lack of an "institutional purchasing power quota." It had also planned to give each employee a bicycle because many of them often came late to work due to the infrequent and crowded bus service; but this plan also came to naught because the factory did not have "bicycle coupons." Finally, it had to turn to the mayor for help in solving all these problems.

A Ridiculous "Rat Tail" Campaign

Among the first joint ventures was the Sino-Japanese Otsuica Pharmaceutical in Tianjin. As a manufacturer of infusion products (made to the GMP standard of the World Health Organization), it impressed visitors with its impeccably clean workshops, advanced equipment and strict management measures. Its products were completely different from those being used in China. First, medicine, bottles and injectors were all disposable, so as to avoid cross-infection from repetitive use. Second, all the bottles were made from polyethylene, which, unlike glass, could resist erosion by medicinal liquid, thus ensuring the quality of the medicine contained within. Third, the drip bottles were different from the traditional ones in that they had a filtering plug to purify the air coming into the bottle through the air hole. These technologies, quite common in today's medical world, were unique at that time. Chinese hospitals, however, having no previous exposure to these types of products, did not show any interest in placing orders. The company, with a large and growing overstock, was on the verge of halting production. It could not find a solution through the market, and so tried the Chinese way – turning to the mayor for help. If one of the first joint ventures in Tianjin was getting into hot water, how could the rest remain cool? After a careful survey, we found that the key solution would be to introduce the products to doctors and hospital authorities. So I suggested that the company invite directors and doctors from various hospitals to their factory, give them detailed product presentations and ask them for advice. It worked. Orders from hospitals came one after the other, some even from major hospitals in Beijing. Medical experts gave positive comments on the products in newspapers and journals. With demand far exceeding supply, the company soon began its second-phase construction to expand production.

Though working the Chinese way helped the company turn the corner, it also experienced some unexpected trouble on its way to success. On one of my visits to Otsuica, the Chinese manager told me that the biggest problem for them at that moment was to hand in 200 rat tails. The neighborhood office was organizing a public health campaign and required all units within the neighborhood to kill off rats and hand in a certain number of rat tails as evidence of their "accomplishments." If any unit failed to meet the requirement, it would be fined five

Peng Zhen (*right*), Li Ruihuan (*middle*) and the author (*left*) visiting China Otsuica Pharmaceutical, July 1984.

yuan per tail. In a factory as clean as Otsuica, where the average cleanliness grade was 10,000, and 1 million at the highest, how could there be any hiding place for rats? Though the fine per se was not burdensome, the reputation of the company could be damaged for "not carrying out the rat-killing campaign." I immediately sent someone to tell the district head to put an end to things like this. Many people wondered why I kept raising this trivial issue on so many occasions. From my point of view, such seeming trifles could do serious harm to the investment environment, especially when there was a tendency to hassle joint ventures. In the eyes of some, joint ventures were like appetizing hot cakes, waiting to be bitten. Once they took the first bite, they could not help wanting more. What they did not realize was that their greed would scare away future investors. Without joint ventures, from whom then could they collect tax, and who would create employment and introduce new technology in the future? So I do not think I was making a fuss for nothing.

There were many other examples of people treating the joint ventures as a piece of meat to feast on. When I was working in Tianjin, I heard a lot of complaints about ridiculous road signs along highways. For example, despite the already low carrying capacity of the highway designed to diverge traffic flow from the Tianjin Harbor, a speed limit was posted, making traffic even slower. Worse still, there was no supervision at all; the speed limit signs were there only for the show. To solve the problem, I sent for the head of the local public security bureau and took him with me to ride along the highways, and had all of such road signs dismantled then and there.

Another example was the television commercial for Wella shampoo and hair conditioner. To make their products better known to consumers, the Sino-German joint venture planned to run an advertisement on TV. They went to the TV station and presented a sample of the commercial, only to be refused. One reason given was that they had never broadcast any commercial for a "foreign brand." What was more, they thought the scene in the commercial, showing a woman (seemingly a foreigner, too) with her long hair flowing about, was indecent. After several rounds of negotiation, the TV station finally accepted the commercial, but the company was required to pay in foreign currency. Since it was extremely difficult to get approval for currency exchange at the official rate, Wella had to pay for the commercial in Renminbi at the market rate, which was several times higher than the normal fee. Once, Schindler needed to mail winter clothes to its staff on a business trip in Switzerland. The post office also asked for payment in foreign currency because Schindler was a joint venture. Hassles like those all had a negative impact on the Chinese investment environment.

From the release of the *Law on Chinese-Foreign Equity Joint Ventures* on July 8, 1979 to the end of that year, only six joint ventures were approved across the whole country. By the end of 1982, the number was no more than 48, with a total investment of US$223 million, of which US$102.5 million came from foreign investors. Of these, 37 were industrial enterprises, with five in the machine-building industry, six in electronics and household appliances, two in textiles, four in food processing, 14 in light industry and handicrafts, three in pharmaceuticals, and one in wood processing, foodstuffs and oil exploration respectively. There were 11 non-industrial joint ventures: three planting or breeding farms, two tourist restaurants, and six others. Most of these joint ventures were in the coastal provinces, with nine in Guangdong, seven in Beijing and Fujian respectively, five in Tianjin and Shanghai respectively, three in Jiangsu, two in Zhejiang and Hubei respectively, one each in Hebei, Liaoning, Shandong, Guangxi, Hunan, Gansu, Xinjiang and Guizhou. As for the investors, 22 were from Hong Kong, 11 from the United States, four from Japan and the Philippines respectively, one from West Germany, Switzerland, Sweden, France, Australia, Thailand, and Norway respectively. Twenty-eight of the joint ventures were set up with investment from overseas Chinese, foreigners of Chinese descent and business people from Hong Kong and Macao, accounting for over 60 percent of the total. Of the 48 joint ventures, 24 were set up with a joint investment of under US$1 million, 12 between US$1 million and US$5 million, six between US$5 million to US$10 million, and another six with over US$10 million. These figures were very small compared with the tens of thousands joint ventures in China today. But it was the success of these pioneering enterprises that helped to win foreign investors' trust in China as a sound investment environment. Through these joint ventures, people in China also saw the benefits brought by joint ventures, such as funds, advanced technology and management expertise. By working together, we have reaped economic returns that are also satisfactory to our partners, and have redressed certain problems in our administrative system. In this sense, the early joint ventures helped us to gain experience and led to the flourishing of more such ventures later on.

Setting up joint ventures was a completely new endeavor for us. To overcome difficulties in the process through more open policies, in early 1983, the Ministry of Foreign Economic Relations and Trade (MOFERT), the State Economic Commission, the State Planning Commission, the Ministry of Finance, and the departments in charge of customs, taxation, banking, and labor, joined hands to conduct a large-scale survey on the situation of joint ventures and to explore approaches for making further progress. The survey concluded that joint ventures were special economic entities representing one of the diversified economic forms in our country. With proper policies and measures, developing joint ventures would improve our national economy, instead of weakening national industries. It was wrong to treat joint ventures as foreign companies, let alone limit or reject them. The survey report proposed to make more flexible policies on taxation, the import of raw materials, and recruitment of workers; to speed up economic legislation; to specify the business autonomy of joint ventures and to protect their legal interests. On March 16, 1983, the State Council approved the report and passed it on to relative local departments, thereby further improving the environment for joint ventures.

With the formulation and enforcement of the *Procedural Regulations for the Law on Chinese-Foreign Equity Joint Ventures*, and complementary laws and regulations, the related policies became more flexible. The investment environment was much improved through measures such as delegating the power of adopting joint ventures to the lower levels, cutting down on taxes, and opening up more markets. From May 11 to 20, 1983, the State Council held the first national work conference on utilizing foreign investment, presided over by State Councilor and MOFERT Minister Chen Muhua. Vice Minister Wei Yuming delivered a report on progress in foreign investment procurement and raised several problems for discussion. At the end of the conference, Vice Premier Yao Yilin stated that it was completely necessary and correct to introduce foreign funds to our economic construction and that this way of doing things had nothing to do with betrayal of national interests. He summed up the achievements China had made in this field of endeavor in three aspects: 1) the building of major projects such as railroads, ports, airports, oil exploration, and mining, and development of special economic zones, all involving foreign investment; 2) initial progress in the development of small- and medium-sized enterprises, tourism, cultural and educational endeavors, with foreign loans or direct investment; and 3) broader vision and better knowledge on our part through cooperation with capitalist countries and capitalists.

Participants of the conference reached a common understanding of joint ventures. By calling on departments at all levels to thoroughly implement the call of the State Economic Commission and MOFERT to do a still better job in running joint ventures, the conference played a positive role in promoting more flexible policies on foreign investment. In March 1984, the central government convened a symposium with participants from some of the coastal cities, for the purpose of further encouraging foreign investment in China. The *Provisions for the Encouragement of Foreign Investment* (the 22 Regulations), issued by the State Council in October 1986, solved many of the problems encountered by foreign-invested enterprises and offered more favorable policies to the export-oriented or technologically advanced ones. The relevant departments of the State Council also formulated more than a dozen rules for the implementation of the *Provisions*, which helped to further improve the investment environment. The result was a new surge of foreign direct investment and its steady growth thereafter.

Here's one example that illustrates how people changed their attitude toward the joint ventures. Quite a few foreign experts worked at the Tianjin Chemical Fiber Plant, an imported project approved by Chairman Mao Zedong and Premier Zhou Enlai. At first, some Chinese staff and workers under the influence of ultra-leftism regarded them as "capitalist spokespersons" and treated them as "targets of struggle." Some others believed that "since we pay them, they must listen to us." To break the ice, the factory management made every effort to encourage the staff and workers to change their attitudes, saying that these experts were merely the employees of capitalists and that we should make friends with them. When disagreement occurs, we should talk with them on an equal footing, instead of imposing our own will on them, or even hurting their feelings. We should respect their expertise and learn from them. In order to give full play to the abilities of these experts, in less than two years, the factory organized 96 technical training sessions with the experts as lecturers and held six seminars to ask about their comments and suggestions on engineering projects and related project management. Every Monday, the factory would hold a regular meeting attended by both the foreign experts and the Chinese staff, which provided a good opportunity for them to work together on technical or managerial issues. Meanwhile, the factory did its best to provide comfortable living conditions for these experts.

All the efforts paid off. Foreign experts began to feel happier at work and in daily life in China. Rotelmann, an electrical engineer from West Germany, was in the possession of a *Handbook on Lightning Protection Grounding*, – an indispensable reference tool for engineering work. During the initial period of tense relation in the office, he would put it away immediately after showing the necessary passages to his Chinese colleagues. But he was gradually softened by the sincerity of his workmates, and before leaving China, the German engineer gave the handbook to the factory staff as a gift.

In June 1980, this seemingly trivial incident was cited in a Xinhua internal report titled "Measures Taken by Tianjin Chemical Fiber Plant for the Motivation of Foreign Experts." Upon reviewing the report, Hu Yaobang had it passed on to related departments with the suggestion: "Please discuss at the regular meeting on international publicity about the effective measures we can take to make this experience available to all units with foreign experts." In July, the State Council held a special meeting to promote the experience.

The Chinese manager of the Sino-US joint venture Beijing Jeep Corporation once told me a very interesting story. His American counterpart once said that before he came to Beijing, he had known little about the Communist Party of China. After he began to work in China, he found that many of the best performing workers were Party members, so he developed an admiration for the Party. The Chinese manager explained that the focus of the factory Party committee was on managing the joint venture well on the basis of equality and mutual benefit. The American manager then asked, "Can I attend your Party meetings?" Thinking he was joking, the Chinese manager told him, "I am afraid you can't, because you are not a member of our Party." Unexpectedly, the American said he would like to become one. We did not know whether he truly understood the nature of our Party, but one thing we could be sure of was that he was satisfied with the running of the company. We took this example as representative of the general situation of most joint ventures in China during that period.

Other Forms of Foreign Investment

When joint ventures got off to a flying start in 1979, other forms of foreign capital utilization also made encouraging progress. Thousands of contracts were signed for small-scale compensation trade projects and processing customer-supplied materials. In addition, we signed contracts for offshore oil exploration, with the United Kingdom, France, the United States, and Japan respectively. According to these contracts, if no oil was found, the explorers had to grin and bear it; on detection of oil, the contracting parties would bid for jointly developing the resource with a Chinese partner. Specifically, the work was to be carried in two stages. During Stage One, all participating companies would work together on geophysical prospecting and share the expenses. The payment would neither be returned, even if a participant failed in the future bidding, nor counted as part of the exploration cost for the company that won the bid. In Stage Two, participants in the prospecting work would bid for joint exploration with a Chinese partner. In less than two years (beginning in 1979), 48 oil companies from 13 countries took part in the first stage of prospecting a sea area of 420,000 square kilometers, completed a seismic investigation along a line of 110,000 kilometers, and detected more than 470 oil-bearing structures. It would have taken us five to six years to complete such an enormous amount of work on our own. Stage Two began in May 1980, with five cooperation contracts signed with oil companies from Japan, the United States and France. In the following two years, a total of 15 producing wells were drilled in the five contracted areas. It was in the Sino-Japanese contract area in the Bohai Sea that oil was first pumped. Moreover, eight of the nine oil wells produced hydrocarbon flow for industrial use. I once joked with Inoue Ryo, chairman of the Nippon Oil Corporation, that the success owed to his name, which, in the Chinese translation, literally means "brightness over the well."

Back then, there was not a single hotel catering to foreign visitors in Tianjin's Tanggu District near the Bohai Sea. So we imported a set of Motor Inn apartments for the foreign experts, who were pleased with our arrangement.

Unlike joint ventures, in which the partners shared profits according to their respective investments, cooperative ventures shared profits according to the approaches and percentages agreed upon in the contract, on the basis of equality and mutual benefit. As contractual economic entities, cooperative ventures were fully based on the contractual agreement that specified the rights, obligations and responsibilities of each party. The Chinese side usually provided land, factory buildings, facilities, workforce and labor services. The guest party would provide capital, technology, equipment, or improved strains of crop or breeds of livestock as direct investment. Cooperative ventures – a flexible and feasible form of business that matched the economic level of China during that period – experienced rapid development. By the end of 1982, China had signed 792 cooperative contracts, involving US$530 million of foreign investment. Guangdong Province topped the list, with 697 contracts and US$410 million of foreign investment. Cooperative enterprises covered such fields as manufacturing, agriculture, aquaculture, fishery, urban construction, transportation, tourism, hotels, culture, education, and public health. They played an active role in stimulating the development of China's industry and agriculture, establishing a comprehensive tourism network and improving people's living standard.

Deng Xiaoping once made an incisive analysis of the absorption of foreign capital, and the establishment of joint ventures, cooperative ventures and foreign-owned enterprises:

The foreign investors will make profits, of course. But our country also gets tax revenues and the employees get payment for their work. In addition, we can learn advanced technology and management experience, as well as information for opening up more markets.

Facts have borne out Deng's analysis. Since the launch of the opening-up policy, industries such as home appliances and telecommunications have actively developed a mixed-ownership economy by absorbing foreign investment and introducing advanced technology. In this way, they have greatly boosted productivity, improved technical competence, and marched into the international market. From what Deng Xiaoping pointed out and the actual achievements we have made, we can conclude that paying a price is inevitable in opening up. Therefore, we need to carefully study the differences and connections between the interest orientations of the partners to joint ventures or cooperative enterprises, so as to bring their initiatives into full play, maximize the benefits and minimize the drawbacks, turn pitfalls into strengths, and strive for the best possible interests at the smallest cost.

5

"Borrowing a Hen to Lay Eggs"

O n May 11, 1969, the *People's Daily* published a report announcing that China had neither internal nor external debt. Being financially independent was then regarded as a virtue of the socialist economy, something to take pride in. Therefore, between 1969 and 1978, the country maintained a conservative financial policy of borrowing neither domestic nor foreign loans. It was not until after the launch of the reform and opening policy that China began to borrow loans from foreign governments and international financial organizations. The loans helped to ease the shortage of funds for economic projects and speed up socioeconomic development.

The "Debt-Free" Era Comes to an End

Deng Xiaoping raised criticism of the conservative "no-debt" financial policy as early as 1978. At a meeting with Hu Qiaomu and others on May 30 of that year, he said:

> The current international conditions are favorable for us. Capitalist countries in the West, out of consideration for their own interests, now hope for China to become stronger. They have problems with surplus capital and are willing to make loans to us. But we don't want to take them. How very stupid! The Four Tigers in the East, South Korea, Taiwan, Hong Kong, and

Singapore, have enjoyed fast economic growth and booming foreign trade. If these countries and regions have been able to develop their economies fast, why can't we?

He later added, "Foreign countries are not afraid to lend money to us. What are we afraid of?"

In June 1978, Vice Premier Gu Mu made a report to the central government after his ground-breaking study tour to Western Europe (described in Chapter One). He raised the question of payment for technology imports. We were then using the internationally accepted method of deferred payment, but the participants of the meeting felt the accompanying interest rates were too high. They believed it necessary to find a new method. After the meeting, Deng Xiaoping had a talk with Gu Mu, saying:

> We need to buy technology from other countries. We must lose no time. Paying interest on the loans is no problem. The sooner we apply new technology in production, the sooner we can pay back the loans. We must resolve to conquer the fear of being in debt.

In July, the State Council called a meeting to discuss principles related to the issue. In addition to the most commonly talked

Gu Mu (*right*) talking with Deng Xiaoping in one of the early days of the reform and opening.

317

about method – using foreign exchange absorbed by the Bank of China from abroad – Gu Mu proposed using various internationally accepted means. After a thorough discussion, the meeting reached a consensus on making use of loans from Western countries and absorbing funds from foreign investors. At a central government work conference, Chen Yun reconfirmed the decision: "We can borrow loans from abroad to ease the shortage of capital."

Some financial organizations in France and West Germany had already expressed their willingness to make loans to China. What we needed most, however, were long-term, low-interest loans.

Borrowing Loans From Japan, a New Experiment

At the beginning of 1979, Kimura Ichizo, a Japanese friend, informed a relevant department of China that the Japanese government offered loans to developing countries through the Overseas Economic Cooperation Fund (OECF) Japan. China could apply for such loans if necessary.

Established in 1961, the OECF is a semi-official organization, with its president nominated by the prime minister and approved by the cabinet. The fund comes from three sources. The first is government finance, which had grown to 834.1 billion yen by the end of 1980. The second is a portion of the savings of Japanese depositors, which is allocated by the Ministry of Finance and which carries interest (for the depositors). The total amounted to 757.6 billion yen by the end of 1980. The third source is the fund's capital and interest. The number and scale of the loans are jointly decided by the Economic Planning Agency, the Ministry of Foreign Affairs, the Ministry of Finance, and the Ministry of International Trade and Industry of the Japanese cabinet. The OECF then signs an agreement for a specific loan with the department authorized by the government of the recipient country and sees to its implementation. In the first few years, the OECF provided loans only to Japanese enterprises for investing in developing countries. In 1965 it began to provide loans directly to developing countries for development projects.

The OECF usually provides two kinds of loans, direct and common. Direct loans are mainly provided to developing countries and are further divided into five types: 1) loans for construction projects, mainly infrastructure, such as transportation and energy. This was the most commonly used type at that time; 2) commodity loans, which are meant to help developing countries improve balance between international revenues and expenditures, and check inflation; 3) loans for resource development and raw materials; 4) a development fund, which is re-loaned to relevant departments of the borrowing countries' by their own development finance organizations; and 5) loans in cooperation with the World Bank. The interests on the OECF loans range from passive to 7.5 percent; the terms of repayment range from ten to 30 years, with grace periods from three to ten-and-a-half years. Conditions for loans may vary from country to country and from project to project. Purchases with the loans need to be made through international bidding within a certain range.

Before the normalization of ties between China and Japan in 1972, the OECF had provided 54 billion yen in loans to the Taiwan region. They were used to build reservoirs, ports, and iron and steel works, with an annual interest rate of 3.5 percent and a 20-year repayment term. From 1965 to 1980, the OECF supplied direct loans to 48 countries and regions. Indonesia had received the largest amount of such loans (as of March 1980), totaling 820.8 billion yen, with the lowest annual rate of 2.5 percent and the highest of 3.5 percent. Most of the loans were used to develop basic industries, oil, chemical fertilizer production, power plants, and to import commodities.

Chinese government leaders took this important information from Kimura Ichizo about the OECF very seriously. In addition, the signing of the *Sino-Japanese Treaty of Peace and Friendship* in mid-August of 1978 created favorable conditions for such cooperation. In May 1979, Bu Ming, Vice Governor of the People's Bank of China, visited Japan to discuss borrowing energy construction loans and loans from private banks. During his visit, he also held discussions with relevant departments about loans from the OECF. When he returned, Bu Ming reported positively on the issue.

Gu Mu Visits Japan for Loan Cooperation

On September 1, 1979, Vice Premier Gu arrived in Tokyo with a delegation including Wang Yaoting, Director of the China Council for the Promotion of International Trade, and Xie Beiyi, Vice Minister of the State Construction Commission. Japanese Prime Minister Ohira Masayoshi met the delegation on September 3. Ohira spoke highly of friendship and cooperation, saying that the Japanese government would do its best to assist and support bilateral economic relations between the two countries while continuing to maintain and develop people-to-people exchanges. Afterward, Gu Mu met with the Japanese Foreign Minister Yoshio Sakurauchi, who appreciated the visit as an opportunity to strengthen the close Sino-Japanese relationship, with special emphasis on aiding China's modernization drive. As for loans to China, he proposed 50 billion yen as the first batch in 1979. With agreement on the Chinese side, Prime Minister Ohira would confirm the loans on his visit to China before the end of that year. Gu and the delegation also paid a visit to former Japanese Prime Minister Tanaka Kakuei, who told his guests that they should have come earlier. He explained that some countries rejuvenated their economies after World War II by making use of foreign capital. It was a common practice in the world today for countries to borrow loans for construction. There was nothing to feel ashamed about. Then he showed the guests several photos taken on his own missions to borrow loans from other countries.

During the visit, some people in Japan indicated that the delegation should express thanks to the Japanese government for providing preferential loans to China. Gu replied that crediting was a mutually beneficial activity. Neither side was obliged to thank the other. Therefore, at the press conference held in Tokyo, he stressed that developing friendly cooperation in all areas was the mutual need of both China and Japan, and would benefit both peoples. At the conference he announced that China would mainly rely on its own efforts to finance construction. At the same time, we would borrow foreign capital and receive loans from all friendly countries under appropriate conditions. China was also planning to join financial organizations of the United Nations and to accept loans from such organizations as the World Bank. Gu Mu confirmed the Chinese government's acceptance of loans from the Japanese government. He also presented to the Japanese government nine infrastructure projects designated for the first batch of loans. That marked the beginning of practical negotiations on loans from the OECF.

In October 1979, the Japanese government sent a delegation to conduct an initial investigation on, and feasibility studies of the projects proposed by China. In December another Japanese delegation visited China and officially confirmed six of the nine projects. On December 7, during his visit to China, Prime Minister Ohira made the commitment to the first batch of loans in the joint communiqué with the Chinese government. The total loans of 330.9 billion yen (approximately US$1.54 billion) would be provided through annual agreements from 1979 to 1984. The annual interest rate would be 3 percent and the period of repayment 30 years, including a ten-year grace period. The six reconfirmed projects were: the expansion of Qinhuangdao Harbor in Hebei Province; the double-track electrical railway between Beijing and Qinhuangdao; Wuqiangxi Hydropower Station in Hunan Province; Yanzhou-Shijiusuo railway in Shandong Province; and the double-track railway from Hengyang (Hunan Province) to Guangzhou (Guangdong Province), including the Dayaoshan Tunnel. At the same time, Ohira announced that, in his capacity as prime minister, he would give free aid to the building of a hospital, today's China-Japan Friendship Hospital in Beijing. This was the beginning of China's use of long-term, low-interest loans from foreign governments.

According to agreement between the Chinese and Japanese governments, the borrower's side was represented by the head of the State Foreign Investment Commission and the creditor's side was represented by the president of the OECF; the Chinese agent was the Bank of China and the Japanese agent was the Bank of Tokyo. On April 25, 1980, the two governments signed exchange letters on the first loan of 50 billion yen for the year 1979, and on April 30 they signed the agreement on the loan. As the fiscal year of the Japanese government starts on April 1, the loan installments began in April 1980. Later, due to a readjustment of China's national economy, two of the six projects were postponed, the double-track railway between Hengyang and Guangzhou (including the Dayaoshan Tunnel) and Wuqiangxi Hydropower

Station. Under an agreement with the Japanese government, the loans of 130 billion yen for these projects were transferred to commodity loans for the continued construction of the first phase of the Shanghai Baosteel and the Daqing Petrochemical Project. As of August 1983, China and Japan had signed five agreements on loans for construction projects, totaling 200.9 billion yen.

The first batch of projects using Japanese loans were all completed within the time limits set in the relevant agreements, with effective results. The second phase of the Qinhuangdao Coal Port was completed in 1984, with an annual handling capacity of 20 million tons. The 300-km, double-track Beijing-Qinhuangdao railway was built in 1984 and began to transport coal in 1985; the entire line was electrified in 1986, increasing transportation capacity by 50 million tons. The 300-km Yanzhou-Shijiusuo railway was built in 1985, with an annual transportation capacity of 12 million tons. The two railways and two ports increased by 35 million tons the annual transportation capacity for Shandong and Shanxi provinces, relieving the huge pressure on transportation at the time. As for the procurement of materials and equipment with loans from the OECF, China won about 46 percent of the international bids that took place in six rounds, second only to Japan among all bidding countries and regions. Back then, the most outstanding problems in China's economic construction were energy and transportation, especially transportation of coal. Energy shortages were responsible for limiting production capacity as much as 30 percent. The early loans from Japan, therefore, were mainly used to improve energy supply and transportation.

In November 1980, Gu Mu, as chief Chinese representative at a Sino-Japanese meeting of government members, talked with the Japanese side about the loan of 56 billion yen (about US$260 million) for that year. On December 5, Vice Premier and Foreign Minister Huang Hua exchanged notes about the loan with Japanese Foreign Minister Ito Masayoshi in Beijing. When the two sides signed the agreement on loans for the year 1983, Vice Premier Wan Li met with Aoki Shinzo, Vice President of the OECF. Both sides expressed full satisfaction with the loan projects. From 1979 to 1983, China borrowed loans of up to 330.9 billion yen from the Japanese government. From 1984 to 1989 the two sides signed agreements on 540 billion yen in loans, including 70 billion yen of trade surplus loans for developing export bases. Over a period of nearly 30 years, the two sides would meet annually to decide the types and amounts of loans for the following year.

At that time, we had three guidelines for our work concerning loans from foreign governments and international financial organizations. The first one was: to do our best to win loans. At the same time, we should be patient. The second was to negotiate with propriety: despite their favorable conditions, loans were to be paid back. Both sides had political as well as economic needs for loans, and would benefit from them. Third, under the principle of equality and mutual benefit, we could make appropriate concessions on specific matters. We basically followed these guidelines in our negotiations. In early 1982, in the wake of a readjustment of government departments, the Ministry of Foreign Economic Relations and Trade was charged with the responsibility for borrowing foreign loans. Minister Chen Muhua, also a state councilor, attended the signing ceremony for the agreement on loans from Japan for that year. In 1998 the Ministry of Finance took over the job.

The relevant statistics show that during the 1979-2007 period, China used 2.54 trillion yen in long-term low-interest loans from Japan for the construction of 255 projects. These included infrastructure projects such as harbors, railways, highways, electric power, gas, agriculture and telecommunications systems. With effective results, they played a positive role in China's construction and development.

The second type of loans from the Japanese government, commodity loans, were meant to subsidize countries with foreign exchange deficits, and were limited to the purchase of equipment and other capital goods for construction projects from the creditor country. The scale, term and interest rate of such loans were decided by the creditor and the borrowing countries through consultation, usually with more favorable terms than commercial loans.

The situation that gave rise to China's commodity loans from the Japanese government was as follows: In 1978, with the aim to speed up economic construction, major leaders of the State Council decided to start a number of large projects in addition to the ones that had already been planned. Import contracts worth US$7.8 billion were signed, including US$6.5 billion for complete sets of equipment. The largest project was Baosteel. Among others were three ethylene projects, with an annual production of 300,000 tons each, in Daqing (Heilongjiang Province) and Nanjing (Jiangsu Province) respectively. There were construction projects for power stations, docks, ports, and 100 sets of comprehensive coal mining units. As too many projects were signed all around the same time, the pressure to carry them all out became enormous. At the end of 1979, the Chinese economy experienced some difficulties. Further pressed by a shortage of foreign exchange, the government had to announce its inability to carry out the contracts. The ethylene project in Daqing and Baosteel projects caught Japan's attention. With the world media making a fuss of the situation, China's reputation, just at the beginning of its reform and opening, was seriously at stake.

In April and May of 1981, the Japanese government, in private-channel communication through Japanese friends such as Yoshihiro Inayama, expressed willingness to continue the contracts in question. Okita Saburo, who was then an advisor to the State Foreign Investment Commission, also facilitated communication between the two countries. He conveyed to China the Japanese government's intention to provide commodity loans. They could be used to help ease the shortage of funds, the cause of the stoppages or delays of projects under contract. When Nikaido Susumu, Chairman of the General Council of the Liberal Democratic Party, met with Deng Xiaoping on his visit to China in September, he mentioned that commodity loans could make up for China's shortfalls in fund and help resume major projects. Nikaido then met with Gu Mu to discuss more details and the two reached agreement in principle.

In October government-level work negotiations settled on the amount, composition, interest rates, and terms of the commodity loans from Japan, which would be composed of three parts. Part One, totaling 130 billion yen, was to be provided by the Japanese government. Part Two was the seller's credit, up to 100 billion yen, from the Export-Import Bank of Japan, with an interest rate of 6.2 percent and 15-year repayment term. Part Three was commercial loans from a syndicate made up of several private Japanese banks. The amount was 70 billion yen and the interest rate would fluctuate with the market. The 130-billion-yen government loans were in Chinese currency, with which China bought fertilizers, steel and medical equipment from Japan. They were used to restart the construction of Baosteel and the Daqing ethylene project. History proved the practice correct. Later, Japan provided loans to China in other forms, such as trade surplus loans.

Through cooperation over loans, China had come into more contact with famous figures in Japan's political and entrepreneurial circles. In June 1981, the two countries jointly launched the Sino-Japanese Forum of Exchange of Economic Knowledge, which has since been held every year, serving as an important channel for high-level persons from the two countries to engage in dialog. It has promoted mutual understanding and provides important advice to the two governments in their respective decision-making.

The agreement on Japanese loans, based on mutual benefit, has promoted friendly cooperation between the two countries. At that time, both officials and ordinary people frequently quoted Premier Zhou Enlai's words: "The Chinese and Japanese peoples should remain friends generation after generation." Beginning with borrowing loans from Japan, China opened up the channels to international financial resources, especially long-term loans with favorable terms. This has helped speed up our country's economic construction over the past 30 years.

Restoring China's Seat in the World Bank

Another major event in the story of China's use of foreign loans was the resumption of its membership in the World Bank.

Back then, the World Bank offered three types of loans. The first type was an interest-free, long-term loan provided through the International Development Association (IDA), to which the World Bank belongs. These were generally called "soft loans," because an annual service charge of only 0.75 percent was required and, with a grace period of ten years, the terms of repayment could be as long as 50 years.

With an average per capita GDP of US$312, China fit the condition, that is, a per capita GDP of less than US$400, for such loans. The formal recognition of China's status in this respect

Deng Xiaoping (*right*) met with World Bank Governor Robert S. McNamara (*left*), April 15, 1980.

was based on an appraisal written by a World Bank delegation to China, and passed at a World Bank Executive Directors meeting in March 1981. Not all projects in eligible developing countries were entitled to "soft loans." The specific conditions of individual projects needed to be considered, too. The second type was a long-term loan with interest. Also called "hard loans," supplied by the World Bank's International Bank for Reconstruction and Development. They were provided to help countries with fairly healthy economies to develop projects. The third type of loan was a mixture of the first two.

Establishing a Guiding Group

In order to make good use of loans from the World Bank and foreign governments, the State Council set up a Guiding Group, with Vice Premier Gu Mu as Director. According to the rules set by the Guiding Group, the State Foreign Investment Commission was responsible for coordination and management of such loans.

On January 13, 1981, the State Council approved the *Report and Proposals on Work Concerning World Bank Loans*. Gu Mu convened a meeting of the relevant ministries and commissions to allocate work. The Guiding Group conducted research on the proper use of medium- and low-interest, and interest-free long-term loans from the World Bank and foreign governments; the division of responsibilities of different departments; and work procedures. The Guiding Group believed that, under the principle of self-reliance, the appropriate use of such loans would benefit our economic restructuring during the Sixth Five-Year Plan period (1981-1984) and the overall development of the national economy in the future. A speech given by Chen Yun at a central government meeting urged us to bear in mind the actual needs and possibilities of our country, follow the guidelines and policies of economic restructuring, pay attention to comprehensive balance, do what our strength allows, carefully choose, plan and properly use such loans. All the relevant ministries were encouraged to play their due part. He stressed that, from feasibility studies to confirmation, and from planning to implementation, everyone should be clear about their responsibilities, and manage the loans under the existing management system and work procedures.

The Guiding Group's job was to coordinate the work of relevant ministries and organizations, keep abreast of the situations, conduct research on problems and raise suggestions to the State Council or the relevant administrative departments. It was not to supersede any department in specific work; the relevant ministries were told they must shoulder their respective responsibilities and closely cooperate with one another.

The following new administrative divisions of labor and guidelines were developed for coordinating and managing our nation's World Bank and foreign loans:

1. The departments in charge were responsible for deciding projects using foreign loans. By following the state's medium- and long-term plans, they were to organize the relevant units and experts to carry out thorough and meticulous research on the plans and resources of products, geological conditions (of production sites), raw materials, fuel and energy, coordination, transportation, and so on. They were responsible for assessing the amount of foreign loans and the amount of corresponding domestic investment, conducting technical feasibility studies of the projects, and evaluating their economic soundness. They would estimate the economic returns of the projects and the

ability to pay back the loans and interests. Their feasibility study reports needed to be practical and reliable. The departments in charge and those cooperating units would be held accountable for any mistakes or impractical proposals in the reports.

2. The State Foreign Investment Commission, the State Planning Commission and the State Construction Commission were responsible for organizing the relevant departments to examine feasibility study reports on projects using foreign loans, in accordance with the relevant regulations and capital construction procedures. The State Foreign Investment Commission was to verify repayment plans in light of the overall balance between imports and exports, and between revenues and expenditures of foreign exchange. The State Planning Commission was to verify domestic complementary investment, considering domestic needs and overall investment, materials supply, and other supplements. The State Construction Commission was to verify project sites, technology, equipment, construction terms, and investment results. The reports would then be examined by the Ministry of Finance and relevant banks before being submitted to the State Council. With approval from the State Council, the projects would be included in the state's long- and medium-term and annual plans. Only then could the Ministry of Finance negotiate and sign agreements.

3. The Ministry of Finance was responsible for negotiating, signing agreements and managing loans from the World Bank and foreign governments, and making repayment plans for the loans and interests. It was also responsible for the relevant domestic credits and debts, and financial affairs, and, together with relevant banks, implementing the strict financial auditing and supervision of the loans. Departments using the loans were accountable to the ministry for economic returns. Non-profit organizations were also required to pay attention to the investment results of their loan projects.

4. Once the loan projects were included in the state plans, the departments in charge were responsible for carrying them out in accordance with existing capital construction procedures. The State Construction Commission was responsible for coordinating and supervising the design, construction and equipment installation. Specifically, the State Construction Commission

would organize the relevant units to set up procedures for bidding, and examining designs and construction. These procedures should comply with relevant regulations, procedures and requirements of the World Bank.

5. According to World Bank rules, all equipment and materials for projects using its loans had to be purchased through international bidding. Chinese enterprises and companies were eligible for such bidding and entitled to certain preferential terms. When making designs for the projects, the relevant departments were urged to adopt, as much as possible, the product and technology standards of which China was capable. Such standards were to be used as technology data for bidding documents. The Ministry of Foreign Trade was responsible for organizing international bidding. The State Machine-Building Industry Commission was responsible for organizing domestic machinery management departments and manufacturing enterprises (companies) to join the bidding for equipment. The Machine-Building Industry Commission would examine the domestic bidding list beforehand. The State Bureau of Material Reserve, together with metallurgy and building materials departments, was responsible for organizing domestic enterprises (companies) to join the bidding.

6. The State Administration of Foreign Exchange and the Bank of China were responsible for foreign exchange management and settlement. Entrusted by the Bank of China, the People's Construction Bank of China (renamed China Construction Bank in 1996) and the Agricultural Bank of China were responsible for supervising the loan processes for the relevant projects. The People's Bank of China was responsible for work related to the International Monetary Fund.

7. The State Foreign Investment Commission set up an Office for Government-Loan Projects for coordinating all the related domestic work. The Office was also under the leadership of the Guiding Group headed by Vice Premier Gu Mu.

The Office for Government-Loan Projects, for its part, was to act as the central coordinator, with a wide array of responsibilities, including: 1) Organizing relevant units to study the rules, procedures and requirements concerning loans from foreign governments and the World Bank, and the practices of

The author at work when he was in charge of government loans at the State Foreign Investment Commission in 1981. Back then, telephone was a rarity. The author "had to go through a back door" to have one installed in his office.

countries that had made use of such loans. Working out procedures and methods that were beneficial to China and appropriate to Chinese realities. 2) Studying, together with relevant departments, and mastering the guidelines and policies on foreign loans, and assisting the responsible departments and those using loans to draft unified plans to negotiate with the creditor side. 3) Organizing relevant departments to provide the creditor side with reports on the progress of projects and other data. 4) Assisting responsible departments in liaising with the offices in Beijing set up by the creditor countries and organizations. 5) Assisting relevant departments to study the economic returns of, and comprehensive issues related to the loan projects; coordinating work between relevant departments and help solve problems that might occur in executing loan agreements. 6) Together with relevant departments, keeping updated with the progress of the loan projects and pushing their implementation and completion. 7) Assisting relevant departments to examine the annual plans for loaning and materials procurement submitted by loan users. 8) Assisting responsible departments to organize bidding for purchases. 9) Supervising loan users in their implementation of loaning agreements and contracts, and in their repayment of loans and interests. 10) Summing up and organizing the sharing and exchange of the situations and experience in negotiations with creditor sides and in project construction. 11) Promptly reporting on the above work to its superiors, dealing with routine affairs and other assignments from higher authorities. 12) Promptly raising questions and providing relevant data to the State Foreign Investment Commission and the Guiding Group.

8. The Ministry of Foreign Affairs was responsible for ensuring that work relating to World Bank and foreign government loans strictly complied with the country's foreign affairs guidelines and policies.

As we were inexperienced in borrowing loans from the World Bank and foreign governments, what we came up with were rather rough considerations. As the work went on, we would emphasize investigation and research, sum up experience in a timely manner, make amendments and complements, and set up more specific rules to ensure the careful planning and orderly implementation of the work.

With approval from the State Council, on April 7, 1981, the above rules and regulations were jointly issued to the relevant departments by the State Foreign Investment Commission, the Ministry of Finance, the State Planning Commission, and the State Construction Commission. From then on, work on World Bank and foreign government loans came under regulated management.

Priority Support for Education

At the beginning, we always tried to obtain interest-free soft loans, given China's status as a developing country eligible for such loans. Since the World Bank provided these loans, it became the target of applications from many departments and localities. Back then, China's education had too many "debts" and remained rather backward in the world. For example, while personal computers were already in common use in developed countries like the United States, none of our institutions of higher education had a computer lab. How could we talk about training science and technology talents? The situation was a far cry from the level required for modernization construction and had to be addressed urgently. Following Deng Xiaoping's instructions on prioritizing education and sci-tech development, the State Foreign Investment Commission and some other departments proposed that the State Council give priority to education if we could obtain soft loans from the World Bank. The State Council approved the proposal in principle. Afterward, the State Foreign Investment Commission, through the relevant channels, sent word to the World Bank that China would only accept soft loans from the International Development Association, which would be used to develop education. World Bank Governor Robert S. McNamara expressed support for the request and intended to have the first loan ready by June 1981, when his tenure was due.

In July 1980, Shahid Husain, Vice President of the World Bank for East Asia and the Pacific Region, led a delegation to visit China. The group made an oral promise to the State Foreign Investment Commission and the Ministry of Finance that the World Bank would provide a first loan of no less than US$200 million to US$233 million to China's institutions of higher education, mainly science and engineering universities and colleges. In September 1980, the World Bank sent a delegation to investigate China's higher education and reconfirmed the Bank's intention to provide the loan. In early November that year, the State Foreign Investment Commission, the Ministry of Education and the Ministry of Finance made a thorough study on how to use the loan and proposed the following:

1. Given the fact that education faced many difficulties and had poor repayment ability, the state should be responsible for borrowing and repaying the loan for education projects, and for distributing it among the relevant institutions. To avoid limitations on capital construction investment during national economic restructuring, the World Bank loan should not be included in the limitation quota. But domestic supplementary investment in Renminbi should be put under such limitations. According to World Bank rules, equipment worth more than US$500,000 must be purchased through international bidding; that worth between US$50,000 and US$500,000 through limited international bidding; and equipment under US$50,000 could be purchased directly. Chinese enterprises were eligible for both

international bidding and limited international bidding, and were entitled to certain preferential conditions.

2. According to instructions given by the central government at a meeting on education on May 11, 1980, education investment should be concentrated on key projects for the fastest and greatest effect possible. Therefore, the World Bank loan should be distributed to key comprehensive universities, multi-disciplinary engineering institutions, and agricultural, medical and normal schools with a strong teaching staff and a sound basis in other aspects. These institutions should use their share of the loan to improve teaching labs and computer-aided training facilities, which could then help improve teaching and research. The loan should also be used to help enlarge enrollment of undergraduate and graduate students, by 30 to 50 percent and 100 percent respectively in five years. The teacher-student ratio in recipient institutions should be raised from the present 1: 3.3 to 1: 7, and they should exchange 5 percent of their teachers with other schools every year. They should also conduct teaching and research with an eye toward training postgraduate and doctoral students, and for research projects assigned by the state.

3. Distribution of the loan should correspond with the recipients' teaching load and capabilities for using the money, such as the strength of teaching and research staff, academic and management level, and even the condition of dormitories. The specific sums should be calculated based on the specific conditions and needs of the recipients. The universities should follow the instructions of the central government on tightening capital construction. They must not use the World Bank loan as an excuse for requesting large capital investment from the state. Existing labs should be renovated or expanded. New ones should be built only if they were already listed in the university's capital construction plan with guaranteed investment. Otherwise the school cannot receive any share of the loan.

4. Based on the above principles, the initial plan for the distribution of the US$200 to US$250 million loan included the following areas:

1) University labs. Prolonged lack of investment had resulted in a severe shortage of teaching facilities. Those we had were rather

backward and, worse still, had been subject to serious damage during the ten-year Cultural Revolution. After the fall of the Gang of Four, some labs had been restored or improved. Even so, key universities and colleges in the country were only able to offer 60 to 70 percent of the necessary basic lab classes. The ratios of classes on specialized subjects and those offering students experience with lab experimentation were even lower. Therefore, priority was to be given to the construction of 44 central labs and computer stations in 26 key comprehensive universities, multi-disciplinary engineering institutions, and agricultural, medical and normal schools. These labs and stations were meant as experimental and data processing facilities for use by the recipient institutions, but also for use by those nearby if possible. The capacity and functions of computers were to be sufficient for the basic training of students, with appropriate consideration for research and management purposes. In general, central labs for analysis and testing purposes would be equipped with instruments of medium-level precision. Together with proper supplementary facilities, they were intended to serve all the schools and departments of a university. Every university, however, was to have their respective focuses. Only one or two key universities or colleges would be provided with high-precision analysis instruments, which were to be shared by other key institutions as well. Repetitive purchases of the same equipment were to be avoided. The idea was to make every effort to benefit more schools with limited investment. In order to make sure that the central labs were appropriately equipped and met the above principles, four specialist groups were set up to do relevant investigations at home and abroad. The results were then discussed by experts and relevant ministries for further analysis. It was then decided that US$104 million to US$140 million would be needed for the construction of university labs.

2) US$48 million to US$50 million would be used for training teachers and improving management of the 26 key higher education institutions. The schools would be able to send 600 to 1,000 teachers abroad for further studies, train personnel in loan management, and buy books and other materials.

3) About US$8 million to US$10 million would be arranged as a fund for follow-up projects and for relevant feasibility studies.

Follow-up projects should help strengthen key disciplines in 43 other science, engineering, agricultural, medical and normal colleges, and colleges for minority students. Future projects should consider expanding the number of basic-discipline universities and strengthening other areas of education – such as the Central Radio and TV University, adult education, middle school and vocational education, the training of teachers from the kindergarten to tertiary level, social science disciplines in higher education, and the production of teaching materials and instruments.

4) A total of US$48 million to US$50 million would be set aside as an expandable fund for unforeseeable expenses, including those incurred from inflation.

The loan would add up to US$200 million to US$250 million, to be used within five years. Of that, 10 percent would be allocated for 1981, about 30 percent for each of the next three years, and any amount left would be arranged for the fifth year. To ensure completion of the projects concerned, about 125 million yuan from domestic sources was allocated as a complementary fund.

The World Bank loan was a huge investment in education at the time. The relevant ministries took it most seriously, emphasizing the need to use the money efficiently and economically. When purchasing equipment, the institutions would be urged to pay attention to its broader uses and economic result, avoiding repetitive purchases and waste. Only equipment that could not be made, or could not be made well in China was to be imported. The Ministry of Education called together experts to review the plans and the universities' wish list of imports. Experts from ten ministries conducted a second review. It was made clear that those who caused serious waste or a bad influence during the course of the loan program would be held responsible. The overall loan plan, after approved by the State Council, was submitted to the World Bank. In November 1980, the World Bank sent another delegation to China to appraise the education loan, and drafted an agreement on US$200 million to US$250 million.

Following World Bank procedures, a delegation of the State Foreign Investment Commission, the Ministry of Finance, the Ministry of Education, and the Bank of China visited the World Bank's US office for negotiations. The first loan agreement between China and the World Bank was signed during that visit. When meeting with the delegation, World Bank Governor McNamara said he was very pleased to see substantial collaboration cemented between the Bank and China before his retirement. He also expressed appreciation for the Chinese government's attention to education and serious attitude and efficient work. He was confident that the project would be a success and hoped the cooperation would further develop and flourish.

As McNamara expected, the first project turned out to be a huge success. The follow-up educational projects, due to careful planning and the thoughtful identification of needs, also proceeded successfully. Nearly 200 higher education institutions improved their teaching and research facilities as a result.

Back then, the Chinese delegates could not find in the United States anything made in the Chinese mainland, but goods made in Taiwan were a common sight. Most of them bought a Taiwan-made cassette player that looked like a brick. But those "rarities" were actually of poor quality; they broke down after very little use. But even those poor-quality gadgets were better than those being produced in the Chinese mainland. Exporting similar Chinese products was out of the question at the time.

Although China started borrowing loans from the World Bank, we were mainly interested in its interest-free soft loans, which were expected to make up at least half of any loan projects. We had many concerns about hard loans, or loans carrying an interest rate. Richard Bumgamer, a high-level World Bank official who was friendly to our country, reminded us that we were too conservative in using loans from his bank. He pointed out that we should not be preoccupied with the interest carried by the loans. Our practice of only accepting loans with an average interest rate of 5 percent (between soft and hard loans), he said, was not based on accurate calculations, because by doing so we neglected the terms of loans. He laid out the logic. Based on the terms of 20 years for hard loans and 50 years for soft loans, the average interest rate would be only 2 percent if we borrowed them half and half; the average would be 2.7 to 3 percent if hard loans made up 60 percent of the total. When hard loans made up 90 percent of the total, the average interest rate would be 7 to 8 percent; even the interest rate on loan packages comprised entirely (100 percent) of hard loans would still be lower than those of commercial loans.

The agreements already signed between China and the World Bank on loans of US$800 million were not enough to support large projects. They would only be regarded as a prelude to more loans in the future. Up to that time, however, China had not proposed the next batch of loan projects. The World Bank was concerned that, without more projects, China would not be able to use more loans in many years to come. Bumgamer suggested that China make loan plans as soon as possible, so as to discuss with the World Bank. The two sides could then select projects together. His suggestion caught the attention of the State Foreign Investment Commission. With the efforts of Gu Mu and other central government leaders, China finally opened a new phase in using World Bank loans to speed up infrastructure construction. Besides education, loans from the Bank in the early years were used in the construction of ports, railways, highways, and energy projects. Tianjin Harbor, the container berth of Shanghai Harbor, and the Beijing-Tianjin-Tanggu Highway were the earliest examples. The World Bank loans played a positive role in training talent, improving the investment environment, and developing the economy as a whole.

At that time, India was the developing country that used the most World Bank soft loans. Due to China's relationship with India back then and other factors, we could not go to India to study their experience. In order to make more and better use of World Bank loans with preferential terms, we organized people to receive short-term training at the Bank's Economic Development Institute (renamed World Bank Institute in 2000). At the same time, and with the help of the World Bank, a Chinese delegation visited Pakistan, the Philippines and Thailand to study their experience. The three countries warmly received us and systematically introduced their organizations working with the World Bank; feasibility studies of projects; procedures for selecting projects and organizing bidding, and for borrowing and returning loans; and ways to make more efficient use of loans. They answered all of our questions and showed us the ports, power stations, institutions of higher education, water plants, and tenements for low-income city residents, which were built with World Bank loans. The Chinese delegates learned a great deal from the hosts' on-site introductions. Among the examples that left the deepest impressions on us was the Karachi Port, which was expanded with a World Bank loan to become a modern international port. Thailand used the loans to build hydropower stations in remote areas and to improve teaching facilities at Chiang Mai University. The Philippines used the loans to build water plants in the countryside and to print primary textbooks for circular use. The lessons we gained from this trip were later applied to China's use of World Bank loans.

We had already witnessed and learned about the huge gap between China and developed countries by going there in person. However, this was the first time that we went to study the experience of developing countries. What surprised us was that the gap between China and these countries was not small either. The impressive things we saw – the advanced facilities and management of Karachi Port; the beautiful and well-equipped campus of Chiang Mai University and the modern Mandarin Oriental Hotel in Thailand (the best hotel in Asia at the time); and the excellent social order and rich commodities of the countries – all made us feel envious. The visits made us feel all the more urgent about the need for reform and opening up; otherwise, China would not be able to stand proudly among the world's countries. During the study tours, I was particularly struck by the following aspects of Pakistan, in addition to the hosts' warm hospitality:

1. The country had excellent social order and the people were content with their lives. Theft was rare, giving us a strong sense of security;
2. Their government officials were well-educated in both general and professional knowledge, and experienced in international cooperation. Although many officials and heads of large enterprises were military men, they had all received higher education in their respective specialties;
3. The market was quite prosperous, filled with products that were not yet available in China;
4. They had fairly good infrastructure and enjoyed stable economic development. The Karachi Port, for example, won our great admiration;

5. The new capital of Islamabad impressed us as a beautiful and scientifically designed city. The Great Mosque, in particular, looked both modern and magnificent;
6. The ancient city of Lahore greatly impressed us with its rich cultural flavors;
7. The port city of Karachi was also a commercial city. It was bustling but pretty safe. Chinese nationals and Chinese Pakistanis there were able to find many opportunities and were contented with their lives.

Of course, we also noticed some problems in Pakistan. The most outstanding was the yawning gap between the rich and the poor. We found the lifestyle of some upper-class people to be no different from that of people in the West. The conditions of poor people in the countryside formed a sharp contrast: some mud dwellings did not even have a door. Inside there was little furniture and the beds were made by fastening a straw-rope mesh to a few wooden sticks. But on the whole, the country and its people left me with very fine impressions, and our visit to Pakistan enabled us to gain much knowledge and experience in using World Bank loans and in building ports.

The *People's Daily* carried a report entitled "First Phase of Chinese-Aided Gwadur Harbor Completed" on December 27, 2004:

People's Daily*'s Chen Yiming reports from Islamabad:* This reporter learned from the China Harbor Construction (Group) Corporation's Pakistan office on December 25 that the main part of the deep-water Gwadur Harbor has been completed toward the end of the first phase of construction in this Chinese-aided project. As planned by the Pakistani government, the harbor is being built in two phases. The first phase consists of infrastructure, including three multi-function docks and a 4.35-km-long approach channel. The second phase includes complementary facilities and upgrading of the berths. Ten more berths will be built during the second phase: three for special containers, one 100,000-ton berth for bulk cargos, and two 200,000-ton berths for oil tankers.

The completion of the Gwadur Harbor will promote economic development of the poor Balochistan Province and the country of

Pakistan as a whole. It will also become the nearest transit harbor for Afghanistan and other inland countries in central Asia.

From the television news on the same day, I learned that the handling capacity of China's harbors had reached 4 billion tons that year, including 61.5 million standard containers, ranking first in the whole world.

While feeling very pleased at the two pieces of news, I could not help recalling my visit to Pakistan over 20 years before. Many changes had taken place in both China and Pakistan during those years, which seemed to have passed quickly by. Just in terms of the construction of harbors, the handling capacity of Karachi Port was 14.5 million tons in 1980, while that of Shanghai Harbor, the largest in China, was only 8.5 million tons. By 2002, however, the comparison had become 25.9 million tons versus 260 million tons, with Shanghai overtaking Karachi by tenfold. Back in the early 1980s, we learned from Pakistan the experience of harbor construction; by the early 21st century, it was our turn to help Pakistan build harbors. Such a dramatic switch was simply unthinkable when we took our study tour to that country.

Managing the Loan Projects

After China established cooperation with the World Bank, for many years to come we enjoyed interest-free soft loans from the International Development Association. As China's per capita GDP and need for loans grew steadily, the ratio of soft loans to hard loans kept shrinking, until we stopped borrowing soft loans altogether in 1999. Loans from the World Bank played a positive role in promoting socioeconomic development in China. In the past, our enterprises used to choose a supplier on their own after several inquiries and comparisons. That practice was likely to spawn corruption. According to World Bank rules, materials procurement and project contracts must go through international bidding. Enterprises in the borrowing country would be preferred, all other things being equal. Therefore, we arranged for the relevant departments to learn the bidding procedures, such as how to call for tenders publicly; how to submit tenders;

how to examine bidding qualifications; how to set the lower limit on bids and how to keep it secret; how to evaluate bids and open sealed tenders; and how to openly solicit public opinions, and so on. An appraisal group was set up to supervise the procedures, to ensure fair bidding and to avoid any illegal practice. Based on experience over a period of time, in 1983 the Ministry of Foreign Trade and the State Economic Commission and some other departments set up the regulations for procurement with World Bank loans. For equipment that could not be made or made well in China, we encouraged foreign companies to join their Chinese counterparts in the bidding. By using the advanced technology of the foreign companies and making the equipment in China, such cooperation could help reduce production costs and upgrade the technology of Chinese manufacturers.

Quite a few pairs of Sino-foreign partners set up joint ventures or jointly bid for projects in third countries. During its expansion period in the early 1980s, Tianjin Harbor bought a large set of hoisting equipment made by the Shanghai Harbor Machinery Factory. Due to poor electromechanical technology, the equipment was often out of order. After several repairs, it broke down altogether. When China used World Bank loans to build its earliest container berths in Tianjin and Shanghai in 1986, we encouraged the Shanghai Harbor Machinery Factory and the Sumitomo Corporation of Japan to jointly produce equipment and bid to supply the relevant equipment. The products of the joint venture soon reached advanced international standards and their brand has become famous both in China and abroad.

In early 1982, the State Council decided to restructure government organizations. At the time, the first batch of projects undertaken in education with World Bank loans were progressing smoothly and negotiations were in process for the second batch of projects in energy and transportation. Since the restructuring would probably result in the merging of the State Foreign Investment Commission, the Ministry of Foreign Trade and the Ministry of Foreign Economic Relations and Trade, and readjustment to some other ministries, the World Bank and foreign governments that had granted loans to China became concerned that our opening-up policy might change. The World Bank even sent Bumgamer, now a high official in charge of loans, to inquire about the situation in China. On February 6, 1982, he discussed three points of concern with me. One, the World Bank had heard about the restructuring of Chinese government organizations. They were concerned that the reform would affect the Bank's loans to the Chinese government, which had begun only recently. They had noticed that some Chinese officials did not seem to concentrate on relevant discussions as much as they used to. Would there be any change to the Office for Government-Loan Projects under the State Foreign Investment Commission? If so, who would be in charge of loans? Two, the World Bank hoped that the Office for Government-Loan Projects would strengthen lateral coordination between relevant departments. A lack of such coordination often caused problems. For example, when discussing a coal project, the Ministry of Coal Mining Industry was familiar with the project itself, but not with the complementary projects such as railways, harbors and power stations. Therefore, they could not make a comprehensive feasibility study of the coal project. The World Bank hoped that staff of the Office for Government-Loan Projects would take part in discussions of as many projects as possible so as to help coordinate all the relevant departments. Three, the World Bank was pleased to learn that the staff of the Office had increased to 30 persons. (It was said that the equivalent office in India had a 200-person staff.) Bumgamer pointed out that it was important to improve the staff's qualifications as well, and that his bank would be happy to assist us in training. He suggested that we select some Chinese students who had studied for degrees abroad to work at the Office for Government-Loan Projects, as they were probably more familiar with international economics and finance than those staying behind in China.

I responded as follows: One, the main purpose of the Chinese government's organizational reshuffling was to clarify the departments' respective responsibilities and to improve work efficiency. This would help further to develop our cooperation with the World Bank. I did not think that the Banking Section under the Office for Government-Loan Projects would undergo any change. Its function would be strengthened rather than weakened. The State Council had specially emphasized that organizational restructuring was not to affect ongoing work. I told Bumgamer that we would take note of his concerns and welcomed him and his colleagues to inform us of any more problems. We would do our best to tackle them. Two, I expressed my appreciation of his suggestion for strengthening lateral departmental coordination. I already required that my colleagues try their best to take part in negotiations for every project. We had already made some overall coordination on coal and transportation projects, but more specific work needed to be done. Three, we were aware of our lack of both theoretical and practical knowledge in international economy and finance. To make up for our English incompetence, in addition to allocating six hours per week for learning the language, we encouraged everyone to study on their own. We were also planning to send some people to study at relevant institutions. I also told Bumgamer that we felt it was important to learn in practice, too, and expressed our thanks to the World Bank for its offer to assist in this respect. I explained that most of the students we sent abroad in recent years were science and engineering majors, with few studying financial and economic management. In the future we would pay attention to the training of specialists in this area.

The suggestions made by Bumgamer proved constructive to our work. The Ministry of Foreign Economic Relations and Trade, established after the organizational reshuffling to take up the management of government loans, further regulated and improved loan management and staff training by drawing on past experience. As a result, work relating to loans from the World Bank and foreign governments continued without any letup.

After China resumed its relationship with the World Bank, we participated in study tours and training sessions organized by the Bank. In an effort to train more people in the departments and localities concerned, we invited Rahatullah Khan, Pakistan's chief specialist in charge of World Bank affairs, to give lectures in China in early 1982. He met with leaders of the State Foreign Investment Commission before giving lectures in different parts of the country. The first lecture was scheduled in Shanghai. Because of its importance, I called the relevant leaders to ask if we needed to bring an interpreter. They told me that they had already chosen one, who had worked at the Bank of China's London Branch for 11 years and who spoke excellent English, of course. When I accompanied Rahatullah Khan into the lecture hall, I was told that most of the audience were high- and medium-level officials. As soon as the lecture began, however, I was disappointed to notice that the translation was wide off the mark. The audience grew puzzled at first, impatient after a while, and upset in the end. I was only grateful that they kept their disapproval under the table until the speaker had left. I had been taking notes from the very beginning and I knew the lecture itself was excellent. But the interpreter knew little about the business of the World Bank. How could he make himself understood? Therefore, to make up for the loss of nearly two hours for the audience, I asked the interpreter to take Rahatullah Khan to his hotel and offered to relate the lecture according to my notes. The audience accepted my suggestion and their warm applause at the end of my talk reassured me that I had got the information across.

In his lectures, Rahatullah Khan touched upon many important topics: the necessity for China to make use of foreign capital in its economic development, selection and the confirmation of foreign-invested projects, unified management for winning foreign investment and aid, the need to have more people work at the World Bank, the suggestion for China to join the Asian Development Bank, and the wish for China to provide more technology services and capital goods to developing countries. He pointed out that China's resumption of World Bank membership would entitle Chinese enterprises to bid for projects funded by the Bank's loans. Back then, the World Bank provided loans for projects worth nearly US$10 billion every year. Due to China's low labor cost and materials prices, Chinese enterprises could be competitive and thus be able to earn foreign exchange for the country. In order to win more contracts, he suggested, interested enterprises should obtain relevant information before publication of invitations for bid. For example, they should get to know the technology requirements of a project, and the types and specifications of equipment to be supplied. Such information could be gathered from relevant embassies in China and China's executive board members in the World Bank. Rahatullah Khan suggested that we set up four to five international contracting companies to engage in irrigation, electricity, highway, and construction projects. Well-known specialists from across the country should be listed as technology leaders of the companies. If we did not have high-level specialists in certain fields, we could invite foreign experts as technology advisors. These specialists could give companies a better chance for recognition by the World Bank. If a Chinese contractor could win the bid for a World Bank project in another country, it would bring along and expand the export of equipment. In order to help project contractors win contracts, it was necessary to establish some consulting companies. These companies should have famous specialists as their consultants. They should also invite high-level specialists with Chinese blood from overseas as part-time consultants. If a consulting company could win projects abroad, it would create favorable conditions for China to win credit contracts. Rahatullah Khan also suggested that some Chinese specialists join the International Think Tank of the World Bank Institute so that they could take part in relevant international affairs discussions. Rahatullah Khan's lectures functioned as a brief course on World Bank affairs and turned out to be of great help to our cooperation with the Bank. Later the State Foreign Investment Commission printed 500 copies of the lectures and distributed them to the concerned departments and localities.

Some of his suggestions were put into practice soon afterward and some are still relevant today. For example, the State Import and Export Commission approved the setup of the first international consulting enterprise – the China International Engineering Consulting Corporation – in April 1982. By attending Rahatullah Khan's lectures, many of the people involved in related work became acutely aware of their lack of knowledge in international economic and trade cooperation. Everybody was eager to learn. Thus we organized more study activities. One was to provide English training to scientists and technicians who often took part in negotiations with foreign counterparts. Most of them had studied English from primary school to college, but had not used it for years. They soon improved their English skills after a short period of training.

On December 14, 2007, I read a report on a fundraising conference in Berlin, organized by the International Development

Association for the purpose of aiding poor developing countries. At the time of the conference, the association had already raised US$41.6 billion. Donating countries promised a record-setting US$25.1 billion in the next three years, while the World Bank would collect US$16.5 billion from within the Bank and from donations for debt reduction or exemption. The money would be used as endowment for projects, and interest-free and low-interest loans to recipient countries from 2008 to 2011. Half the money would go to Africa. For the first time in history, China became a donating country to the World Bank and a funding member of the International Development Association.

The report has given me much food for thought. Only eight years before, China was still a country receiving aid from the International Development Association. There were many reasons for our dramatic shift from recipient to donor country, but the fundamental one was the reform and opening-up policy, initiated by Deng and resolutely pursued by our country. While signifying China's socioeconomic development, the change also demonstrates that the country's peaceful development has enabled it to shoulder greater international responsibilities.

Diversifying Sources of Foreign Loans

With the success of financial cooperation with Japan and the World Bank, we sped up the pace and expanded the sources of foreign loans. Many developed countries, while expressing wishes to provide us with such long-term commercial loans as buyer's and/or seller's credits, also took steps to establish cooperation with us over government loans with favorable terms.

Loans from foreign governments were low-cost and similar to aid due to their favorable terms. They were either interest-free or came with an annual interest rate of 2 to 3 percent. The repayment period ranged from 20 to 30 years, including seven to ten years of grace, during which the debtor was required to pay only the interest. Generally speaking, compared with the market interest rates, at least 35 percent of such loans were "aid" in nature.

Following Japan, the Belgian government promised to provide its first government loan to us in October 1979. After bilateral negotiations, the first Sino-Belgian financial agreement was signed on April 30, 1980, for a soft government loan of 300 million Belgian francs. Of the total, 20 percent was designated as Belgium's investment in the Sino-Belgian joint ventures of Shanghai Bell and Xi'an-Janssen Pharmaceutical. This was another indication that Western countries are good at using the interest-free or reduced-interest loans to develop cooperative relations with other countries.

Importing Program-Controlled Telephone With Loans

China was one of the most underdeveloped countries in telephone technology, which has undergone several phases of development since the early battery telephone, that is, the hand-cranked telephone, which was first used in China in the later years of the Qing Dynasty (1644-1911). That was followed by the step-by-step system, the crossbar system, coded system, program-controlled system, and the most recent digital-controlled system. In the mid-1980s, the telecommunications system in our country was so small in both scale and volume, and the technology so backward, that the difficulty of placing phone calls became a sweeping social problem. While developed countries had already entered the era of program-controlled telephone, China was using step-by-step and crossbar telephones in large numbers, and in its rural counties, the battery system that belonged in the age of the Qing-Dynasty Empress Dowager Cixi was still in use. In the 1970s, the coding system was adopted on an experimental basis during construction of the Second Auto Works. Due to technical faults, it was given up and the crossbar system was resumed. After the country opened up to the outside world, however, backward telecommunications posed one of the obstacles to attracting foreign investment. For example, during negotiations over the Jianguo Hotel and the Great Wall Sheraton Hotel, which were both joint ventures, the foreign investors expressed serious concern about telecommunications problems. This constituted the background of the Sino-Belgian Program-Controlled Telephone Project. However, it would take time to build the plant, import and apply the technology, and go into production. To meet the urgent need for efficient telecommunications service, the State Foreign Investment Commission suggested that we import several sets of program-controlled telephone equipment for Beijing, Shanghai, Tianjin, and Guangzhou, with loans from the Japanese government. After rounds of consultations, China and Japan signed the 1984-1988 agreement on loans for the expansion of telecommunications in Tianjin, Shanghai and Guangzhou on October 26, 1984. Later on, the two countries signed the 1992-1993 agreement on loans for long-distance-call projects in Beijing, Shenyang and Harbin. Guangzhou and Tianjin were the first two cities to import 40,000-line program-controlled telephone facilities because they had already built operation rooms originally for the purpose of expanding their old telephone systems. When I visited the Tianjin Telephone Bureau, I noticed that the 40,000-line program-controlled telephone system took up only one tenth of the space originally planned for a 10,000-line crossbar system. The usual noise (on par with the racket of a textile mill) disappeared. The new system was also much more efficient and reliable. The early import of program-controlled telephone technology and Sino-foreign joint investment greatly promoted program- and digital-controlled telecommunication technology and manufacture in our country.

The third government loan China accepted was the 43.6 million Dinars committed by the Kuwait Fund for Arab Economic Development in 1981. Part of the loan was used to build the Xiamen International Airport, Anhui Ningguo Cement Plant and Xinjiang Chemical Fertilizer Plant.

In 1981 we began negotiations with the Italian government over cash aid and loans. After the proposed plans were examined and evaluated, a Chinese delegation, headed by Wei Yuming, Vice Minister of Foreign Economic Relations and Trade, visited Rome. I acted as his deputy and Zhu Rongji, from the State Economic Commission, was a consultant. On July 16, after more than a week of negotiations, Wei Yuming and Italian Vice Foreign Minister Roberto Palleschi signed the *Summary of Sino-Italian Talks on Three-Year Economic, Technological and Financial Cooperation*. The main contents of the agreement were:

1. The Italian government agreed to provide an endowment of US$29.7 million for the 15 projects proposed by the Chinese government, mainly the Beijing First Aid Center and other medical facilities.

2. The Italian government agreed to provide a low-interest government loan of US$148 million for another nine projects proposed by the Chinese government. The annual rate was 2.25 percent, with a repayment period of 13 years, including two years of grace.

3. In May 1982, during a visit to China, the Italian Vice Foreign Trade Minister signed an agreement on Italian export loans totaling US$170 million for 50 projects. If formal contracts on individual projects could be signed by the end of the year or in the first half of 1983 for a few complex projects, the annual interest rate would remain at 7.5 percent. (According to regulations of the Organization of Economic Cooperation and Development, the annual interest rate had already been raised to 10 percent by that time.) Furthermore, the Italian government would provide 15 percent government loans for some of the projects as cash payment advances.

4. The Italian government agreed in principle to provide US$500 million in export loans for the Southwest Energy Development Project, a US$5 million endowment for the feasibility research and US$6 million government loans for the design expenses. Because of its huge scale, the project

Wei Yuming (*third from right*), Zhu Rongji (*third from left*), the author (*second from left*) and other Chinese delegates in July 1982 in Italy, where they signed the *Summary of Sino-Italian Talks on Three-Year Economic, Technological and Financial Cooperation.*

could only be finalized after Italian experts' on-site inspections and further negotiations.

These examples clearly indicated the Italian government's intention to develop long-term friendly cooperation with our country. In fact, China is one of only four developing countries with which the Italian government has signed long-term economic, technological and financial cooperation programs.

I still retain fresh memories of working in cooperation with Italy. The earliest country to develop an interest in our opening-up policy, Italy began negotiations with our Ministry of Agricultural Machinery Industry for technological renovations of the Tractor Plant of Luoyang as early as 1977. Even before agreement was reached, they had already arranged living accommodations for Chinese trainees. In spite of many setbacks in the negotiations, they pushed on and reached agreements with Luoyang and Shanghai on tractor projects, and with Nanjing on the Iveco automobile project.

At the start of the negotiations in Rome, our Italian counterparts underestimated our knowledge and negotiation capabilities on inter-government loans. When we asked who should propose a plan, they said that they would do that. But they had not prepared a draft plan and, due to a lack of coordination between the negotiators from different departments, little progress was made in the first few days. As the Italian government was in constant reshuffling at that time, we were afraid that any further delay could nullify the previous efforts. We therefore suggested that we propose a plan for discussions, and they consented. Since we had gained experience through cooperation with Japan and the World Bank, and had conducted preliminary assessments of the loan projects, we smoothly reached agreement with our Italian counterparts after constructive discussions.

Italian Policemen: Refusing to Bend the Law

While in Rome, another incident occurred that left a lasting impression on me. One Sunday, the commercial attaché of the Chinese Embassy offered to take us for a tour of the city in a van newly imported from West Germany. When we came back to the van at our first scenic spot, we found that two policemen were questioning our driver. Not able to speak Italian, the man was struggling to explain to them with a few words he knew and gestures. It turned out that the policemen were trying to detain the van because it had not been registered for a license plate and all the customs papers had been left behind in the Embassy. The driver did not have any certificates with him. When we rejoined him, the driver confidently told the policemen through the interpreter that the van was the property of the Chinese Embassy and that the passengers were Chinese government delegates invited by the Italian government. Hearing this, one of the policemen told us politely that they welcomed the Chinese guests, but if they let the vehicle go, they would be neglecting their duty. He would be severely punished if his colleague reported this to the authorities. They asked us to let them take the vehicle to the police station, where it would well taken care of. Since it was the property of our embassy, the policemen reassured us, we should have no problem reclaiming it if we went through the Foreign Ministry with the relevant documents. Though our original plan for a city tour failed to materialize, we learned a good legal lesson. The following day, when we mentioned the incident to our Italian friends, they expressed regret for our inconvenience, but assured us that the policemen would do the same even with their government ministers.

Developing Dairy Production With Danish Loans

Though small in territory, Denmark is a large exporter of foodstuffs such as meat and dairy products. Back then, food, especially dairy products, was in short supply in our country. Milk was a rarity even for small children and elderly people, not to mention adults in general. We therefore inquired about the possibility of borrowing preferential loans from the Danish government to import advanced technology for cow breeding and dairy-product processing. Thanks to the efforts made by the Chinese Embassy in Denmark and the descendants of the founder of the East Asiatic Company, which had a long-time trade relationship with China, as well as other Danish friends, the Danish government responded enthusiastically and expressed a willingness to provide long-term interest-free loans.

In November 1981, the Danish government sent a delegation to China, headed by Mogens Isaksen, Director of the Danish International Development Agency. From our list of potential partners, they selected the Beijing Milk Company, Anda County Creamery (Heilongjiang Province), New China Sugar Refinery (Jilin Province), and Guangzhou Light Ceramsite Plant, and offered a loan of 125 million Danish Krones. Representatives of the two governments signed the agreement in Beijing on April 19, 1982.

Hu Yaobang Supports the Implementation of Loan Projects

In September 1982, we reported that the Anda County Creamery could go into trial operation in the last quarter of 1984 and full operation the following year, with the capacity for processing 200 tons of fresh milk daily and producing 7,000 tons of milk powder annually. Hu Yaobang wrote on the report:

> About 20,000 milk cows are needed, and they should be bred within a distance of 50 kilometers. Otherwise, it will be difficult to keep the milk fresh. Please take this into consideration.

After we reported to him what we had done, Hu commented:

> Well done! Now I feel relieved. There are still many ways to attract foreign investment and cooperate with Third World countries. I look forward to new breakthroughs.

The milk supply was significantly improved after we used the foreign government loans to help build a number of dairy projects, import fine cow breeds and introduce advanced breeding and milk processing technologies.

After Japan and Belgium promised to offer us government loans in 1979, more countries followed suit to establish long-term cooperation over favorable loan projects. These included Kuwait, Italy, Demark, Sweden, Switzerland, Australia, Austria, West Germany, Spain, the United Kingdom, France, Norway, Finland, Canada, the Netherlands, and Luxemburg. Having accumulated new knowledge and experience, and aiming to cut costs, we conducted friendly negotiations with the lending countries through simplified procedures and on more favorable terms. For instance, West Germany agreed to cut the annual interest rate of its government loans from 2 percent to 0.75 percent; Denmark turned its interest-free government loans (accounting for 40 percent of its mixed loans) into endowment; Canada increased the ratio of interest-free government loans from the original 30 percent to 40 percent of its second batch of mixed loans.

In the process of using foreign loans, however, we also came across some impostors who took advantage of our lack of knowledge of foreign countries and international finance at the start of opening up. Some used "favorable loans" as bait and later turned them into usurious loans; some promoted low-quality equipment at unduly high prices; others laundered illegal funds by taking advantage of the loopholes in Chinese legislation; and still others simply disappeared after defrauding us of large commissions. For a time, fraudulent information ran rampant, invariably claiming to offer us loans of billions of US dollars. Some swindlers went so far as to say they were already holding talks with our embassies in foreign lands. Although investigations revealed all those "cakes falling from heaven" to be frauds, and despite public warnings by authorities, cases of fraud still occurred from time to time in the years that followed.

By the end of 2007, according to statistics, the World Bank and foreign governments had agreed to provide China with favorable loans of US$104 billion in total, of which US$82.8 billion had actually been used for 2,679 projects in 31 provinces, autonomous regions and municipalities directly under the central government.

In terms of industry, nearly 50 percent of the loans were used on energy, transportation and telecommunication projects, which helped restructure the industry and coordinate the national economic development. More specifically, the World Bank and foreign governments provided US$18.1 billion in loans for energy projects such as power stations, coal mines and oil fields; US$29.1 billion for transportation projects such as harbors, railways and airports. All of these were key national projects. We built, among others, the Tianshengqiao Hydropower Station, which increased the power generating capacity by about 5 million kilowatts and the nation's annual electricity output by 20 billion kilowatt hours. The annual production capacity of raw coal grew by about 50 million tons. Besides helping maintain production of the Shengli Oilfield in north China, the loans were also used to build new oilfields, which added to the production capacity of crude oil. We built the Shijiu Harbor in Shandong Province, and expanded the harbors of Qinhuangdao (Hebei Province), Qingdao (Shandong Province), Lianyungang (Jiangsu Province), and the first container berths of the harbors of Tianjin and Shanghai. Twenty-three new berths were built for ships at or above 10,000 tons. As a result, the handling capacity of harbors increased by over 60 million tons annually. These projects have significantly contributed to the development of our foreign trade. They also have facilitated the transportation of coal from Shanxi Province to other areas, and from the north to the south for industrial production. The Yanzhou-Shijiusuo railway, the double-track and electrification projects for the Beijing-Qinhuandao, Zhengzhou-Baoji railway, and Hengyang-Guangzhou railways (with a total length of 1,800 kilometers), increased the nation's annual transportation capacity by more than 100 million tons. The Beijing-Tianjin-Tanggu Highway, the first high-standard freeway in China, was also built with such loans. Other major projects included the Xiamen International Airport, a mini-bus plant in Tianjin with an annual output of 20,000 and a light-truck project in Nanjing with an annual output of 60,000. All these have significantly helped to improve transportation in our country.

More specific statistics concerning the use of loans from foreign governments are as follows:

1. US$545 million was used to improve telecommunication facilities, including optical cable, in several dozen cities. Among the major projects were the Huaihe Digital Micro-wave Electric Circuit, the Sirius Satellite Ground Station and Naval Satellite Ground Station. These have helped us to receive information from all over the world in a timely fashion, to improve internal communications and to promote the economic development.
2. US$421 million was used to renovate 13 metallurgical enterprises. These helped to raise iron and steel output and quality, made up for shortages in certain products, improved the quality of the products, and saved expenses in foreign currency. US$1.236 billion was used to build 27 petrochemical and chemical projects;

US$221 million was used to build 23 construction materials projects. These projects helped agricultural production in a variety of ways.

3. US$500 million to US$600 million was used to build or renovate 72 mechanical and electrical enterprises, which helped promote technological advancement in industry. Successful examples abound. With interest-free loans from the Danish government, the Anda County Creamery imported the designing and manufacturing technologies for two kinds of licensed products. The imported technologies filled the gaps in our industry and enabled us to make equipment for spraying, drying and evaporating milk at the international advanced level. As one of the first group of large- and medium-sized key enterprises slated for technological innovation during the Seventh Five-Year Plan period (1986-1990), the Chongqing Telecommunication Equipment Plant under the Ministry of Post and Telecommunications imported from Italy – with loans from the Italian government – a Pulse Coding Modulation (PCM) equipment production line. In October 1986, along with the contract coming into effect, the plant started to produce complete sets of PCM equipment at the 1980s international standard, filling a technological gap and saving us large amounts of foreign currency in the years to come, thus playing a significant role in improving telecommunications in our country. The Dayaoshan Tunnel, a double-track electrified railway tunnel built with Japanese loans, is one of the longest of its kind in the world. With imported advanced excavating machines, we armed a mechanized excavating team. New technologies, chiefly large-diameter, full-face rock drills for one-step excavation, were used for the first time in the construction of a new railway tunnel. The new excavating technologies were later effectively applied in the construction of the Beijing Subway and Jundushan Tunnel on the Dalian-Qinhuangdao railway.

4. Some of the loans were used to build or renovate a number of enterprises with a focus on the production of export products and products that we had to buy from other countries. Moreover, we used US$400 million of foreign loans

355

and donations in poor and remote areas to help local people beat poverty.

5. Of the 340 textile and light industrial projects, 72 mechanical and electrical projects, 27 petrochemical and chemical projects and 23 building materials projects, the majority focused on export products or import substitutes. In particular, the 100 billion yen in trade surplus loans were used almost entirely for export-oriented projects. The Jilin Paper Mill, built with loans from the Swedish government, and equipped with E61 paper production lines imported from Sweden, went into full operation in April 1988. By June 1989, it had produced 55,000 tons of 49.5 grams/square meter of offset printing newsprint, with quality reaching the government standard, and exported 14,200 tons for US$4.36 million, with profits and taxes totaling 39.21 million yuan.

By now China had shed its obsession with a "debt-free" economy. In fact, foreign loans had become the lubricant for industrial development. Through practical work and training, a large number of management and technical talents have come to the fore. The economic achievements made possible by aid and loans were monumental. Clearly it was not only feasible, but also highly beneficial to use favorable international loans to make up for shortfalls in capital funds and advance our country's socioeconomic development.

6

Foreign Trade Reform's Rough Beginning

In January 1950, the Central People's Government promulgated a new customs import and export tariff, which put foreign trade under state control. This was to remain a state policy for the next three decades, with imports and exports basically subject to the uniform management of specialized companies under the Ministry of Foreign Trade, which in 1982 was merged into the Ministry of Foreign Economic Relations and Trade (MOFERT, renamed the "Ministry of Foreign Trade and Economic Cooperation," or MOFTEC in 1993).

This highly centralized foreign trade system, born of the circumstances of the time, played an important role in abolishing imperialist powers' trade prerogatives in old China, carrying out the socialist transformation of private import and export firms, breaking the economic sanctions imposed on China by Western powers, and rehabilitating and developing the national economy. However, its drawbacks also became increasingly pronounced with changes in the domestic and world situations and with the development and expansion of the national economy. To begin with, the annual national import and export plan and the biannual Chinese Export Commodities Fair, also known as the "Canton Fair," could barely keep pace with an ever-changing market. Second, at the time, export commodities were purchased by local branches before they were sold abroad by their head companies according to unified plans, a practice that alienated producers from sellers, and detached industries from trade organizations. Third, monopolies and rigid

357

Premier Zhou Enlai visiting the textiles hall of the Spring Canton Fair, May 15, 1967. The Premier made sure that the Canton Fair ran without disruption even during the Cultural Revolution (1966-1976).

central planning over imports and exports made it impossible to mobilize the enthusiasm of all quarters. Fourth, the system whereby the state, not the companies, bore the sole responsibility for profits and losses resulted in poor economic outcomes. Fifth, foreign trade was deemed only a means to "supply each other's needs and regulate surpluses and shortages," to the neglect of its role in the international division of labor and international competition, as well as the importation of advanced technology and capital.

After the fall of the Gang of Four, economic construction was accorded due importance. Reform of the foreign trade system was put on the agenda amid earnest appeals from all corners. This became a hot topic at a State Council meeting (in July of 1978) to discuss principles. In his concluding speech at the meeting, Vice Premier Li Xiannian said:

> South Korea, Singapore, Hong Kong, and Taiwan are such small countries and regions but their imports and exports are much larger than ours. Can't we surpass them? To increase exports, some of our administrative systems and approaches must be reformed. For instance, we should adopt exchange rate quotations

in foreign trade, and allow manufacturers to engage in direct export and to retain part of foreign exchange revenues.

With Deng Xiaoping's support, the central government held a work conference in April 1979 to review and analyze the issues associated with the foreign trade system, with a goal to reform it step by step.

Breaking the Monopoly Over Foreign Trade

At the time, China's foreign trade was too small to satisfy the nation's huge demand for foreign exchange for construction and development. How to tap the nation's potential in its abundant cheap labor and other resources to expand foreign trade and increase foreign exchange revenues through exports thus became a pressing concern. On August 13, 1979, the State Council promulgated the *Regulations on Issues Concerning Vigorous Development of Foreign Trade and Increase of Foreign Exchange Revenues*, stipulating that all regions and departments should develop export commodities by all means and actively source non-trade foreign exchange revenues. The *Regulations* also called for an overhaul of the existing foreign trade and other administrative systems with a view toward mobilizing the enthusiasm and initiative of all quarters to do a good job in managing foreign trade and other undertakings that could add to the nation's foreign exchange revenues.

Based on its investigations from 1979 to 1982, the State Import and Export Commission (SIEC) pinpointed three impediments to the work to increase foreign exchange revenues through expanding exports: the monopolistic foreign trade system that inhibited the relevant organizations' interest in increasing exports; the low quality and limited variety of export commodities as a result of low manufacturing technology; and the losses incurred in exports that had become a heavy financial burden on the state. The State Import and Export Commission suggested that relevant industrial departments, regions and industrial manufacturing enterprises directly take part in foreign trade, and expand production by technically transforming export-oriented manufacturing enterprises via compensation trade and other approaches. The Commission also urged local governments to appropriate a certain amount of local foreign exchange reserves and revenues from exports to back up the production of export commodities.

To remedy the "heavy losses" resulting from export commodities, the Commission began investigations into local enterprises in March 1981. The practice in foreign trade at the time was to calculate profits and losses of imports and exports as a whole, in which the profits from imports (in some years customs tariffs and industrial-commercial taxes were included) were generally used to offset the "losses" in exports. The export losses in 1980 amounted to 3.2 billion yuan. Export commodities with "losses" above 70 percent (or 40 percent based on the internal settlement price for foreign exchange earned through trade) were categorized as "heavy-loss" products. The year 1980 saw 462 kinds of "heavy-loss" commodities, totaling US$1.108 billion. Investigations revealed four causes for "heavy losses" in export commodities: 1) over-priced imported raw materials, and high domestic taxes, industrial profits and purchase prices, which accounted for two thirds of the total "heavy losses"; 2) poor management in production, circulation and foreign trade; 3) commodities made for export that paired raw materials purchased at high prices with outdated manufacturing technology: an example was the Chinese-made pocket-size radios that sold for US$2 each, as compared with Japanese-made radios that sold for US$8 to US$10; 4) the high production costs and low prices of a few export commodities, such as grass meal, leaf meal and other feedstuffs purchased at high prices to help subsidize some poor areas.

In November 1981, the State Import and Export Commission submitted the *Report on an Analysis of Heavy Losses Incurred by Export Commodities and Proposed Solutions* to the State Council. Among other things, the Report proposed to: 1) formulate incentive export policies, and actively reform the egalitarian "big pot" system in such areas as industry, finance and foreign trade; 2) increase coastal cities' autonomy in processing imported materials and require enterprises to bear sole responsibility for their own profits and losses, with the aim to transform coastal Shanghai, Tianjin and other cities into export processing centers; 3) to relax controls on foreign exchange and domestic loans to facilitate the import of advanced technology and support export-oriented production, to set aside 0.5 percent of the foreign exchange revenues from exports in 1981 (about US$85 million), to support the production of export commodities; 4) to establish joint industrial and trading companies (or joint industrial, agricultural and trading companies) to deal in export commodities along specialized lines, to establish specialized import and export companies (for example, dealing in a particular category, such as silk products) that combine central and local management, and to set up pilot business entities affiliated to export companies and export-industry associations. The *Report* suggested that in the course of the reform, it was imperative to follow such principles as separating government administration from enterprise management, integrating industry and trade, and to do away with old conventions. Quotas should be set and every enterprise should be responsible for its own profits and losses on the basis of the export costs of individual goods. The enterprises would enjoy their rights and interests alongside responsibilities.

To meet the requirements of the State Council, during the 1979-1982 period the State Import and Export Commission conducted a series of investigations and, on this basis, began coordinating with relevant departments to transform the monopolistic foreign trade system by decontrolling power. In Guangdong and Fujian provinces, special policies and flexible measures were enforced to expand their administrative power over foreign trade. Local foreign trade companies were set up to deal in commodities that were locally produced or needed, and that did not fall into the categories subject to unified state management. At an August 1979 symposium on the export work of Beijing, Tianjin and Shanghai, the State Import and Export Commission granted the aforementioned policies to these cities. A month-long national import and export work conference convened by the Commission on November 20, 1979 further delved into foreign trade reform, extending decision-making power to Liaoning, Hebei and other provinces and regions along the coasts or the Yangtze River, as soon as their conditions became mature. At the conference, the Commission outlined reforms in the following five aspects:

First, grading and classifying export commodities. The past rigid practice in which exports were exclusively managed by the foreign trade corporations under the Ministry of Foreign Trade was reformed by entrusting the export of some commodities to localities and relevant departments, while provinces, municipalities and autonomous regions were allowed to establish specialized trading companies to handle the export and import of local commodities. Furthermore, the foreign trade corporations under the Ministry delegated the import and export rights on certain commodities to their branches in Beijing, Tianjin and Shanghai municipalities, and Guangdong, Fujian and Liaoning provinces. Relevant departments of the State Council were allowed to set up companies to supply export commodities. Apart from the 11 foreign trade corporations under the Ministry of Foreign Trade, the State Council also allowed its metallurgical, machine-building, weaponry, aviation, and shipbuilding departments to set up their own companies and to export commodities produced by factories under their administration. The establishment of these industrial and trading companies shattered the monopoly of foreign trade and marked a good beginning in the effort to diversify foreign trade entities, even though it fell short of separating government administration from corporate management.

Second, expanding the rights of manufacturing enterprises to engage in foreign trade and setting up various pilot companies that combined both manufacturing and trading. For instance, the Shanghai Toy Company was given the green light to export its products and import raw materials. The Beijing Arts and Crafts Company, and the Beijing Special Crafts Export Company began to coordinate production and sales under overall planning. Industrial departments and trading companies also jointly set up factories to produce export commodities, such as the titanium sponge factory run by the China Minmetals Corporation and the Sichuan Provincial Metallurgy Department.

Third, developing the export of commodities processed with imported materials. In November 1981, Beijing was the venue of a State Council meeting of representatives from Beijing, Tianjin, Shanghai, Liaoning, Hebei, Shandong, Jiangsu, Zhejiang, and Guangxi (Guangdong and Fujian provinces had just been granted special policies and therefore did not attend it) to discuss foreign economic relations and trade. Also present at the meeting were leaders of the State Import and Export Commission, the State Planning Commission, the State Economic Commission, the Ministry of Finance, the Ministry of Foreign Trade, and the Ministry of Transport and Communications. The meeting arrived at a consensus to readjust taxation and use other means to help coastal regions expand their exports of finished commodities processed with imported materials. To that end, the meeting decided that the import of raw, semi-finished and subsidiary materials, accessories and components, and packaging materials needed for producing export commodities should be exempt from customs tariffs and industrial and commercial taxes on imported goods. Agreement was also reached to further expand the coastal regions' foreign trade rights, put their foreign trade businesses under both central and local leadership, and entrust foreign trade accounting to local management on the basis of unified responsibilities, rights and interests. By taking the 1981 profits and losses in export as base numbers, the losses were to be offset with a special fund from the central coffers, while the profits were to be delivered to the state treasury. As to profits and losses incurred in exports after 1982, the profits were to be included in local budgets, while the losses would be included in central or local budgets according to respective responsibilities of the enterprises using foreign exchange.

Fourth, adopting an internal settlement price for foreign exchange revenues from exports, and increasing the portion of such revenues to be retained by localities so as to encourage them to expand exports. The exchange rate between the US dollar and the Renminbi, as set by the People's Bank of China was 1: 1.8 at that time. The over-valuation of the Renminbi resulted in serious losses in exports, and it was impossible to devaluate the Renminbi within a short time. The State Import and Export Commission had carried out numerous investigations and calculations, held more than 100 discussions to seek a solution, and finally came up with a dual exchange rate scheme. While the official exchange rate was to remain unchanged, as of 1981 the foreign exchange revenues earned from exports within state plans were to be settled at a rate of 1: 2.8 between the US dollar and the Renminbi. This practice came to an end after the official exchange rate dropped below the 1: 2.8 ratio. To guarantee the foreign exchange needed for local imports, the government introduced a system that allowed an average province or municipality to retain 10 percent of the foreign exchange revenues from exports, but raised the portion to 25 percent for Guangdong and Fujian provinces and, for a certain period of time, 50 percent for ethnic autonomous regions.

Fifth, establishing foreign trade organizations overseas. In 1980, the China Import and Export Corporation under the

Ministry of Foreign Trade established agencies in Tokyo, London, Paris, and Hamburg. The staff consisted of people dispatched by various import and export corporations, thereby turning these agencies into joint working bodies.

For the convenience of local exports, the former rigid division of work among export ports (carpets, for example, were shipped via the Tianjin Harbor, and tea was shipped via the Shanghai Harbor) was adjusted according to the rational flow of export commodities to ensure that they could be shipped to the ports nearest to their origins.

A number of laws and regulations on management coordination were formulated to correspond with the new situation in which the nation's foreign trade was handled through diverse channels. The years 1980 and 1981 alone saw the promulgation of 15 regulations, including:

- *Procedures on Special-Purpose Loans for Production of Export Manufactured Goods;*
- *Interim Provisions on Export Licensing System;*
- *Procedures on Client Management;*
- *Regulations Governing the Division of Work on Export Commodities Between National Foreign Trade Corporations and Provincial Foreign Trade Companies;*
- *Procedural Regulations on Factories Specializing in Export Commodities Production;* and
- *Procedural Provisions on Producing Bases for Export Farm and Sideline Products*

The central government put a premium on the reform of the foreign trade system. Toward the end of July 1981, upon reading a SIEC report on the basic situation in foreign trade (along with the relevant strategic conceptions, policies and measures), a top leader pointed out:

The significance of foreign economic relations and trade should be recognized from a strategic vantage point. In our economic work there are two forces, two battlefields and two resources. We should mainly rely on our own efforts, and supplement those with external support. We should make the most of internal resources without neglecting external ones. There being a domestic battle-field and an international battlefield, we should not only enhance our abilities to work at home but also be able to go international. We should ask ourselves whether there is a foothold for us in the world market? The biannual Canton Fair itself represents a policy of self-seclusion. Many of the markets in the world are mere blank spots for us. Foreign trade will have no way forward if we continue to allow one department to monopolize it. We must bring the resources of provinces and municipalities into full play. We must emancipate our minds, shake off old conventions and fight our way onto the world market.

The monopolistic foreign trade system was the joint outcome of the trade embargo imposed by the West, the dire shortage of foreign exchange, and a highly centralized planned economy. Reforming the system was tough going, because barter trade with the Soviet Union and other countries was then a major part of our foreign trade, because monopoly over the foreign trade system – a typical field of central planning – had been in place for 30 years, and because its reform was circumscribed by other areas of the economy such as planning, finance, foreign exchange, and taxation.

The drawbacks of this outdated foreign trade system gradu-ally became more obvious – particularly as we had more encounters with the foreign markets and as the economy itself expanded. The reform and opening policy could not work unless the old system was transformed. Because decentralization of power meant that some departments had to readjust or even lose their established interests, Vice Premier Gu Mu and the State Import and Export Commission were under immense pressure at that time. Whatever the difficul-ties, however, reform was the only way out. Without knowing this background, people today can hardly understand the harsh reality and the crucial nature of reform back then. Breaking the monopoly over imports and exports, for instance, may look like a minor step now, but considering the deep-rooted history of this monopoly, and the oppositions and obstacles encountered, it was nothing short of a huge breakthrough in Chinese foreign trade history.

Some of the ideas for reforming foreign trade that were suggested in the early 1980s were adopted on a trial basis.

The other ideas were shelved because of impediments in the economic system, but were later proved correct by a new round of foreign trade reforms that began in the late 1980s. These reforms included abolishing the old monopolistic foreign trade system, separating foreign trade corporations from their local branches, decentralizing foreign trade management, allowing factories and research institutes to run their own foreign trade businesses, separating government administration from enterprise management, adjusting the exchange rate, adopting a tax rebate on export commodities, and requiring the relevant organizations to be responsible for their own profits and losses.

Reform Brings About New Vitality

On September 15, 1984, the State Council approved the *Propositions on Foreign Trade Restructuring* submitted by the Ministry of Foreign Economic Relations and Trade (MOFERT), and set forth three basic principles for the reform: first, to strip government administration from enterprise management, so that the only task for the MOFERT was to put the nation's foreign trade under its administration; second, to introduce an agent system in foreign trade; third, to combine industry and trade, technology and trade, and import and export. Specifically, in the course of foreign trade reform, government administration would be separated from enterprise management, with foreign trade subject to the administration by the MOFERT and by the provincial committees or bureaus in charge of foreign trade and economic cooperation. Foreign trade enterprises were allowed to do business free from intervention from administrative departments at any level, while exercising independent accounting and bearing the responsibility for their own losses and profits thereof. These principles were correct beyond doubt, but their implementation was delayed because the State Import and Export Commission, which had been coordinating the reform had by then been merged into the MOFERT.

Nevertheless, as the defects of the old foreign trade system became more and more apparent with the expansion of the opening-up policy, local governments' demands for the relaxation of control and decentralization of power became stronger.

Under the leadership of the State Council and with the support and coordination of the State Commission for Economic Restructuring, the MOFERT conducted careful investigations and overcame many difficulties before implementing the following major reforms in the foreign trade system in the middle and late 1980s:

First, reform of the exchange rate system and the export subsidy scheme. The exchange rate between the US dollar and Renminbi was then fixed at 1: 2.8. In other words, for each US dollar earned through export, a foreign trade company could only get 2.8 yuan in settlement at a state-designated bank. The government would then subsidize the company for the evident "losses," based on the swap costs of different commodities. Abolishing these subsidies would call for an adjustment of the exchange rate, which in turn would cause a substantial devaluation of the Renminbi and probably give rise to economic and social turmoil. To avoid such risks, the MOFERT decided to gradually adjust the exchange rate, and in the meantime allow foreign trade companies to retain a portion of their foreign exchange revenues, which could be either used to finance imports or swapped at the real market exchange rate to make up for swap costs. Hence the coexistence of two exchange rates at the time, which were later merged into one so that foreign trade companies could settle their export earnings at state banks based on the market exchange rate. Thereafter the practice of foreign exchange retention and foreign exchange swap markets were naturally abolished. By the 1990s, when the foreign exchange earnings from foreign trade became freely swappable, all the above-mentioned practices and phenomena had disappeared.

Second, the implementation of the policy of tax rebate on export commodities. The adjustment of the exchange rate alone could not fully make up for swap costs. The common practice of most countries was to impose taxes on all domestic commodities, such as consumption taxes and value-added taxes. Tax payments for commodities not for home sale were to be refunded when exported, based on legal certificates. China practiced the value-added tax system, according to which taxes for export commodities should likewise be refunded or else manufacturers could not compete with their international rivals on an equal footing. However, as the value-added tax system came late in China and the improvement of tax collection system took time, some companies resorted to cheating to claim tax rebates for export commodities. Such illegal practices largely diminished with the development of the tax collection system, and in particular, the establishment of the National Network for Computerized Auditing of Value-Added Tax Invoices, also known as the "Golden Tax Project."

Third, reform of monopoly on foreign trade, and decentralization of foreign trade authority. The focus of the foreign trade reform initiated in 1984 was to streamline government administration and to decentralize power. Specifically, the specialized foreign trade companies under the MOFERT, foreign trade companies under other departments and local foreign trade companies needed to be separated from their former governing bodies so as to engage in independent accounting, take responsibility for their own profits and losses, and gradually develop into professional and outsourcing companies. Various foreign trade corporations also cut ties with their provincial branches, a move to give them a free hand and inspire their enthusiasm for foreign trade. The autonomy was later extended to foreign trade companies at city and county levels, whose tasks until then had been to procure export commodities for higher-level companies, manufacturing enterprises and research institutes. To better facilitate the administrative function of the MOFERT, the financial management of all foreign trade companies was then put under the supervision of the Ministry of Finance. The restrictions on the business scope of foreign trade companies were lifted, so that they could deal in a range of commodities. They were also encouraged to engage in the processing and manufacture of export products, and to act as agents for manufacturing enterprises.

Fourth, the implementation of guidance plans to replace mandatory export quotas for foreign exchange revenues from exports. To remedy the drawbacks of extreme egalitarianism in foreign trade enterprises where everybody "ate from the same big pot regardless of individual performance," the contract responsibility system was implemented. In some foreign trade enterprises, a "joint-stock system" – which allowed employees to purchase part of the enterprises' incremental shares on a voluntary basis – was later introduced on a trial basis. The experiment proved successful over the years. Of course, because of the constraints from the process of economic restructuring as a whole, and particularly because most of the reforms were carried out under the planned economy, the results were bound to be circumscribed. Nevertheless, they laid the foundation for further in-depth reforms.

Most people realized that it was totally unrealistic to rely on a dozen or so national import and export corporations for major development of foreign trade in a country with more than a billion people. That realization alone, however, could not solve the problem. Given the administrative and management systems, and the mentality and practices based on monopoly over many years, even a minor step would meet unreasonable opposition. The reforming breakthroughs made in the 1980s resulted in the following achievements: in 1988, the separation of foreign trade corporations from their branches and subsidiaries throughout the country; the decentralization of foreign trade power, whereby 100 scientific and research units were given the right to engage in foreign trade; the synergies between trade and industry, between trade and technology, and the transformation of foreign trade enterprises through such synergies; the readjustment of exchange rates; the replacement of export subsidies by tax rebates on export commodities; the system for trading companies to bear the responsibility for losses and profits; and the substitution of administrative approval of foreign trade rights with a new registration system. By the end of 2007, a total of 634,000 enterprises had been granted the right to foreign trade.

Fear of chaotic competition was at the core of monopoly. However, competition is the bottom line of a market economy. Only with competition can there be economic vitality and progress. What's more, chaos is not a matter of course. It can be avoided through institutional, management and legislation reforms, which is something that should be done in a socialist market economy. Therefore, we must not give up eating for fear of choking, so to speak. After all, is monopoly, itself, immune from chaos?

Prior to the foreign trade reform, I was once faced with a difficult question: Which company to choose to handle the nation's export of drawnwork* products? Such a question may seem superfluous today – any registered enterprise can do it. But it was a hard decision to make under the monopoly system in which all imports and exports were handled by the foreign trade corporations under the MOFERT. To make the situation more complicated, under the fixed and over-valued exchange rate system at the time, the subsidies to different export commodities had to be readjusted according to the changing purchase prices at home and the export prices abroad. In order to prevent the practice of exporting only those commodities with lower swap costs for higher government subsidies, the government banned all foreign trade companies from dealing in export commodities other than those officially designated to handle them.

The Ramie War

The causes and effects I have illustrated in the foregoing might be unintelligible to those who have not experienced them. Actually, they could confuse even those entrusted to manage them. Here's an example: For some time before the reform, the swap cost of drawnwork products was so low that it caused a tough scramble among several companies – the China National Textiles Import and Export Corporation (Chinatex), the China National Native Produce and Animal By-Products Import and Export Corporation (China Tuhsu), and the China National Arts and Crafts Import and Export Corporation (CNACIEC) – to expand exports. They vied with each to procure ramie (the major raw material for making the cloth for drawnwork products), from the countryside. As a result the purchase price of ramie soared from four yuan to 16 yuan per kilogram, and the rug was pulled from underneath the nation's drawnwork exporting business. The relevant departments of the MOFERT tried to coordinate the situation but to no avail. I had no choice but to call a meeting

---

* Drawnwork is a form of textile design, achieved by pulling threads from even woven cloth, in a kind of "reverse embroidery." (*Translator*)

of the general mangers of the three companies. The man from Chinatex claimed that drawnwork was a textile product and the man from CNACIEC contended that it was a handicraft. The leader of China Tuhsu argued that ramie was a native product, and went so far as to declare that anything that flew in the sky, grew on the ground or was raised by man was either native produce or an animal product, and was therefore well within his company's business domain. He fell just short of saying that all commodities on earth should be left to their management. Having failed to persuade the three general managers to make concessions and reach an agreement by taking the nation's overall interests into consideration, I had no alternative but to announce the following verdict: The raw materials associated with ramie, such as ramie balls, belonged in the business scope of China Tuhsu, while CHINATEX was to deal in products that were fashioned out of textiles and decorated with drawnwork, such as tablecloths, napkins and clothing, and CNACIEC was to handle commodities that were mainly drawnwork, such as drawnwork shawls. I added that this new division of business scopes should be strictly followed, and no trespassing of each other's territories was allowed. When I announced the verdict, I knew it was only a temporary "armistice agreement," rather than a thorough settlement of the issue.

There were many more examples of this nature, such as panic purchases of eel fries and cocoons, in those years. In fact, any export goods with low swap costs were likely to draw trading companies into conflict and to overstep their respective business lines. The purchase prices were bid up while export prices bid down until the government could no longer afford the ever-increasing subsidies and had no alternative but to withdraw the commodities in question from the international market. This problem, however, was certainly not caused by the national foreign trade corporations, which bore no hard feelings against each other. The fault was with the established system.

I remember that when I declared the separation of foreign trade corporations from their local branches and subsidiaries, some general managers complained that they could not live without their "arms and legs," that is, the branches and subsidiaries. I replied:

We have cut off your "arms and legs," and more than that, we are going to take away your patron – the MOFERT. But we have left you a most precious thing – your brains. With your pool of talented foreign trade personnel, I believe you can do a much better job.

As I expected, all the trading corporations that actively transformed their structures and carried out reforms in earnest, such as those dealing in grain and cooking oil, chemical products, and machines, all developed into mainstay giants in the nation, while a few others that were slow in adopting new concepts of economic management and clung to old monopolies could not survive market competition and therefore got left behind. The reform of the foreign exchange system also enabled people to see the importance of exchange rates for the nation's foreign trade, finance and economic development.

Blazing a New Trail for Mechanical and Electrical Products Exports

All mechanical and electrical products were then purchased by foreign trade companies with exclusive exporting rights. The problem with this practice was that market demand information could not be fed back to manufacturers in a timely fashion, and as a consequence, mechanical and electrical products often fell behind international demand, and were often overstocked. Mechanical and electrical products made up only a tiny portion of the nation's total export volume. In 1981, for instance, China exported US$620 million worth of mechanical and electrical products, or 2.97 percent of the nation's total exports. The figure for Japan was US$102.9 billion, or 67.6 percent of its total export volume of US$152 billion. In South Korea, where the total export was about the same as ours, mechanical and electrical products made up 22.5 percent of the total amount. India only had half the amount of our total export, but its export of mechanical and electrical products was twice as much as ours. Even in comparison with some other developing countries and regions, we still lagged far behind in this area.

Based on our research and comparative studies with other countries, we found that many factors were tipped in favor of Chinese mechanical and electrical exports. First, China had plentiful material and labor resources. Actually our labor cost was lower than that of developed countries and even some developing countries as well. Second, China already had built up a relatively complete industrial system and an ancillary industrial foundation, along with 3 million or so master machine tools. Third, China already had developed a considerable technical force in research and development, design and trial production, and technological processes. Fourth, we already had accumulated some preliminary knowledge and experience in marketing mechanical and electrical products in the international market. Fifth, backed by a vast home market, the mechanical and electrical industry in China was less risky than in countries whose industries hinged on the world market. The development of mechanical and electrical exports, therefore, would be a most promising area for us, so long as we took active measures and brought our advantages into full play. It could even make headway so long as product quality, marketing networks and management system could be properly handled.

I illustrated these ideas in an essay entitled "Propositions on Furtherance of Exports of Mechanical and Electrical Products," which was published in the December 18, 1982 issue of the *Economic Research References*, a journal run by the Research Center of the Secretariat of the Party Central Committee. Some of my proposals were later put into practice.

One example was my proposal to gradually replace purchases of mechanical and electrical products for exclusive sales, with an agent system, with foreign trade enterprises acting as export agents for manufacturers. Compared with exclusive sales, the agent system bound the exporters and manufacturers together on the basis of shared interests, which helped to optimize their respective strengths in marketing and technology. Eventually, the agent system became a major practice in foreign trade, and has now been widely applied in foreign trade enterprises.

Another proposal I raised in the article was the introduction of an incentive-based system to evaluate companies' performances in mechanical and electrical exports. Because outdated technology was a prevailing problem in the production of mechanical and electrical products in those days, most exporters set higher technical demands for export products than domestic ones. Thus the export products cost more in terms of time and labor, and incurred financial losses, which greatly dampened the producers' enthusiasm. To redress the situation, my suggestion was to appraise and award the exporters based on both revenues and costs.

Through decades of ceaseless efforts, the Chinese mechanical and electrical industry has markedly improved its international competitiveness. By 2007, its exports amounted to US$701.17 billion, compared to US$620 million in 1981, and accounted for 57.6 percent of the nation's total export. With that quantum leap, China's foreign trade structure, long dominated by primary products, textiles and other light-industry products, had shifted its weight to mechanical and electrical and high-tech products.

GATT Membership: From Rejection to Re-entry

As is now well known, China submitted its application for resumption of its status as one of the contracting parties to the General Agreement on Tariffs and Trade (GATT) in 1986, and it took a long 15 years before it became a full member of the World Trade Organization (WTO) in 2001.

Back on March 24, 1948, China put its signature on the final document of the UN Conference on Trade and Employment held in Havana, thereby becoming a member of the Executive Committee of the Interim Commission for the International Trade Organization. On April 21, 1948 China signed the Protocol of Provisional Application of GATT, and on May 21 the same year it became one of GATT's original signatories. The People's Republic of China declared upon its founding in 1949 that with respect to the various multilateral agreements the old Chinese government concluded with foreign countries, it would make a close examination of their worth so as to come up with separate decisions for their recognition, annulment, revision or reinstitution. The Taiwan authority declared on March 6, 1950, in the name of "Republic of China," to withdraw from the GATT, which then requested the New China government to take over the seat left by the Kuomintang government. Yet, due to historical reasons, we then deemed it as a "rich men's club" and refrained from joining it. After 1971, however, with the successive restoration of China's legitimate seat in the United Nations and many other international organizations and institutions, our view of the GATT began to change.

We moved to resume relationships with the GATT during the early 1980s. In August 1980 China accepted an invitation to a meeting organized by the Executive Committee of the Interim Commission for the International Trade Organization, and in 1981 joined the Multifibre Agreement (MFA) negotiated through the GATT Textile Committee, and it also became a member of the latter.

On December 25, 1982 the Ministry of Foreign Economic Relations and Trade – together with the Ministry of Foreign Affairs, the State Economic Commission, the Ministry of Finance and the General Administration of Customs – submitted to the State Council a report for joining the GATT, which noted that China's trade with the GATT's members had been rising as a result of its reform and opening policy, accounting for approximately 80 percent that of China's total foreign trade. Therefore, whether we joined GATT or not, the various decisions it made would have a bearing on us directly or indirectly. In the wake of China's joining the World Monetary Fund and the World Bank, the problem of joining the GATT was the next item on the agenda, and to safeguard China's legitimate interests we proposed to join the GATT.

In the face of its mounting world economic and trade activities, China had an immediate need for a stable international environment and, with its economic system and foreign trade regime becoming increasingly market-driven, the country possessed the initial conditions for joining the multilateral trade system. On December 31, 1982, Chen Muhua, then Vice Premier, wrote this instruction on the above-mentioned report submitted by the five departments: "I'm inclined to agree to the proposal; kindly request instructions from Wan Li, Zhang Jinfu and Ji Pengfei." The mentioned state leaders soon give their reply in the affirmative.

The State Council then approved a decision to go ahead with the necessary preparatory work and to send in promptly the re-entry application. It was felt at the time that striving for the restoration of China's membership in the GATT would be more advantageous than joining as a new member. For one thing, this would be in keeping with our common practice of requesting seat resumption as we did with other international organizations and institutions. For another, we could thus be saved from prolonged "accession" negotiations with other major GATT contracting parties. With these considerations in mind, we laid out our principled stand: 1) We would request the resumption of China's status as a contracting party to the GATT; 2) The Chinese government stood ready to enter into substantial negotiations with other major contracting parties to this end; 3) China, still a developing country, should enjoy the favorable treatment accorded to other developing countries.

Acting from these principles the departments concerned sped up their preparations. Starting from 1982 China had sent non-voting delegates to GATT contracting-party assemblies, councils and other meetings. The relevant persons were also making visits to Hungary, Pakistan, the former Yugoslavia and other countries to learn their experience and lessons in gaining entrance into the GATT. Non-official negotiations were also conducted with a score or more of states and regions, including the United States and the European Community (EC).

Following a series of deliberations and preparation, Qian Jiadong, China's Permanent Representative to the UN and Other International Organizations, submitted (via Madan G. Mathur, Deputy Director-General of GATT), a note of application to Director-General Arthur J. Dunkel. The full text follows:

Honorable Sir Director-General,

I have the honor to inform Your Excellency that the government of the People's Republic of China, recalling its being one of the contracting parties to the General Agreement on Tariffs and Trade (GATT), considers now to be the time for China to seek the resumption of its status as such in the GATT.

China is currently implementing a fundamental state policy of opening up to the outside world while enlivening its domestic economy, and will adhere to this policy in the future. The government of the People's Republic of China believes that China's ongoing economic reform process will contribute to the expansion of economic and trade relationships with other contracting members. China's involvement in the GATT's work as a contracting party would be instrumental to the attaining of GATT's objectives. China is a developing country and the Chinese government expects it to receive the same treatment accorded to other developing contracting parties.

China is prepared to enter into negotiations with other contracting parties on the restoration of its status in the GATT, and it would to this end provide information about its economic and foreign trade regime.

We would be very grateful if Your Excellency could circulate this request of the PRC to all of the other contracting parties for their consideration.

I avail myself of this opportunity to renew to Your Excellency the assurance of my highest consideration.

Qian Jiadong,
Permanent Representative to the UN
and Other International Organizations
July 10, 1986

Thus, China prepared to hold a series of multi- and bilateral negotiations concerning foreign trade regime evaluation, tariffs reduction and multilateral market access. Within a year the Sino-European talks were formally set in motion. In June 1987 with the approval of the State Council I led a delegation to Brussels, the location of the GATT headquarters, to begin the first round of formal discussions with the EC. At the meeting, I expounded China's basic stance on requesting the resumption of its GATT membership, and a consensus was reached about the choice of director for the Chinese working group and the working procedure. Unexpectedly, however, the negotiations thus begun were to last as many as 15 years!

Why did it take so long? From my personal experiences, I think, in retrospect, apart from the harsh terms and unreasonable demands raised by some industrialized countries, it was mainly due to the following reasons on our part.

First, a lack of acquaintance with the GATT. China began intensive research with regard to the GATT only after handing in its re-entry application, and our contact with it started as late as the early 1980s. On August 4, 1980 China attended the meeting of the Executive Committee of the Interim Commission for the International Trade Organization as one of the 18 supervising member states and voted for the election of Director-General Arthur J. Dunkel. In November 1982, the Chinese government sent its first non-voting delegation to the 38th Assembly of GATT State Parties. During the meeting

377

the delegation consulted with the Secretariat concerning China's re-entry problem. Mr. Dunkel provided opinions on relevant legal matters, while legal experts from the Secretariat told us that, unlike joining other international organizations, China's re-entry to the GATT required substantial negotiations with other major contracting parties and undertook to make tariff reduction and meet the relevant commitments. It was not until 1984, when China obtained observer status, did we begin to have closer contacts with the GATT and its contracting parties.

Second, in the early days, not a few people at home regarded the GATT as a "rich men's club." They were worried that the GATT demand for opening home markets would be detrimental to China, a developing country whose foreign trade served the main purpose of regulating home supply and demand and earning foreign exchange. On November 16, 1971, the GATT adopted the resolution to cancel Taiwan's observer's status, and on November 18, Premier Zhou Enlai ordered the Ministry of Foreign Trade and Ministry of Foreign Affairs to study what attitude China should take toward the GATT and how to make our stand known to the world. On the basis of careful studies, the two ministries presented a report to the State Council with the view that from a long-term point of view, entering the GATT would benefit us politically and economically, but the GATT's most-favored-nation rule might become an impediment to the Chinese policy of treating different nations differently. Furthermore, GATT membership called for certain commitments from member states, and it took time to know the GATT and its activities thoroughly. Thus the report of the two ministries recommended postponing the relevant procedures. Indeed, this view sounded reasonable at the time. It was only after the country's foreign trade had grown substantially that rejoining the GATT was put on the nation's agenda.

Third, joining the GATT would involve one-by-one negotiations with the contracting parties that raised such requests. These parties, proceeding from their own interests, would put forth this or that demand, some rational, others not, and still others likely to put us at a serious disadvantage. Every contracting party had the veto power on the applicant party. Such being the case, a hard "bargaining" process was inevitable. Actually, among all the negotiations over China's GATT re-entry, and later WTO accession, those with the United

States were the most difficult and complex. In the early 1990s the US Trade Representative was a lady named Carla A. Hills, who often wielded a stick and threatened us with sanctions at the talks. She was the tough-talking lady sitting across the negotiation table from Wu Yi, China's newly appointed Vice Minister of Foreign Economic Relations and Trade.

I can remember a discussion held in 1991 over intellectual property rights. Our position in the talks was clear: intellectual property protection, as required by the United States and other countries, accords with China's own interests. Only when intellectual property was duly protected could research and innovation results be free from infringement, and science and technology be developed. We wanted to enhance cooperation with other countries so that intellectual property could be effectively protected. However, the American side, for its part, not only lacked the good faith for cooperation but made an arbitrary attack on us, even accusing China of being an intellectual thief. Unable to tolerate the slander any longer, Chinese representative Wu Yi immediately cited the case of the involvement of US troops, as part of the Eight-Power Allied Forces, in burning, killing and looting in China, and she pointed out that this, indeed, was the behavior of a robber!

During the Fourth Asia-Pacific Economic Cooperation (APEC) Ministerial Meeting, held in Bangkok in September 1992, I myself had talks with the same American Trade Representative on the same topic. She charged that many Chinese chemical and pharmaceutical products had been produced by the uncompensated use of American patents, which constituted an infringement of American intellectual property. Consequently, she demanded on behalf of the US: 1) compensation for those products thus produced in the past; 2) compensation for such products presently under production, or the production be stopped; 3) negotiations conducted and compensation paid before the production of new chemical and pharmaceutical products using American intellectual property. Among the three demands, as we saw it, the first was utterly absurd, the second not quite so, but absolutely unacceptable, as it would seriously jeopardize Chinese public interest, and the third was negotiable.

Consequently, I made this clear to her: "Your first demand is as unfeasible as it is absurd. Let me ask: Can you tell for sure how many such products has China produced in the past? I am pretty sure neither you, nor even we ourselves, are in a position to know exactly. How can you talk about compensation without knowing the facts? Your second demand, namely, that compensation be made or production be stopped, is also unpractical. Leaving a host of Chinese patients anguishing for lack of medicine to cure their illness is in no way compatible with the humanitarianism that you have always championed. Besides, who of all Chinese could make such a promise for compensation – even if there was one such person, he or she would be removed from office and punished. As for the third demand you raised, I think it could be solved through a "win-win" negotiation based on respect for intellectual property rights." Ultimately, the talk wrapped up with a principled agreement in accordance with the view of our side.

The fourth reason I believe our GATT membership negotiations became protracted was that we were somewhat hamstrung by our nation's own development. China was backward in technology, with a weak industrial base. I still remember, in Sino-foreign joint venture negotiations conducted in those days, that we were still adhering to the "three old principles": 1) all the products turned out by the joint ventures should be sold abroad, so as not to let them grab the domestic market; 2) the products should be manufactured within Chinese borders and should have an increasing proportion of "domestic content" lest we be reduced to a mere assembler; 3) each joint venture should be responsible for its own foreign exchange balance. Sometimes when foreign businessmen asked to balance the foreign exchange through import substitution, we could not readily agree, because the foreign exchange used for imports was under the control of the foreign imports department, while joint ventures belonged to the manufacturing department and an accommodation between the two systems could not easily be found.

These were the most knotty problems in joint venture negotiations, which we met, for instance, in talks with the German company Volkswagen in 1978. We asked to use homemade auto parts, a suggestion that the Germans had agreed to in principle. Yet, after checking out the relevant factories, they got the impression that the technology and equipment belonged in their grandfathers' era; moreover, the overwhelming majority of the domestically made auto parts sent to them for appraisal had not come up to the German quality and security standards. It was only after hard bargaining that the Germans barely agreed to adopt, in the Santana model, China-made tires, radios and the nameplate inscribed with the two Chinese characters meaning "Shanghai." Together they accounted for a mere 2.7 percent of the total value of the auto parts. The very nameplate itself, the sign of commercial credit, was of inferior quality and murky in appearance, the two Chinese characters dimly visible. Because of this, at the time I gave them a rather severe criticism. As if this were not enough, the raw stock for the production was not delivered on a timely basis; moreover, the steel plate (rolled by the 1.7-meter rolling machine, then the most advanced in the Wuhan Steel Works) was too narrow for producing the car shell. Under such circumstances, how could we expect to counter the external impact on our automobile industry that was bound to occur after China joined the GATT or WTO? It was this, and other concerns that prompted us, ahead of the accession to the WTO, to draw up the country's first industrial policy regarding automobile production, to put into force a series of measures for enhancing technique and increasing the share of the "domestic content" in production, especially the policy of coupling the import tariffs with the "domestic content" rate. All these had paved the way for the upsurge in the development of the Chinese automobile industry that transpired after we entered the WTO.

Fifth, the Chinese departments taking part in the negotiations were often widely divided in opinions. Some were worried about possbile foreign impact on their own departments, and the others were out to scramble for greater departmental interests. Internal quarrels frequently occurred, while the Ministry of Foreign Economic Relations and Trade, which was then in charge of the external negotiations, was caught in the middle and found it hard to find middle ground. I told the Chinese negotiators, "Just bring these people to the negotiation table and let them speak their minds. Don't talk on their behalf. In this way, they can hear what the foreigners have to say, and the foreigners can also hear out our industrialists." This approach of mine proved to be quite effective, as each department ceased to proceed from departmental interest in the talks, and began to adopt an overall perspective instead.

Sixth, due to the unreasonable demands and obstruction by the United States and a few other contracting parties in the negotiations, China failed to re-enter the GATT as a contracting party member, thereby missing the opportunity to become a natural member of its replacement organization, the World Trade Organization (WTO) upon its establishment on January 1, 1995. This turned China's application for status restoration in the GATT into one for "accession" to the WTO – an entirely different concept. Although the subsequent negotiations were not quite starting anew, it became more complex and prolonged, as the WTO is much wider in content and scope and with a varied application procedure.

The seventh, last and most fundamental reason is that we were not fully prepared at the time. First, China had long been implementing a planned economy and, although market-oriented reform got underway following the decision to reform and open up, it was not actually until 1992 that the establishment of a socialist market economic system became a clear policy decision. The planned economy China was then following could not fit well within GATT's framework of rules and regulations based on market economics, and this is the fundamental factor that prevented substantial progress from being achieved in the negotiations. Second, with the functions of government and the enterprises still confused together, enterprises in China then were not operating independently, but were government-run. It was not until 1998 that the state-owned enterprises began to decouple from government departments. Third, there were difficulties involved in tariff reduction. One of the essential policies enshrined in the GATT was tariff reduction and concessions. Yet, the mere mention of a slight reduction of import tariffs would meet with rallied attacks from various departments in China. As the Director of the Tariff Commission of the State Council, I then felt deeply the troubles involved. The breakthrough in the problem came with President Jiang Zemin's announcement (on three different occasions, in the APEC non-official meetings) of China's voluntary tariff reduction and the commitment to lowering those for industrial products to 10 percent. The measure proved to be very beneficial to China's participation in the international division of labor.

These were the problems we had been tackling amidst 15 years of negotiations, development and reform, some only getting solved through final resolutions from the top level. Historically, there have been many disputes concerning the advantages and disadvantages, and fear that the latter would outweigh the former. As it was, Chinese accession to the WTO came down to the negotiations between the United States and China, and at some critical moments President Jiang Zemin asked Premier Li Peng, Foreign Minister Qian Qichen and Wu Yi to personally join the negotiations so that a decision could be reached on the spot. In retrospect, we can see that the advantages of joining the WTO far outstripped the disadvantages, and the Party's Central Committee made the right decision to pursue it.

The WTO, as well as the GATT are organizations based on market economics, and the decision to join them shows our resolution to implement a market-oriented economic and trade regime. In the course of the negotiations, China's foreign trade regime has undergone corresponding changes, triggering a market-oriented reform process starting with the foreign trade sector, which then led the way. It adopted a series of measures, such as reducing mandatory plans, deregulating pricing for foreign trade commodities; cutting down on administrative controls in foreign import and export trade; stressing the role of regulation in foreign trade played by tariffs, exchange rate and tax revenue; stepping up the construction of a legal system for foreign trade; and drafting the *Foreign Trade Law*. The *Bulletin of the Ministry of Foreign Economic Relations and Trade,* to be updated for circulation at irregular intervals, was also launched to increase the transparency of China's foreign trade policy. In addition, they have followed international rules and made revisions to relevant laws and regulations such as the *Law on Chinese-Foreign Equity Joint Ventures*, the *Law on Chinese-Foreign Contractual Joint Ventures* and the *Law on Foreign-Funded Enterprises*. A total of 2,300 documents were sorted through, with 830 annulled and 325 modified, which have paved way for building a foreign trade system under the socialist market economy that is compatible with prevailing international practice.

With each step forward achieved in the reform of the foreign trade regime, the development of foreign trade began a new phase. The deepening of the reform, and the accession to the WTO in particular, has pushed China's reform and opening up to a new stage and contributed to the development of an open economy and improvement of the socialist market economic system.

7

Learning Along the Way

Coming off long years of seclusion, China was running short of competent professionals in foreign economic relations and trade in the early days of the opening-up era. Bringing forth a vast contingent of such talents became the order of the day. That was why Deng always put a premium on study and learning. Shortly after his comeback to power in 1977, he called on the entire Party membership to study and learn:

> We need to study and be good at it, for there is no room for sophistry in science. We are resolved to push the modernization drive and have made a state policy of it. To be good at studying and learning is what it is all about. To excel in this field, we have got to learn faster and better. We need to be able to study well if we are to achieve the Four Modernizations.

During a conversation with Vice Premier Gu Mu, Deng made some important instructions on cultivating the needed professionals in the early stage of opening up to the outside world.

With a history of several hundred years, the Western market economy has grown into a relatively systematic and integral system with a complete array of operational mechanisms. It has many scientific and rational elements that we can draw upon in restructuring our economic system and building socialism the Chinese way. Opening up not only gave us an excellent opportunity to get to know and absorb the advanced expertise and experience of the Western economic system, but also prompted us to carry out reforms, without which we would have no way of cooperating with foreign investors. It was out of this objective need that study and training became all the rage in this country.

Learning to Swim by Swimming

Theoretically speaking, it is not difficult to study, but not easy to put what one has learned into practice. In the early stages of the opening-up effort, the most pressing task of study was to get people to let go of themselves, refresh their ideas, and genuinely understand the great strategic significance of reform and opening up from an ideological perspective. A principal approach in those years was to get people to study the relationship between opening up and the nation's rise and fall in history. At the same time, relevant materials – collected from the United States, Japan, West Germany, France, Spain, Hungary, Romania, Yugoslavia, Singapore, Brazil, Mexico and India, as well as from Hong Kong and Taiwan through Chinese embassies and consulates and other channels – were reprinted and distributed for study and discussion. Sending delegations abroad to gather first-hand information, and discussing with foreign government delegations to China, were another approach to catching up on the outside world. The State Import and Export Commission and other departments urged their staff members to submit detailed reports on their findings after returning from short-term training and inspection tours of other countries and regions. The reports were then selected and handed out as reference materials. The Commission's leaders took the lead in studies and lecturing staff members on the basics. With Gu Mu's approval, Wang Daohan served as a part-time professor in Peking University. Zhou Jiannan, Wei Yuming, Jiang Zemin and other leaders also lectured at the Party School of the Party Central Committee, the State Construction Commission and the PLA General Political Department. All these efforts helped the staff quit closed-minded ways of thinking and arrive at a consensus on the opening-up policy.

Many business practices that are commonplace nowadays were entirely new to us in the early days of opening up. These included many of the practices discussed in the foregoing chapters, such as joint ventures, three-plus-one trade (the practice of combining export-oriented processing work with customer-supplied materials, designs or samples plus compensation trade), feasibility studies, hard and soft loans, and open bidding. Those of us working in this field were very much like the first person to try tomato. Left with little time to learn the ropes systematically, we had to plunge right into it like diving into the water and learning to swim to avoid drowning. As a result, everyone was learning a lot, and very quickly, about such things as: what a joint venture was like, how to do a credit check on a joint venture partner, what to say at the negotiation table, how to go about feasibility studies, how to bring two enterprises from different social systems under the same roof to accomplish something for mutual benefit, what was to be written or avoided in a contract or a business constitution, what legislation or policies the country needed, how to deal with conflicts with reigning institutions and management methods, and how to arbitrate disputes between joint venture partners.

The State Import and Export Commission attached great importance to training its staff in this regard and invited foreign experts to give lectures from Day One. According to Li Hao, then a member with the Commission, Gu Mu once followed Deng's instruction to invite Armin Gotowski from Germany to lecture in China in the latter half of 1979 as one of the second group of foreign experts invited to help out after the opening-up policy was adopted. The first group included Japanese experts Kite Saber and Sakisaka Masao.

Gotowski, who served on the five-member Supreme Consultation Committee of West Germany and as head of the Hamburg Institute of International Economics, is a good friend of China. During his stay in China, he not only briefed State Council leaders on the business practices in his country and answered their questions, but also gave a number of lectures on the market economy to government officials, economists and scholars in Beijing. His vivid descriptions of West Germany's market economy made a deep impression on his audience.

After World War II, West Germany, like many other European countries, faced the decision as to what path to take. Some European countries, which adopted a planned economic system, recovered slowly and their people were having a hard time making ends meet.

According to him, if a potato fell onto the street, everyone who saw it would scramble for it. In West Germany, the population was divided on whether to go on with a planned economy that served to tighten up the screws, or to adopt a market economy that called for decontrolling prices and decentralizing the market, while using such economic levers as tax revenue to redistribute social wealth, with due consideration to fairness. To avoid what was happening in neighboring countries, the government finally adopted what was called a "social market economy," which tided West Germany over economic difficulties in a few years' time. Gotowski would conclude his lectures by saying that what he had talked about could only serve as reference for China, a large country totally different from his country. In fact, the German expert's lectures came as something of a conceptual "breakthrough" for China's government officials, who had the planned economy deeply ingrained in their minds, and opened their eyes to the market economy.

Learning Contract Law the Hard Way

I remember someone once sought me out about a joint venture contract. I had previously negotiated joint venture contracts with foreign partners and knew that these documents were thick and had a lot of appendices. Seeing him with nothing in his hand, I asked, "What contract did you sign? Where is it?" He reached into his pocket and produced two pieces of paper with the heading "Joint Venture Contract" written at the top of the first page. When I ran over the content, I was shocked. Not only did it fail to conform to any norms or legal standards of a contract, but its content was ridiculous. Nearly every clause was nonsense or empty verbiage. Everything that was essential was left out, and everything that was included was irrelevant. I still remember one clause that went like this: "If a dispute arises in the course of carrying out this contract, both sides should settle the dispute through friendly negotiations based on equality and mutual benefit." Of course there was nothing wrong with the wording of this sentence. The point of a contract, however, is to point out ways to address those disputes that cannot be settled through friendly negotiations, such as what to do when a dispute arises and where to go for arbitration. Issues like these, which call for solutions that work, were commonplace among the earliest group of joint ventures in this country.

To better prepare myself for negotiations with foreign investors, I took a course on international business law given by a foreign professor in Peking University. I also put my staff through a one-year remedial English training course, so that they could communicate with foreigners directly at the negotiation table. When the State Import and Export Commission invited the Hong Kong lawyer Huang Xian to lecture on law twice a week in the Western Hills of Beijing, all those responsible for foreign investment work attended, never missing a single one. In addition, experts from among Chinese living abroad and Hong Kong compatriots, as well as Western scholars, were also invited to give lectures on economics, law and contracts. Beginning in May 1980, we sent a dozen staff members for six- or 12-month studies and internships in universities, law firms and other organizations in Hong Kong, Canada and the United States. Meanwhile, with assistance from the UN Industrial Development Organization, Chinese delegations also attended foreign investment meetings held in the Southeast Asia region to learn what other countries were doing in absorbing foreign investment and endorsing foreign-invested projects. Senior experts from consulting firms, universities, research institutes and foreign-related departments were also invited to give lectures or hold seminars. This intensive learning period enabled us to lay down the principles in a couple of years for the drafting of legislation concerning foreign investment and joint ventures.

Learning to Conduct Feasibility Studies

Western entrepreneurs conduct feasibility studies before making investment decisions, but people in this country knew little about it before the adoption of the opening-up policy. Leaders of the State Import and Export Commission were perhaps the first to realize the importance of feasibility studies. They lost no time to have relevant references translated into Chinese and the *Outline on Feasibility Studies* drafted. The *Outline* played no small part in ditching the long-standing "planning – initial designing – technical designing – engineering designing" procedure under the planned economy and in rectifying people's obsession with the technicalities of things to the neglect of the importance of market survey, environment and safety evaluation, cost accounting, investment risks and repayment.

Take, for example, the production of steel cord for making steel radial tires, which were twice as expensive as ordinary tires on the international market. China began developing radial tires as early as 1958, but took some 20 years to turn out 300,000 radial tires by the end of 1980. Only 150,000 of them were steel radial tires. Sensing a profit opportunity in this, the Hubei Steel Wire Factory decided to import technology and equipment to produce steel cord in 1980. However, the project ran aground after failing to win government approval for lack of feasibility studies. After the factory completed its market and economic studies, it petitioned for resumption of the project. According to the petition, if they were allowed to import, through compensation trade, a production line with an annual output of 2,000 tons of steel cord (to be sold for US$5,000 per ton), the factory could earn US$10 million in foreign exchange every year and recoup the costs within four years. After I read their report, I asked them to do some supplementary analyses before giving my go-ahead to their project.

Training Talents Against All Odds

In those years, all the localities were stressing the importance of study and talent. I had been personally involved in it during my 1983-1986 tenure as vice mayor of Tianjin. At a 1984 central government forum on opening more coastal cities, Deng urged us to do a good job in grooming talents. We kept his instruction in mind as we prepared for establishing the Tianjin Economic and Technological Development Zone. When we set about forming a preparatory team for the zone, we were frustrated that we could not find enough open-minded people who spoke some English from among those on the government payroll. When Mayor Li Ruihuan asked me what was to be done about the situation, I suggested choosing 200 functionaries who spoke some English and send them to foreign trade training courses at Nankai University and the Tianjin Institute of Finance and Economics.

With Li's approval, I asked the Municipal Education Commission to begin recruiting immediately. I thought people would flock in to enter their names, but to my dismay, Yu Su, deputy director of the Commission, told me that only 70 had applied for the 200 slots when the three-day application period expired. "Did those who know English not want the job?" I asked. "That wasn't the problem," she answered. "People came in droves to my office every day. But their employers refused to write recommendation letters for them."

Now I saw where the snag was and reported it to Li. The mayor asked me to convene a mobilization meeting and ask all the municipal government's department leaders to heed the overall interest and release those who wanted to apply for the new job. At my request, Li also agreed to invest the recruitment office with the power to admit eligible candidates who came without a recommendation letter.

At the mobilization meeting, I elaborated the prospects of opening up the coastal cities and establishing the development zone and what good it would do the economy and living standard of Tianjin. My speech was interrupted repeatedly by warm applause. Seeing that the audience had become elated with what they had heard, I came straight to the point. "It looks to me that all of you are willing to let go of your people to show that you all stand for the training program for the development zone," I said. "However, it doesn't matter if some of you don't like the idea. The recruitment office will just go ahead and accommodate the applicants – with or without recommendation letters." To my surprise, that statement of mine drew another round of applause of approval. In the next two days, more than 1,400 government employees sent in their applications, and 200 were selected and sent to the foreign trade training courses.

Drawing a Lesson From a Passenger's Complaints

Another way by which we braced ourselves for the opening-up endeavor was to render a willing ear to what foreign experts and overseas Chinese had to say about how they felt about things happening in our country.

On September 8, 1980, the Letters and Calls Bureau of the General Office of the Party Central Committee received a letter from Mrs. Fan née Chou, an American of Chinese descent. In this letter, addressed to Deng Xiaoping and Hu Yaobang, Fan expressed her gratitude for the warm hospitality her fellow countrymen had accorded her and her brother, daughter and two other family members during a recent trip to the mainland. However, she said, her good feelings were somewhat marred by what had happened on July 17, when she and her companions went through customs inspection after arriving at the Shanghai Hongqiao Airport from Hong Kong. She had carried with her one pocket watch, four Enicars, four cheap wristwatches for ladies, and 48 pairs of glasses to be used as gifts for her hometown relatives. Customs confiscated eight of the watches and all of the glasses, on the grounds that they were smuggled goods. Her offer to pay customs duties was ignored. According to Fan, two other passengers from the same flight, a 71-year-old pianist and a Chinese-American, were treated the same way. They haggled with the customs officers until 11 o'clock, and ended up paying duties on some of the gifts. The other articles were confiscated. That experience with the Chinese customs officers left an awful impression on her and her fellow passengers, she said.

"We love our motherland heart and soul," she continued in her letter. Her husband used to be one of the ten engineering technology authorities and head of the technological steering committee in Taiwan, but he gave up his position and comfortable life in Taiwan and settled down in the United States, "because of his love for the mainland," according to Fan. As president of the board of directors of an agency for six major tobacco companies in the United States, she said, she herself was popular with Chinese communities in America. That was why she felt utterly wronged when she was accused of "smuggling" during her recent homecoming visit. She said that the purpose of her letter was not to try to recover the eight watches, but to appeal to the Chinese authorities not to do anything detrimental to the sentimental attachment between overseas Chinese and their motherland. Even though the government made a few hundred bucks from the customs duties, she asserted, the damage done to people's good feelings would be immeasurable. She urged the authorities to be discreet and scrupulous when handling articles brought to China by overseas Chinese passengers, and to strictly differentiate gifts from smuggled goods.

On September 14, Hu Yaobang wrote on the letter, "Would Comrade Gu Mu please give the problem due consideration." The following day, Gu issued the directive: "Comrade Zhou Jiannan, please summon the relevant parties to investigate this matter and offer a solution." The State Import and Export Commission then instructed the General Administration of Customs to investigate the incident. On November 24, Jiang Zemin signed a report on the findings of the investigation to Gu Mu, in which he stated:

> According to the results of the investigation, what the customs officers did was in compliance with customs regulations, but they failed to do a meticulous job in clarifying the facts about Mrs. Fan's case. The fact was that only one watch and 48 pairs of sunglasses were in Fan's possession. The other undeclared articles belonged to her brother, Zhou Dongcheng, a Chinese citizen fresh from a visit to the United States. Therefore, the person in question should be Zhou, instead of Fan. It was inappropriate for the Shanghai Customs Office to censure Fan alone. For that reason, her objection to the Customs' decision was understandable, and we should draw a lesson from it. It is our opinion that in handling cases like this, the Customs should take the differences in circumstances and between people into consideration. In cases involving Mrs. Fan or any other Chinese who have lived overseas for a long time, if their undeclared articles violate the customs limits by only a small margin – in Fan's case, it was only one watch and 48 pairs of glasses, and if they have admitted their wrong doings, our customs officers should go out of their way to explain the rules to them, exempt them from duties or levy duties at a cut-down rate, and then let them go. To equate this type of cases with smuggling is just far-fetched.

On November 26, Gu Mu wrote on the investigation report, "Pass this on to Vice Chairman Deng and Comrade (Hu) Yaobang for their examination." On November 27, Hu instructed, "Care should be taken to handle different situations differently." Deng also gave his consent on the report.

These instructions immediately galvanized customs officers around the country into a drive to revamp their passenger service.

In those early days of opening up, they were dealing with similar cases on a daily basis. Uppermost on their minds were the ubiquitous questions: How to be strict with law enforcement while remaining cordial to the passengers? How to uphold principles while handling cases according to their merits? And how to be fair and square in handling cases and make overseas compatriots feel at home right after they set foot on the motherland? The top leaders' concern with the overseas Chinese's well-being was nothing short of an eye-opener to the customs officers across the country.

Learning-along-the-way experiences like this stood us in good stead in the early days of opening up. During my visit to the Massachusetts Institute of Technology, a professor at the Sloan School of Management said to me, "We are amazed by how quickly you enact legislation for foreign investment procurement. You have accomplished in a few years' time what it took us [Westerners] decades or even a hundred years to accomplish. You have shown an admirable spirit for learning."

Accelerating Training for the Opening-Up Effort

In response to Deng's instructions to excel at studying such subjects as foreign trade, international economics, finance and law, foreign languages, and training skilled personnel, the State Import and Export Commission undertook the important task of training people in the skills needed to help carry out the opening-up effort.

We had groomed quite a few professionals in foreign economic relations and trade in the years when central planning and a monopolistic foreign trade system held sway. These people had contributed tremendously to the country's foreign economic relations and international trade. The way they had been trained, however, could not apply in the opening-up era. The dire shortage of skilled personnel was having a bottleneck effect on the new opening-up effort. While asking people to learn along the way, we must put some of them through full-time training and studies to turn them into a new type of experts to take on the mission of developing the nation's foreign economic relations and trade and implementing the opening-up effort.

Setting up a school to serve this purpose was put high on the agenda. It also gained the consent and support of the UN Development Programme. That task fell on the shoulders of Wang Daohan, and was taken over by Jiang Zemin when Wang was moved to another government post. Consultations with the World Bank Institute for International Development and Harvard University led to an agreement to establish an international economic management college with the assistance of the World Bank Institute and Harvard. The guideline of the new college was to turn itself into a world-caliber institution by combining our own bootstrap efforts with the assistance of international counterparts. Students were to be chosen from among college lecturers and college-educated, experienced government functionaries, and be put through a few years of intensive studies for postgraduate degrees.

In February 1980, the State Import and Export Commission authorized the Beijing Institute of Foreign Trade to sign an agreement with the University of California to open a joint English training center in September. The center was to comprise four departments: 1) an English department, offering oral and written English courses ranging from six to 12 months to prepare the students for business negotiations with foreigners or further studies; 2) a department of short training programs that catered to the learning needs of in-service high- and medium-ranking government officials engaged in international economic affairs; 3) a graduate school, where government functionaries with a college degree and some work experience could take two-year courses on international economics, finance, business management, public finance, international business law, tax law and development economics, and graduate to become business leaders or teach college; 4) a consultancy and research department that was to conduct studies in international economics, trade, finance and law, and to run an international economic information center to serve the nation's decision-making purposes.

The joint English training center would have an administrative committee with members from the State Import and Export Commission, the Ministry of Foreign Trade, the Ministry of Foreign Economic Liaison, the Ministry of Finance, the Ministry of Education, the Chinese Academy of Social Sciences, the Bank of China, Peking

University, Renmin University of China, the University of International Relations, and the Institute of Foreign Trade. There would also be a consultation committee composed of experts, professors and university presidents from home and abroad.

With the approval of the State Council, the joint English training center was to be built at Nanxinzhuang Village near Fragrant Hills in Beijing's western suburbs. However, because the school buildings could not be finished overnight, makeshift classrooms were set up on the nearby Zhongzhi Farm, so that the first group of 1,000 students chosen through entrance exams could start studies right away. The Canadian International Development Agency, under the auspices of the UN Development Programme, sent foreign teachers to open one-year English courses on international law and trade. Despite their short duration, these courses effectively helped the students catch up on much needed knowledge and improve their English proficiency. At their commencement, the students were able to deliver reports in fluent English, to the delight of their foreign professors and Jiang Zemin, who came all the way to attend. Some people were so impressed that they compared the center to the Anti-Japanese Military and Political University at Yan'an during World War II. Although it existed for only two school years, it produced hundreds of talents for the opening-up policy, and came down in history as a harbinger for running colleges in China in collaboration with the world's elite universities.

In an organizational reshuffle in 1982, the joint English training center became the English Training Center for Economics and Trade of the Beijing Institute of Foreign Trade. It continued to recruit foreign experts to teach lessons and send faculty members abroad for further studies, while grooming more professionals for the opening-up endeavor. In 1984, the Beijing Institute of Foreign Trade was renamed the University of International Business and Economics, and became the first Chinese university to have its academic degrees recognized in the United States. Other colleges and universities followed suit to set up their own foreign trade institutes and departments. Among them, the Tianjin Institute of Finance and Economics, established with the approval of the State Education Commission, developed a two-year MBA program in collaboration with Oklahoma City

University. The program, allowing both universities to confer Master's Degrees to the graduates, set a precedent for running credit education under Sino-foreign partnership.

Sending Students Abroad After a Long Hiatus

After the adoption of the opening-up policy, Deng quickly resumed sending large numbers of students abroad to study after a decade-long hiatus. It was a daring decision, given the fact that the mental shackles of the Cultural Revolution were still stultifying people's minds, the country was still in seclusion and the state coffers were almost empty.

Chinese students stopped going abroad shortly after the Cultural Revolution began, although a small number of them were arriving in a few selected countries from 1972 on. In the aftermath of the decade-long chaos, science and technology in this country was in a state of flux, education fell short of society's learning needs, and every field of endeavor was crying out for talents. During a conversation with leaders of the Changsha Institute of Technology on July 23, 1977, or six days after he returned to power, Deng said it was imperative to learn advanced technology from foreign countries. "You could buy their technological materials and compile them into textbooks, or send your students abroad to learn it," he said. He repeated his idea of sending students abroad in a discussion with Vice Premier Fang Yi and Minister of Education Liu Xiyao on August 1. Addressing a symposium on science and education a week later, he reiterated once again, "Accepting homecoming scholars of Chinese descent is one thing we can do to develop science and technology, but sending students abroad to study is definitely another step we can take."

On June 23, 1978, during a conversation with Fang Yi, Jiang Nanxiang, and Liu Xiyao after hearing a report by Tsinghua University leaders, Deng said:

I'm for sending more students to foreign countries for the main purpose of learning natural sciences. We should send them by the thousand instead of in single digit. Let me ask the Ministry of Education to make a study of it, for it is worth the money and the effort. This is one of the major things we can do if we want to see quick results in boosting our nation's science and education in five years. The steps we are taking now are too slow. We should quicken our steps by all means, and widen the avenues as we go along. On the one hand, we must work hard to upgrade our universities, and on the other hand, we must also send people to other countries. Only thus can we make comparisons, and see the difference between our universities and foreign counterparts. Our administrative system over students studying abroad should also be changed. On no account should we keep them under rigid control. They can live on campus, or with hosting families. We should allow them to come back during summer vacations, so that they can see what is happening in the motherland. The Ministry of Education should set up an office to run overseas student affairs, and send people to countries where there are many Chinese students to see how they are doing and what problems they have. Don't be afraid of problems, because most of the students studying abroad are good. It doesn't matter if a few people did something wrong.

This speech was of epoch-making significance, for it ushered China's overseas studies program into a new stage of development. Shortly afterward, the Ministry of Education submitted a report on increasing the number of students to pursue studies abroad. This step was not lost on international media, which saw it as a "signal" of the beginning of an open China, "a step hitherto unseen in the communist world," or "a convincing evidence of China's political self-confidence." The chain of events that followed testified that this step was not just a symbol of the opening-up policy. It gave great impetus to the endeavor to swing the nation's doors wide open to the world.

In July 1978, US Presidential Science Advisor Frank Press extended an invitation to Vice Premier Fang Yi, asking him to dispatch a Chinese government delegation to the United States for consultations on an exchange student program. On July 10, Deng received an American science and technology delegation headed by Press, and told him, "Your suggestion about exchange students is a very positive one, and we agree with you totally. As to your plan to accept 500 students in the immediate future, I'm afraid we may suggest more." Through further consultations the two countries arrived at an understanding in October. After that, China reached agreement on the same issue with many other countries, including Britain, Egypt, Canada, the Netherlands, Italy, Japan, West Germany, France, Belgium and Australia.

Few people realized that December 26, 1978, which happened to be a Christmas Day for Westerners, was a landmark date on the Chinese agenda for the opening-up policy in its infancy. That evening, the first group of 50 visiting scholars, in their thirties or forties, the youngest at 32 and the oldest at 49, took off from Beijing for two years of studies in the United States. Before their departure, Vice Premier Fang Yi met them and gave his last-minute advice. Zhou Peiyuan, Chairman of the China Science and Technology Association, and Li Qi, Vice Minister of Education, saw them off at the airport.

Earlier, in May and June, 23 strictly chosen straight-A students had begun their studies in Canada, Britain, France, Japan, Australia and New Zealand. Another 1,777 students went abroad the following year. Indeed, once the nation's doors were open, a popular desire, held in check by long years of political and ideological campaigns, poured out all of a sudden in an "exodus" of students on a scale never experienced before in Chinese history.

As a matter of fact, since the mid-1840s, thousands of Chinese youths had studies overseas and returned to build a stronger China. Among them were Li Dazhao, Zhou Enlai, Zhu De, Zhan Tianyou, Yan Fu, Lu Xun and Cai Yuanpei, to name just a few. Deng himself went on a work-study program in France in 1920 and moved on to Moscow Sun Yat-sen University in 1926. Look at modern Chinese history, and we will find the departure of Chinese students to other lands and their homecoming had an intimate connection with the endeavor for national salvation, rejuvenation and transformation.

In 1847, Yung Wing (1828-1912) went to the United States in the company of the American missionary Samuel Robins Brown, and became the first Chinese to study abroad in modern Chinese history. He spent eight years working and studying part time and returned to China a Yale University graduate.

The first group of students sent abroad by the Chinese government consisted of 120 boys, between the ages of 12 and 15. They were sent to the United States in four consecutive groups from 1872 to 1875. The original plan was for them to study abroad for 15 years, but for a number of reasons, they were all brought back in 1881. A group of nearly 100 naval cadets were sent to Europe to study in 1887, and when they returned they assumed leadership positions in the Chinese Navy at all ranks. In 1903, large numbers of students began going to Japan to study, some on government scholarships and some at their own expense.

After the Eight-Power Allied Forces sacked Beijing, the Qing government was forced to sign the Treaty of 1901 and pay 450 million taels of silver in indemnity. In 1907 American President Theodore Roosevelt proposed using the American share of the indemnities in excess of the country's actual expenses in the war to build universities in China and to bring Chinese students to schools in the United States. The following year, American Congress approved the president's proposal. Great Britain, Japan and France followed suit. In 1909, China began sending students to the United States on the war-indemnity program. China established the Tsinghua School in 1911 to select students to study in the United States.

France endorsed a similar program in 1912, and Chinese students arrived there to work and study. Many of them was to become pillars of society. After the October Revolution of 1917, the Soviet Union established the Communist University of the Toilers of the East in Moscow (KUTV) for the education of ethnic minorities in the far-east Soviet Union and youths from other Asian countries. In 1925, the KUTV Chinese Department was renamed Sun Yat-sen University in memory of the pioneer of democratic revolution of China. Many early Party leaders had studied in both universities.

After the founding of the People's Republic, great importance was attached to sending students abroad to study. In August 1948, not long before Liberation, the Party Central Committee approved the selection of 21 young people from its Northeast Bureau to be sent to the Soviet Union to study science and technology. Between 1950 and 1952, China reached agreements with the Soviet Union and a number of Eastern European countries on educational exchange, and set up a leading group to oversee this work, led by Nie Rongzhen, Li Fuchun and Lu Dingyi. In April 1956, Chairman Mao wrote *On the Ten Relationships*, in which he said:

> Our policy is to learn from the strong points of all nations and all countries, learn all that is genuinely good in the political, economic, scientific and technological fields and in literature and art. ... Even when one day our country becomes strong and prosperous, we must still adhere to the revolutionary stand, remain modest and prudent, learn from other countries and not allow ourselves to become swollen with conceit. ... We must ... go on doing so [learning from other countries] after the completion of scores of five-year plans. We must be ready to learn even ten thousand years from now.

According to statistics, China sent nearly 10,000 people to the Soviet Union and Eastern Europe for study and internships between 1950 and 1960. Upon their return, they became experts and key personnel in every field of endeavor and played an important role in our country's construction and development.

Later, when relations with the Soviet Union became tense, we began sending people to Western countries.

While accelerating the pace of sending students abroad, New China was also eagerly expecting Chinese students to return from abroad. Those who had studied abroad for many years were homesick and eager to return to their motherland. The American, British and Japanese governments put up one stumbling block after another, but many managed to come home, including Li Siguang and Qian Xuesen. Most of the returnees went right to where they were most needed in the 1950s and 1960s.

Deng showed great concern for the exchange students after they were dispatched abroad after 1978. During his January 1979 US visit, he found time to meet the first 50 visiting scholars sent to the United States, exhorting them to study diligently and, once they were back after their studies, render good service to the country and the people. He would repeat this idea during many other meetings with representatives of Chinese students studying abroad. He also wrote calligraphic names for the Western Returned Scholars Association of *China*, and the *China Scholars Abroad,* the magazine devoted to Chinese students studying abroad.

In addition to sending students abroad, Deng was also mindful of how to accommodate and arrange those who had returned to China. Meeting the Chinese-American mathematician Shiing-Shen Chern on August 25, 1984, he promised to provide more favorable conditions for returned students. On July 16, 1985, after hearing reports by Hu Qili (member of the Secretariat of the Party Central Committee), Vice Premier Fang Yi, Song Jian (Minister of the State Science and Technology Commission), Yan Dongsheng (Vice President of the Chinese Academy of Sciences), and Zhou Guangzhao (Vice President of the Chinese Academy of Sciences), Deng said:

> People are the most valuable of all wealth. The tens of thousands of students studying abroad are valuable assets that we want to do everything we can to get them to come home. We should strengthen our ties with them. We shall attract them in two ways. One is to run postdoctoral stations. The other is for the special economic zones and the open seaboard cities to offer them jobs. We also need to think of other ways to get them back.

On September 12, 1988, Deng stressed:

> We have tens of thousands of students studying abroad, and it is important to create suitable working conditions for them after they come back. ... Otherwise, these people will not come back. If that happens, it will be a great pity to the country. ... It is necessary to raise the status of intellectuals from the "ninth category" during the Cultural Revolution to the "first category, because, after all, science and technology are the foremost productive force, and intellectuals are part and parcel of the working class. These are my opinions on education, science, technology, and intellectuals, opinions that I am expressing as a strategic principle and a strategic step.

During his south China tour in 1992, Deng turned to the subject again in one of his remarks:

We hope all those who are studying abroad will come back. All of them may return, and once they are back, proper arrangement will be made for them in life and work, regardless of their previous political attitudes. This policy should stay unchanged. They should be told that if they want to make their contributions, it would be better for them to come home.

With reform and opening going in depth, and with steady policy improvement, the nation laid down a new policy to aid those wanting to study overseas, encourage those who have finished their studies to return, and allow them to come and go freely. According to statistics, 134,000 students went abroad for studies in 2006, or 155.8 times the 1978 figure of 860. A total of 1.067 million studied abroad during the 29 intervening years, including 218,000 on government scholarships; and 143,000 or 66% of them had returned to serve the country. In 2007 the number of government-sent students totaled 12,402, a 51% increase over what it was in 2006.

Studying abroad can be a turning point in a person's life. For China, it is a way to cultivate scientists, engineers, educators and other professionals badly needed in implementing its opening-up policy. When they return, they have acquired up-to-date knowledge and technology, advanced ways of thinking, and a global vision, factors that qualify them as history makers in various fields of national socioeconomic development. What is more, studying abroad is also a good way to increase understanding, contacts and friendship between China and the outside world.

Borrowing Foreign Brains by Recruiting Experts

Recruiting experts from other lands is an important component of the opening-up policy. At the beginning of reform and opening up, we lacked experience and personnel in all areas. Deng addressed this situation in a conversation with Wan Li, Yao Yilin, Fang Yi and Song Ping on July 8, 1983. He said:

We should make use of the intellectual resources of other countries by inviting foreigners to participate in key development projects and other construction projects in various fields. In our modernization drive we lack both experience and know-how. We should have no qualms about spending a bit more on recruiting foreigners. It doesn't matter whether they stay here for a long time or a short time, or just for a single project. Once they are here, we should make the most of their skills. … As a matter of fact, they have been quite willing to help out.

Deng also stressed that it is not enough to see recruiting foreign experts as an ordinary policy. Instead, it should be carried out unremittingly as a long-term strategy.

Acting upon the spirit of Deng's instructions, the Party Central Committee and the State Council drew up the *Decision Concerning Recruiting Foreign Experts for the Four Modernizations* on August 24, 1983. The *Decision* stated that, other than making full use of foreign investment and importing advanced technology, it was conducive to the modernization drive to bring in foreign experts, Chinese living abroad and foreign citizens of Chinese decent in particular, in a planned and measured way. As walking books of knowledge, foreign experts can never be replaced with equipments, books, materials or blueprints. Bringing in technology along with talented people from abroad would be extremely beneficial to digesting and assimilating advanced foreign science and technology and management experience. It would enable us to get things done in a cost-effective way, and accelerate the pace of development. To bring in talented foreigners, the *Decision* stated, we must make use of all channels, official, semi-official and non-governmental channels included, and seek the help of international organizations. Proceeding from the modernization drive's urgent needs, we should focus our recruitment work on engineers and managers. Government departments and economic organizations may also invite foreign experts to serve policymakers as consultants or, where appropriate, assume technical or management responsibilities.

On September 7, the central authorities decided to establish the Central Leading Group for Recruiting Foreign Experts to Facilitate the Four Modernizations, which was composed of Vice Premier Yao Yilin, Vice Premier Fang Yi, State Councilor Zhang Jinfu and State Councilor Song Ping, with Yao Yilin as group head and Zhang Jinfu in charge of day-to-day work. Two days later, the State Council held a plenary session to relay Deng's ideas and the Central Committee's decision, and made plans for the recruitment work. Thirty famous scientists and university leaders attended the session.

Hearing a recruitment work report on September 12, Yao Yilin and Zhang Jinfu instructed that recruited foreign experts should be accommodated with solicitude and good pay; that the recruitment effort should be combined with foreign trade; and that priority should be given to those foreign experts who possessed mature technology in such fields as energy conservation, new pharmaceuticals, synthetic ammonia, bioengineering and computer software. On September 26, the State Council issued procedural regulations on administrative issues, procedures, funding and accommodations concerning the work to recruit foreign experts.

In the same month, Nankai University sent in a request for approval on its decision to invite the Chinese-American mathematician Shiing-Shen Chern as director of the university's Institute of Mathematics. This was the first request of its kind put on the table of the Central Leading Group for Recruiting Foreign Experts.

Sensing the potential impact of this appointment on the international learning community, Zhang Jinfu instructed the Leading Group to earmark 120,000 yuan a year for three consecutive years for it. With that amount of funding, Nankai University was able to finish the appointment procedure on Chern and built him a house. When I called on the professor at his residence, he told me that the house was so large that he could spare a room for doctoral students. After he took up his post, Chern invited world-renowned scholars to international meetings held at regular intervals at Nankai, and brought outstanding experts to fill openings in his cooperative research projects. As a result of his efforts, mathematical researches went up a notch at Nankai University.

The recruited foreign experts contributed remarkably to all fields of endeavor in China, such as macroeconomic decision-making, technological upgrading and product development. During their service they helped solve a great deal of technical and management problems for their Chinese colleagues. Three hundred foreign engineers and mangers were recruited to work in China in 1984. In 1985, the number rose to 1,102, while 3,200 Chinese engineers, managers and administrators received training in foreign countries. Later, Goh Keng Swee, former Deputy Prime Minister of Singapore, and Pao Yue-kong, the well-known entrepreneur from

Hong Kong, became advisors for the State Council on affairs related to the economic development of Chinese coastal regions.

During a conversation with Goh on May 15, 1985, Deng told him:

> To make the modernization drive work, we cannot do without knowledge and talent. But this is exactly where our Achilles' heel lies. We are running short of knowledge and talent. We brought you in because we wanted you to give us knowledge. Apart from people like you, we shall expand our recruitment work to invite retired experts and engineers from a wide range of developed countries to help out. If they like, they may work as our advisors or take responsible positions in our companies.

To better communicate with professional organizations abroad, the China Association for International Exchange of Personnel and the China International Talent Exchange Foundation were established in November 1985, with Zhang Jinfu as director of both organizations. Branch offices were set up in the United States and Japan and in Hong Kong, to serve as important talent-recruiting conduits.

A Foreign Manager Brings New Expertise

In November 1984, the Wuhan Diesel Engine Plant signed a two-year contract with Werner Gerich from West Germany to serve as its general manager. This was the first time for a Chinese factory to hire a foreign manager, which caused a sensation nationwide. State Councilor Zhang Jinfu, who arrived in Wuhan on a work tour of Hubei Province a few days later, applauded it as "a bold step."

The first thing Gerich did upon arriving at the plant was to tighten up quality control. When he found that the plant accepted components and parts from other factories without quality inspection, leaving its testing instruments and equipment dust-covered, he immediately fired the deputy general manager in charge of quality control. That move triggered off a lot of controversy. Some argued that a Party-appointed leader should not be dismissed off-hand; others wondered whether a factory could remain socialist under a foreigner manager. The Wuhan municipal leaders, however, were adamant in their support of Gerich and his move for the simple reason that a factory could not survive without sound product quality. To ensure product quality, Gerich made a point of inspecting one workshop after another, toting a bag that carried three tools: a vernier caliper for precision measurement, a magnet to draw scruffs hidden in machines, and a pair of white gloves to see whether the machines were polluted.

Apart from quality control, the German general manager took a series of other reform steps in his Chinese factory. One such step was to overhaul the pay system, so as to motivate his employees and trim the bloated workforce. He also introduced modern expertise to transform the management. Under his diligent and dexterous leadership, the Wuhan Diesel Engine Plant Wuhan took on a new look, and its product quality improved substantially. Small wonder then, that Premier Zhu Rongji nicknamed Gerich "Mr. Quality."

In view of the controversy surrounding Gerich's reforms, Zhang Jinfu sent a Central Office for Recruiting Foreign Experts team to investigate the case, and found out that Gerich's measures had cut the factory's problems to the quick and won the hearts of its workers and staff. The investigation ended with the Symposium on Gerich's Factory Management Experience held by the Office along with the State Economic Commission and Wuhan University. Gerich, who had worked at the Wuhan Diesel Engine Plant for only two years, was remembered for his "loyalty to work, bold reforms, sensible management, and great contributions to Chinese corporate transformation and Sino-German friendship." The awards he received included the Friendship Award of the People's Republic of China, the Cross of Merit of Federal Germany, and a permanent residence card in China. In April 2005, the State Administration of Foreign Experts Affairs and the Wuhan Municipal Government jointly had a bronze statue of him erected at a downtown industrial park in Wuhan.

Boosting Self-Reliance With Foreign Intellectual Resources

The Central Leading Group for Recruiting Foreign Experts developed a style of work that combined the recruitment of talents from other lands with the import of expertise and equipment. A good case in point was Baosteel.

During its first phase of construction, Baosteel imported a large quantity of equipment from Japan. Going against the belief that the client is King, however, the Japanese side neither provided the blueprints nor transferred its technology. What was more, the company had to pay for its workers' training in Japan.

Drawing a lesson from that experience, when Baosteel put up two second-phase construction projects – a US$500-million hot-rolling mill and a US$300-million continuous casting installation – for international bidding, it demanded that the winner of the bid should transfer the relevant software while supplying the equipment, allow Chinese experts to participate in designing, manufacturing and training, and cover the expenses incurred by these experts. After the SMS Demag Consortium of Federal Germany won the bid, they constructed a building to accommodate Chinese experts working and training in Germany. Some 1,000 Baosteel engineers participated in designing, manufacturing and training, and completely mastered the technology in the process. Consequently, more than 90 percent of the blast furnaces built during the steel works' third construction phase were homemade. The aforementioned Japanese company was alarmed, and soon ditched its "over-conservative" mentality.

Baosteel's success story prompted governments at all levels to bring in needed talents to promote local economic development in various ways. For example, to solve the nagging problem of port congestion, the Tianjin Harbor invited Torii Yukio, the harbor master of Kobe, Tianjin's sister city, as a consultant. With Kobe's help, the handling capacity of the Tianjin Harbor increased from 12.87 million tons in 1982 to 18.56 million tons in 1985. Port congestion was dramatically eased, and ships' waiting time shortened as a result. In a similar vein, Heilongjiang Province invited the Japanese rice experts Fujihara Chosaku and Hara Shoichi to teach Chinese experts how to grow cold-region rice by breeding rice seedlings on dry beds, with the result that per-*mu* rice yield more than doubled, and rice became one of the major farm crops in the province. Through incorporation and innovation, the Japanese rice-growing technique gradually found its way into warm and moist regions in the south, and at last spread nationwide. Similar cases of success were also reported from various parts of the country.

Better to Buy a Fishing Pole Than a Fish

In the early 1980s, I learned that Tianjin Municipality had mastered a British beer fermentation technology by recruiting experts and acquiring software for GBP£36,000, just one fourth the cost to buy a complete set of the equipment. In 1984, the Chinese embassy to Great Britain suggested that Tianjin and Hunan adopt the British technology and equipment to produce beer on a small scale (that is, an annual production of 3,000 to 5,000 tons). Ideal for small breweries and easy to learn, the technology in question called for small investment, saved energy, and greatly shortened the fermentation cycle. The Austin Brewery of Great Britain, which owned this technology, had already sold 34 sets of such brewing equipment worldwide.

The State Science and Technology Commission accepted the embassy's suggestion and decided to purchase one set of such equipment and have it installed in Hunan Province as a Spark Program project. In early 1984, after consulting Austin experts invited to China and making a fact-finding tour of the British brewery, the Tianjin Municipal Sci-Tech Exchange Center also saw fit to transplant the brewing technology in Tianjin.

With the approval of the municipal government and the consent of the Central Office for Recruiting Foreign Experts and the Spark Program Office of the State Science and Technology Commission, the Tianjin Friendship Beer Technology United Company decided to buy the technology and recruit British experts so that it could be designing and building the needed equipment on its own. Acting on a contract signed between the two partners, Austin sent its experts and provided its blueprints to assist Tianjin in producing beer in a variety of British flavors. The contract was worth GBP£36,000, just one quarter what Hunan had paid for the purchase of a complete set of equipment.

In a little more than one year's time, the engineers and technicians of Tianjin drew up a new design based on Austin blueprints, made the needed equipment, and installed it in a 400-square-meter workshop on a local farm. Under the hands-on guidance of the British experts, the equipment was fine tuned in a trial run until it yielded four kinds of British beer – European style, brown ale, mild beer and sweet stout. The British experts judged that the beer made in Tianjin basically met British standards and had the authentic flavor of fermented beer. Experts invited by the Tianjin Office for Recruiting Foreign Experts and the Spark Program Office to taste the beer spoke highly of its inviting color and mild but pure taste.

According to a Tianjin Science and Technology Commission report, the Tianjin success with the new brewery bore out five advantages of the British beer-making technology: 1) Small investment, as the brewery's total cost was one third that of a domestic counterpart with the same production capacity; 2) a fermentation cycle of three to seven day was one fifth that of the domestic technology; 3) great variety, as a single production line could turn out five flavors of beer, and low cost, because instead of 100 percent wheat, the equipment allowed for 30 to 40 percent of rice in the raw material; 4) low energy consumption, as the new brewery consumed 20 percent less water and 28 percent less electricity than breweries using Chinese brewery technology; and 5) it could be readily patterned after and products could gain easy access to the international market.

What had happened in the new Tianjin brewery testified to the proverb that goes, "It is better to teach someone how to fish than to give him a fish." Inspired by the Commission's report, I sent Zhang Jinfu a note on August 12, 1987:

> I'm sending some material about a successful case of bringing in foreign experts and software for your review. As things stand now, people are given to importing hardware, to the neglect of foreign expert and software.

After Zhang Jinfu received my letter, he immediately instructed the Central Leading Group for Recruiting Foreign Experts to distribute it. An article concerning this case was published in the journal *Experts Recruitment Trends.*

In 1988, the Central Leading Group for Recruiting Foreign Experts was renamed the State Council Leading Group for Recruiting Foreign Expert. In March 1993, the leading group was disbanded, and replaced by the newly founded State Administration of Foreign Experts Affairs. Practice over the past 30 years has proved that recruiting experts from other lands is a promising and efficient undertaking that "costs a trickle but yields a lot." As the implications of this strategic policy sank in, the number of experts coming to work in China increased hundredfold, while hundreds of thousand were sent abroad for training. The role of foreign experts in our nation's industry, agriculture, science and education, commerce and trade can never be belittled.

Learning Modern Management Is a Revolution

Under the planned economy, enterprises were administrative units, all means of production belonged to the state or a collective, and all the manufacturing activities were run by the government. The enterprises had little decision-making power, with the state making plans for what and how much to produce. Moreover, all the products were purchased and then distributed by the state, and no business accounting was required; the state was responsible for both profits and losses, and payments were the same to all no matter how much effort one put into work. This "big pot" practice smothered the initiative of workers and killed the vitality of enterprises. From 1956 to 1977, the original value of fixed assets generated by state investment increased by 9.2 times, but the amount of profit made by state-owned enterprises only increased by 5.5 times, and the revenues they turned in only increased by 2.5 times.

Deng Xiaoping paid close attention to the problem the moment he resumed his leading position, and began considering how to break away from the fossilized system by learning management methods from other countries.

At a meeting with Hu Qiaomu and some other colleagues on March 28, 1978, Deng pointed out, "We have a most urgent problem to deal with, and that is management." The problem was most outstanding when China began importing technology and equipment. Some enterprises did not know how to run their imported production lines, nor could they understand or accept the related management know-how. As a result, many imported installations could not perform efficiently, and some enterprises even became laughing stocks because they could not operate the foreign things properly. The call for "loosening control" from enterprises ran high, and the academic circles also put forward a theory on "enterprises as self-governing bodies," appealing for autonomy of enterprises.

On the afternoon of September 13, 1978, Deng arrived at Benxi City in Liaoning Province after visiting the Democratic People's Republic of Korea, and began his inspection tours in northeastern China. He traveled for several thousand kilometers in the three provinces there, speaking emphatically on two major issues: seeking truth from facts and learning advanced management methods from abroad. In his own words, he was "lighting up fires everywhere" to break down the rigid system in both ideology and practice.

On the morning of September 16, after hearing a report from the Huolinhe Coal Mine then under construction on importing technology from Federal Germany, he said:

> If you intend to import technology, you should also learn the relevant management methods and follow the production process step by step. A leading group should be established at the very beginning to take charge of everything, from direct negotiation and contract signing to the organization of production according to the management methods from Germany. For enterprises like this, you need to carry out a complete revolution. Reformism won't work. All imports should stick to this principle; otherwise, the enterprise is not qualified to import anything, and we would remain backward forever. We should learn hard and go abroad to make field studies, and to watch how enterprises are managed there.

While inspecting Anshan Iron and Steel Works on the afternoon of September 18, Deng stressed again:

> Socialism should manifest its advantages, and should not be what it is now. If we are to stay this poor after 20 years' practice, then why should we embrace socialism? We must carry out a revolution in both technology and management to develop production and increase the income of the workers. ... It's high time that we transform the superstructure now.

After returning to Beijing, Deng personally took charge of the revision and finalization of a speech at the Ninth National Congress of the Trade Union of China (1978), and added in some of the major remarks he had made in northeastern China. On October 8, Deng forwarded the draft to Hua Guofeng, Ye Jianying, Li Xiannian, and Wang Dongxing. On October 10, he added two more paragraphs to the draft:

1. Carrying out these reforms is in the interest of all the people of China. Otherwise we won't be able to change the current

backward conditions in production technology and management.

...

2. Under the leadership of the Party committee, the director or manager should be responsible for the operation of an enterprise. A powerful steering system for production should be established.

...

He then wrote to Hua Guofeng and Li Xiannian, "I have reviewed the speech for the Trade Union congress again, and added two paragraphs, which are important changes." This speech later evoked great repercussion nationwide.

On the afternoon of December 13, 1978, Deng delivered a speech at the closure of a work meeting of the central government. Concerning economic reform he said:

We must learn to manage the economy with economic methods, learn from the experts, and study advanced management methods from abroad, since we don't have the expertise. Not only do the newly imported enterprises need to adopt advanced methods (from abroad), the existing enterprises should also learn to do so. Before a unified overall plan for the whole nation is put on the table, we can begin doing it step by step, starting from one area and one industry, until it becomes routine. Departments under the central government should allow and encourage enterprises to undertake experiments of this kind.

To put Deng's ideas into practice, Li Xiannian, then in charge of industry, asked the State Economic Commission to organize a delegation to study corporate management and product quality in Japan. After coming back to China, the delegation submitted the *Investigation Report on Industrial Corporate Management in Japan*, with suggestions on how to learn the scientific enterprise management expertise in capitalist countries. Subsequently, training courses were opened nationwide for the study of the know-how and experience of quality management in Japan and Western countries, and to popularize modern management knowledge among corporate managers. Meanwhile, some places began pilot projects in reforming the management system of their enterprises.

Bonus Experiment in Sichuan

On February 1, 1978, Deng stopped over in Chengdu on his way to a foreign country. While listening to a work report from the provincial leadership of Sichuan, he emphasized:

> I have said earlier that two problems might hold us back. One is agriculture, for food provision is no easy matter, and the other is industry management, which we are not good at.

He then added:

> As for rural policies and urban policies, the central government needs to straighten them out, and local governments should do the same. We should give overall consideration to this issue, instead of handling it in bits and pieces. However, local governments are entitled to certain flexibility so that they can address whatever problems within their capacity.

This was why Deng mentioned later in his visit to the northeast that "I lit up a fire in Chengdu as well."

The Sichuan provincial government lost no time in conducting a survey and arrived at the following conclusions: To achieve industrial modernization, it is entirely necessary to import some advanced foreign technology and equipment and build some modern enterprises with state investment; but our foothold should be secured on learning advanced experience and speeding up the modernization and transformation of old enterprises. Soon afterward, Sichuan decided to try out bonus and piecework wages in 218 pilot enterprises.

For the first time in their careers, the workers truly experienced the benefit of "more pay for more work"wage system, and their enthusiasm surged. As a result, their attendance rate, output and product quality all improved tremendously, while their consumption of raw materials dropped rapidly. Almost all the pilot enterprises overfulfilled state-set production targets in an all-round way, with output, quality and profit reaching all-time highs.

The Power of Advertising

Having tasted the benefits of bonus and piecework wages, Sichuan immediately started exploring ways to expand the decision-making power of six enterprises, including the Ningjiang Machine Tools Works in October 1978. At that time, the production capacity of Ningjiang was 500 to 600 machine tools, with the pillar products approaching world-advanced level. But because these products were subject to planned allocation by the state, they were kept long in stock. In 1979, the factory decreased its output to 300 units, despite the fact that purchasing orders kept flooding in from companies in need of such machine tools. Under the planned economy, the factory was not allowed to sell its products without authorization. According to the regulations, the state was responsible for supplying raw materials, allocating products, deciding technical innovation, handling profits and losses, and distributing wages, and enterprises had no final say whatsoever. Ningjiang was once investigated for "disposing of state-allocated products without permission," just because it had sold some overstocked products.

During the experiment with enlarging factories' decision-making power, the First Ministry of Machine-Building Industry and the Sichuan government decided to reform the state-mandated product allocation method in Ningjiang, and allowed the factory to base production on sales. To ensure success of the reform, the factory managers decided to advertise their products, as enterprises in foreign countries did. On June 25, 1979, an advertisement of the machine tools of Ningjiang was printed in an eye-catching space on the fourth page of the *People's Daily*. The impact was like "a stone that stirs up huge waves."

The market was opened up. In just two months, Ningjiang signed sales contracts on 1,300 machine tools with clients from all over the country, which was four times the factory's state-alloted output. All the while, letters and telegraphs and buyers arrived in a constant stream. The 7-mm automatic lathe produced by Ningjiang was of top quality, and its highly competitive producer price of 9,500 yuan put great pressure on other domestic machine tool factories, forcing them to improve their management, cut costs and lower prices. The Shanghai 11th Machine Tools Works, for example, began sales promotion as well.

However, the advertisement of Ningjiang also aroused a lot of controversy. In the views of some economists and government officials in economic administration departments, as means of production, machine tools should not be circulated as commodities. That view corresponded with traditional Marxist theories. So they were worried and opposed to the Ningjiang practice of selling their machine tools and even advertising them in the newspaper. Public opinions and clients, however, voiced their encouragement and support for Ningjiang. On August 5, the *People's Daily* published a front-page commentary headlined "Directly Linking Sales to the Market Satisfies Both Sides." The editor's note said, "We hope that more people who are devoted to reform will come to the fore, emancipate their minds, brave the adversities and take an active part in this kind of reform, so that they can gain more experience and bring about results as early as possible, thereby enabling economic construction to proceed at a faster speed." The *People's Daily* also opened a special column on this topic, and contributors expressed different views. Bo Yibo said, "The commercial of the machine tools works has performed a meritorious deed for the economic restructuring of China."

Advertising began to catch on in some cities immediately after the reform and open policy was adopted. Advertisements flourished in the media and in the streets. At first the populace felt quite amazed. What people were not aware of was that advertising was commonplace in foreign countries. It had been so in China, too, before it disappeared during the Cultural Revolution.

After 1979, professional advertising companies sprang up one after another in Beijing, Shanghai and Guangdong. Foreign businesses also began running commercials in China for their products and companies. By September 1979, seven newspapers and five TV stations had carried commercials for foreign products. From April to September 1979, the revenues of the Shanghai Advertising Company from foreign companies added up to US$700,000. The Guangdong TV Station netted an advertisement revenue of HK$800,000 by July, and signed HK$3 million worth of commercial broadcasting contracts with foreign businesses. Enterprises from the United States, Europe and Japan rushed to sign contracts with Chinese media to run their own commercials. Those in Hong Kong and Macao lost no time in advertising their products in the mainland as well.

All this raised quite a few eyebrows. Some people even considered the commercials "an embellishment of capitalism." Relevant departments and media organizations, on the basis of discussions and consultations, came up with the *Report on Foreign Commercials Run by Newspapers and Radio and Television Stations* on September 13, 1979. While confirming the necessity of advertising, the report raised more restrictions than constructive suggestions. On September 18, Hu Yaobang wrote on the draft of the report: "I think the restrictions you have proposed are too many and too tight. Your minds are not open enough. We should believe that the staff of newspapers, radio and TV stations is doing a good job." As for the report's suggestion to limit the commercials to homemade products, he wrote: "It's better not to set limits like that." About the suggestion to ban commercials on cigarettes, alcohol and cosmetics, he wrote: "Commercials of cigarettes and alcohol may be banned, but those of cosmetics seem all right to me, other consumables even more so." Hu's instructions were later issued to relevant departments and local governments, which greatly stimulated the development of the advertising industry.

But localities acted upon these instructions quite differently. In April, 1980, a government department in Beijing issued the document *No Window Commercial Contracts Shall Be Signed With Foreign Business People From Now On*. In July the same department instructed, "No commercials shall be put up in the subway now or in the future." And in August they raised suggestions on banning foreign commercials in Beijing. This chain of events aroused dissatisfaction and doubts among foreign business people. On October 13, 1980, the 508th issue of *Report on Current Affairs* published by the *People's Daily* carried an article titled "Cancellation of Window and Bulletin Commercials Aroused Doubts Among Foreign Businesses" in response.

On October 16, Gu Mu urged Wei Yuming, Vice Minister of the State Import and Export Commission, to look into the issue and come up with a solution. After holding two group discussions, Wei submitted a special report to Gu Mu, saying that both advertising and the looks of the city should be taken into consideration. On the one hand, the report argued, Beijing was the capital city of China with many historical and scenic sites, so it should present a neat and tidy appearance. On the other hand, foreign enterprises should be allowed to set up some commercials, which would help expand China's economic and technological exchange with other countries, broaden the horizons of the general public, and increase foreign exchange

417

revenues. Therefore, Beijing could develop advertising in a guided and controlled way. The report also suggested that an advertising law be made as soon as possible. Gu Mu, Wan Li, Wang Renzhong, Yao Yilin, Ji Pengfei and some other leaders approved the report. It was not until 1987 that the *Procedural Provisions on Advertisements* was promulgated, which provided a stable environment for the industry.

While the flourishing of advertising as a marketing tool indicated an enhanced sense of competition in Chinese enterprises, the Ningjiang Machine Tools Works and other pilot enterprises gained a new lease on life by expanding their autonomy and participating in market competition. On July 9, 1979, a national conference on industry and communications was held in Chengdu to promote their experience. During the conference, the State Council arranged discussions about five documents concerning decentralizing management power and allowing enterprises to keep a bigger portion of their profits, including the *Regulations on Expanding Management Autonomy of State-Owned Industrial Enterprises*. With some revisions, the five documents were issued on July 13 to relevant departments, which were required to carry out experiments in a well-organized manner. Six ministries, including the State Economic Commission and the Ministry of Finance, selected eight large- and medium-sized state-owned enterprises in Beijing, Tianjin and Shanghai (the Shoudu Iron and Steel Company, the Tianjin Bicycle Factory, and the Shanghai Diesel Engine Works included) as the pilots for expanding enterprises' final say in production planning, use of funds, sales, profit allocation, and employment. By June 1980, the number of pilot enterprises had reached 6,600, which accounted for 16 percent of all the industrial enterprises listed in the national budget, 60 percent of their total output value and 70 percent of their total profit. From 1981 on, even greater autonomy was granted to all state-owned enterprises.

Historic Choice: To Establish a Market Economy by Opening Up

After he resumed leadership in 1977, Deng had to face a serious question: to mend the traditional planned economic system here and there, or to move on and make a fresh start?

At that time, under the influence of "leftist" ideology, people generally believed that socialist countries could only implement a planned economy, under which all the main industrial and agricultural products were subject to central purchase and supply planning, and barred from the market. Naturally there was no opportunity for markets to grow for consumer goods, production materials and means of production.

On November 26, 1979, Deng met with Frank B. Gibney, Vice Chairman of the Board of Editors, Encyclopedia Britannica, Inc., and Paul T. K. Lin, Director of the Center for East Asia Research of McGill University of Canada, and some other guests. During the meeting, Deng expounded his thoughts on market economy in a comprehensive manner for the first time, and raised the idea of developing market economy in a socialist society. He said:

> It is definitely wrong to say that market economy only exists in capitalist societies, and that there is only a capitalist market economy. Why shouldn't socialist countries develop market economy? This should not be labeled capitalism. ... Socialist countries can also develop market-oriented economies.

Deng Xiaoping (*right*) meeting with Frank B. Gibney (*center*), Vice Chairman of the Board of Editors of Encyclopedia Britannica, Inc., and Paul T. K. Lin (*left*), Director of the Center for East Asia Research of McGill University of Canada. At the meeting Deng for the first time clearly expounds the concept that socialist society can also develop a market economy. (November 26, 1979)

This concept broke away from the long-standing mistaken idea that only capitalist societies could have market economies, and brought about a grand ideological liberation. Soon afterward, people began learning and practicing market economy all around China.

Special Economic Zones were the "testing fields" for learning and practicing market economy. At the start, the central government clearly specified that the economies of the zones would be regulated by the market. The Shekou Industrial Zone was the first to adopt market practices in its construction. At its establishment in 1979, the central government granted the China Merchants Group the right to borrow from foreign banks. In fact, the construction of Shekou had mainly relied on foreign funds, with the first loans coming from banks in Hong Kong. Marketization of the sources of funds rendered a market orientation to business operations. First of all, in project construction, Shekou followed the requirements of the investors and the practices of Hong Kong. The bidding for, and contracting of projects ended the frequent delays caused by construction teams assigned by administrative departments.

The Effect of a Four-Cent Bonus

In the construction of a dock, Shekou followed the example of Hong Kong enterprises by awarding bonuses for extra-quota work done. Specifically, the quota for each truck on one shift was 44 loads, and the driver would get two cents for fulfilling each load within that quota, and was entitled to a bonus of four cents for every load done above the quota; bonuses for bulldozer drivers, excavator operators and the support crew would be based on the quota fulfillment and extra-quota work. This method mobilized the initiative of the workers, and the average number of loads for one cart reached 99.4, with the 55.4 extra loads raising the per-day bonus per driver to 1.62 yuan. However, according to regulations of relevant departments, workers' bonuses were not to exceed the workers' wages for 1.5-2 months of work, so Shekou was forced to stop the practice. The enthusiasm of the workers was dampened, efficiency dropped from 99.4 loads per truck per day to 32.2, and the whole building site turned from a boiling pot to a bowl of cold water. The construction speed slowed dramatically, making it impossible for the dock to be completed and put to use on time, which, in turn, would delay foreign investors in setting up factories in Shekou.

Hu Yaobang learned of this situation from an internal reference of the Xinhua News Agency dated July 30, 1980. He immediately made the following instruction:

> Please ask Gu Mu to look into the matter. I remember when the central government was discussing bonuses, no one present agreed to the regulation that workers' bonuses should not exceed their wages for 1.5-2 months. Then why did the State Labor Administration set regulations like this? And why is the Ministry of Transport and Communications acting so assertively? It seems that some of the departments are not conducting reform in the real sense of the term, but are still muddling along by setting regulations and issuing orders. How can we achieve the Four Modernizations this way? Please bring this up at the meeting of leaders in charge of finance and economy.

On July 30, Gu Mu made instructions on another document:

> Would (Zhou) Jiannan and (Jiang) Zemin please consider this: Now that special policies are applied there, Shekou can totally bypass regulations of the Ministry of Transport and Communications and the State Labor Administration. Please inform Guangdong (the province where Shekou is located) if you do not have a second opinion.

The next day, Jiang Zemin made arrangements to implement Gu Mu's instructions and informed the leaders of Guangdong, requiring the relevant departments there to do a good job.

Upon receiving Hu Yaobang's instructions on August 1, Gu Mu added his comment: "I have told Guangdong not to carry out this regulation. Guangdong enjoys special policies and flexible measures, and should not be limited by those regulations in the first place." Soon afterward Shekou resumed bonuses for extra-quota production.

In Shekou, foreign-funded enterprises led the way in operating following market rules. In September 1979, the first joint venture in Shekou – the Chun Wang Industrial Gases Company – was established, and in the following two years, several hundred operative companies and joint ventures settled there. The sources of funding, legal status, shareholders' rights and interests, operation, and management of these enterprises all followed the rules of a market economy, which required Shekou to adopt corresponding ways of administration.

Later on, Shekou began adopting a manager accountability system, under which the enterprises would decide for themselves the number of staff and workers, the targets of cost and profit, and allow reasonable flow of staff and talents – enterprises could fire workers and workers could quit their jobs. Market-oriented reform was also carried out in the wage and housing systems. Measures in Shekou soon spread to the whole Shenzhen Special Economic Zone. They were later summarized into two characteristics: an export-oriented economy and management based on market mechanisms.

In the spring of 1984, Deng approved Shekou's practices while inspecting the special economic zones. Later, with the opening up of 14 coastal cities and Hainan Island, market mechanisms caught on rapidly, and were having a model effect nationwide. Consequently, market concepts like efficiency, competition and exchange at equal value were gradually accepted by the general public. New economic entities like private businesses, township enterprises and companies involving foreign investment emerged one after another. New words and phrases like "bonus," "street vendor," "bargaining," "working for a boss (as opposed to working for the state under the planned economy)," "going into private business," "job-hopping," and "firing" somebody (as opposed to lifelong employment under the planned economy) became everyday expressions.

Researchers Get a First Taste of the Market Economy

Zhongguancun used to be a small village in the north of Beijing. In 1952, the Chinese Academy of Sciences was founded here, where the Peking and Tsinghua universities, and some other higher education institutions were located. Over the years, it had developed into a compact district for high-tech talents, but could not bring this advantage into full play for a long time.

In October 1980, Chen Chunxian, a researcher with the Chinese Academy of Sciences went to the United States to observe and study Route 128 in Boston and Silicon Valley in California. He focused on learning about the "technology development zone" and the market mechanism of closely connecting production, teaching and research. After returning to China, Chen wrote a report suggesting a "technology development zone" be established in Zhongguancun, to turn it into the "Silicon Valley of China." He also suggested that scientists and researchers should learn from their counterparts in the United States, borrow money by themselves and establish joint-stock factories, so that their research results could be turned into productivity promptly.

Chen Chunxian's ideas won support from the Beijing Association for Science and Technology, which agreed that Chen could start a service company in the name of the Plasma Science Society with the authorization of the Association. The Association even lent him 500 yuan, and helped him open a company account at the bank. On October 23, 1980, Chen and 14 researchers from the Chinese Academy of Sciences launched the first private technical business in China at Zhongguancun – the Beijing Plasma Science Society Advanced Technology Service Association. They drafted their operation principles by following the market operation methods in the United States: scientists and engineers step out of research institutes; follow the patterns of commercialization of research findings and market economy; give up appropriations from state treasury and state-appointed positions; raise funds on their own; take responsibility for their own management, profits and losses; and enjoy decision-making autonomy in accordance with the law. These principles later became the common practices of enterprises in Zhongguancun, which soon grew into an eye-catching "electronics street."

This phenomenon also raised questions such as "What is the task for researchers?" and "Should a research institute set up businesses?" In January 1983, an internal reference reflecting related disputes was submitted to high-level officials in the central government. Hu Yaobang, Hu Qili, Fang Yi and some others leaders affirmed that Chen should be commended because he was leading a new trend and doing the right thing.

In May 1988, during the crucial period of its development, Deng approved the establishment of the Zhongguancun Science and Technology Garden, which further promoted its function as a grand market in stimulating the development of the science and technology industry.

In the process of learning and practicing market economy, many innovations and explorations emerged in different parts of the country, to which Deng always gave his approval. For instance, small-scale private businesses at the beginning of reform and opening up were the most active in learning and pursuing market practices. Their hiring of laborers gave rise to questions about exploitation and a call for restrictions, to which Deng responded, "My suggestion is to wait for a couple of years before drawing any conclusion; if we make any change now, people will say that our policy has changed and may get worried." In another example, when farmers in the south of Jiangsu Province developed township enterprises by adopting market economic practices, some people accused them of disturbing the economic order, and said they should be stopped. On February 6, 1983, Deng took a work tour to Jiangsu, where the local officials reported to him: the development of collectively-owned enterprises had largely relied on a flexible mechanism of operation, the mechanism of a market economy. From raw materials and the sources of funds to the sales of products, everything depended on the market. On hearing this, Deng said firmly, "It seems that market economy is very important!"

Deng's ideas to open still wider to the world and develop a market economy were soon reflected in Party documents. In June 1984, the Party Central Committee began drafting the *Decisions on Economic Restructuring*, to be discussed at the Third Plenary Session of the 12th Party Central Committee.

On October 20, 1984, the Third Plenary Session of the 12th Party Central Committee approved the *Decisions*, which pointed out that quickening the overall reform of the economic system with the focus on cities was the most urgent need of national development at present. The basic task of the reform was to establish a dynamic socialist economic system with Chinese characteristics. The *Decisions* also stressed that in order to transform the planned economic system, the first thing was to break away from the traditional ideology that set the planned economy against a market economy. It must be clearly understood that the law of value should be consciously followed in a socialist planned economy, which was actually a planned commodity economy based on public ownership. The full development of a commodity economy was a prerequisite for economic modernization in our country, and therefore could not be bypassed in the development of a socialist economy.

After the *Decisions* was passed, Deng pointed out in his speech:

The *Decisions* is an example of political economics that combines the basic Marxist theories and China's socialist practices. This is my evaluation. But I should wait for five years before saying this, when it has been proved correct.

After this plenary session, the market-oriented reform of the economic system gradually unfolded.

Although the concept and practices of market economics grew up and matured in capitalist countries, we have learned it through reform and opening up. In an important speech at the Central Party School on June 9, 1992, Jiang Zeming made it clear that the economic restructuring in our country was designed to establish a socialist market economic system, a statement that was reconfirmed at the 14th National Party Congress. China's learning process of market economy is of profound and lasting historical significance.

*   *   *

Opening up to the outside world is a basic state policy, the only way out for socialism with Chinese characteristics and for the great revitalization of the nation. It is also an important part of Deng Xiaoping Theory.

By opening up to the outside world, drawing on foreign experience, expanding economic and trade cooperation with foreign countries, and procuring foreign funds, technology and management expertise, we have blazed a new trail and greatly sped up the process of industrialization and modernization. Our comprehensive national strength, economic power and people's living standards have improved enormously. The nation's total import and export value reached US$2,173.8 billion in 2007 – 105 times the 1978 figure of US$20.6 billion. By the end of 2007, the actual total inflow of foreign investment reached US$780 billion, and export-oriented economic entities had provided over 100 million jobs. From 1978 to 2007, China's GDP increased from 1 percent to more than 5 percent of the world total, and the total import and export value grew from less than 1 percent to around 8 percent of the world total. In 2007, China contributed more than 10 percent of the growth in the world economy, and over 12 percent of the growth in international trade. The Chinese economy has become an important and integral part of the global economy.

After 30 years' exploration and practice, the opening-up efforts have won popular support and brought about remarkable achievements and benefits to the nation. China's international status in the opening-up era has improved noticeably, thanks to its growing contributions to the world economy and to peoples in other parts of the world.

With each passing day, our experience in opening up continues to become richer and our people continue to learn more about international rules; the integration of domestic and international markets, and of domestic and international resources also continues to grow closer. Never before have China and the rest of the world needed each other so much.

Looking forward, China still has a long and challenging way to go. At the international level – with the continuous deepening of economic globalization and the irreversible trend of interdependence between nations – active adaptation is the necessary choice for China in its pursuit of peaceful development. At home, on the one hand, China still lags far behind developed countries in innovation capability, cutting-edge technology, high-end brands, and people's living standard. Therefore, we still have a long way to go before catching up with moderately developed countries when New China celebrates its 100th anniversary, a target set by Deng. On the long path of opening up, we still have many problems to solve and numerous difficulties to overcome. On the other hand, opening up to the outside world has obviously stimulated the economic growth of China, so we cannot afford to neglect its status and effects. Both the external environment and domestic needs, therefore, dictate that we must continue to persistently devote major efforts toward opening up.

In a talk during his crucial 1992 work tour to the south, Deng said firmly, "We would come to a dead end should we fail to adhere to socialism, reform and opening up, develop the economy, and improve the people's livelihood," and "The fundamental policies must be maintained for 100 years, unswervingly." These resounding remarks fully demonstrated Deng's firm determination on China's socialist reform, opening up and modernization drive. His heroic spirit in spite of formidable obstacles will forever encourage the Chinese people in their efforts to build socialism with Chinese characteristics, a fundamental policy of the Party.

In 1998, when summarizing the Party's major historical experience of reform and opening up for the last 20 years, Jiang Zemin pointed out:

> Historical facts have fully proved that the development of China cannot be separated from the rest of the world, and that construction cannot succeed behind closed doors. Opening up to the outside world is in accordance with the characteristics of the present times and the world's economic and technological development, and is the inevitable choice for China to speed up its modernization construction. This is a basic state policy that we must adhere to for a long period. China is a large, developing socialist country with a huge population. We can never rely on others for our construction, but should always emphasize independence and self-reliance. For economic development, our long-term strategy is to rely on domestic resources and expand domestic demands. At the same time, we also need to open up in our construction efforts, including the use of foreign investment, introduction of advanced technology and everything progressive. We need to learn from other countries, including developed capitalist countries, all the advanced ways of operation and management that

Deng Xiaoping met with Jiang Zemin, November 9, 1989.

reflect the law of modern, socialized production. We should combine developing and expanding the excellent traditional culture of our nation with actively learning all the achievements of human civilization; combine expanding domestic markets with utilizing foreign resources and expanding international market; combine revitalizing the domestic economy with opening up to the outside world. Only in this way can there be a continuous drive to socialist modernization in our country. In the process of opening up, we must always pay attention to safeguarding national sovereignty and socioeconomic security, watch out for and resolve the impact of international risks, and watch out for and resist the invasion of all sorts of decadent ideologies and lifestyles. In today's world of multi-polarization and increasing economic globalization, we must further improve relevant policies, continue to expand opening up, enriching its form and content, and enhancing its quality and standard.

In his report to the 17th National Party Congress, Hu Jintao pointed out:

Facts have incontrovertibly proved that the decision to begin reform and opening up is vital to the destiny of contemporary China, that reform and opening up are the only way of developing socialism with Chinese characteristics and rejuvenating the Chinese nation, that only socialism can save China and that only reform and opening up can develop China, socialism and

Deng Xiaoping met with Hu Jintao, October 19, 1992.

Marxism. As a great new revolution, reform and opening up are not to be plain sailing or be accomplished overnight. Essentially they accord with the aspirations of the Party membership and the people and keep up with the trend of the times. The orientation and path of reform and opening up are entirely correct, and their merits and achievements can never be negated. To stop or reverse reform and opening up would only lead to a blind alley.

It is exactly because our Party and all the people have persisted in the state policy of opening up, continuously emancipated our minds, deepened the reform, and kept pace with the times, that we have been able to make the tremendous achievements of today.

When I review Deng Xiaoping's important thoughts and guidelines about opening up, and as I look back on the early years, I have further strengthened my belief: The rise of any nation should, without doubt, mainly depend on its own efforts. However, self-reliance and opening up to the outside world, and utilizing both domestic and international resources and markets are mutually complementary rather than contradictory. Opening up to the outside world is not just an expedient, but a basic state policy in which we must persist for a long time, not just for the time being, but also into the future, even after China has become a developed country.

Postscript by the Translators

When China observed the 30th anniversary of the adoption of its open policy, the world it had embraced with open arms was engulfed in an unprecedented "financial tsunami," uncertain of when the economy would bottom out. It was against this dismal international background that Li Lanqing's *Breaking Through – The Birth of China's Opening-Up Policy* was released in China in late 2008. This coincidence, however, makes the launch of this book opportune in many ways. The book takes a retrospective look at a pioneering episode of Chinese history that began three decades ago. Its narrative carries a celebratory tone about the triumph and heroism of the trailblazers of the opening-up policy, but its message is no less forceful: In times of adversity, hope lies in "breaking through" or away from the status quo, and the source of strength to envision the future most probably lies grounded in history.

The idea for *Breaking Through* stemmed from an interview with Li Lanqing conducted by the Central Literature Publishing House in Beijing, in preparation for commemorating Deng Xiaoping and the 30th anniversary of the reform and opening-up policy. That deep and inspirational dialog was the catalyst for this book. Shortly after it came off the press, it stood out among a series of similar titles and became the topic for a wave of symposiums, discussions and book reading gatherings. Apart from its commemorative purpose, its value as a history book and a reference tool for theoretical research speaks for itself.

The stories told in *Breaking Through* run the gamut – from the conception of the idea of opening up as a fundamental state policy, and the birth of special economic zones, to the introduction of foreign technology and equipment, the use of foreign direct investment and low-interest foreign government loans, to the restructuring of the foreign trade system, and the "borrowing" of intellectual resources from other lands.

As its subtitle – The Birth of China's Opening-Up Policy – suggests, these and other events took place from 1978 through 1984, or the "first phase" according to the author's groupings of the first 30 years of the opening-up policy in his preface to the Chinese edition of his book. It was a period that saw China begin to rise to its feet from the damage of the Cultural Revolution and start afresh by groping its way into uncharted territory. The road ahead was littered with obstacles: a scarcity of supplies, brittle social institutions, and conservatism, just to name a few. Showing extraordinary grit and determination, the second generation of the top leadership, centered around Deng Xiaoping, broke through the nation's ideological and institutional encirclement and gradually put the nation on a road to sustainable development. That short span of time, undeniably the watershed that preceded the now-famous "China miracle," cannot be overlooked in studies of the first 30 years of reform and opening – or of the first 60 years of the People's Republic, no matter what your field of interest.

In *Breaking Through*, Li Lanqing's knack for weaving personal and historical experience and philosophy comes across in a succession of firsthand accounts that are often humorous and insightful. His narration – whether telling a story about a public debate over whether a socialist newspaper should carry commercials; or about how a four-cent bonus shocked state leaders dwelling in Zhongnanhai; or recounting a saying that likened a Chinese-foreign joint venture to a marriage between a capitalist and a communist – frequently and vividly drives home the fact that many of the things we take for granted in China today, were either taboo or unknown in the China of three decades ago. These stories, comparing the past with the present, touch upon many facets of the reform and opening and give a personal touch to the history of trials and tribulations the nation has weathered to become what it is today.

The author's unique persona has been a decisive factor behind *Breaking Through's* reception in China as an influential work and something of a sensation. A 340,000-word memoir of this kind on the early years of reform and opening by a senior Chinese official – one who served as a Politburo Standing Committee Member and two tenures as Vice Premier of the State Council – is unprecedented in Chinese publishing history. What we would like to stress here is the fact that the author, a policy insider, is an authoritative voice on this subject.

As early as 1978, Li Lanqing was the first man to petition the central government to adopt Chinese-foreign equity joint ventures. After that petition was granted, he personally presided over relevant negotiations with foreign investors, and went on to become a drafter of legislation on joint ventures. In 1982, as Director General of the Foreign Investment Administration under the Ministry of Foreign Economic Relations and Trade, he was a zealous advocate for the birth of the earliest batch of joint ventures on Chinese soil. Beginning from 1983, as Vice Mayor in charge of foreign affairs of Tianjin Municipality, he guided the establishment of the Tianjin Economic-Technological Development Zone and the transformation of Tianjin Harbor. Starting in 1986, while serving first as Vice Minister and then Minister of Foreign Economic Relations and Trade, Li orchestrated negotiations over China's membership in General Agreement on Tariffs and Trade (GATT) and World Trade Organization (WTO). He became a national leader in 1992, and was appointed head of the National Leading Panel for Foreign Capital Work in 1994. Li served successively as Politburo Member and Standing Committee Member and Vice Premier of the State Council before retiring in 2003. His interpretations of that episode of Chinese history in which he was both a trailblazer and a decision-maker, naturally, are devoid of the far-fetched observations and wild guesswork of an outsider, and are interspersed with "inside stories" that serve to enhance the credibility and accuracy of his narration.

Another significant feature of *Breaking Through* is its wealth of historical data. The relationship between remembrance and history is a much-debated topic among readers, writers and scholars alike. The rise of "oral accounts of history" has elevated remembrance, that is, *his-story*, to the level of history (*history*). The key to the authenticity of remembrance, however, lies in whether it can be validated with historical data. This book is imbued with some 330 declassified files, documents, hand-written scripts and pictures hitherto little known to the public, over and above a cornucopia of quotations, facts and figures. Many of them were brought to light for the first time in this book. The author has meticulously collected and collated historical documents and data for his book. These include an image of a three-page, 400-word outline, of seven topics, in Deng's own handwriting, for his famous speech "Emancipating the Mind, Seeking Truth from Facts, and Looking Toward the Future in Unity." (That speech, delivered on December 13, 1978, set the tone for the landmark policy discussions on reform and opening that took place at the Third Plenary Session of the 11th Party Central Committee, which opened five days later.) As the author states, "...I wrote my book in all seriousness, in which my writing ability was secondary. The authenticity of historical facts was foremost on my mind because I did not want to say anything that might mislead our readers." It is that conscientious attitude that makes this a trusted history book.

As translators of this English edition, we had the good fortune to be immersed in this book for ten months, to run over its text repeatedly, and to ponder every word and expression of it. The more deeply we became absorbed in it, the more we were captivated by its unadorned conversational language and mesmerized by its epic-like scale. We also were stirred by Li Lanqing's relentless fidelity to history, his passion for the subject, and his ingenuous analysis and reflections.

Our personal communications with some readers also revealed that, despite different interpretations of what the book is all about due to differences in perspectives, we can agree that *Breaking Through* has shortened the distance between us, as individuals, and our destiny as a nation. It has enabled us to understand "where China came from" and to become more concerned with "where China will go."

It is out of this desire for "shortening the distance" that we introduce the English edition of *Breaking Through* to our overseas readers. If the Chinese edition has served the purposes of "shortening the distance" between us and history and arousing the Chinese people's sense of mission for the nation, we present this English edition with the hope of bringing China closer to the world.

To achieve that end, the distance between languages must be spanned in the first place. Our experience in translating Li Lanqing's *Education for 1.3 Billion* in 2004 came in handy, but *Breaking Through* is different from that book in two ways. First, it dwells on a period of time that is earlier and a lot more special to China. Second, with a far more complex and diverse coverage, ranging from politics and economics to science and technology, education, diplomacy, commerce, finance and industry, it is nothing short of an encyclopedia on the opening-up policy. The rapid succession of Party and government positions the author held during that short period could be perplexing to overseas readers. Furthermore, the book's narrative style, a delight for native Chinese speakers, was daunting to translate for English readers. And we were torn between two choices: a verbatim rendition from Chinese into English, or a flexible translation approach that would be friendlier to non-Chinese speakers. Verbatim translation is likely to spawn language barriers, but will flexible rendition spoil the integrity and brilliance of the original text? That is the sixty-four thousand dollar question for those of us who make a living as translators.

Fortunately, we were not left alone to handle this complex translation issue, as we had the support of a whole team behind us. Everyone involved – the author, editors and translators – contributed their suggestions. Through repeated deliberation, we hammered out a translation guideline that called for inserting background information where needed, and deleting or rewriting some of the terms and passages that might not make sense to non-Chinese speakers. An index was added to provide valuable references and to facilitate reading. It was, indeed, a labor of love to work out the proper English solutions for words and expressions that, in Chinese, vividly convey some specific meanings, but if ill-translated, might baffle our foreign readers.

It is fitting that the English edition of *Breaking Through* is co-published by Oxford University Press and the Foreign Language Teaching and Research Press. The former is a world-renowned university publishing house, and the latter, the leading university press in China. Both are run by universities in which knowledge and culture are taught and carried forward. By undertaking this co-publishing project in time for the 60th anniversary of the founding of the People's Republic of China, OUP and FLTRP are inviting readers across the globe to learn something about China from this book by an authoritative source so that we can better share the future of the world.

We are indebted to Simon Li, Sun Yiyi, and Lam To Kwan of Oxford University Press, whose cogent, resourceful advice helped shape the editorial and translation guideline for this complex translation project. We are grateful to Daniel Clutton and Mary J. Child for editing the translated text with great expertise and attention to the minute detail, and to Feng Yunsheng, Wang Jianping, Chu Shijia, Zhao Xianquan, Liu Jingsong, and Wang Bin of the Office of Li Lanqing at Zhongnanhai for their unstinting assistance to us in the tedious task of verifying facts and figures and the translation of a host of institutional and personal names. Our heartfelt thanks are also due to our FLTRP colleagues who aided us in numerous ways and played no small part throughout the translation, editing and proofreading process: Copy editors/translators Zhang Lixin, Ren Xiaomei, Zhong Zhilan, and Peng Lin; translators Chen Haiyan, Zhou Ziping, Tong Xiaohua, Zhen Qiang, and Zeng Zhen; and editors/data researchers Yi Lu, Chen Yinan, Zhu Meng and Lu You.

Glossary of Names

An Zhiwen	安志文
Aoki Shinzo	青木慎三
Bai Xiangguo	白相國
Bo Yibo	薄一波
Brown, Samuel Robins	布朗
Bu Ming	卜明
Bu Zhaomin	卜昭敏
Bumgamer, Richard	彭加拉
Cai Yuanpei	蔡元培
Cao Yunzhang	曹蘊章
Carter, Jimmy	卡特
Kuang-piu Chao	曹光彪
Chen Chunxian	陳春先
Chen, Clement, Jr.	陳宣遠
Chen Jinhua	陳錦華
Chen Muhua	陳慕華
Chen Yang	陳揚
Chen Yun	陳雲
Shiing-Shen Chern	陳省身
Chiang Kai-shek	蔣介石
Susana Chou	曹其真
Chuang Shih-ping	莊世平
Cohen, Jerome	科恩
de Gaulle, Charles	戴高樂
Delair, Pierre	德萊爾
Deng Liqun	鄧力群
Deng Xiaoping	鄧小平
Deng Yingchao	鄧穎超
d'Estaing, Giscard	德斯坦
Duan Wei	段為
Duan Yun	段雲
Dunkel, Arthur J.	鄧克爾
Engels	恩格斯
Fang Xiao	方曉
Fang Yi	方毅
Fei Jiaji	費家驥
Feng Tianshun	馮天順
Henry Fok Ying-tung	霍英東

Fujihara Chosaku	藤原長作
Fung King Hey	馮景禧
Gan Ziyu	甘子玉
Geng Biao	耿颱
Gerich, Werner	威爾納‧格里希
Gibney, Frank B.	弗蘭克‧吉布尼
Goh Keng Swee	吳慶瑞
Gotowski, Armin	古托夫斯基
Gu Ming	顧明
Gu Mu	谷牧
Gu Nianliang	古念良
Gu Wenguang	顧文廣
Gu Xiulian	顧秀蓮
Guan Tianpei	關天培
Guo Chao	郭超
Guo Moruo	郭沫若
Han Suyin	韓素音
Han Yuanzuo	韓元佐
Hara Shoichi	原正市
Hills, Carla A.	卡拉‧西爾斯
Hu Guangbao	胡光寶
Hu Jintao	胡錦濤
Hu Juewen	胡厥文
Hu Qili	胡啓立
Hu Qiaomu	胡喬木
Hu Yaobang	胡耀邦
Hu Zi'ang	胡子昂
Hua Guofeng	華國鋒
Huang Hua	黃華
Huang Shimin	黃施民
Huang Xian	黃賢
Hunter, John	亨達
Husain, Shahid	夏希德‧侯賽因
Inoue Ryo	井上亮
Isaksen, Mogens	莫根斯‧伊薩克森
Ito Masayoshi	伊東正義
Ji Chongwei	季崇威
Ji Dengkui	紀登奎
Ji Pengfei	姬鵬飛
Jia Shi	賈石
Jiang Nanxiang	蔣南翔
Jiang Qing	江青

Jiang Zemin	江澤民
Jin Xiying	金熙英
Kahn, Herman	赫爾曼·康恩
Kang Keqing	康克清
Kang Shi'en	康世恩
Khan, Rahatullah	烏拉赫·汗
Kimura Ichizo	木村一三
Laxalt, Paul	拉克索爾特
Richard Charles Lee	利銘澤
Lei Renmin	雷任民
Lenin, Vladimir	列寧
Li Chunguang	李春光
Li Dazhao	李大釗
Li Fakui	李發奎
Li Fuchun	李富春
Li Gu	李固
Li Guotang	李國堂
Li Hao	李灝
Li Hongzhang	李鴻章
Li Jingzhao	李景昭
Li Ka-shing	李嘉誠
Li Lanqing	李嵐清
Li Peng	李鵬
Li Qi	李琦
Li Ruihuan	李瑞環
Li Siguang	李四光
Li Xiannian	李先念
Li Youzhang	李有章
Liang Lingguang	梁靈光
Liang Xiang	梁湘
Liao Chengzhi	廖承志
Lin Biao	林彪
Lin Jianqing	林澗青
Paul T. K. Lin	林達光
Lin Zexu	林則徐
Liu Ningyi	劉寧一
Liu Tianfu	劉田夫
Liu Tianjiu	劉天就
Liu Xiwen	劉希文
Liu Xiyao	劉西堯
Liu Yiu-chu	廖瑤珠
Lu Dingyi	陸定一

Lu Xun	魯迅
Lu Xuzhang	盧緒章
Lu Zifen	陸自奮
Luo Baoyi	羅抱一
Luo Ruiqing	羅瑞卿
Ma Bin	馬賓
MacArthur, Douglas	道格拉斯·麥克阿瑟
Ma Chengde	馬成德
MacLehose, Murray	麥理浩
Ma Dayou	馬大猷
Ma Hong	馬洪
Ma Jingfu	馬敬夫
Ma Man-kei	馬萬祺
Ma Meili	馬玫麗
Ma Tianshui	馬天水
Mao Zedong	毛澤東
Mathur, Madan G.	馬吐
McNamara, Robert S.	麥克納馬拉
Murphy, Thomas	湯姆斯·墨菲
Nie Rongzhen	聶榮臻
Nikaido Susumu	二階堂進
Nixon, Richard	尼克松
Ohira Masayoshi	大平正芳
Okita Saburo	大來佐武郎
Palleschi, Roberto	帕萊斯基
Pao Yue-kong	包玉剛
Pao Siu-loong	包兆龍
Pei Chao	裴潮
Peng Chong	彭沖
Peng Deqing	彭德清
Peng Zhen	彭真
Pompidou, Georges	蓬皮杜
Press, Frank	弗蘭克·普雷斯
Qian Jiadong	錢嘉東
Qian Junrui	錢俊瑞
Qian Qichen	錢其琛
Qian Xuesen	錢學森
Qian Zhiguang	錢之光
Qin Wenjun	秦文俊
Qiu Chunfu	丘純甫
Rao Bin	饒斌
Ren Zhongyi	任仲夷

Rong Yiren	榮毅仁
Roosevelt, Theodore	羅斯福
Rotelmann	羅德曼
Saito Hiroshi	齋藤英四郎
Sakisaka Masao	向阪正男
Run Run Shaw	邵逸夫
Shen Tu	沈圖
Shi Qingye	石青野
Shi Ruji	史汝輯
Shi Yumin	史裕民
Song Jian	宋健
Song Ping	宋平
Song Yifeng	宋一峰
Su Buqing	蘇步青
C. B. Sung	沈堅白
Takasaki Tatsunosuke	高碕達之助
Takeiri Yoshikatsu	竹入義勝
Tan Zhenlin	譚震林
Tanaka Kakuei	田中角榮
Tang Aoqing	唐敖慶
Tang Hong	湯紅
Tian Yinong	田一農
Torii Yukio	鳥居幸雄
Ulanhu	烏蘭夫
Wan Li	萬里
Wang Bingqian	王丙乾
Wang Daohan	汪道涵
Wang Dongxing	汪東興
Wang Douguang	王斗光
Wang Heshou	王鶴壽
Wang Hongwen	王洪文
Wang Quanguo	王全國
Wang Renzhong	王任重
Wang Ruilin	王瑞林
Wang Runsheng	王潤生
Wang Shoudao	王首道
Wang Shuming	王書明
Wang Xuan	王選
Wang Yaoting	王耀庭
Wang Zhen	王震
Wei Nanjin	魏南金
Weitz	維茨

Wei Yuming	魏玉明
Wei Yuan	魏源
Weng Jianxin	翁建新
K. C. Wong	王寬誠
Wu Bosen	吳伯森
James Tak Wu	伍沾德
Wu Jianmin	吳健民
Wu Nansheng	吳南生
Wu Wenjun	吳文俊
Wu Yi	吳儀
Ying Sheung Wu	胡應湘
Xi Zhongxun	習仲勛
Xiang Nan	項南
Xie Beiyi	謝北一
Xie Hua	謝華
Xie Shuangqiu	謝爽秋
Xing Lu	邢路
Xu Dixin	許滌新
Xu Zhiming	許智明
Xue Muqiao	薛暮橋
Yan Dongsheng	嚴東生
Yan Fu	嚴復
Yang Jun	楊峻
Yang Shangkun	楊尚昆
Yang Shixian	楊石先
Yang Wei	楊威
Yao Wenyuan	姚文元
Yao Yilin	姚依林
Ye Fei	葉飛
Ye Jianying	葉劍英
Ye Zhiqiang	葉志强
Ye Zilong	葉子龍
Yoshihiro Inayama	稻山嘉寬
Yoshio Sakurauchi	園田直
Yu Guangyuan	于光遠
Yu Qiuli	余秋里
Yu Su	于愫
Yuan Geng	袁庚
Yung Wing	容閎
Zeng Dingshi	曾定石
Zha Quanxing	查全性
Zhan Tianyou	詹天佑

Zhang Chunqiao	張春橋
Zhang Jinfu	張勁夫
Zhang Pinghua	張平化
Zhang Quan	張荃
Zhang Xunfu	張勛甫
Zhang Yun	章蘊
Zhao Jing	趙靜
Zhao Yiwen	趙藝文
Zheng Guanying	鄭觀應
Zheng Tuobin	鄭拓彬
Zhou Dongcheng	周東成
Zhou Enlai	周恩來
Zhou Guangzhao	周光召
Zhou Jiannan	周建南
Zhou Li	周力
Zhou Peiyuan	周培源
Zhou Xuancheng	周宣城
Zhou Zijian	周子健
Zhu De	朱德
Zhu Rongji	朱鎔基
Zhu Xuefan	朱學範
Zhuang Yanlin	莊炎林

Index